Foreword by
Daniel Negreanu

Swayne's
ADVANCED DEGREE
in Hold'em

CHARLEY
SWAYNE

Published by ECW Press, 2120 Queen Street East, Suite 200,
Toronto, Ontario, Canada M4E 1E2
416.694.3348 / info@ecwpress.com

Library and Archives Canada Cataloguing in Publication

Swayne, Charles B
Swayne's advanced degree in hold 'em / Charley Swayne.

ISBN-13: 978-1-55022-866-3
ISBN-10: 1-55022-866-6

1. Poker. I. Title. II. Title: Advanced degree in hold 'em.

GV1251.S93 2009   795.412   C2008-907550-1

Cover and Text Design: Tania Craan
Typesetting: Florence Aliesch
Printing: Transcontinental
1   2   3   4   5

Printed and Bound in Canada

ECW PRESS
ecwpress.com

Carol has never seen one hand of poker, not even on television. When I proudly showed her my WSOP Academy instructor website she asked, "What's a wooosop?"

No man has ever had a more wonderful wife than Carol, or better sons than Joe, Brian, and Chuck.

CONTENTS

Foreword

You know they say that poker is a game that takes five minutes to learn but a lifetime to master. It may take a little more than five minutes to learn, but it does indeed take a lifetime to master. When I first started playing Hold'em, books and training devices were few and far between. We are straight up spoiled today! There is an abundance of poker training tools out there that claim to make you a better all-round player; however only a few give you a serious return on your investment.

As you may know, I'm constantly trying to learn more about the game and add more weapons to my poker arsenal. Most of the stuff I read is commonplace and a dime-a-dozen. However, *Swayne's Advanced Degree in Hold'em* really grabbed my attention through several cutting edge concepts. The PATL (Passive Aggressive Tight Loose) and Advanced PATL matrices, Swayne's Win Factors and Relative Strength Evaluations (just to name a few) are a direct result of Charley's extensive academic background and thorough understanding of the game. Charley's innovative concepts not only will give you the opportunity to become a great poker player, they will allow you to play with unmatched confidence. I was so impressed with his school of thought that I asked him to join my Poker VT team at the very start. It turned out to be quite the good decision. Not only does Charley have an in-depth, easy-to-use mathematical strategy, he and I developed the ever-so-challenging N-SPAT (The Negreanu-Swayne Poker Aptitude Test) seen on Poker VT.

So why would I back Charley's book? The answer is quite simple. *Swayne's Advanced Degree* is like nothing I have ever seen before and offers readers of all experience levels, even the weak little fish, the tools necessary to become a better Hold'em player. Contrary to what you may believe, I'm all for feeding the fish knowledge. After all, it's better for the competitive nature of the game I love.

Daniel Negreanu
April 2009

CHAPTER 1

Introduction

Just what you wanted to see when you opened the book. A disclaimer. Of course I am covering my tail. Neither Advanced Degree Poker, LLC, I, my sons, nor this book guarantees you anything. I do not guarantee you will win. Everything in this book is for your information only. This book may not be construed as offering you any type of advice with regard to poker gambling. It is your responsibility to evaluate the information presented in this book. It is also your responsibility to follow the laws that apply in your state or country with regard to playing poker. If you are unsure about the status of playing poker consult your own attorney. I, the publisher, and anyone else involved with this book do not endorse or guarantee anything presented in this book. You assume all responsibility for your actions. If you do not agree to any of these conditions, immediately return this book from the place you purchased it for a full refund. If that place does not give you a full refund, immediately write directly to me, Charley Swayne. Give me the name, address, and phone number of the retailer who refused to give you a full refund. Include the book and receipt, and I will send you a full refund of your purchase price. The address is Advanced Degree Poker, LLC, N. 1964 Crestview Place, La Crosse, WI 54601, USA.

How important is poker?

The first day of poker class. The professor wheeled a cart into a packed room. On the cart were a very large glass jar and four boxes. He silently filled the jar with golf balls from one of the boxes. He asked the students if the jar was full. "Yes," was the response.

He then opened another box which contained pebbles. He poured the pebbles into the jar with the golf balls, making sure to shake the jar so some pebbles made their way to the bottom. "Now is the jar full?" The class agreed it was.

Another box with sand. The sand went into the jar. He again asked the class if the jar was full. A very loud, "Yes!" was heard.

Then out of the last box he pulled out a can of beer. He then proceeded to fill the jar to the brim.

As the laughter quieted down, the professor said, "The golf balls are the truly important things in your life. Your family, honor, health, service to others, and for some of you God. The pebbles are important but if you lost the pebbles you could start over. Pebbles are your wealth, job, fame, friends, money, and possessions. The sand is the fun things in your life, stuff you could do without but you enjoy doing. Hobbies, pastimes, relaxing."

"What would happen if we put the sand in the jar first? You couldn't get the golf balls or pebbles in. If you filled your jar with sand first, there would be no room for your family, your health." A long pause. "Poker is sand. For some, poker is pebbles. But, poker should never become golf balls."

The students were silent for a few seconds. Finally, one asked what the beer represents. The answer: "No matter how much you have, there is always room for a beer."

Now the real introduction

Welcome. This intro is brief. All of the usual things you find at the start of a book are at the end of this one because if you are like me, you want to get to the meat of something fast.

The more you know, the less you fear. I will show you how to know more than most of your opponents. It is assumed you know how to play. If you are a beginner there are several books in Appendix A which will give you all the basics.

Knowledge and skill

Certain skills and specific kinds of knowledge are necessary to be a great hold'em player — similar to the wheels of a bicycle. You need the back wheel to guide your decisions. You need the front wheel for your actual decision making.

The knowledge is math. This is your back wheel. Without knowing the math, decisions are based on a hunch. Knowing the math guides you into profitable decisions. Then there is a broad range of strategies, tactics and skills which include having the guts to bet hard, bluffing, semi-bluffing, check-raising, reading your opponents and their hands. These skills are your front wheel. You use these to decide how to play the hand. For shorthand I will lump all of these poker strategies, tactics, and skills under the term psychology, psych. You need to be both Spock and Kirk. Figure 1.1 shows the relative importance of math knowledge versus psych skills depending on the type of hold'em game played.

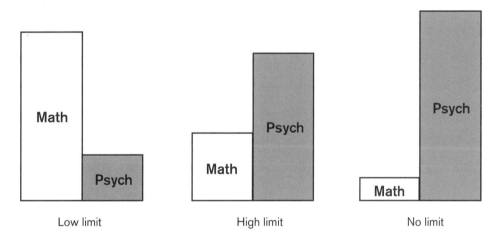

Relative importance of math knowledge and psych skills depending on type of hold'em played

Figure 1.1

Is this book for you?

This book will more than satisfy limit players who need a superior blend of psych skills and math knowledge and **who expect to win a minimum of 1.5 big bets per hour.** Unless you are playing others who know what you will learn, it is possible **TO MAKE A LIVING PLAYING HOLD'EM,** even playing low limit. For example, if you simultaneously play four $3/$6 tables on the net, you should expect to win $9 per table per hour or $36 per hour. If you play low limit, $10/$20 or less, your primary focus should be the math. If you play high limit, $30/$60 and up, your emphasis needs to be on the psych skills. If you want to be a great limit player you need both and this book is definitely for you.

If you want to focus on no limit tournaments, it is a long road to becoming good. If you play no limit, you make the most money by playing the people rather than the cards. And here's what I mean by a long road. Before you can become a good no limit player you must become a great player at limit. And before you become a good no limit tournament player, you must become good at no limit cash play.

From this moment until the No Limit Chapter, we speak and focus primarily on limit. The No Limit Chapter, Chapter 11, will build on your limit expertise and then show you what it takes to become good at no limit cash. Then, and only then, will you be ready to learn the tortoise small ball play to get through major no limit tournaments.

This is a book only for one who is very serious about his game, not the casual player, not the player primarily out for fun, although there is a section for beginners in Chapter 9 which shows those starting out an oversimplified method for play. Although written in a conversational tone, **this is more like a college text**, than the traditional poker book.

The beginner, unless he is serious about the game, and certainly the casual player, will find the concepts too complicated and cumbersome to understand and apply.

Importance of skills during each round of betting

During your first round of limit your knowledge of math is most important and becomes less important as betting continues. Notice how much more important your psych skills are on the flop and turn. No limit requires a greater emphasis of psych skills on the flop as that's where most of the moves are made.

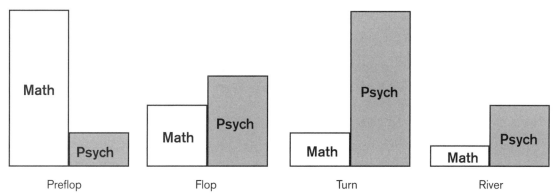

Importance of math knowledge and psych skills during each round of limit betting

Figure 1.2

Degree of difficulty

Figure 1.3.a illustrates the degree of difficulty of each betting round in low limit. If you haven't played much when you first read Chapter 9 you will probably disagree but preflop play is relatively easy. Eventually you will understand how easy preflop play is compared to the flop and turn.

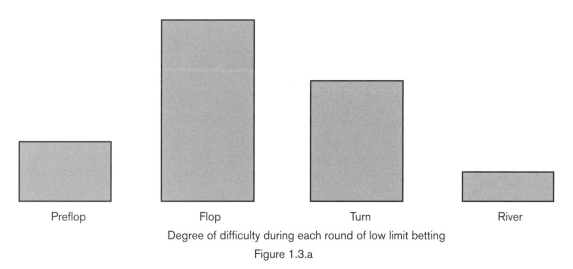

Degree of difficulty during each round of low limit betting

Figure 1.3.a

Notice in figure 1.3.b the turn is the most difficult street with high limit and no limit, as those games require many more difficult decisions on the turn, especially in no limit.

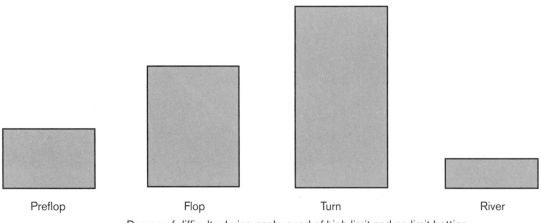

Degree of difficulty during each round of high limit and no limit betting

Figure 1.3.b

Postflop play

From the above figure it is obvious postflop play is the most important part of a hand. We will take a lot of time developing starting hands and the flop, insuring you are an expert for these two betting rounds, before you are introduced to extensive postflop play. You will find most of your opponents have only poor to good postflop skills. Your ability to play as an expert postflop will separate you from the vast majority of opponents.

Book outline

Here's the general outline of the book:

First, psych skills are emphasized.
- You will be introduced to a basic model of passive/ aggressive and tight/loose, and learn how to use that model to develop your psych skills.
- A definitive chapter on reading opponents and hands.
- A chapter on a foolproof way to deceive every opponent.

Then we start to move into areas which are math based.
- How to study the board.
- Playing the blinds.
- A chapter with lots of numbers.
- The relative strength of hands depending on how many opponents you have.
- An advanced mathematical model of passive/aggressive and tight/loose.

- The seven determining factors for every limit hand. They are:
    - How loose or tight the table is.
    - How passive or aggressive the table is.
    - Your card strength.
    - Number of opponents.
    - Position.
    - The horse.
    - Pot size.
- An extensive and exhaustive analysis of all seven factors. Toward the end there is a blending of math knowledge and psych skills with the Betting Chapter. After that, we move into no limit where we will have to add an additional three determining factors to the seven above:
    - The type of no limit game.
    - Stack size.
    - Unlimited betting.

Then we examine how to play no limit tournaments. Last, there is a special math based chapter on the casino game, Ultimate Texas Hold'em.

Even though most of the introduction is in the very back, more of a postface than a preface, there are a few important topics which need to be covered.

Experience

Education only goes so far. Experience is the comb nature gives us when we are bald. Experience is the name we give our mistakes. You need to be a balding mistake maker. With experience you will develop the patience and discipline needed to only play and stay in hands where you have a positive Expected Value.

How do you get experience? Play, play, play. You should play a minimum of 250,000 hands before you consider yourself experienced. All of these hands should be played using computer practice, micro limit, or low limit tables.

Do not play for real money until you are experienced.
Real money is money you care about.

Pre-computer players would play 30–35 hands an hour at a casino or at a home game. In a five-hour night, with no toilet breaks, they could get 150–200 hands played. Over a year they might play a total of 8,000. It would take them 30 years to play 250,000 hands. Sure, some played three times as much and got their experience in only a decade. Those are the ones whose spouses divorced them, so they had the time to play more.

But you have computer software available; both Poker Academy Pro and Wilson Turbo are excellent; they allow you to play several thousand hands a week. You can play several tables on the internet at once. Use a big screen and you can get four tables on one computer screen or you can stack several tables on one screen. Play four speed tables and you can play over 200 hands an hour, well over a 1,000 a day. After a few months you can add another monitor and play eight tables at once. Do the math. It just depends on how much time you want to put in to become experienced. Two years? One? It is up to you. Then, and only then, should you play for real money.

Why play so many hands? So that you gather the full range of experiences. You'll receive pocket Aces over 1,100 times. You will see some players defy all reason and draw all the way to the river and beat you. But the most important things you will learn are the patience and emotional stability to wait for the right cards and the discipline to make the right decisions on how to play or fold your hand.

Some experts learn superior postflop skills from coaching, seminars, books and experience. Others from experience alone. But the ability to get away from a marginal hand and read an opponent must include experience.

Simple but not easy

Every effort has been made to simplify an extremely complex subject. Some steps have been left in so expert players can follow the logic to see if they agree. Many of the laborious and mathematical formulas, statistical details, and several thousands of pages of data have been omitted. Even though we believe the material is presented in the easiest-to-understand manner, you need to know mastering all of the concepts will not be easy. The only place success comes before work is in the dictionary.

Good or world class

One of the benefits of teaching is helping a student with his/her life's plan. I don't know the answers, but I do know the questions. We spend several hours finding out what they are good at and love to do. Where their "good at's" and "love to's" converge is their natural strength; why they were put on this earth. Once we discover this intersection, it is surprisingly easy to then choose how they should spend the rest of their life. Many ask about their weaknesses. My advice is always the same. Spend most of your time building on your strengths; do not focus on compensating for weaknesses. This approach works well throughout life as we can always find others or other ways to compensate for our weaknesses.

Why bring this up? Because it doesn't work with poker. You are in a one-person business. No one but you can make up for a weakness. You can choose to be a good player or a world class player. This book will, at a minimum, make you a good player. If good is your objective you will learn those things that are part of your natural strengths and look over and perhaps become familiar with those details that don't excite you.

If you choose to be a great player you must learn and do everything. Becoming great demands doing and learning some things which are not fun. Accept the fact you cannot overcome a weakness naturally; it does take extra practice. The true difference between ordinary and extraordinary is extra. Compensating for weaknesses may not be enjoyable but becomes bearable if you look at it through the lens of a march toward being the best. You cannot fail to know which hands you can play and when. You must be patient and wait for the right hands. You must be selectively aggressive. You can't skip the 10,000 practice readings of the board (yes, that's one assignment). You must know the minimum bets needed in the pot before you can even consider drawing to an inside straight. You must keep a complete and thorough log. It goes on and on. No matter what your personality you are going to find things in this book you don't like or want to do. But every step will increase your competitive advantage. The choice is yours. Good or world class. Commercial: If you go to *PokerVT.com*, Mr. Daniel Negreanu and I willl personally teach you to be world class.

Making a living by being a good player

Is it possible to make a living playing hold'em by being good? Yes, but it is a grind if you are only winning 1 big bet per hour. There are too many good players. Good players are everywhere. Good is not nearly good enough. If you really want to make a living working this game, you must become world class. You must be able to consistently, over a long period of time, make at least 1.5 big bets per hour in limit. How about no limit? Carefully study figure 1.4.a. No limit, especially no limit tournaments, cannot be thoroughly mastered until you work your way up the pyramid.

The foundation is low limit. Figure 1.4.b reinforces the concept to play ¼ million hands of low limit before you start playing for money you care about.

Limit is so important that over 80% of this book is dedicated to you becoming a great low and high limit player. The least expensive, but best way to become good at no limit, is to first become world class at limit. If you don't there will be holes in your game and the best players will exploit those holes.

Once you are consistently making 1.5 big bets per hour in high limit, you are ready to start no limit. You will apply the same concepts learned in limit to no limit cash games. You will then move into no limit tournaments where the blinds go up fast. Here you will find a different style of play is required. Then, and only then, are you ready to play professional no limit tournaments. Tournaments where the blinds go up slowly and everyone starts off with deep stacks. At this level, you must be proficient in every possible style of play. And we'll show you how.

This is a long road, but it leads to success.

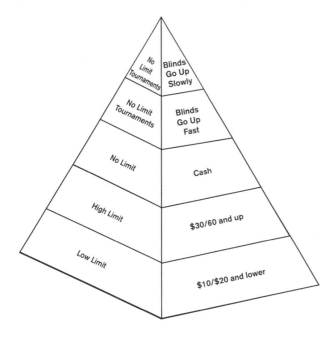

Figure 1.4.a

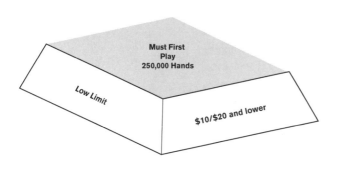

Figure 1.4.b

Repetition

Some concepts, principles, or numbers are so important, but too easily missed, that they are repeated often. And some things don't lend themselves to part of a logical progression so they appear out of nowhere.

Errors

Some of the concepts and the bulk of the data in this book are original. You will see the results of billions (no typo) of calculations. And we have checked and rechecked everything. But, when breaking fresh ground, with new ideas, new numbers, and new charts, I certainly may have made a misnake or two, or more. I'd like to say they were hidden in there to see if you could find them, but that's not true. If you find an error, or several, please write me and let me know.

Gambling

What's the difference between winning $1,000 and not losing $1,000? The adrenaline rush of winning a $1,000 pot is the only difference. Mathematically there is no difference. Chasing with a bet here and a bet there (here a bet, there a bet, everywhere a bet, bet) when the numbers are wrong is gambling and will end up costing you much more than $1,000. If you know the numbers you will know when to fold early and will not chase unless the numbers are right. You must learn how to catch and release.

Luck is where preparation meets opportunity. Knowing the numbers is the preparation. Using your psych skills and playing the numbers, not the bookie kind, is a true limit hold'em opportunity. You are going to create your own luck.

Playing the numbers in limit is not gambling. Gambling is failing to use your psych skills and follow the numbers. Gambling is getting bored and playing A9 — a hand you may only play in very limited circumstances. That may cause you to think a little. No limit does require you to gamble and guess now and then. But, following the numbers will keep you out of hands you are likely to lose and put you in hands you are likely to win. Following the numbers will keep you from betting when you have a low Expected Value draw and insure you bet when you have a high Expected Value draw. When you are finished with this book, whether you decide to devote yourself to limit or no limit, your decisions will be based on a combination of numbers and psych, not hope.

Begin with the end in mind

When you complete your first reading, you will have been exposed to hundreds of concepts and details. You are not done. The end comes only when all of the tactical details mesh together in your mind into a strategy which allows you to see the whole at a glance. How do you get to this level? You will have to learn one concept. Play and apply it. Then another concept. More play and more application. Learn and do. Do and learn. If you keep at it persistently, making a small improvement every day, you will not feel a breakthrough, but eventually you will see everything. The imprecise will have turned into the certain. When you get to that point, you will play with a confidence your opponents can smell.

Summary

- Poker is not the most important thing in life.
- A blend of superior math knowledge and psych skills is needed in hold'em.
- Postflop play separates the good from the great.
- Don't play for real money until you are experienced.
- **To make a living at this game, being good is not good enough. You must become world class.**
- Becoming world class requires work.
- The most efficient path to becoming an expert in no limit, is to first become a world class limit player.
- The concepts in this book are simple, but not easy.
- It takes a long time to see everything at a glance.

Improvement with homework and tests

Homework is given. Most assignments do not include a suggested amount of time or number of practices. You know when you are familiar, then good, then competent, then expert. Some work is nothing more than a brief review. Some will take months to complete. Many students tend to fast forward through some critical learning steps. To get the maximum benefit, you should complete all the homework.

You will find three tests and a final exam. The answers are in the back in Appendix E. If you miss anything, do not go forward until you understand the correct answers.

Homework

- Play 250,000 low limit hands before you play for real money.

CHAPTER 2

The Swayne PATL Matrix

This page describes the model which will be used as the foundation for the entire book.

Passive versus Aggressive
A passive player doesn't raise much. An aggressive player raises a lot. Figure 2.1.a illustrates the difference.

Tight versus Loose
A tight player plays few hands. A loose player plays lots of hands. See figure 2.1.b.

Creating the matrix   2.1
Now we combine the concepts by using a matrix as a basic model. A matrix is a box with other boxes in it. It is used to help make decisions or understand information in a two-dimensional way.

The matrix we will use is called the PATL matrix. It is pronounced "pat-tell" and rhymes with paddle; the P stands for passive, the A for aggressive, the T for tight, and the L for loose.

At times the matrix will be used to describe an individual player, as shown in figure 2.1.c. Other times it will describe an entire table, as in 2.1.d. Before you continue, make sure you completely understand both figures.

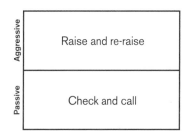

Figure 2.1.a

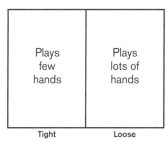

Figure 2.1.b

Individual PATL matrix

Figure 2.1.c

Table PATL matrix

Figure 2.1.d

Figure 2.2.a

Figure 2.2.b

The rest of this chapter gives you specific conditions you will find, as well as overall tactics and strategies for you to use, in each quadrant. A quadrant is a specific box within the PATL matrix. Since each section is accompanied by a figure, this chapter has numerical subdivisions, such as 2.1 above, which has figures 2.1.a-d included, 2.2 is the next section, which has figure 2.2.a-e included, and so on.

The merry-go-round

As you go through the next few chapters it will feel as though you are going around and around the PATL. You are. Why? Because the later chapters build on earlier ones. Having a complete and thorough understanding of the basic PATL will insure an easy transition to a more advanced model.

Identifying players   2.2
Where they are
The worst players are loose. The best players are tight. You will find a gaggle of poor players at loose tables.

Aggressive/tight games are played by the best players. If you expect to be a winner at a tight table, you must be a good to great player.

Mistakes

Your brilliant play is not where you make your profit. Profit comes from players who make poor decisions. The more mistakes, the poorer the player. **You want to play against loose players.**

Alcohol is your ally, as long as you are not a user. When loose players drink they make even more mistakes. *Ein Prost.* You don't have to be a great player at a loose table. You just have to be better than most of those in the game.

Their names

Figure 2.2.c shows the names, at least the polite ones, more experienced players use to describe others.

The noise tipoff

Most loose tables are loud, as opposed to the quiet-as-a-tree tight tables.

The chip clue

Another sign as to the flavor of the table is how the players' chips are stacked. Loose players tend to stack their chips poorly. The messier the looser. Passive/tights have their chips stacked neatly, in exactly the same heights, and sometimes in a creative pattern. Some go so far as to align the marks on the sides of chips together. This is a readable indication that this player is disciplined and will patiently wait for the right hands to play. Aggressive/tights either mirror the passive/tights or go one better by having very tall precise stacks.

When betting, many experienced aggressives have a special or unusual manner of putting their chips in the pot. Likewise, when they fold, look for a skillful twist of the cards in the air, or other practiced fold.

Where to find players   2.3
Type of Hold'em

Passive/loose players tend to play low limit. You will find passive/tights mostly at low limit tables, grinding away to win their 1 big bet per hour. Aggressive/loose players don't last long at high limit. Aggressive/tights, the best players, focus on high limit and no limit.

Special note. We will find in the no limit chapter there are specific types of no limit tournaments where this matrix does not hold.

Strategic and tactical decisions   2.4
Cost to benefit

The primary reason you want **a passive/loose table** is it **gives you your best return on your investment**. This doesn't mean you win the biggest pots with a passive/loose game; it means that when you do win, you win a lot compared to what you had to invest in the pot.

Target size

You can bag a passive/loose player with a shotgun. An expert sniper is needed for the aggressive/tight.

	Tight	Loose
Aggressive	Professional	Maniac
Passive	Rock	Calling station

Figure 2.2.c

	Tight	Loose
Aggressive	Quiet	Conversation, laughter, noisy
Passive	Quiet	Conversation, laughter, noisy

Figure 2.2.d

	Tight	Loose
Aggressive	Chips stacked precisely and tall	Chips not neat
Passive	Chips stacked neatly	Chips not neat

Figure 2.2.e

	Tight	Loose
Aggressive	High limit No limit	Low limit No limit
Passive	Mostly low limit; some no limit	Low limit

Figure 2.3

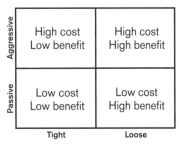

	Tight	Loose
Aggressive	High cost Low benefit	High cost High benefit
Passive	Low cost Low benefit	Low cost High benefit

Figure 2.4.a

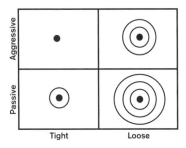

Figure 2.4.b

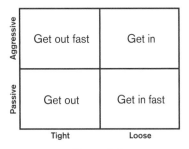

	Tight	Loose
Aggressive	Get out fast	Get in
Passive	Get out	Get in fast

Figure 2.4.c

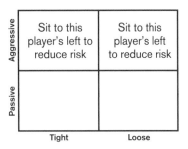

	Tight	Loose
Aggressive	Sit to this player's left to reduce risk	Sit to this player's left to reduce risk
Passive		

Figure 2.4.d

Get in or get out

The most important strategic decision you can possibly make is whether to get in a game or get out of it. You want a passive/loose table and you must avoid aggressive/tight games. As you sign in at the casino, hand the pit boss a green chip and tell him you want the loosest table. If that doesn't work, use the clues in the previous sections and your own observations about the amount of raising, calling, and number of players in each hand to decide which is the table for you.

Once at a table adjust your play to the personality of the game. By personality we mean where the table fits on the PATL matrix. Adapt. Become a chameleon. Once you know how the table is playing, become one with the table (Ah yes, grasshopper). Blend in up to a point. The reason we say up to a point is when the table is loose, you will be somewhat tighter. If the game is extremely tight you will be slightly looser. When play is passive, you will be more aggressive. After you have read all the chapters, you will have a better understanding of these concepts.

Choosing your seat

If the most important decision you can make is whether or not to get in a game, **the second most important decision is choosing your seat.** Loose players will choose their "lucky" or "favorite" seat. You will understand seat position is extremely important at certain tables. One philosophy is to reduce your risk. Another strives to provide you with the most potential profit.

Reduce your risk

To reduce your risk the seat you choose is extremely important if you are going to play at an aggressive table. **You want to be seated to the left, preferably immediately to the left, of the most aggressive bettor.**

The two most important elements of risk are how much information you have and how much you must bet. If the aggressor is on your right, you will have a lot of information before you decide to play. You will know what some of your opponents have done and what the aggressor has done, before you make your decision. If you are on the button, you will actually know what all of your opponents have done. That information reduces your risk. Second, if the aggressor is on your left, you must constantly worry about being re-raised if you bet with just marginal drawing cards, and your risk is increased because you will have to put more in the pot just to stay in the hand.

How much you lose at an aggressive table is directly related to where you sit. Too many inexperienced players underestimate this strategic decision. Although you may not be able to choose your seat when you first sit down, once you have determined who the most aggressive bettor is, ask the dealer if you can move to one of the seats to the left of him when it opens up. The dealer should then place a seat change button on the table indicating you have priority for a seat change.

Choosing your seat at a passive game is not very important. However, if you find there is a player who tends to raise more than the rest of the table, ask the dealer if you can move to his left when a seat opens up. Always moving to the left of the most aggressive bettor will save you money.

Make more money

There is another school of thought which says you should have the loosest players to your right as money tends to flow to the left. The reasons are that players to the left always have more information than those on the right, and loose players provide the most opportunity for profit. You should be aware some very respected players and authors prefer loose players, especially aggressive/loose, to their left. I respectfully disagree. I want opponents who can cause me the most trouble on my right.

Another advantage of having tights immediately to your left is it increases the likelihood you can steal their blinds.

	Aggressive		Sit to this player's left to make more money
	Passive		Sit to this player's left to make more money
		Tight	Loose

Figure 2.4.e

The best of both worlds

Although the opportunity will seldom occur, figure 2.4.f shows the best seating arrangement possible as it keeps both the aggressive and loose players to your right, and the passive/tights to your left.

Passive Tight	Passive Tight	Passive Tight	Passive Tight	Your seat	Aggressive Loose	Aggressive Tight	Passive Loose	Passive Loose

Ideal Seating
Figure 2.4.f

Yin and yang

What do you do if you find an aggressive on your left? Turn the bad into good. When we get to the Betting Chapter you will find when you enter a hand, you will normally be raising. With an

	Tight	Loose
Aggressive	High cost to stay in hand	High cost to stay in hand
Passive	Low cost to stay in hand	Low cost to stay in hand

Figure 2.5.a

	Tight	Loose
Aggressive	Large pot size fluctuations	Large pot size fluctuations
Passive	Small pot size fluctuations	Small pot size fluctuations

Figure 2.5.b

	Tight	Loose
Aggressive	Extreme bankroll swing	Extreme bankroll swing
Passive	Small bankroll swing	Moderate bankroll swing

Figure 2.5.c

	Tight	Loose
Aggressive	A few moderate wins	A few big wins
Passive	Series of small wins	A few big wins

Figure 2.5.d

	Tight	Loose
Aggressive	Worst chance to recoup losses	Best chance to recoup losses
Passive	Little chance to recoup losses	Moderate chance to recoup losses

Figure 2.5.e

aggressive/loose on your left, you can just call, as he is likely to do the raising for you. With the aggressive/tight on your left, since he will be playing fewer hands than the aggressive/loose, you should enter with your usual raise.

What you will find at the table   2.5
Cost to stay in the hand

Everyone's cost to play, including yours, will be high at any kind of aggressive table.

Pot size fluctuations

The biggest pots will be at an aggressive/loose table. The smallest at a passive/tight table. It is difficult just to stay ahead of the rake at a passive/tight table while at a loose table the rake is of minor concern.

Bankroll swing

You can win or lose the most at an aggressive table. It will cost you dearly to see the river and often several bets just to see the flop. If you are playing at an aggressive/loose table you must avoid two traps. Trap number one is getting discouraged by being way down. Trap number two is when you are way up and start believing you can win with losing hands.

Wins

You will win your biggest pots at a loose table. When you win at an aggressive/tight table, the pots are OK, but not great. Remember it is extremely important to stay out of these games. At a passive/tight table the best you can hope for is accumulating small wins. You want to avoid these games too.

Recoup losses

Players who are down often either look for an aggressive/loose game or try to turn the table they are playing at into an aggressive/loose game.

Your best chance of recovering losses is at an aggressive/loose table. If you don't have the experience to play in this game, you will find it will turn out to be your best chance of increasing your losses. Do not try to recoup losses at an aggressive/loose table until you have the experience to do so.

Bad beats

In any kind of loose game you are going to have bad beats. Passive/loose players believe in luck and love to see the river, even though mathematically they should not continue. If the pot is large, which it will be often at an aggressive/loose table, advanced players who understand Expected Value, or "pot odds," know it is often correct to play to the river, even with a low pair or other low percentage hand. Before you finish this book, you will understand and know how to use Expected Value.

At an extremely passive/loose 10-handed table, with the best starting hand you can get, AA, you will win 30% of the time. That means your AA will lose 70% of the time. No whining allowed. Bad beats are part of playing in any loose game.

Position   2.6
Who understands and uses position?

Position is where you are seated relative to the dealer. The later your position the more information you have, so your risk is minimal, and you can better control the play. A passive/loose does not understand position. The aggressive/tight not only values his position, but when in middle or late position, uses it aggressively.

General comment

Preflop the importance of position is greatest at an aggressive/tight table and least at a passive/loose table. The value of position also increases when there are fewer opponents.

Always remember in any game you always win more money, or are able to cut your losses, with good position. If you are in late position and a passive/tight raises before it is your turn to act, you will know to fold hands such as AJ or KQ.

Opponents   2.7
Who will lead?

Aggressives want control. The aggressive/loose just wants to be the top dog at the table. The aggressive/tight strategically understands hold'em rewards aggression and the long-term winners bet, raise, and re-raise. Aggressives often battle each other hard to achieve betting dominance.

	Tight	Loose
Aggressive	Few bad beats	Some bad beats
Passive	Few bad beats	Many bad beats

Figure 2.5.f

	Tight	Loose
Aggressive	Values position and uses it aggressively	Undervalues position
Passive	Values position	Doesn't understand position

Figure 2.6.a

	Tight	Loose
Aggressive	Position extremely important	Position very important
Passive	Position important	Preflop position not important; postflop position important

Figure 2.6.b

	Tight	Loose
Aggressive	Takes control of the hand	Takes control of the hand
Passive	Seldom takes control of the hand	Will not take control of the hand

Figure 2.7.a

	Tight	Loose
Aggressive	Raises if hits or on a good draw	Raises
Passive	Calls if hits or a very strong draw	Calls

Figure 2.7.b

	Tight	Loose
Aggressive	Opponents sometimes bluff	Opponents often bluff
Passive	Opponents never bluff	Opponents seldom bluff

Figure 2.7.c

Passive players hate to play against aggressives. Passives are, as you would expect, passive; they do not try to take control of a hand. The passive/tight may understand how important aggression is, but it is not in his personality to use it. The passive/loose does not understand the importance of aggression.

When players raise or call

The passive/loose calls. Fortunately for you he calls too much and chases too much. The passive/tight calls with a very strong draw and will just call even when he catches and has the best hand. The aggressive/loose will raise because the word "call" is not in his vocabulary. The aggressive/tight raises if he hits, is on a good draw, smells weakness, or has position.

Bluff

Bluffing occurs most at aggressive and least at passive tables. It is most frequently used at aggressive/tight tables and least at passive/loose. The passive/tight opponent will never bluff. You should avoid bluffing against passive/loose opponents as it is common for a player to call on the river because he "wants to see it." He who tries to bluff a loose player is a poor player. You can bluff tight players. The best bluff is against one, at most two, tights.

Your most effective bluffing, especially in no limit, is with small pots.

	Tight	Loose
Aggressive	Preflop easier to read hands; postflop difficult	It is almost impossible to read these hands
Passive	Easy to read these hands	Difficult to read preflop hands; postflop easier

Figure 2.8.a

What's important for you   2.8
Reading hands

The more aggressive the table, the more important reading hands becomes. Having said that, it is almost impossible to read aggressive/loose players.

A long cut, not a short cut, to becoming a great poker player is to take a year or two and become a casino dealer. When a casino dealer plays in a game — most must play at a casino other than where they work — he is usually the best at reading hands of anyone at the table. A dealer knows from the experience of seeing so many hands how to recognize betting patterns and physical tells. Often he can predict precisely not only what the winner has, but also the cards of others in the hand. The next chapter teaches how to read hands.

Deception

Deception is extremely important at tight tables. Deception is worthless at a passive/loose table unless your remaining opponents are aggressive/loose.

Type of play

Against loose tables straightforward play is best. Bet when strong; check when weak. At tight tables bluffing, deception, check-raising, and other advanced plays work.

Preflop   2.9
Preflop raising and calling

Figure 2.9.a shows the relative frequencies of opponents' preflop decisions at each type of table.

At a passive/loose table you will think a bunch of crows are in the casino. All you hear is "caw, caw, caw." Actually what you are hearing is "call, call, call." You will be calling a lot too; not as much as everyone else, but you can play a lot of hands at this table.

Notice that at tight tables, preflop folding is more prevalent than raising or calling.

Your play will be different than others.

1. You will fold more than your opponents.
2. You will call less often, even at loose tables.
3. When you do play a hand, you will enter with a raise more often at a loose table than your opponents.

	Tight	Loose
Aggressive	Deception important	Deception somewhat important
Passive	Deception important	Deception not important

Figure 2.8.b

	Tight	Loose
Aggressive	Advanced play OK	Straight-forward play works best
Passive	Advanced play OK	Straight-forward play works best

Figure 2.8.c

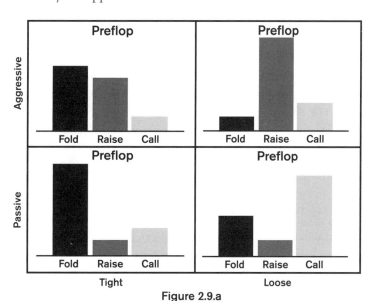

Figure 2.9.a

	Tight	Loose
Aggressive	Moderate preflop pot size	Very large preflop pot size
Passive	Very small preflop pot size	Large preflop pot size

Figure 2.9.b

	Tight	Loose
Aggressive	You will play very few hands	You will play some hands
Passive	You will play few hands	You will play the most hands

Figure 2.9.c

	Tight	Loose
Aggressive	You will fold good hands often	You may fold a few good hands
Passive	You will fold good hands	You will not fold good hands

Figure 2.9.d

	Tight	Loose
Aggressive	High cards High pairs win frequently	Pairs and draws win frequently
Passive	High cards High pairs win frequently	Pairs and draws win frequently

Figure 2.9.e

	Tight	Loose
Aggressive	Some opponents see flop	Many opponents see flop
Passive	Few opponents see flop	Many opponents see flop

Figure 2.10.a

Preflop pot size

Count on it costing you a lot just to see the flop at an aggressive table. Why? Opponents at an aggressive table like to be, well, aggressive. They love the words "raise, re-raise, and cap." It won't cost you much to see flops at a passive table.

Number of hands you will play

You will play the most hands at a passive/loose table. You will play the least at an aggressive/tight table. Chapter 9 will go through exactly how many hands you can play at various types of tables.

How often you will fold

Both preflop and postflop you will be folding more against tight opponents than loose ones. Similarly, you will fold more against a passive's bet than an aggressive's.

Winning hands

At a tight table, because you and your opponents will be playing fewer drawing cards, high cards and high pairs are frequent winners. At a loose table, drawing hands, including low pairs, turn into winners more often on the turn or river than in a tight game as loose players hang on, hoping to catch a miracle card. Chapter 9 will show you the drawing hands you will play at a loose table that you would not play at a tight one.

The flop   2.10
Opponents see flop

At an extremely passive/loose table almost everyone stays in to see the flop. Amazing. The vulture in good players loves it. At an aggressive/loose table over ½ the players see the flop. An aggressive/loose table is OK, but not nearly as nice as the extremely passive/loose table.

Flop folding

Figure 2.9.a showed preflop folding. Few stayed in preflop on tight tables, more on loose tables. Correctly reading figure 2.10.b takes a few extra seconds. The chart shows the tendency of those who stayed to see the flop to then fold, raise, or call.

Once the flop is shown, even passive/loose players tighten up. You will see most of the folding on the flop appears on loose tables. Beware of those on tight tables, or tight players at a loose

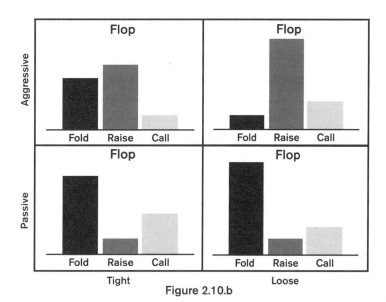

Figure 2.10.b

table, who do not fold on the flop. They either have a good hand, are close to making a good hand, or, if aggressive, believe they can bluff you into believing they have a good hand.

Even though there is not a tendency on the flop to raise at a passive table, if you have a made hand or have a solid semi-bluff opportunity — for example an open-ended straight or four flush — you should raise.

Bet draws to get these players to fold

If on the flop you have a draw and you want your opponents to fold, betting may get tights to fold. Loose players will make their decision based on what they think they have; your bet will not impact their decision to stay or fold.

Free card play works

You raise in late position preflop or on the flop and if you miss, you hope the previous callers check to you so you can see the next card without a bet. At any kind of aggressive/tight table the free card play won't work. These opponents know the play and will not check based on your raise. Likewise, the aggressive/loose won't check — not because he understands the play, he just doesn't know how to check. If your opponents are passive/loose, the free card play works very well.

	Tight	Loose
Aggressive	Bet draws to get these to fold	Betting draws will not get these to fold
Passive	Bet draws to get these to fold	Betting draws will not get these to fold

Figure 2.10.c

	Tight	Loose
Aggressive	Forget free card play	Forget free card play
Passive	Free card play may work	Free card play will work

Figure 2.10.d

	Tight	Loose
Aggressive	Some showdowns	Many showdowns
Passive	Few showdowns	Almost always a showdown

Figure 2.11.a

	Tight	Loose
Aggressive	This opponent will bluff heads up on river	This opponent will bluff heads up on river
Passive	This opponent will not bluff heads up on river	This opponent will not bluff heads up on river

Figure 2.11.b

	Tight	Loose
Aggressive	May bet if you missed	Check if you missed
Passive	May bet if you missed	Check if you missed

Figure 2.11.c

	Tight	Loose
Aggressive	Don't worry about scare card on the river	Beware of scare card on the river
Passive	Don't worry about scare card on the river	Beware of scare card on the river

Figure 2.11.d

	Tight	Loose
Aggressive	Don't worry about runner runner	Beware of runner runner
Passive	Don't worry about runner runner	Beware of runner runner

Figure 2.11.e

Turn and river   2.11
Showdowns

A showdown means you have to show your cards on the river, usually against just one or two opponents.

Count on a lot of showdowns at loose tables, with the most at passive/loose tables. Too often at a passive/loose table someone wants to keep his opponent "honest" and is foolishly willing to spend a big bet just to do so. Let others pay the big bet and you will get the information for free.

Bluffing heads up on the river

River bluffs work best when it is heads up. Figure 2.11.b shows when your opponents are most likely to river bluff. When should you bluff on the river? Only when your remaining opponent is tight or the pot is large and bluffing is your only way of winning the pot. This will be covered again in the Betting Chapter.

What to do if heads up on the river and you missed

Good players can be bluffed. Poor players can't. If you are first to bet heads up on the river and you missed, unless you are resigned to fold, you should bet, raise or re-raise against a tight player. Always check against a loose player.

Beware of a scare card on the river

Many loose players stay to the river. Watch out on the river for an A or K as loose players play A-anything, K-anything, and will stay for the turn if the flop shows their third flush card or a third card for a straight. Back off on raising against a loose opponent with any of these types of river scare cards.

Runner runner

This means the turn and river cards. Against tight opponents you don't have to worry much about a runner runner flush or straight. As stated above, this is not so with loose opponents.

The player you must first become

An aggressive/tight. The aggressive/tight steals blinds, starts off with a strong hand, or tries — especially in no limit — to get everyone to fold to him on the flop. Will you always play as an aggressive/tight? No, and we will show you when you don't when we get to professional no limit tournaments.

Summary

- The PATL matrix is the underlying foundation for everything in this book.
- There are identifying characteristics for players and tables in each PATL quadrant.
- You want to play at loose tables and avoid tight ones.
- Where a table and your opponents fit in the PATL determines your playing strategy.

Homework

- Be able to place every table in the table PATL matrix.
- Be able to place every person in the individual PATL matrix.

CHAPTER 3

Reading Opponents and Their Hands

Taking good to great — knowing when to hold them and when to fold them

In the first chapter one figure showed you how important your math knowledge is compared to your psych skills during each round of betting. Others illustrated how difficult each round of betting is and as you may recall, the turn is the most difficult to play in no limit and high limit. We have combined the findings of those two figures into figure 3.1. Your math knowledge will allow you to maximize your Expected Value during each round of betting. Your psych skills, especially important on the flop and turn, determine your decisions.

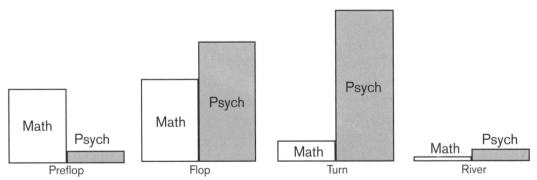

Combination of play difficulty and knowledge/skills needed during each round of betting

Figure 3.1

Reading opponents and their hands is a psych skill you can develop. It uses a combination of betting patterns and physical tells. The first part to learning this skill is gathering information on how an opponent plays his hands, which will help you read hands later.

You must first read your opponents. Watch and learn how each person plays and what they do to tell you what they have. You do this so you can read their hands, but **before you can read a hand, you must, MUST, <u>MUST</u> know each opponent on an individual basis**.

This chapter's findings are not mathematically determined but empirical, which means they are the result of extensive observations. When pure math is used, as it will be in later chapters, the results are science. When observations alone are used, it is a mix of art and science. Slimy, imprecise words such as "tends" and "usually" need to be added to almost every sentence.

This chapter depends heavily on your understanding of the PATL matrix. As you go through, you will see how hands are played for each type of player. The first part will describe the general hand strength of each type of individual PATL opponent. The second shows the physical changes which occur with each type of player. The next few pages give specific postflop hands and how various opponents play them. This section also includes the strength of the hands on the turn and river.

You are going to learn not just what cards each opponent will play, but most important, how he plays those cards.

Part I – General hand strength

Experience level

The first thing you need to do is determine an individual player's experience level. The level will range anywhere from someone who has never set foot in a poker room to another who plays eight days a week. It is fairly easy to determine one's experience level by their conduct at the table. A player who doesn't understand the blinds or betting structure is an inexperienced player. Another, who converses with others at the table by "talking the talk," or who is on a first-name basis with them is more than likely experienced.

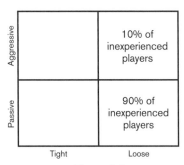

Figure 3.2

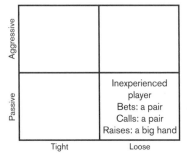

Figure 3.3

The inexperienced player — predominantly passive/loose

If you are playing with inexperienced players, you are playing with opponents who, for the most part, are bad. It isn't their fault they are bad; they just don't have the experience yet. With an inexperienced player you are less likely to run into slowplaying or check-raising. All this player knows is if he makes some sort of hand, he will bet. With a draw he won't bet but will call. So if an inexperienced player bets, there is a good chance he has something. Now something could mean a lot of things. He might not have a strong hand but he thinks he does. Often he will bet any pair he made on the flop thinking that it is automatically a good hand. Or he could have a small pocket pair. Many inexperienced players go all the way to the river with a small pair no matter what the board shows. Likewise, he could have had a big hand but didn't raise because he didn't know when to raise.

90% of inexperienced players fall into the passive/loose area and 10% into the aggressive/loose quadrant. Aggressive/loose inexperienced players are usually young and have watched too much no limit on TV.

When trying to read an inexperienced player's hand, keep it simple. The obvious holds true. If he is calling, he more than likely has a pair. And he may call all the way to the river with nothing more than a low pair. If he asks how much he can bet, he has a big hand.

The experienced player

There are many more variables with the experienced player. You must place each player's style in the PATL matrix. For the rest of this chapter, unless otherwise noted, we are discussing experienced players.

Probable distribution of hands

Where a player fits in the PATL matrix determines the range of hands he will play. Even a superficial placement of an opponent in his PATL gives a good indication of his probable distribution of hands. As you would expect, and will see in the next few pages, since tights play fewer hands, their range of hands will be a lot stronger than loose players'.

Passive/tight

This player has a small arsenal of hands he plays and you can tell what he has within a few cards.

When he comes into a preflop pot without raising, he has two face cards, a pair, a high Ace, AT or better, or suited connectors 87 or higher.

If he raises preflop he has AA, KK, QQ, or AKs. If he re-raises, he has AA and AA only. Another sure bet is if he raises from either of the blinds, he has AA.

If he is betting on the flop, make your read from the high cards on the board. If he calls a two flush flop he probably has a four flush. If he bets and there is a three flush on the board, he probably has a flush. Likewise, if there are three in sequence or close sequence, especially higher cards, his betting will be similar if he hit a straight.

If he stops betting, the board has delivered something that can beat him.

Aggressive/tight

As with the passive/tight opponent, **he usually only plays good to premium hands**. The difference is when he has strong cards, even a strong draw, you may run into a check-raise. You will hear "raise" and "re-raise" as long as he is in the hand.

This player is slightly more difficult to pinpoint than the passive/tight because he seems reckless. But when he shows his cards, you will see he was playing only top cards or strong draws. That's your key to knowing this player is aggressive/tight — not aggressive/loose.

Passive/loose

He plays almost any two cards, sees at least the flop, but folds quickly when he misses. This player is more difficult to read preflop.

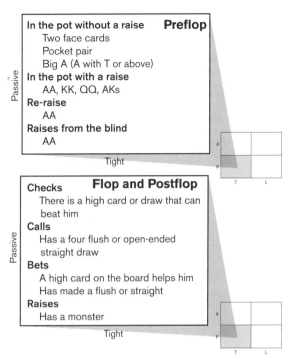

Reading the passive/tight player's hands

Figure 3.4

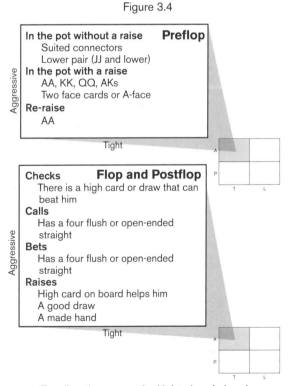

Reading the aggressive/tight player's hands

Figure 3.5

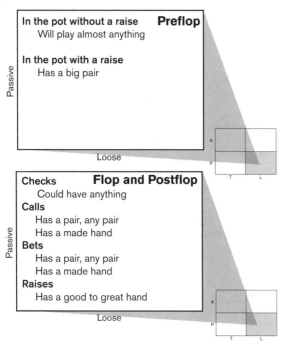

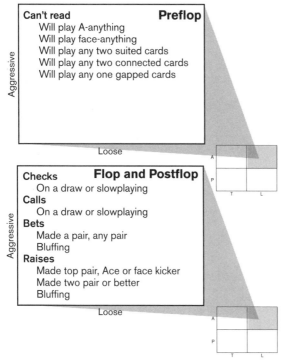

Preflop

In the pot without a raise
Will play almost anything

In the pot with a raise
Has a big pair

Flop and Postflop

Checks
Could have anything
Calls
Has a pair, any pair
Has a made hand
Bets
Has a pair, any pair
Has a made hand
Raises
Has a good to great hand

Reading the passive/loose player's hands

Figure 3.6

Preflop

Can't read
Will play A-anything
Will play face-anything
Will play any two suited cards
Will play any two connected cards
Will play any one gapped cards

Flop and Postflop

Checks
On a draw or slowplaying
Calls
On a draw or slowplaying
Bets
Made a pair, any pair
Bluffing
Raises
Made top pair, Ace or face kicker
Made two pair or better
Bluffing

Reading the aggressive/loose player's hands

Figure 3.7

On the flop it is worth raising or check-raising to see if this player really has something. When faced with a raise, he will fold unless he has a made hand, an open-ended straight, or four flush draw. Remember, this is where you will also find most of the inexperienced players.

Aggressive/loose

Almost impossible to put on a specific hand. He plays any two cards and when he is in, which is almost every hand, it is raise, re-raise, and cap. He will have wild swings in his bankroll, and will often tilt when he is losing. If he is dominating the table, as he often will, the table will become aggressive/loose just because he is playing.

When two or more are at the same table, the entertainment value is great. Although I refrain from telling too many stories, I did have the pleasure of playing at a table where seat three straddled, the next player raised in the dark, the player after that re-raised in the dark, and the next player capped it in the dark. Not a card dealt and it was capped. That's extreme aggressive/loose.

When at an aggressive/loose table, you will not be playing many hands but when you do play, you will be paid off much more often than not. As far as reading the aggressive/loose player's hand, you can't. He could have anything.

Ease of reading summary

Figure 3.8 summarizes the ease in reading hands

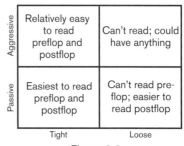

	Tight	Loose
Aggressive	Relatively easy to read preflop and postflop	Can't read; could have anything
Passive	Easiest to read preflop and postflop	Can't read preflop; easier to read postflop

Figure 3.8

based on where the player fits in the PATL matrix both preflop and postflop.

Part II – Physical changes

Tell trends

We are going to review how players tend to react and tell you what they have. But, in order for you to know if the trends presented on the next few pages hold true for a particular player, let's repeat something.

You must watch and learn how each person plays and what they do to tell you what they have. You do this so you can read their hands, but before you can read a hand, you must, MUST, <u>MUST</u> know your opponents.

It will not be enough to just place each person in the PATL matrix, although that is the starting point. Becoming a great player requires you to pay much more attention to what they do to tell you what they have. It will pay you handsome dividends if you take the time to watch your opponents as they get their cards. Too many players, mostly loose ones, are just looking at their cards. The best players are observing the other players and their reactions as they receive their cards or as the board cards come out.

The trends presented are just that, trends. With your observations you must confirm, or deny, which, if any, trends apply to those around the table.

Dress

Some players dress as they play. Conservative dress would indicate a passive/tight. Flamboyant clothes signify loose play. A neat appearance, including even a hair style or close shave, all lean towards a tighter player.

Occupation

Some friendly table talk and you will be able to find out what they do for a living. Although not definitive, what a person does for a living tends to tell you the type of player they are.

Bad hand – knows when beat

Tight players get out of a hand if they think they are beat even when they hold AA. Loose players will stay for almost any kind of a draw.

	Tight	Loose
Aggressive	Casual dress	Flamboyant dress
Passive	Conservative dress	Casual dress

Figure 3.9

	Tight	Loose
Aggressive	Executive Attorney	Attorney Lower level worker Student
Passive	Doctor Teacher Accountant	Middle manager

Figure 3.10

	Tight	Loose
Aggressive	Knows when beat and folds	Doesn't know when beat; stays in hand too long
Passive	Knows when beat and folds	Doesn't know when beat; stays in hand too long

Figure 3.11

	Tight	Loose
Aggressive	Usually no change in manner of protecting cards	May protect cards differently depending on hand strength
Passive	May protect cards differently depending on hand strength	Usually doesn't protect cards at all

Figure 3.12

Protects cards

This tip is a change in the usual manner a player protects his cards. Better players tend to put a chip on their cards when they are going to play them but not when they are going to fold. Many will put more chips on their cards than usual if they either have a very good hand or intend to bluff. With a good hand, others move their cards closer to them or have their hands, the ones connected to the arms, over the cards. Again, see what is the usual pattern, if any, and look for changes.

Bad hand — cards off the table

When a player holds his cards an inch or two off the table preflop, he will tend to fold. This occurs with almost every loose player, and even with some aggressive/tight players. Knowing this, if you are in early position, you should be able to predict the size of the preflop pot.

Good hand — change in mood

If a loose player has a good hand, he tends to change his mood from whatever it was before he saw his hand, to something totally different. He may become more quiet and serious as though he is saying, "it is time to focus." The loose player also tends to act faster than usual, act out of turn, or may try to put in a big bet when it is a smaller betting round. Not true with the tight players. A change you may perceive with a tight is he may protect or cover his cards more than usual.

Stops conversation

In 3.15 another change a tight player shows is he will stop conversing with another. In 3.14 above note how the tight player's mood remains constant no matter what he has or doesn't have.

Bad hand — continue conversation

All players tend to continue their conversations when they have a bad hand, but if tight players are engaged in a conversation and get a bad hand, they definitely continue their conversation. Some passive/tights will whine about their cards, but most passive/tights just don't engage in any conversation. A passive/tight player is a passive/tight person.

	Tight	Loose
Aggressive	Some will fold if cards held off the table	Will fold if cards held off the table
Passive		Will fold if cards held off the table

Figure 3.13

	Tight	Loose
Aggressive	No change in expression or mood with a good hand	Noticeable change in expression or mood with a good hand
Passive	No change in expression or mood with a good hand	Big change in expression or mood with a good hand

Figure 3.14

	Tight	Loose
Aggressive	May stop conversation with a good hand	
Passive	May stop conversation (but seldom is having one) with a good hand	

Figure 3.15

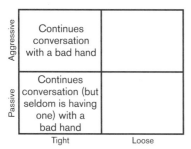

	Tight	Loose
Aggressive	Continues conversation with a bad hand	
Passive	Continues conversation (but seldom is having one) with a bad hand	

Figure 3.16

Good hand — chips come in slowly

A player's hands, the ones connected to their arms, not the cards they hold, reveal much — although if you could see their cards that would help even more. A good tell is any change in how a player puts in his chips, compared to his usual pattern. Generally, tight players who have a good hand tend to put their chips in slowly; almost as though they are saying "I don't want to chase anyone out." To a lesser extent the same applies to the aggressive/loose player.

Bad hand — chip action

Loose players tend to give away a bad hand by either putting in their chips very slowly or throwing them in reluctantly, in a manner inconsistent with their usual bet. Both actions say, "I know I'm going to lose. I know I don't belong in this pot." The aggressive/tight will also throw in his chips differently when he is on tilt, which isn't often.

Tilt

Players on tilt play foolishly. They play poor hands, raise too much, and chase too much. **Any opponent on tilt provides you with excellent profit potential.**

The aggressive/loose is the one who will tilt most often. Reading his hands is impossible, but if you see him throwing in his chips, especially after losing a big hand, he is probably on tilt. The passive/tight may simmer or sometimes complain after a bad beat, but he does not tilt. The aggressive/tight does not go on tilt when playing at an aggressive/tight table; these are his peers and he accepts the way they play. If the aggressive/tight is outdrawn by a passive/loose, he may be on tilt for a few hands, but pulls out of it rapidly.

Fast check

Passive opponents who immediately check are letting you know they either missed or are on a draw. Aggressive opponents who do the same are either on a draw, or, if in early position, may be waiting to check-raise.

Fast call

An opponent who calls quickly usually does so for one of two reasons. First, he is most likely on a draw. This is the case for most opponents. Second, if he is an aggressive/loose, he may be letting you know he is going to stay in the hand until there is a

	Tight	Loose
Aggressive	Chips come in slower than usual with a good hand	Chips sometimes come in slower than usual with a good hand
Passive	Chips come in slower than usual with a good hand	

Figure 3.17

	Tight	Loose
Aggressive	Throws them in with a bad hand only if on tilt	Reluctant to put chips in or throws them in with a bad hand
Passive		Reluctant to put chips in or throws them in with a bad hand

Figure 3.18

	Tight	Loose
Aggressive	Occasionally on tilt	Tilts most often
Passive	Does not tilt	Doesn't know what tilt is

Figure 3.19

	Tight	Loose
Aggressive	Usually no read but may be ready to check-raise	Completely missed or preparing to check-raise
Passive	Missed	Missed or on a draw

Figure 3.20

	Tight	Loose
Aggressive	On a draw but usually too disciplined to fast call	On a draw
Passive	Usually won't call quickly	On a draw

Figure 3.21

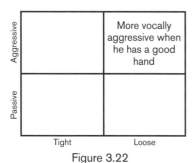

	Tight	Loose
Aggressive		More vocally aggressive when he has a good hand
Passive		

Figure 3.22

	Tight	Loose
Aggressive		Shows good hand to others preflop and on flop
Passive		Shows good hand to others preflop and on flop

Figure 3.23

	Tight	Loose
Aggressive		Sometimes forgets to read the board with a good hand
Passive		Sometimes forgets to read the board or doesn't know how to read it

Figure 3.24

	Tight	Loose
Aggressive	Will not look at cards	After looking at hole cards, bets; has a flush or high flush card
Passive	Will not look at cards	After looking at hole cards, bets; has a flush or high flush card

Figure 3.25

	Tight	Loose
Aggressive	Will not look at cards	After looking at hole cards bets; has a straight or straight draw
Passive	Will not look at cards	After looking at hole cards bets; has a straight

Figure 3.26

showdown. Good, but not excellent players, with a marginal catch on the flop or a medium pocket pair, may use the fast call on the flop as a false show of strength. Their objective is to get to the river with at least one free card.

Good hand — more vocally aggressive

An aggressive/loose player who has a good hand tends to not only be aggressive with his betting, but also becomes louder and engages in more aggressive talk with others at the table. In addition, his body posture — sitting up straight or moving towards the table, will represent confidence.

Good hand — showing his card or cards

On the flop, observe if a player shows his cards to others watching. If the player shows only one card he has a small pocket pair; he is letting the onlooker know he needs to hit another for a set. If the player shows both cards to another preflop he has a big pocket pair. Also on the flop, if he shows his cards to another before he bets, he has hit top pair with a good kicker. On the turn or river, anytime he shows his cards after he checks, he missed.

Good hand — forgets to read the board

Some loose players, especially the passive/loose who has a great hand or gets wrapped up in his good hand, tend to forget to read the board, or ignore the board, failing to see they are beat.

Two or three suited on flop

Loose players will look at their cards to see if they have one or two of the suited flop card. On a three flush after a loose player has looked at his cards and bets, he likely has a flush or a high flush card. The same can be said for the turn or river when a flush card hits.

Straight draw on the board

Similarly, when there is a straight draw on the board, loose players will look at their cards to see if their cards fit. If they look for more than an instant, they have cards which are close. If the straight draw on the board is not sequenced and they take an extra long look, they definitely have cards which are close to making a straight. If they then bet they either have an open-ended straight draw, a made straight, or a pair.

Unusual tells from loose players

Observation will reveal some very unusual tells, mostly from loose players. The reason these do not apply to tights is because the tights are so much more experienced. More clues are available from an opponent's body than from his voice or face.

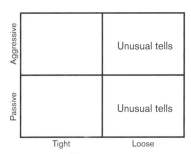

Figure 3.27

- The loose player acts strong when he is weak and weak when he is strong. Poker master Mike Caro is right.
- He goes out of his way to show disappointment. Good hand.
- He looks at his hole cards once or twice during the hand. This indicates he does not have a pocket pair. The tight player seldom checks his cards at any time throughout the hand as he has memorized his cards.
- Conversely, the player who usually looks at his cards at least twice during a hand and now does not look at all has a pocket pair.
- He blinks faster than usual. He is bluffing.
- He normally sits erect, but curls up when he bets. A bluff.
- Any unusual sign of being nervous, such as a garbled sentence, usually signals a bluff.
- He calls immediately on the flop with a two flush on the board. He has a four flush.
- He flicks the corners of his cards. He is unhappy with the hand.
- His lips are different when he has a good versus a poor hand, perhaps they press together with a poor hand and are not touching each other with a good hand. The key to this tell is a change. Watch for a change in pattern. Also applies to some tights.
- His posture becomes more straight or he moves towards the table. Good hand.
- When he has a bad hand he folds his arms.
- Preflop he looks at his cards and quickly grabs his chips. Good hand.
- Calls a bet fast. Weak hand or still on a draw.
- Checks fast. Weak hand, still on a draw, or if an aggressive player, may be waiting to check-raise.
- The hand, the one connected to the arm, not his cards, of a passive/loose does not normally shake but it shakes now or he fumbles putting his chips in the pot. He has a good hand.

- He looks at his cards and looks at his chips. He is going to bet.
- The aggressive/loose player gets his cards and puts something on top of his cards, such as a chip. He is going to bet.
- Caro says, and I can confirm, if a player — my experience indicates a loose player — looks away he has a better hand than if he looks at you.
- The player whose first card is an Ace rubs it on the table until he receives his second card.
- The loose player will often change his expression or smile when you ask him if he got the card he wanted, especially on a showdown.
- Whenever you see a no limit player look at each card as they come instead of waiting and watching opponents, you can assume this player is loose.

The only way to pick these up is to watch and learn.

Part III — Postflop hands

Flop betting pattern

This next portion of this chapter deals with the tendency of players to call, bet, or raise depending on the flop and where the player fits in the PATL matrix. As in the previous section, these trends are for individual players, not the overall table personality. When you discover a player's betting pattern, it will usually not change. When a player does change his betting pattern, it indicates he is a great player. Beware this opponent. Deception is described more fully in the next chapter.

A spike in betting

The passive raises preflop. You know he has a high pocket pair. The caller turns into a raiser. Unless he is an aggressive/loose, he either hit or has a great draw. If there is no flush or straight draw on the board, the passive has caught top pair with the highest possible kicker, two pair, or a set.

Monster flops

Any flop with two high cards is dangerous. A flop with three high cards is treacherous. If two or more of these high cards are suited, look out! Beware, beware, beware. If there are two or more opponents betting and raising on the flop, unless you either have a great hand, not just a good hand, or you have a

	Tight	Loose
Aggressive	Watch out for spike in betting	
Passive	Beware spike in betting	Beware spike in betting

Figure 3.28

	Tight	Loose
Aggressive	Either completely missed or is slowplaying when checks	Beware; usually only checks on flop when he has hit something big
Passive	Checks if missed	Checks if missed

Figure 3.29

positive Expected Value draw to a great hand, get out. In later chapters both positive Expected Value draws and monster flops will be covered in more detail.

The preflop raiser who checks on the flop

The passive player missed. If one or more high cards are on the board, the passive player has a pocket pair, but there is an overcard on the board. If low cards are on the board the passive player has AK or AQ suited or unsuited. The aggressive/tight either completely missed or is slowplaying his set-or-better. The aggressive/loose doesn't like to check. He tends to automatically bet out on the flop unless he hit something big and is waiting to trap on the turn. In a minute, with figure 3.32, we will expand this thinking.

Turn reading

By the turn, you should be able to put most players, other than the aggressive/looses, on as few as one or two specific hands.

The river

The party's over. You should know where you stand with everyone, except the aggressive/loose and sometimes the aggressive/tight.

Position betting gives more clues

In addition to knowing the PATL and other information, understanding how position affects opponents' betting is useful. Before we profile how betting patterns are linked to position, review figure 3.31 which shows how the table is unfolded to facilitate presentation. For a 10-handed table some other authors may use slightly different definitions of early, middle, or late position, but these are our definitions.

Figure 3.32 gives the tendencies of betting depending on position. This will be the last piece in the reading opponents puzzle. There are some comments in this figure which will be more fully explained in the Betting Chapter. For example, "May be looking for information" means a player is using his position and betting to see how strong other players' hands might be.

	Tight	Loose
Aggressive	**Call** Has a good hand **Bet** Has a good or the best hand **Raise** Has a good or the best hand	**Call** Missed; not much of a hand **Bet** Could have anything **Raise** Could have anything
Passive	**Call** Has a good or very good hand **Bet** Has the best hand **Raise** Has the best hand	**Call** Has any pair **Bet** Has any high pair, any kicker **Raise** Has a good to great hand

Turn and River reading
Figure 3.30

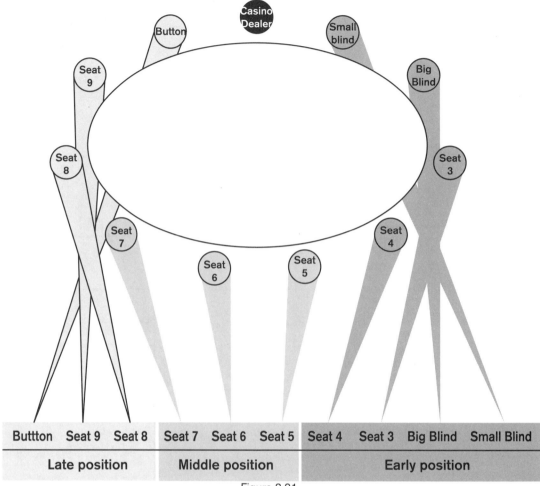

Buttton	Seat 9	Seat 8	Seat 7	Seat 6	Seat 5	Seat 4	Seat 3	Big Blind	Small Blind
Late position			Middle position			Early position			

Figure 3.31

A "continuation bet" means a player in late position raised in the previous round of betting, and continues to represent a strong hand even though he may have missed. A "position bet" means the opponent is in late position and bets regardless of strength.

Showdown information

Regardless of whether you are still in the hand, pay attention anytime anyone is forced to show their cards or voluntarily shows them. This point cannot be overemphasized. Mentally replay the hand. Almost every player plays the same cards the same way in the same situation. **Knowing the betting pattern of each and every opponent** can't help but make you money, but it **becomes vital when you get to no limit**. An expert has superior postflop skills. One is knowing how an opponent tends to play a hand. You can't become a professional without developing this skill.

	Late Position	Middle Position	Early Position
Preflop			
Check	Nothing or poor draw	Nothing or weak draw	Nothing or medium draw
Call	Poor draw	Acceptable draw	Good draw
Bet	Any kind of draw	Medium pair or good draw	High pair or good draw
	May be looking for information		
	Could be a position bet		
Raise	Pair or good draw	Medium pair or strong draw	High pair or A-face suited
	Possibly trying to buy button		
	Possible free card play		
Re-raise	Believes he has a hand or extremely strong draw much better than the raiser		
	May be trying to isolate		
Calls a raise	Believes he has a hand or potential hand not just equal to the raiser, but better than the raiser		
Cold calls 2 bets	Believes he has a hand or monster draw (A-high face suited) much better than the raiser		
Flop			
Check	Nothing	Nothing or medium draw	Nothing, low pair, weak draw
Call	Weak draw, several callers	Medium draw	2nd pair, acceptable draw
Bet	At least a pair	Good pair or good draw	Strong pair or good draw
	Possibly looking for info		
	May be a continuation bet		
Raise	At least a pair	Top or 2nd pair	Top pair or nut draw
	Acceptable or better draw	Good draw	
	May be looking for information		
Re-raise	Top or 2nd high pair	Top pair or better	At least top pair
	Strong or nut draw	Nut draw	
	May be trying to isolate		
	May be a continuation bet		
Calls a raise	Believes he has a hand or potential hand not just equal to the raiser, but better than the raiser		
Cold calls 2 bets	Believes he has a hand better than the raiser or extremely strong draw		
Turn			
Check	Nothing	Nothing, weak or slowplay	Nothing or slowplay
Call	Still on a draw	Still on a draw	2nd pair or still on a draw
Bet	A pair or better	2nd pair or better	High pair or better
	May be a continuation bet		
Raise	A pair or better	2nd pair or better	High pair or better
	May be a continuation bet		
Re-raise	At least high pair	More than just high pair	More than just high pair
Calls a raise	Believes he has a hand or potential hand not just equal to the raiser, but better than the raiser		
Cold calls 2 bets	Believes he has a hand better than the raiser or extremely strong draw		
River			
Check	Nothing	Nothing or not much	Nothing or not much
Call	Something but not strong	Something but not strong	Something but not strong
Bet	Something	Something good	Something very good
	Could be a bluff if heads up	Could be a bluff if heads up	Could be a bluff if heads up
Raise	At least high pair	At least high pair	Two pair or better
	Could be a bluff if heads up	Could be a bluff if heads up	Could be a bluff if heads up
Re-raise	Believes he has the best hand		
Calls a raise	Believes he may have the best hand		
Cold calls 2 bets	Believes he may have the best hand		

Figure 3.32

Create opponent profiles

You will play the same opponent many times in your poker career, even on the net. One of the easiest but most overlooked techniques to increase profitability is to keep a written log on each opponent. Among the most important questions: Where do they fit in the PATL? Do they defend their blinds or allow a steal? What is their betting pattern? What are their physical tells?

Put each opponent on a hand

As the hand develops it becomes easier to predict your opponents' cards. **Using logic** to reduce and eliminate possibilities, you should use each of the following tools available to **deduce what they have**:

1. Their betting pattern throughout the hand.
2. Where each opponent falls within the PATL.
3. Physical tells.
4. Their position.
5. Your study of the board, which will be discussed in chapter 5.

Numbers

- A straight draw can be identified on the flop 68%, almost ¾, of the time.
- The flop will have two or more of the same suit 60% of the time.
- The majority of pots are won by the player who has paired the top card on the board with a good kicker.

No tell routine

If you don't want to be read, follow the exact same routine every time. This sounds easy, but will take a great deal of discipline. The best TV example is Chris Ferguson. His routine is flawless. Here is what you must master:

- What you do when you look at your first two cards.
- What you do when you are going to fold.
- What you do and say when you are going to bet.
- What you do and say when you are going to raise or re-raise.
- Protect your cards in a consistent manner.

Your objective is to make every situation exactly the same so no one knows what you are going to do before it is your turn to act, for example:

- Your chips are going to have to go in the pot exactly the same way every time.
- When you announce you are going to bet, raise, or re-raise the sound and intensity of your voice must be the same every time.
- When you look at your first two cards you must always take exactly the same amount of time before you decide if you are going to fold or bet.

Here are a few hints for the inexperienced player:

- As soon as you get your cards do not look at them but place a chip on them.
- Preflop, take a look at your cards only when it is your turn to act.
- Have a mental count such as "One Mississippi" before you fold or announce you are going to bet, raise or re-raise.
- Have a small bet ready and a big bet ready in exactly the same place next to your cards.
- Do not reach for or look at your chips until you have completed the "One Mississippi" count.
- Either immediately memorize your cards — expert players do this but even they sometimes forget what they have — or look at your cards in exactly the same way during every round of betting.
- Your posture and hand position must be the same throughout the entire hand.
- Other than when you look at your opponents to see their reaction when they receive their cards or when cards come out, your eyes must focus on the same place.
- Whatever your natural facial expression is, it must stay constant.
- Practice putting your chips in the same way every time you bet, raise, and re-raise.

Find a routine you are comfortable with and then ensure you do the same thing over and over and over. That's the only way a good player can't read you. When you are no longer in the hand, that's the time to change posture, engage in a conversation, or just to relax. But you still should be watching those in the hand as the cards come out or as they act. Also note which cards they play depending on their position; this is valuable information for later play.

Summary
- To take good play to great play you must be able to read hands. You can develop this skill.
- Putting each opponent in the PATL is the first step.
- You must know each opponent well beyond their PATL by studying their ability and personality.
- Opponents tend to have certain physical tells depending on where they fit in the PATL.
- Opponents tend to have certain betting patterns depending on the flop and where each fits in the PATL.
- Create a written profile on every opponent.
- By the turn, you should be able to put most opponents on a few specific hands.
- On the river, you should know where you stand with most players.
- Becoming a no tell player takes long hours of practice.

Professionals
Later you will find specific recommended hands. The more you play the more you will see expert players playing with a wider range of hands than those recommended, even when out of position. The reason these professionals play a wide range of hands is because their hand reading skills are so advanced, they are confident they can either outplay their opponents postflop or fold when they are beat.

Special thanks
Andy Blum, the best hand reader I have ever known, helped me with most of this chapter. Andy is a dealer and has watched over 2,000,000 casino hands. Andy, under 30 at the time of this writing, is so good he not only can predict the winner of almost every hand but will give the exact cards the player has before they are turned over. You will be seeing a lot of Andy in the poker world in years to come.

Homework

- Learn which opponents conform to the PATL predictions and which don't.
- Watch opponents as they receive their cards and as the cards are dealt to learn how they react.
- Learn how opponents bet based on their position.
- Know every betting pattern for every opponent.
- Develop and use your no tell routine.
- Put every opponent on a hand or a range of hands; put everyone in a showdown on a specific hand.

CHAPTER 4

Deception

Introduction

If you play the same hands the same way every time, experienced players will know what you have. They know how to read your hand because they watch and learn how you play. You become predictable. Everyone has a predisposition to play the same hands the same way all the time. Even if they use deception, players tend to try to deceive with similar hands in similar ways. Under pressure, such as a big pot or short stacked, almost every player reverts to what has worked in the past and plays in their comfort zone. When you are playing in your comfort zone that's when it is easiest for experienced players to put you on a hand. **Deceiving tough opponents so they never know what you have is not the sign of a good player; it is that of a great player**. Your deception prevents anyone from exploiting your play.

How do you find a random way to mix up your betting patterns so it becomes impossible for your opponents to read your hand? Simple. And once you understand this technique no one will ever be able to read your hands again. You let your cards tell you what to do. Huh?

A basic and advanced system are explained. Once you understand both, it won't take you 10 minutes to develop your own. Understanding what follows will allow you to make your personal deception system as simple or complex as you wish.

These techniques do not determine if you are going to play a hand. That decision is made by using later chapters. But if you are in a hand, you will be able to change your play so no one knows what you have. Additionally, as stated in Chapter 2, and again reiterated in figure 4.1, these concepts only have a major impact when you are playing at a tight table. If you are playing at a loose table there is little need to bother with deception unless you are down to tight opponents. The only time you should use deception at a loose table is when you are playing opponents who play with you often.

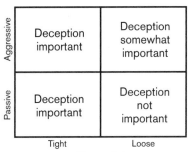
Figure 4.1

Occasionally you will end up playing passively with a high pair and will lose a pot you would have won if you had bet strongly right from the start. Your deceptive play will more than make up for this occasional loss as your pots will be bigger when you do win.

The key to Swayne random deception

When you look at your first two cards, one is on your left and one is on your right. You must pick one side which is going to tell you what to do. If you are right handed, the easiest card to pick is the one on your right, and if left handed, the card on the left.

You then must decide how much you want to mix up your play. On the next page are systems for both basic and advanced deception. Examples will be used to illustrate the concepts. Create your own system from these examples.

The pattern is to deceive preflop, deceive on the flop, and then to play your hand as you normally would on the turn and river. You will see that in the same hand you often will be flipping deception patterns; you will often use one style preflop and a different one on the flop.

Basic deception

Assign one color to passive and the other to aggressive as shown in 4.2.

Preflop if your right hand card is red, you will be aggressive; if black, passive.

On the flop use the middle card turned up by the dealer to tell you what to do. If red, go aggressive; if black, passive.

On the turn and river play as you normally would.

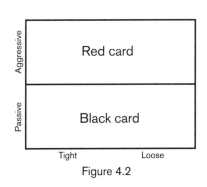
Figure 4.2

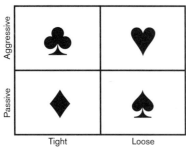

Figure 4.3

Advanced deception

The more you hide information from top opponents, the more you will win.

This technique will result in complete deception on every hand, as you will be flipping all over the PATL. Assign a suit to each quadrant, such as shown in figure 4.3.

Preflop assume you are using your right hand card to tell you how to deceive. Let's suppose that card is a ♥. That ♥ corresponds to the aggressive/loose quadrant. So preflop you play and physically act aggressive/loose.

On the flop again use the middle card turned up to tell you what to do. Let's suppose that card is a ♦. In figure 4.3 it indicates this is a passive/tight player. So now you switch both your play and physical actions to that of a passive/tight.

On the turn and river using your cards to deceive is over; play as you normally would.

For those who want to use deception, but not as much

Some students like the idea of deception, but are uncomfortable using it on every hand. A simple solution is to use a variation of the basic passive or aggressive deception; however, instead of using a color, which will result in deception ½ the time, pick one suit to indicate what to do, which will result in deception ¼ of the time.

Another layer of deception

As you become more advanced, you will find in no limit it is better to adjust your raises based on the skill level of your opponents. When we get to the no limit chapter you will be shown how to add this technique as another layer of deception.

Flopping a monster

If you flop a monster at a predominately loose table with a few tights at the table, always use the middle flop card to determine how you bet. You are going to have to show your cards at the end anyway, and you want to make sure the tights are consistently confused.

A monster on the turn

This will be your only exception to playing as you would normally play on the turn. When you hit a hand on the turn you think will be the winner, use the turn card — either the color or the suit, depending on which type of deception you are using — to determine how you will play this round.

Deception against the best players

You will not always be the best player at the table, even though we all think we are. The better your opponents, the more you must use deception. In a later chapter we will discuss how to place an opponent not just in a PATL quadrant, but in a specific portion of the quadrant. In other words you will be able to gauge just how good a particular player is.

Playing bad cards

As mentioned earlier experienced opponents tend to stay in against loose players. If you are perceived as loose this helps you win larger pots. The best way to appear loose is to play bad cards. When playing trash you must play all the way to the river and make sure you show your cards.

A bad play made in front of players not familiar with you within the first few minutes of arriving establishes you as a loose player. As soon as you have two low unsuited connectors or two trash flush cards play them all the way to a showdown.

After awhile the better players will see you are playing smart. To keep them off balance wait until you have the button, again with either any two flush cards or any two connectors, bet as though you have bullets, and stay in the hand until the end. To keep you from doing this too often you may use a card code such as both flush cards must be red, the connectors must contain a 5, or similar random methods to tell you when to play bad cards.

Showing good cards

We will cover stealing blinds later. One time you should voluntarily show good cards is when you have successfully stolen the blinds and you actually had good cards, which won't be often. Another will be when you are playing extremely aggressively, which will be most of the time in limit and cash no limit, and you win with strong cards without a showdown. The reason to show good cards is to convince opponents when you are in a hand, you are strong.

If you are playing aggressively with poor cards, avoid showing a bluff.

Summary
- **Deception is a sign of a great player**.
- You can use your cards to be randomly deceptive.
- Deception is always important at tight tables.
- Your style of play will often vary preflop and postflop.
- On the turn and river play as you normally would, unless you have a monster on the turn.
- **Occasionally** playing bad cards helps you win bigger pots.

Homework
- Develop, practice, and use your own method of deception.

CHAPTER 5

Boardology

If you are an experienced player, you don't need this chapter; skip to the last section of this chapter and do the "future assignment." But, if you have not played your 250,000 hands, you will have to learn to study the board.

The expensive mistake

Many good books have a chapter on reading the board. Almost all inexperienced players skim that chapter because they believe reading the board is so obvious, of course they will see what's there. But until you are experienced, here is the mistake you will make over and over unless you learn what to study and how to study. You have been limping on a draw and hit a card on the river, sometimes on the turn, that makes your hand. When the card hits you become aggressive, only to get re-raised and end up losing the pot. What happened? You only saw the card helping you when, in fact, it helped someone else more. Impossible you say. You would have certainly seen that card helping someone else more than it helped you.

Until you have played your 250,000 hands, and have learned to see the entire board, there is a natural psychological reaction when you think your overpair is the best hand or a card hits which makes your hand. **You ONLY see what you have or the card that helped you,** not how that card may have helped an opponent. What's worse, even though you swear it will never happen to you again, it happens over and over. Believe it or not, this selective focus occurs in all facets of human endeavor; it is just easier to see in poker.

How to clearly see the board

There are two paths to seeing the board:

1. You make the expensive mistake of failing to clearly read the board so often and lose so much money that eventually you learn what to do. If you give an electric shock to a lab rat every time it does something wrong, it eventually learns. If you choose this path, you are the rat.
2. You practice reading the board and make it part of your game.

We're going to focus on #2. The rest of this chapter is not very long, and you may not enjoy the assignment at the end, but completing this assignment will save you money and is necessary if you choose to be great.

Practice on every hand

In a later chapter you will find you must fold much more than you probably are used to. How does that help you learn to read the board? You get to practice on every hand. It doesn't cost you anything extra. At a casino or home game you will see over 30 flops, turns, and rivers every hour and many more on the internet.

Why not the nuts first?

Most books which include a chapter on reading the board suggest you first figure out what is the best possible hand, the second best hand, and so on. They then identify the three main categories of hands:

1. Pairs, two pairs, sets, trips, boats, quads
2. Straights
3. Flushes, which include straight flushes.

With our procedure you will still identify the nuts, the second nuts, and so on, as well as the three main categories of hands, but you will now first look for the most difficult to see possibilities.

Board reading rules

Before you start to read the board, review these rules:

Straights

- The possible straight is everywhere. 68% of the time a straight draw can be identified on the flop.
- QJ or JT on the flop, unless it helps you, is likely to help several opponents.
- When the board pairs, the number of straight draws goes down.
- When the board has two pair or three of a kind, a straight is unlikely.
- On the river there can be as many as four different straights possible.

Flushes

- The flop will have two or more of the same suit 60% of the time.
- When all the cards through the turn are the same color, either a flush or a flush draw is possible.
- When all the cards through the river are the same color, a flush is possible.

Both straights and flushes

- When the board offers both a flush and straight possibility, there is double the chance a draw will hit.

Pairs, sets, trips or better

- The top card on the board is important as a potential pair because the majority of pots are won by the player who has paired the highest board card with a good kicker or has a pocket overpair.

Monster boards

- Boards with all high cards should have hit at least one player.

Maximum information; minimal cost

The flop gives you the most information at the least cost. This doesn't mean you will play a lot of hands and pay to see the flop; it does mean when you are in the hand you will see 60% of the board for a minimum investment.

You need answers

Here's how to make reading the board a natural part of your play. You must ask yourself each of the following questions for every flop, turn, and river whether you are in the hand or not. It takes thousands and thousands of hands of asking and answering every one of these questions before reading the board becomes effortless.

The Flop

Answer these in exactly this order. **Straight questions are first because they are the easiest to miss.**

1. Straights
   a. Could someone have made a straight?
      i. If so, what is the highest possible straight?
      ii. What is the 2nd highest possible straight?
      iii. What is the 3rd highest possible straight?
   b. Is there a straight draw on the board?
      i. If so, what is the highest possible draw?
      ii. What is the 2nd highest possible draw?
      iii. What is the 3rd highest possible draw?
2. Flushes
   a. Could someone have made a flush? Obviously a three flush must be on the board.
   b. Could someone have a flush draw? Not a backdoor; is there a two flush on the board?
3. Pairs, two pairs, trips or better
   a. What is the top card on the board?
   b. Are two pairs possible? Almost always yes.
   c. Are trips possible?
   d. Is a set possible? Almost always yes.
   e. Is a boat or better possible? The board must be paired.
4. If play stopped now
   a. What is the best possible hand?
   b. The 2nd nuts?
   c. The 3rd nuts?
   d. The 4th nuts?
   e. The 5th nuts?
5. Judging by what has taken place so far
   a. Which opponent appears to have the best hand?
   b. What do you think he has?

The Turn

Similar questions, but the answers regarding straights become slightly more difficult with the fourth community card.

1. Straights
    a. Could someone have hit a straight?
        i. If so, what is the highest possible straight?
        ii. What is the 2nd highest possible straight?
        iii. What is the 3rd highest possible straight?
    b. Are there straight draws on the board?
        i. If so, what is the highest possible draw?
        ii. What is the 2nd highest possible draw?
        iii. What is the 3rd highest possible draw?
        iv. What is the 4th highest possible draw?
2. Flushes
    a. Could someone have made a flush?
    b. Could someone have a flush draw?
3. Pairs, two pairs, trips or better
    a. What is the top card on the board?
    b. Are there two pairs on the board?
    c. Are two pairs possible?
    d. Are trips possible?
    e. Is a set possible?
    f. Is a boat or better possible?
4. If play stopped now
    a. What is the best possible hand?
    b. The 2nd nuts?
    c. The 3rd nuts?
    d. The 4th nuts?
    e. The 5th nuts?
5. Judging by what has taken place so far
    a. Which player appears to have the best hand?
    b. What do you think he has?

The River

1. Straights
    a. Could someone have hit a straight?
        i. If so, what is the highest possible straight?
        ii. What is the 2nd highest possible straight?
        iii. What is the 3rd highest possible straight?
        iv. What is the 4th highest possible straight?

        b. Are any of the possible straights made with runner runner? Which?

  2. Flushes

        a. Is the board three or more flushed?

        b. Is runner runner the only way a flush could have been made?

  3. Pairs, two pairs, trips or better

        a. What is the top card on the board?

        b. Are there two pairs on the board?

        c. Are two pairs possible?

        d. Are trips possible?

        e. Is a set possible?

        f. Is a boat or better possible?

  4. Hand ranking

        a. The nuts?

        b. The 2nd nuts?

        c. The 3rd nuts?

        d. The 4th nuts?

        e. The 5th nuts?

  5. Before the cards are turned over

        a. Which player has the best hand?

           i. What do you think he has?

        b. Which player has the second best hand?

           i. What do you think he has?

The answer is yes

There are several questions which will almost always have yes as the answer:

The Flop

Is there a straight draw on the board?

Could someone have a flush draw?

Are two pairs or a set possible?

The Turn

Is there a straight draw on the board?

Can someone have a flush draw?

Are two pairs or a set possible?

The River

Could someone have a straight?

Are two pairs or a set possible?

The straight problem

Losing to an unseen straight, or one you don't see until you are raised, is the biggest challenge when reading the board. After the flop, reading straights becomes even more hairy.

Straight possibilities on the flop

More straights can be made when cards are sequenced than with gaps. Also, more straights can be made if the board cards are in the middle than at an end. These two concepts will be detailed in the Numbers Chapter.

Side notes. A straight must contain a 5 or a T. When you hold JT and make a straight, unless the board shows KQT9 through the turn or river, or shows QJT98 on the river, you automatically have the nut straight.

Flop is three in sequence

If the flop is three in sequence, such as **7 6 5**, players could have a straight with

$$9\ 8\ \mathbf{7\ 6\ 5}$$
$$8\ \mathbf{7\ 6\ 5}\ 4$$
$$\mathbf{7\ 6\ 5}\ 4\ 3$$

Seeing a straight possibility when three flop in sequence is easy. But make sure you see all the possible straights. When there is a flop with three in sequence, especially when that flop is in the middle, for example 765, as opposed to an end such as A23, not only are there three possible straights on the flop, many other cards may come into play to make a straight on the turn or river.

Flop has a gap in sequence

Suppose the flop is **8 6 5**; that is there is one gap in the sequence. Players could have flopped a straight with

$$9\ \mathbf{8}\ 7\ \mathbf{6\ 5}$$
$$\mathbf{8}\ 7\ \mathbf{6\ 5}\ 4$$

Any player holding a 7 now has an open-ended straight.

Two gaps

What if there are two gaps such as **8 5 4**? A player must hold 76 to have a straight.

$$\mathbf{8}\ 7\ 6\ \mathbf{5\ 4}$$

Three or more gaps

If there are three or more gaps, there are no made straights possible at this point, and there is only one potential straight draw.

Double inside straight draws

Some are well disguised and are frequently missed by less than experienced players. There are several different ways to have this draw on the flop. Double inside straight draws, known among most players as double belly busters, can be formed when you have connectors or gapped cards. Here are some examples of double inside straight draws: you have 89 and the flop is 57J or 6TQ; one gap, you hold 79 with the flop 356, 58J or TJK; two gaps, you hold 8J and the flop is TQA or 579; three gaps, 7J with a flop of 9TK or 589; or even five gaps, 7K with the flop 9TJ.

The shared Ace

An A can form straights at both the upper and lower end. If the flop is **A Q 3** there are six straight draws possible. Each is an inside straight draw.

A K **Q** T
A K **Q** J
A Q J T
A 2 **3** 4
A 2 **3** 5
A 3 4 5

A word on possible upper end straights

Beware of a flop of three high unpaired cards if they don't help you. Many at the table will now have a straight draw, or worse, a made straight.

Straight flop conclusions

The closer the sequence, the more dangerous the flop is to you if you didn't catch.

Straights on the turn

Additional made straights are possible, and many more straight draws become possible.

Four in sequence

If the cards on the turn are **9 8 7 6** there are three possible made straights

J T **9 8 7**
T **9 8 7 6**
9 8 7 6 5

In addition, someone holding QJ has overcards and an inside straight draw to the nut straight.

Three in sequence, the 4th with one gap

If the cards on the turn are **8 7 6 4** there are three possible made straights

$$T\ 9\ \mathbf{8}\ \mathbf{7}\ \mathbf{6}$$
$$9\ \mathbf{8}\ \mathbf{7}\ \mathbf{6}\ 5$$
$$\mathbf{8}\ \mathbf{7}\ \mathbf{6}\ 5\ \mathbf{4}$$

A player with JT has a draw to the nut straight.

Partial sequence, partial gaps

If the cards on the turn are **9 7 6 4** there are three possible made straights

$$T\ \mathbf{9}\ 8\ \mathbf{7}\ \mathbf{6}$$
$$\mathbf{9}\ 8\ \mathbf{7}\ \mathbf{6}\ 5$$
$$\mathbf{7}\ \mathbf{6}\ 5\ \mathbf{4}\ 3$$

Anyone with an 8 or 5 now has an open-ended straight

$$\mathbf{9}\ 8\ \mathbf{7}\ \mathbf{6}$$
$$\mathbf{7}\ \mathbf{6}\ 5\ \mathbf{4}$$

An opponent with a J8 has not only an open-ended straight but a draw to the nuts.

Double inside straight draws

The player has 8 J. The flop is 6 9 Q. The turn is a 5. The player now has a double inside straight draw.

$$\mathbf{5}\ 6\ 8\ 9\ J\ \mathbf{Q}$$

Straight on the river

Five cards are now exposed. The number of possible straights may increase.

Five in sequence

Relatively easy to see. If the community cards are **8 7 6 5 4**, obviously everyone has a straight. Anyone holding T9 has the nut straight. Anyone holding a 9 is probably the winner. Anyone holding a 3, or even AA, has nothing and will only play the board.

Four in sequence

No substantial difference from the flop, except when there are one or two gaps — especially at the end. These gaps hide straights you may not have anticipated on the turn.

If the cards on the turn are **9 8 7 6** there are three possible made straights as explained in the turn section above. But notice what happens if a J hits on the river. Anyone with a T would have

$$J\ T\ \mathbf{9}\ 8\ \mathbf{7}$$

Anyone with a QT would have the nut straight.

The shared Ace

There are sometimes two straight possibilities on the river with the shared Ace. The cards through the river are **T Q A 3 5.** Two possible straights.

T J **Q** K **A**
A 2 **3** 4 **5**

Inexperienced players often see the possible treetop, but miss the wheel.

The difficult to read gaps

When all the community cards are out, if there are several cards close or partially sequenced, reading ALL the straights becomes more difficult. We cannot overemphasize this point. Reading gaps correctly every time is not easy to learn, but it can be done.

The cards through the river are **9 7 6 4 2.** What are all the possible straights?

T **9** 8 **7 6**
9 8 **7 6** 5
7 6 5 **4** 3
6 5 **4** 3 **2**

Four possible. It is easy to identify and expensive if you miss one.

Extra cautions

Most of the examples used were picked intentionally using cards with a numerical rank. Even though we all know a face card is higher in rank than those with a numerical rank, it is much more difficult for the brain to process possible sequences when those sequences involve a face card; if two face cards or an Ace and a face are involved, the ability to "see" the sequences actually decreases. Also, all of the examples are arranged in an easy to see order. That's not the way you will see them on the board and unless you practice mentally putting them in order as the board is revealed, it is difficult to see every possible straight. It does take a lot of practice, focus, and concentration to be able to read all the possible straights.

Flushes

A flush is much easier to see. But again, beware the river card making a three flush on the board, especially if there were two of that suit on the flop, or if there was a free turn card. The inexperienced player who doesn't practice reading the board will miss more than one flush on the river.

The river

He had J9s. The flop was 994. Aggressive/loose table. Lots of raising and re-raising. The turn was a K. At the showdown his opponent flipped over Q9. He mucked his cards. Too bad he was so absorbed with his opponent's kicker he forgot to read the river, an A. He missed the split pot. Your supposedly great author did just that. Grrrrrrrrr. Expensive mistake. Lesson learned.

Conclusion

If the board shows there are several cards that can beat you, the longer you remain in the hand, the more aggressive you must be. This will again be stated in the Betting Chapter.

Summary

- Inexperienced players fail to read the board.
- Inexperienced players see cards that help them, not cards that may help others.
- Reading the board successfully saves money.
- Board reading requires getting answers to specific questions.
- A straight is the easiest to miss.
- As you will see below, a massive amount of homework is needed to make board reading a natural part of your play.

Homework

Here is your assignment. Some readers may find it is not fun, but it needs to be done. Go to an internet hold'em site. Focus on one speed table. Take out a tablet of paper or make many copies of Appendix B. For every flop, turn, and river you are to quickly answer every question. Two hours a day for 10 weeks or 5,000 hands — whichever comes first. After that, one two hour session per week for the next year. That's another 5,000 hands. When you have completed this assignment — and, of course, are now doing the same thing for every hand you play or watch — you are well on your way to becoming proficient at boardology. Before you begin playing four or more speed tables on the internet simultaneously, complete at least your first 5,000 boardology hands, otherwise you will find it extremely difficult to properly read the board every time. Practice does not make perfect. Perfect practice makes perfect.

Future assignment

Mark your calendar to read this page a year from now. When reading the board becomes natural, your next assignment is to merge each opponent's individual PATL with the cards needed to make a specific hand. Example. The flop is A35. Who might have the wheel? Would a passive/tight ever play 42 even if they were suited? Not unless he was in the big blind without having to call a raise. The chance of the passive/tight having a straight on the flop is between zero and zip. Would a passive/loose play a 42? Yes, and they don't even have to be the same color. This is an enjoyable exercise to keep you entertained, and help you become a better player, as you fold lots of hands at a casino or home game. But it only can be done after you are an accomplished boardologist.

CHAPTER 6

Playing the Blinds

Blinds are risky

Beginners and intermediates lose too much money playing their blinds. And we are not talking about the money you have already put in before the hand starts. That money is gone. It's not yours anymore.

Why is more money lost in the blinds? Several reasons. First, the inexperienced player calls a small blind because he can get in for what he perceives to be a cheap bet. Second, if he doesn't hit a hot flop, he tends to stay in the hand too long chasing. Third, even when he hits, his payout is less than if he were in late position. Last, and this is the most important reason, inexperienced players do not realize how much risk they have when they play a blind or any hand in any early position.

Risk is determined by how much information you have and how much you must bet. In the blinds, and obviously the big blind, your risk is low for the first round of betting. You actually have more information preflop and are required to bet either nothing or a small amount to stay in the hand during this betting round. Figure 6.1.a shows you the preflop risk for the first round

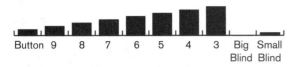

Button 9 8 7 6 5 4 3 Big Small
                                   Blind Blind

Risk during the first round of betting (preflop)

Figure 6.1.a

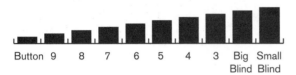

Button 9 8 7 6 5 4 3 Big Small
                                   Blind Blind

Risk during the second round of betting (flop)

Figure 6.1.b

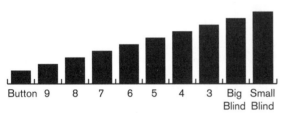

Button 9 8 7 6 5 4 3 Big Small
                                   Blind Blind

Risk during the third round of betting

(on the turn)

Figure 6.1.c

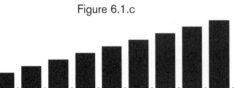

Button 9 8 7 6 5 4 3 Big Small
                                   Blind Blind

Risk during the last round of betting

(on the river)

Figure 6.1.d

of betting. Your risk in the blinds is either nothing or extremely low.

You were OK for the first betting round. You have a little information, but from now on you aren't going to know much about your opponents' cards until it is too late. There are three more betting rounds to go. You will have to bet with the least amount of information during this next round and you have no idea if you are going to be raised or re-raised if you do bet. You are the first to give information to your opponents. Your opponents have the info, you don't. The more information you have the less risk. The less info you have the greater your risk. And your risk is greatest from early position. Look at your risk in figure 6.1.b during the second round of betting.

Third betting round. It gets worse. Bets are doubled. Twice as much risk as the second round.

Fourth betting round. More big bets with high risk.

The Swayne risk/position graph

We have added the risk players incur through all four betting rounds. This is the sum of the risk of each individual betting round. Now look at the figure 6.2. That's your total risk depending on your position. Look at how much risk you incur in early position, even if you are in the blinds. How cheap does that small blind bet look now?

Controlling the size of the pot

A tremendous additional benefit with good position is that you will usually have the ability to control the pot size. A perfect storm. Controlling the pot size and low risk. When we get to the no limit chapter you will see how important this is. When we go through Negreneau's small ball strategy for no limit tournament play, position will turn out to be extremely important.

Defending your blinds

This means calling a small bet when you are in the small blind or calling a raise from either blind position. Usually a bad play, unless, of course, you have playable cards.

How to play the blinds

Your job is not to gamble. Your job is to win money. Part of winning is keeping your risk low. Your risk playing the blinds is outrageous compared to late position. Part of winning money is not losing it. As important as the risk is even if you do end up winning the hand, the size of the pot will not be nearly as big if you were in late position because you were forced to give away information to the rest of the table.

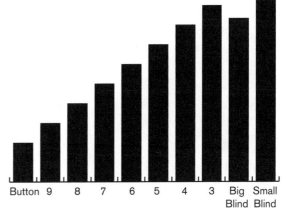

Total risk incurred during all four
rounds of betting
Figure 6.2

Until you are an experienced player and know how to play from an early position, be very, very careful playing a blind. Losing your blind is much less expensive than calling all the way to the river. Specifics: Until you have played your 250,000 hands, which will be no less than 50,000 blinds, here's how you should play your blinds:

Preflop

Other than the big blind for free, until you are experienced, only play small blind cards as if you were on the button. You will find out in a later chapter which hands these include. Unless you have decided to disguise a strong hand, the only time you will raise or re-raise is with AA, KK, or AKs.

Flop

Fold unless you have:
> The highest board pair, at least 99 or better.
> An open-ended straight draw.
> A four flush.
> Another miracle flop such as two pair, trips.

OK to be aggressive with three or fewer opponents. Otherwise, limp.

Turn and river

OK to be aggressive if your opponents have been thinned out to one or two tight players or you believe you have the best hand. Otherwise limp.

Blind bluff

When in an unraised big blind, if the board on the flop shows a small pair or low trash cards, even if they don't help you, a bluff is in order.

Playing the small blind with suited cards

Some experts recommend you call a small blind if you have suited cards. In the next chapter you will be introduced to probability and later learn how to use Expected Value. Here are some numbers which help decide if you should call with two suiteds. If you play two suited cards, you will have either a flush or at least two pair 5% of the time on the flop. If the flop is two of your flush cards, giving you a four flush — which happens 12% of the time — you will hit a flush by the river ⅓ of the time. In addition, we have to consider the rank of your top hole card as an opponent could make a higher flush.

Playing the small blind with connected cards

The same analysis can be used if you have two unsuited connectors, unless they are close to the low end, that is, A2, 23, or 34. You will either flop a straight or at least two pair 5% of the time. If the flop gives you an open-ended straight, you will catch a straight ⅓ of the time by the river. We also have to consider you hitting the low end and someone else hitting the high end as well as what happens when there are three or more flush cards on the board. Without going through all of the math, as you'll get more than enough in the next few chapters, you should call with two unsuited connectors not at the low end, or two sub-par suiteds if all of the following conditions are met:
  1. You are sure your big blind won't raise you.
  2. Your call is not more than ½ the big blind. Some games, such as $3/$6, require your call to be ⅓ of the big blind.
  3. There are 5 or more other callers in front of you.

Reduced bet and probability

In a later chapter you will also be shown the likelihood of winning with various preflop hands. Once you are experienced, you can use the fact that if you are paying a ½ small blind bet the probability of winning theoretically only has to be ½ what it normally must be in order to see the flop. We say theoretically because figure 6.2 tells us we cannot use strict proportionality to adjust for the increased risk. Here's what we can say. Marginal hands may be played from the small blind, but only by those who have played no less than 50,000 blinds.

In no limit you will find you must aggressively defend your blind at least 75% of the time against a lone raiser in late position, even though you will have to play many low probability hands.

Summary
- Inexperienced players underestimate the risk of playing the blinds.
- Lack of information and being early to bet are the reasons playing the blinds is risky.
- The total risk when playing blinds for all four rounds of betting is extremely high.
- When you win a blind hand the payoff is low.
- You must play blinds conservatively until you are experienced.

Homework
- Review the total risk incurred when playing the blinds or early position.

1. Poker should never become:
   - ❏ A. Sand
   - ❏ B. Pebbles
   - ❏ C. Golf balls
   - ❏ D. Beer

2. In which type of hold'em game is math knowledge most important?
   - ❏ A. Low limit
   - ❏ B. High limit
   - ❏ C. No limit
   - ❏ D. The importance of math knowledge is the same for every type of hold'em game

3. In which type of hold'em game is the use of psych skills the most important?
   - ❏ A. Low limit
   - ❏ B. Pot limit
   - ❏ C. High limit
   - ❏ D. No limit

4. Before you become a good no limit player, what must you do first?
   - ❏ A. Become a casino dealer
   - ❏ B. Become a great limit player
   - ❏ C. Play well over 500,000 hands
   - ❏ D. All of the above

5. In limit hold'em, knowledge is most important during what betting round?
   - ❏ A. Preflop
   - ❏ B. Flop
   - ❏ C. Turn
   - ❏ D. River

6. In limit hold'em, psych skills are most important during what betting round?
   - ❏ A. Preflop
   - ❏ B. Flop
   - ❏ C. Turn
   - ❏ D. River

7. In low limit hold'em, which TWO rounds of play have the most combined difficulty?
   - ❏ A. Preflop and river
   - ❏ B. Flop and river
   - ❏ C. Turn and river
   - ❏ D. Flop and turn

8. In high limit and no limit hold'em, which betting round has the highest degree of difficulty?
   - ❏ A. Preflop
   - ❏ B. Flop
   - ❏ C. Turn
   - ❏ D. River

9. You should play a minimum of _____ hands before you consider yourself an experienced player and begin to play for real money.
   - ❏ A. 10,000
   - ❏ B. 25,000
   - ❏ C. 100,000
   - ❏ D. 250,000

10. An aggressive player is one who _____ and a passive player is one who _____.
   - ❏ A. Raises a lot; Re-raises a lot
   - ❏ B. Calls a lot; Raises a lot
   - ❏ C. Checks and calls; Checks
   - ❏ D. None of the above

11. A tight player is one who _____ and a loose player is one who _____.
   - ❏ A. Plays few hands; Plays many hands
   - ❏ B. Plays few hands; Plays hands aggressively
   - ❏ C. Plays many hands; Plays few hands
   - ❏ D. Plays about 40% of their hands; Plays about 50% of their hands

12. Of the following, which is a characteristic of a passive/tight table?
   - ❏ A. Many players in the hand
   - ❏ B. Lots of raising
   - ❏ C. Few players in the hand
   - ❏ D. None of the above

13. A(n) _____/_____ table has four or more players in the hand and lots of raising.
   - ❏ A. Aggressive/tight
   - ❏ B. Aggressive/loose
   - ❏ C. Passive/tight
   - ❏ D. Passive/loose

14. A(n) _____/_____ table has few players in the hand and little raising.
   - ❏ A. Aggressive/tight
   - ❏ B. Aggressive/loose
   - ❏ C. Passive/tight
   - ❏ D. Passive/loose

15. The worst players are _____ and the best players are _____.
   - ❏ A. Loose; passive
   - ❏ B. Loose; tight
   - ❏ C. Tight; loose
   - ❏ D. Tight; passive

16. Typically, the most skilled players are found playing at what type of table?
   - ❏ A. Aggressive/tight
   - ❏ B. Aggressive/loose
   - ❏ C. Passive/loose
   - ❏ D. Passive/tight

17. Which of the following players typically make the most mistakes?
   - ❏ A. Passive players
   - ❏ B. Tight players
   - ❏ C. Aggressive players
   - ❏ D. Loose players

18. Typically, a table that is loud usually means the majority of the players are _____, and a table that is very quiet usually means the majority of the players are _____.
   - ❏ A. Tight; loose
   - ❏ B. Loose; tight
   - ❏ C. Tight; passive
   - ❏ D. Passive; tight

19. Which of the following type of table typically gives you the best return on investment?
   - ❏ A. Passive/tight
   - ❏ B. Aggressive/tight
   - ❏ C. Passive/loose
   - ❏ D. Aggressive/loose

20. Which of the following limit tables should you avoid playing at the most?
   - ❏ A. Aggressive/tight
   - ❏ B. Aggressive/loose
   - ❏ C. Passive/tight
   - ❏ D. Passive/loose

21. You want to be seated to the immediate left of what kind of player?
 ❏ A. Passive
 ❏ B. Aggressive
 ❏ C. Conservative
 ❏ D. Tight

22. At what kind of table will you find the smallest average pot sizes?
 ❏ A. Aggressive/tight
 ❏ B. Aggressive/loose
 ❏ C. Passive/tight
 ❏ D. Passive/loose

23. At an extremely passive/loose 10-handed table, on average you will lose about what percentage of the time when you start with pocket Aces?
 ❏ A. 20%
 ❏ B. 30%
 ❏ C. 60%
 ❏ D. 70%

24. Which of the following is an advantage of having late position?
 ❏ A. You have minimal risk
 ❏ B. You have a great amount of information
 ❏ C. You have control over the play during the hand
 ❏ D. All of the above

25. Which of the following players values position and uses it as a weapon when he has it?
 ❏ A. Aggressive/loose
 ❏ B. Aggressive/tight
 ❏ C. Passive/loose
 ❏ D. Passive/tight

26. After observing one of your opponent's tendencies for quite some time, you have noticed that he usually does the following: raises if he is on a good draw, raises when he has position or smells weakness, and plays few hands. We can conclude that this player is probably what type of opponent?
 ❏ A. Passive/loose
 ❏ B. Aggressive/loose
 ❏ C. Aggressive/tight
 ❏ D. Passive/tight

27. Which of the following opponents is the least likely to bluff?
 ❏ A. Aggressive/loose
 ❏ B. Passive/loose
 ❏ C. Aggressive/tight
 ❏ D. Passive/tight

28. True or False: Deception is extremely important when playing at a tight table.
 ❏ A. True
 ❏ B. False

29. Which of the following opponents tend to raise preflop the most?
 ❏ A. Aggressive/tight
 ❏ B. Aggressive/loose
 ❏ C. Passive/loose
 ❏ D. Passive/tight

30. You should play the least amount of hands at which type of table?
 ❏ A. Aggressive/tight
 ❏ B. Aggressive/loose
 ❏ C. Passive/loose
 ❏ D. Passive/tight

31. True or False: Compared to tight tables, high cards and high pairs are more frequent winning hands at loose tables.
- ❏ A. True
- ❏ B. False

32. Generally, more than ½ the players dealt cards see the flop at which type of table?
- ❏ A. Aggressive/tight
- ❏ B. Aggressive/loose
- ❏ C. Passive/tight
- ❏ D. None of the above

33. Against what type of opponent will the free card play work best?
- ❏ A. Passive/tight
- ❏ B. Passive/loose
- ❏ C. Aggressive/tight
- ❏ D. Aggressive/loose

34. Which of the following scenarios on the river make it correct to attempt a bluff?
- ❏ A. The pot is small
- ❏ B. The remaining opponent is loose
- ❏ C. The remaining opponent is tight
- ❏ D. The remaining opponent is aggressive

35. True or False: Generally, good players can be bluffed; however, poor players cannot be bluffed.
- ❏ A. True
- ❏ B. False

36. In no limit, the importance of psych skills is highest during which betting round?
- ❏ A. Preflop
- ❏ B. Flop
- ❏ C. Turn
- ❏ D. River

37. During which two betting rounds is math knowledge most important?
- ❏ A. Preflop and river
- ❏ B. Preflop and flop
- ❏ C. Preflop and turn
- ❏ D. Flop and turn

38. Which of the following opponent tends to play almost any two cards, sees at least the flop, and folds promptly when he misses?
- ❏ A. Passive/loose
- ❏ B. Passive/tight
- ❏ C. Aggressive/loose
- ❏ D. Aggressive/tight

39. Which of the following type of opponent is typically the hardest to read?
- ❏ A. Passive/loose
- ❏ B. Passive/tight
- ❏ C. Aggressive/tight
- ❏ D. Aggressive/loose

40. True or False: Compared to tight players, loose players often know when they are beat, and fold quickly.
- ❏ A. True
- ❏ B. False

41. What does it typically mean when a player holds his cards off the table preflop?
- ❏ A. He is going to bet
- ❏ B. He is going to call
- ❏ C. He is going to fold
- ❏ D. He is going to re-raise

42. What kind of opponent typically does not have a change in mood or expression when they have a good hand?
- ❏ A. Tight
- ❏ B. Loose
- ❏ C. Passive
- ❏ D. Aggressive

43. What does it usually mean when an opponent continues a conversation when they are in a hand?
    - ❏ A. They have a good hand
    - ❏ B. They have a bad hand
    - ❏ C. They are on a strong draw
    - ❏ D. They are confident that their hand is the winner

44. In most cases, what does it mean when a tight player puts his chips into the pot slower than normal?
    - ❏ A. He has a good hand
    - ❏ B. He has a bad hand
    - ❏ C. He has a marginal draw
    - ❏ D. He is trying to scare away opponents

45. Which of the following opponents has the tendency to go on tilt most frequently?
    - ❏ A. Aggressive/tight
    - ❏ B. Passive/tight
    - ❏ C. Passive/loose
    - ❏ D. Aggressive/loose

46. True or False: A loose player typically acts weak when he is strong and acts strong when he is weak.
    - ❏ A. True
    - ❏ B. False

47. On the flop, a straight draw can be identified _____ percent of the time.
    - ❏ A. 35%
    - ❏ B. 48%
    - ❏ C. 55%
    - ❏ D. 68%

48. Against what kind of opponent is the use of deception the least important?
    - ❏ A. Passive/tight
    - ❏ B. Passive/loose
    - ❏ C. Aggressive/tight
    - ❏ D. Aggressive/loose

49. Deception is most important at which type of table?
    - ❏ A. Tight
    - ❏ B. Loose
    - ❏ C. Passive
    - ❏ D. Aggressive

50. One of the only times you should voluntarily show your hole cards is when you have stolen the blinds with a strong starting hand.
    - ❏ A. True
    - ❏ B. False

51. What is the maximum number of straight possibilities when all five community cards are out?
    - ❏ A. 3
    - ❏ B. 4
    - ❏ C. 5
    - ❏ D. 6

52. The flop will contain two or more of the same suit what percentage of the time?
    - ❏ A. 33%
    - ❏ B. 45%
    - ❏ C. 60%
    - ❏ D. 68%

53. When reading the board, what type of hand is the easiest to miss and therefore should be focused on first?
    - ❏ A. Flushes
    - ❏ B. Trips
    - ❏ C. Straights
    - ❏ D. Two pair

54. How many different straights are possible when the flop is 7 8 9?
   - ❏ A. 2
   - ❏ B. 3
   - ❏ C. 4
   - ❏ D. 5

55. The level of risk is determined primarily by what two factors?
   - ❏ A. The number of opponents in the hand and the amount of information you have
   - ❏ B. How much you have to bet and the size of your chip stack
   - ❏ C. The size of your chip stack and the number of opponents dealt cards
   - ❏ D. How much information you have and how much you have to bet

56. The total amount of risk incurred during all four betting rounds is greatest from what position?
   - ❏ A. Early
   - ❏ B. Middle
   - ❏ C. Late
   - ❏ D. The button

57. Which of the following hands should you raise or re-raise preflop from the small blind?
   - ❏ A. AA
   - ❏ B. KK
   - ❏ C. AKs
   - ❏ D. All of the above

58. Until you are experienced, how should you play when you are in the blinds?
   - ❏ A. Aggressive
   - ❏ B. Tight
   - ❏ C. Fancy
   - ❏ D. Loose

See Appendix E for answers

CHAPTER 7

The Numbers Chapter

Part I — Probability and hand frequency

Probability

Almost every number in this chapter depends on your chance of winning — a probability. Using probability doesn't mean you are going to win every time. Probability is not good for short-term results. It is great for long-term results. The reason probability doesn't work well in the short term is clumps of unusual things can happen, strictly by chance. It is possible that if you flipped a coin it could come up heads 10 times in a row. But, if you flipped it 10,000 times, you would end up with close to 5,000 heads and 5,000 tails. That's the long term, when probability works. Low limit is perfect for probability; and you need to know the numbers for high limit and no limit. You are going to use probability to win over the long term.

"It's not the seat. It's the meat in the seat."

Is there a rush? Yes. Both positive and negative. You will get several good hands close together and may go an hour without getting a playable hand. On average, you should never experience a rush. But, in the short run, things might not turn out to be average. A rush will happen for the same reason the coin came up heads 10 times in a row. By chance. The reason is because of something in statistics called random variation. You don't need to know the mathematical background, but here's what you need to know. **You should never play as though you are on a rush.** You should never keep A8 because "8's are hot today" or play poor hands because the deck is "warm." You must play each hand as if the previous hands have no effect on the hand you are playing. They don't. What happened in the hand you just played has absolutely no effect on what happens in the next. There is a benefit to being on a rush, but it has nothing to do with math. Most of your opponents believe in rushes and will be cautious if you come out firing; a good time for one of your infrequent bluffs. Another thing. If you flip a coin 10 times and it comes up heads every time, is a tail more likely to come up on the next flip than a head? If you said "yes," wrong. The coin has no memory. A flipped coin could come up heads 11 times in a row, but now you know this happens just by chance. The coin has such a small brain it doesn't know it just landed heads up 10 times in a row, and doesn't think it is due to come up tails. The cards can't remember any better than a coin can. You can't play a hand as though the cards have a memory.

Each betting round

Preflop there are 169 hands we study. There are actually 1,326 possible preflop starting hands but once we neglect specific suits and take into account the possible flush, we focus on 169 hands. Once you have seen your first two cards there are 19,600 different possible flops. There are 1,081 possible turn and r i v e r combinations. Taken individually there are 47 turns and 46 rivers.

50-50

If there are 169 hands which can be dealt, some of my students believe if they play the top 84 hands — 169 hands/2=84.5 hands above average and likewise 84.5 hands below average — they will win ½ the time. Although that seems logical to a few students, unless you are playing against only one other opponent, it doesn't work out that way. It turns out there are only certain hands that can be played which give you a positive Expected Value of winning and the number of those hands is well below 84. Sometimes probability and common sense are not the same. One more point. Just because you can win or lose a hand doesn't mean you have a 50-50 chance of winning or losing. Thinking this way will cost you a ton of money. If you buy a powerball ticket you will either win the $200,000,000 or not win. You know you do not have a 50-50 chance of winning. The same thing applies to your hands. You do not have a 50-50 chance of winning every time you play. Your chances are much lower and you must use probability to enhance your likelihood of winning.

Hand frequency

Some hands come up more frequently than other hands. At first, that doesn't seem logical. Let's think about it. How many ways can AK unsuited come up? You could have:

A♣ K♥	A♠ K♥	A♦ K♥	A♥ K♣
A♣ K♦	A♠ K♦	A♦ K♣	A♥ K♦
A♣ K♠	A♠ K♣	A♦ K♠	A♥ K♠

Obviously, there are 12 different ways AK unsuited can happen.

How about AK suited?

A♣ K♣	A♦ K♦	A♠ K♠	A♥ K♥

Hmmm. Only four ways to get AKs. Does that mean you will get AK offsuit three times as often as you will get AKs? Yes it does.

How about pairs? Let's take QQ.

Q♣ Q♥	Q♠Q♥	Q♥Q♦
Q♣ Q♦	Q♠Q♦	
Q♣ Q♠		

Wow. There are only six ways to make a specific pair.

Even though there are 169 different hands, you now know some hands will come up more frequently than other hands, so statements such as these will not surprise you:

- You will get AA once every 221 hands.
- You will get AK once every 110.5 hands.
- You will get AKs once every 331.5 hands.
- You will get a pair once every 17 hands.

Part II — The Swayne hand pyramid

Figure 7.2.a shows all 169 possible hands in the form of a pyramid. I first saw a similar figure in the form of an arrow in one of Bill Burton's books. I have tested the pyramid with focus groups and have found it to be extremely effective for learning. We will use the hand pyramid extensively throughout the rest of the book.

```
                                                AA

                                          AKs  KK  AK

                                    KQs AQs  QQ  AQ  KQ

                              QJs KJs AJs  JJ  AJ  KJ  QJ

                        JTs QTs KTs ATs  TT  AT  KT  QT  JT

                  T9s J9s Q9s K9s A9s  99  A9  K9  Q9  J9  T9

            98s T8s J8s Q8s K8s A8s  88  A8  K8  Q8  J8  T8  98

      87s 97s T7s J7s Q7s K7s A7s  77  A7  K7  Q7  J7  T7  97  87

76s 86s 96s T6s J6s Q6s K6s A6s  66  A6  K6  Q6  J6  T6  96  86  76

65s 75s 85s 95s T5s J5s Q5s K5s A5s  55  A5  K5  Q5  J5  T5  95  85  75  65

54s 64s 74s 84s 94s T4s J4s Q4s K4s A4s  44  A4  K4  Q4  J4  T4  94  84  74  64  54

43s 53s 63s 73s 83s 93s T3s J3s Q3s K3s A3s  33  A3  K3  Q3  J3  T3  93  83  73  63  53  43

32s 42s 52s 62s 72s 82s 92s T2s J2s Q2s K2s A2s  22  A2  K2  Q2  J2  T2  92  82  72  62  52  42  32
```

The Swayne hand pyramid

Figure 7.1

Figure 7.2.a

											AA												
									AKs	**KK**	AK											
							KQs	AQs	**QQ**	AQ	KQ											
					QJs	KJs	AJs	**JJ**	AJ	KJ	QJ										
			JTs	QTs	KTs	ATs	**TT**	AT	KT	QT	JT									
		T9s	J9s	Q9s	K9s	A9s	**99**	A9	K9	Q9	J9	T9							
	98s	T8s	J8s	Q8s	K8s	A8s	**88**	A8	K8	Q8	J8	T8	98						
87s	97s	T7s	J7s	Q7s	K7s	A7s	**77**	A7	K7	Q7	J7	T7	97	87					
76s	86s	96s	T6s	J6s	Q6s	K6s	A6s	**66**	A6	K6	Q6	J6	T6	96	86	76			
65s	75s	85s	95s	T5s	J5s	Q5s	K5s	A5s	**55**	A5	K5	Q5	J5	T5	95	85	75	65	
54s	64s	74s	84s	94s	T4s	J4s	Q4s	K4s	A4s	**44**	A4	K4	Q4	J4	T4	94	84	74	64	54
43s	53s	63s	73s	83s	93s	T3s	J3s	Q3s	K3s	A3s	**33**	A3	K3	Q3	J3	T3	93	83	73	63	53	43
32s	42s	52s	62s	72s	82s	92s	T2s	J2s	Q2s	K2s	A2s	**22**	A2	K2	Q2	J2	T2	92	82	72	62	52	42	32

Column frequency	1	2	3	4	5	6	7	8	9	10	11	12	**13**	12	11	10	9	8	7	6	5	4	3	2	1
Hand frequency	4	4	4	4	4	4	4	4	4	4	4	4	**6**	12	12	12	12	12	12	12	12	12	12	12	12
Total frequency	4	8	12	16	20	24	28	32	36	40	44	48	**78**	144	132	120	108	96	84	72	60	48	36	24	12

Suited hands frequency = 312 (24%) **Paired hands frequency = 78** (6%) Unsuited hands frequency = 936 (70%) Total frequency of all hands = 1,326 (100%)

Figure 7.2.a

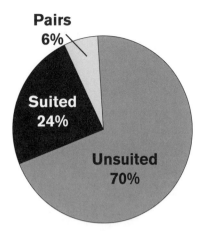

Pairs
6%

Suited
24%

Unsuited
70%

Figure 7.2.b

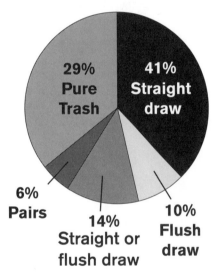

29%
Pure
Trash

41%
Straight
draw

6%
Pairs

14%
Straight or
flush draw

10%
Flush
draw

Figure 7.2.c

Hand frequency and the pyramid

To ensure you understand how often suiteds, pairs, and unpaired/unsuiteds occur, look at figure 7.2.a. You will receive a pocket pair only 6% of the time, the middle column; suited cards, the left hand portion of the pyramid, 24% of the time; and unpaired/unsuited cards, right portion, 70% of the time.

Figure 7.2.b shows these proportions in a pie chart.

Looking at the frequency of hands in a different way

To change your viewpoint you must change your point of view. We will now look at the same total hands illustrated a different way. Figure 7.2.c shows you how frequently you will have:

- A straight draw, that is you could form a straight, but the cards are not suited.
- A flush draw, suited cards which could not form a straight.
- A straight or flush draw; these cards could form either a flush or a straight or a straight flush.
- Pairs.
- Pure trash.

Figure 7.2.d allows you to look at the various portions of the hand pyramid. At the top part of the figure you can compare the straight flush draws to the straight draws not suited. It looks like there is the same number of straight flush draws as pure straight draws. But the pie chart in figure 7.2.c said the pure straight draws occur 41% of the time and straight flush draws occur 14%. A puzzle? No. Suited cards occur less frequently than non-suited cards

Don't think you will be able to play all the hands shown as other than "pure trash." In Chapter 9 you will learn that a lot more of the hands shown above may not be pure trash, but they are trashy enough you won't be able to play them. A9 is included as a trash hand, but later you will find there are a few times, although not often, you can play this hand.

```
                              AA
                         AKs  KK  AK
                     KQs AQs  QQ  AQ KQ
                 QJs KJs AJs  JJ  AJ KJ QJ
             JTs QTs KTs ATs  TT  AT KT QT JT
         T9s J9s Q9s K9s      99     K9 Q9 J9 T9
     98s T8s J8s Q8s          88        Q8 J8 T8 98
 87s 97s T7s J7s              77           J7 T7 97 87
 76s 86s 96s T6s              66              T6 96 86 76
 65s 75s 85s 95s      A5s     55  A5             95 85 75 65
 54s 64s 74s 84s      A4s     44  A4                84 74 64 54
 43s 53s 63s 73s      A3s     33  A3                   73 63 53 43
 32s 42s 52s 62s      A2s     22  A2                      62 52 42 32
```

Straight or flush draws   *Straight draws not suited*

```
                         A9s      A9
                     K8s A8s      A8 K8
                 Q7s K7s A7s      A7 K7 Q7
             J6s Q6s K6s A6s      A6 K6 Q6 J6
         T5s J5s Q5s K5s          K5 Q5 J5 T5
     94s T4s J4s Q4s K4s          K4 Q4 J4 T4 94
 83s 93s T3s J3s Q3s K3s          K3 Q3 J3 T3 93 83
 72s 82s 92s T2s J2s Q2s K2s      K2 Q2 J2 T2 92 82 72
```

Flush draw   *Pure trash*

Figure 7.2.d

Part III — Odds, probability, pot odds, and Expected Value

My objective in explaining these topics is to take something which appears complex to some players and make it simple. Every step is shown and in some cases, to ensure ease of understanding, even obvious steps are shown. This is a long section. If you already understand these topics, skip them. If you are unsure, let's learn. This discussion will focus on limit, but when we get to no limit the same principles will apply.

Odds

The odds are 14 to 4. "14 to 4" is the way odds are said. 14:4 is the way odds are written. The left hand side, the 14, could mean how many times something will happen or "odds for." Or it could mean how many times something won't happen or "odds against." Poker players use "odds against." The left hand side of the 14:4, the 14, means how many times something won't happen and we compare it to the right side, the 4, which means how often something will happen. Said another way, for every 18 events, it won't happen 14 times and it will happen 4 times.

To make the 14:4 easier to understand and use, we want to get the right hand side to 1, so we know how many times something won't happen compared to the 1 time it will happen. We can divide both sides by the same number and the odds don't change. To get the right hand side to 1, we divide the 4 by 4. But if we divide the right hand side by 4, we also have to divide the left hand side by 4.

14/4 and 4/4 is the same as

$$\frac{14}{4} : \frac{4}{4}$$
$$= 3.5:1$$

The odds of 14 to 4 are the same as 3.5 to 1. But if it is an even fraction most people don't say the odds are 3.5 to 1, they say the odds are 3½ to 1. It won't happen 3½ times for every 1 time it will happen.

Now to cards

You have two clubs in your hand and two more clubs hit on the flop. What are the odds against you catching another club on the turn? Remember the left hand side of odds is how many times something won't happen and the right hand side is how often it will happen. We want to find out

How often we won't catch a club : How often we will catch a club

To find the left hand side, the "how often we won't catch a club," we need to find out how many cards won't help us make the club flush.

$$\text{How many cards won't help} \quad = \quad \begin{array}{l} \text{How many cards we don't know} \\ - \text{ how many cards will help} \end{array}$$

How many cards don't we know? We know the 2 in our hand and the 3 on the board so we know 5 cards. There are 52 cards in the deck minus the 5 we know, so the number of cards we don't know is 47.

How many cards will help? There are 13 clubs in the deck, and we know where 4 of them are, so there are 9 remaining clubs that will help.

The left hand side of odds,

$$\text{the number of cards that won't help} \quad = \quad \begin{array}{l} \text{the 47 cards we don't know} \\ - \text{ the 9 that will help} \end{array}$$

$$= \text{ 38 cards}$$

Now let's find the right hand side, which is how often something will happen. That's the number of cards that will help us. We already calculated that number; there are 9 cards that will help.

So now we know both sides of the odds

$$\text{38 cards : 9 cards}$$

We cancel out the word "cards"

$$38 : 9$$

And we want the right hand side to be 1, so we divide both sides by 9

$$38/9 \text{ and } 9/9, \text{ which is the same as}$$

$$\frac{38}{9} : \frac{9}{9}$$

And we get $\qquad$ 4.2 : 1

The odds against you catching a club on the turn are 4.2 : 1, said "4.2 to 1." The left hand side, the 4.2, is how often you will not catch a club compared to the right hand side, the 1, which is how often you will catch a club. The left hand side is how many times it won't happen compared to the right hand side, which is how often it will happen.

Probability

Suppose you believe you have a 1 in 10 chance of winning a hand. To find the probability you divide the chance you have of winning the hand by the total number of chances. In this case

$$\frac{\text{Chances of winning}}{\text{Total chances}} = \frac{1}{10}$$

$$= 0.1, \text{ often expressed as } 10\%.$$

Your probability of winning is 10%. That's what probability is, your chance of winning.

The relationship between odds and probability

Chance of occurring	% probability	Odds
½	50%	1 to 1
⅓	33%	2 to 1
¼	25%	3 to 1
⅕	20%	4 to 1
1/10	10%	9 to 1

Figure 7.3.a

Does the temperature feel different if one person says it's 0 degrees Centigrade and another says it's 32 degrees Fahrenheit? Of course not. The temperature is still the same, freezing. They are just measuring the same thing in a different way.

That's the same with odds and probability. They are both measuring the same thing, just in a different way. Odds tell you the chance of losing. Probability tells you the chance of winning. As you review figure 7.3.a you will see the relationship among probability, odds, and chance.

Do you mean to tell me if I am a 4 to 1 dog, that I don't have a 1 in 4 chance of winning? That's exactly what we mean. And this is a mistake too many players who don't really understand odds make. If you are a 4 to 1 dog, that's 4:1, you have a 1 in 5 chance of catching, not a 1 in 4 chance.

Just as we can convert Fahrenheit to Centigrade or Centigrade to Fahrenheit, we can convert odds to probability or probability to odds.

Converting odds to probability

Take the number on the left side of the odds and add it to the number on the right side of the odds, then divide that number by the number on the right side of the odds.

If the odds are 4:1, we add the left number to the right number

$$4+1 = 5$$

Then we divide the number on the right by that number

$$= \frac{1}{5}$$

$$= 0.20 \text{ or } 20\%$$

Converting probability to odds

Convert the probability into a fraction by first converting the percentage probability into a decimal probability and then dividing that decimal by 1.00. Subtract the bottom number of the fraction from the top number. That number goes on the left hand side of the odds and the top number of the fraction goes on the right side of the odds.

If the probability is 20%

$$20\% \text{ is the same as } 0.20$$

Divide the decimal probability by 1.00

$$= \frac{0.20}{1.00}$$

$$= \frac{1}{5}$$

Subtract the top number of the fraction from the bottom number

$$5 - 1 = 4$$

Take that number and put it on the left hand side of the odds

$$4:$$

Take the top number of the fraction and put it on the right side of the odds

$$:1$$

And you have the odds

$$4:1$$

Do we use odds or probability?

Usual poker language is in odds. But, we will use probability. Probability is much simpler to use and understand.

Presentation of Probabilities

Probabilities will be expressed as a percent. Some are carried out to a few decimal places, such as 0.6745%. In most cases, unless it is less than 1%, it will be rounded off to the nearest whole percent, such as 32%.

Some probabilities are for specific events, such as the probability you will be dealt suited connectors, which is 4%, or the flop will contain exactly a pair, which will occur 17% of the time. When useful, the probability will also be shown in terms of "once every so many hands." You will receive suited connectors once every 28 hands.

If there are many events which could help you, you will see the phrase "at least." That means we have calculated all the probabilities of anything that could help you, added them all together, and then rounded the result to the nearest percentage.

For example suppose you have AK. The top part of figure 7.3.b shows all the good things that could happen on the flop, the individual probabilities of each, then the total, then that total rounded off. You don't need to know all of the individual numbers. All you need to know is if you have AK the probability of you getting something good on the flop is 33%, 1 in 3.

The bottom portion shows you what happens if you have AKs. This improves your probability of getting something good on the flop by 11%.

AK

Probability of exactly one A on the flop	14.4796%
Probability of exactly one K on the flop	14.4796%
Probability of exactly one A and one K on the flop	2.0204%
Probability of AA on the flop	0.6745%
Probability of KK on the flop	0.6745%
Probability of AAK on the flop	0.0459%
Probability of KKA on the flop	0.0459%
Probability of AAA on the flop	0.0051%
Probability of KKK on the flop	0.0051%
Probability of QJT on the flop	0.3265%
Total probability of getting something good on the flop	32.7551%
Which will be rounded off to	33%

AKs

Same as above	32.7551%
Plus two more cards of the same suit on the flop	10.9439%
Total probability of getting something good on the flop	43.6990%
Which will be rounded off to	44%

Figure 7.3.b

Pot odds

In poker language, pot odds are the $ odds which the pot is offering. The $ odds the pot is offering is the amount of money in the pot compared to the amount of money you must pay to stay in the hand.

Suppose there is $50 in the pot and you must bet $10 to stay in. The pot is offering you $50 for your $10 or, said another way, you are risking $10 to win $50. In odds language we would write this as

$$\$50:\$10$$

We can cancel out the $ signs and it would be

$$50:10$$

Just as we did with odds, we want to get the right hand number to 1.

50/10 and 10/10 is the same as

$$\frac{50}{10} \cdot \frac{10}{10}$$

And we get

$$5:1$$

The pot is offering you $50 for your $10 and we have changed that into 5:1. The pot is offering you 5:1.

Another way to arrive at the same odds is

$$\text{Pot odds} = \frac{\text{How much is in the pot}}{\text{How much you must bet}}$$

$$= \frac{\$50 \text{ in the pot}}{\$10 \text{ to call}}$$

$$= \frac{\$50}{\$10}$$

$$= \frac{50}{10}$$

$$5:1$$

Let's take three examples all with your bet being $10, but with pots of $30, $50, and $100.

Pot size	$30	$50	$100
Your bet	$10	$10	$10
Pot odds	3:1	5:1	10:1

Using pot odds

We want to compare the chance of catching to the size of the pot. We are going to compare the odds against improving, that is the odds, to the $ odds which the pot is offering; that is pot odds. Why? To help you decide whether to stay in or fold postflop, usually when you are on a draw. We will use the following criteria:

Anytime the pot is offering you more than your odds against, as long as you believe if you make your hand it will be the winner, you stay in the hand. Said another way, if your pot odds are greater than your odds of winning, continue in the hand.

Anytime the pot is offering you less than your odds against, you fold.

In our flush example a few pages ago, we saw that our odds for catching the flush were 4.2:1. If the pot is offering us $50 for our $10 bet, the pot is offering 5:1. Anytime the pot is offering you more than your odds against, as long as you believe that if you make your hand it will be the winner, you stay in the hand. The pot is offering more than the odds against. 5:1 is more than 4.2:1. With this example you would stay in the hand.

Let's say you have the exact same flush draw, but now the pot is $30 and it will cost you $10 to call. The pot is offering you $30 for your $10. $30:$10 or 30:10 or 3:1.

The pot is offering you 3:1 and your odds are 4.2:1. Anytime the pot is offering you less than your odds against, you fold. The pot is offering you less than your odds. 3:1 is less than 4.2:1. You fold.

If you are thinking about implied odds, we'll discuss that later.

Expected Value

You have seen the term Expected Value a few times. Expected Value is a term used in statistics which means the probability of winning times the amount you can win minus the probability of losing times the amount you must bet to see if you win.

$$\text{Expected Value} = \frac{(\text{probability of winning})(\text{pot size})}{-(\text{probability of losing})(\text{amount you must bet or call})}$$

A positive Expected Value is good. It means over the long run you will win more than you will lose. A negative Expected Value is bad. Over the long run you will lose more than you will win. Expected Value is used extensively from now on to put you in positive Expected Value situations and keep you out of negative ones. You will win more and lose less using Expected Value.

Using Expected Value

In a few pages you will see a chart showing you how many bets must be in the pot before you should play. One question I get asked often is if the probability of catching specific cards doesn't change, why must we have a certain number of bets to stay in a hand?

Let's go through an example. To make this example easier to understand, we will ignore the rake. We have our four flush on the flop again. What's the probability of making a flush on the turn?

$$\text{Probability of catching} = \frac{\text{Number of cards left in the deck to make the flush}}{\text{Number of cards we don't know}}$$

$$= \frac{13 - 4}{47}$$

$$= 0.19$$

$$\text{Probability of not catching} = 1.00 - \text{Probability of catching}$$
$$= 1.00 - 0.19$$
$$= 0.81$$

So far we know several parts of the Expected Value, EV, equation

$$\text{EV} = (0.19)(\text{pot size}) - (0.81)(\text{amount you must bet}).$$

In this example we'll assume no one has raised, so it will cost you 1 bet if you call.

$$\text{EV} = (0.19)(\text{pot size}) - (0.81)(1 \text{ bet}).$$

Here's where the pot size comes into play.

If the pot had 3 bets, your Expected Value would be

$$\text{EV} = (0.19)(3 \text{ bets}) - (.81)(1 \text{ bet})$$
$$= \text{-0.24 bets}$$

A negative Expected Value, -0.24 bets, means if we played this hand with this size pot several thousand times, we would, over the long run, lose an average of 0.24 bets for every hand we played. Not a good deal.

How about 4 bets in the pot?

$$\text{EV} = (0.19)(4 \text{ bets}) - (.81)(1 \text{ bet})$$
$$= \text{-0.05 bets}$$

Expected Value is still negative. Not good. We need a positive Expected Value.

5 bets

$$\text{EV} = (0.19)(5 \text{ bets}) - (.81)(1 \text{ bet})$$
$$= \text{+0.14 bets}$$

All right. A positive Expected Value.

6 bets

$$\text{EV} = (0.19)(6 \text{ bets}) - (.81)(1 \text{ bet})$$
$$= \text{+0.33 bets}$$

7 bets

$$EV = (0.19)(7 \text{ bets}) - (.81)(1 \text{ bet})$$
$$= +0.52 \text{ bets}$$

If there are 7 bets in the pot, our Expected Value is a positive 0.52. If this is a $10/$20 limit table, and there are 7 small bets in the pot on the flop with our flush draw, the amount we could win in the pot is $70. If we call and no one raises it costs us $10. Assuming we win with our flush that means if we played this hand the same way thousands and thousands of times we would win 0.52 X our bet, or 0.52 X $10, or on average, $5.20 for every hand we played. That's a good deal.

It does not mean you will win every time, or close to every time, but as long as you base your play on positive Expected Value, you will win over time.

What has changed in our example? Has the probability of getting a flush card changed? No. The probability is the same. The only change is the amount in the pot and that in turn changes the Expected Value.

The relationship between pot odds and Expected Value

Does it matter to your car if you fill it up with gallons or liters of gas? Just as odds and probability are the same way of saying the same thing, so too are pot odds and Expected Value.

Anytime the pot is offering you more than your odds against that means the same thing as a positive Expected Value. Whenever you have a positive Expected Value that means the same thing as the pot is offering you more than your odds against. Gallons or liters.

Big pots on the button with a trash hand

You see it all the time. A 10-handed table, almost everyone in, and when it gets to the player on the button he says, "Pot odds," and calls or even raises with 86. If he flops two pair, trips, or a straight, he is thinking of winning a monster pot. And if he does flop trips or a straight, or even an open-ended straight, he will probably win that monster pot. But what are his chances? What is the probability he will do so? What's his Expected Value?

I'll give you a few probabilities now so we can figure this out. With a trash hand such as 86, you will flop two pair 2% of the time. Your probability of flopping trips is 1%. A straight 1%. By the river the board will pair, but not give you a full house, 16%

of the time; when that happens your bottom two pair are usually worthless. So you will win less than 4% of the time, but let's just round it off to a 4% probability of winning. Let's see how that pays off.

If you raise on the button there could now be as many as 14 small bets in the pot. You catch on the flop. In all likelihood, if it is a very loose table, once the flop betting is done there might be as many as another 8 small bets in the pot. We are now up to 22 small bets, or 11 big bets. The turn gets another 4 big bets in and the river another 4. There are 19 big bets in the pot and you win.

We'll also assume that if you don't catch on the flop, you will fold. Since you raised on the button your loss would be 2 small bets or the same as 1 big bet.

Does this strategy work out? Let's forget you being outdrawn when you stay in. Let's forget pots smaller than 19 big bets. Let's forget about the extra bets you have to spend when you win and those you spend when you are outdrawn. Let's look only at you winning 19 big bets 4% of the time compared to losing 1 big bet each time you fold on the flop.

You win $(0.04)(19 \text{ big bets})$ or 0.76 big bets on average. You lose $(.96)(1 \text{ big bet})$ or 0.96 big bets on average. Your net loss is 0.96 big bets − 0.76 big bets or 0.2 big bets every time you play this hand. Your loss is actually more because we assumed a monster pot and ignored the extra bets you would have to put in when you catch.

At a $10/$20 table, if you lose at least 0.2 of a big bet on average, that means you lose at least $4, on average, every time you play this hand.

Does this change when you are playing no limit? Sure, because the amount in the pot can be much greater which might turn your Expected Value positive. But it usually isn't.

Do we use pot odds or Expected Value?

Just as odds are traditionally used by poker players, so are pot odds. But we will use Expected Value because it is simpler to use. Simpler is always better. We won't use the term pot odds much anymore, but when we do it means the same thing as Expected Value, just expressed in a different way.

Part IV — Preflop

Preflop straight draws

Straights are not as straightforward as you would expect. You have the possibility of having:

Connectors. Within connectors you will have those:

In the middle	JT, T9, 98, 87, 76, 65, 54
Two from the end	QJ, 43
One from the end	KQ, 32
At the end	AK, A2.

One gap. These are separated from being connected by one card rank. Within one gaps there are those:

In the middle	J9, T8, 97, 86, 75, 64
Two from the end	QT, 53
One from the end	KJ, 42
At the end	AQ, A3.

Two gaps. Separated from being connected by two card ranks. As above you will have those:

In the middle	J8, T7, 96, 85, 74
Two from the end	Q9, 63
One from the end	KT, 52
At the end	AJ, A4.

Three gaps. Separated from being connected by three card ranks. Within these gaps there are those:

In the middle	J7, T6, 95, 84
Two from the end	Q8, 73
One from the end	K9, 62
At the end	AT, A5.

Straights

So what? Here's some of the so what. First, if you have connectors in the middle, such as 87, you have four possible ways of making a straight.

$$J T 9 \textbf{8 7}$$
$$T 9 \textbf{8 7} 6$$
$$9 \textbf{8 7} 6 5$$
$$\textbf{8 7} 6 5 4$$

If you have a one gap hand in the middle, such as 86, there are now three possible ways of making a straight.

$$T 9 \textbf{8} 7 \textbf{6}$$
$$9 \textbf{8} 7 \textbf{6} 5$$
$$\textbf{8} 7 \textbf{6} 5 4$$

With two gaps you have only two ways to make a straight.

T **9** 8 7 **6**

9 8 7 **6** 5

And with three gaps you have only one way to make a straight.

8 7 6 5 **4**

Also the closer you are to the end, the less chance you have of making a straight. For example, if you have A2 there is only one way to make a straight.

A 2 3 4 5

There are some more nuances but they are of only academic interest. Here's what you need to know about your straight draw:

- The chances of making a straight go down substantially the more gaps you have.
- The closer to the end you are, the lower your probability of catching a straight or straight draw.

Preflop flush draw

You will have suited cards 24% of the time. But what about your opponents? In figure 7.4.a the graph shows the probability of at least one opponent also holding two of the same suit as you. At a 10-handed table, if you hold two flush cards there is a 36% chance — about ⅓ — that someone else also has two of your suit.

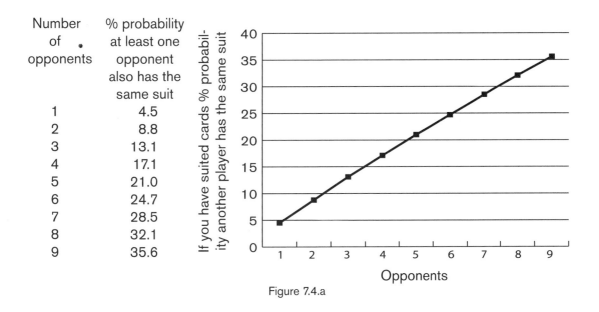

Number of opponents	% probability at least one opponent also has the same suit
1	4.5
2	8.8
3	13.1
4	17.1
5	21.0
6	24.7
7	28.5
8	32.1
9	35.6

Figure 7.4.a

Your highest suited card	% probability an opponent who has the same suit has a higher ranked card
3	100.0
4	100.0
5	98.2
6	94.6
7	89.0
8	81.8
9	72.7
T	61.8
J	49.1
Q	34.6
K	18.2
A	0.0

Figure 7.4.b

Figure 7.4.b is even more interesting. Assuming both you and an opponent have the same suit, this graph shows, depending on your highest card, the probability of your opponent holding a higher card. Many authors say to bet cautiously unless you have one of the top two flush cards in your hand at the river. Their advice is based on years of playing flush hands but intuitively it doesn't seem right. It is good advice. The graph shows if your highest flush card is a T, an opponent holding the same suit has a 62% chance of holding a higher card than you. If you have J high it is essentially a coin flip. You are the clear statistical favorite only if you have a Q or above. Of course, if the A, K, or Q, or more than one is on the board, you must make an adjustment. For example, if the K is on the board, you are the statistical favorite if you hold the J. If the A and Q are on the board, you are favored if you hold the T.

The Swayne preflop straight and flush draws

The left hand column of the graphs in figure 7.4.c summarizes your straight possibilities. The vertical scale axis is the same for all graphs on the page so you can easily compare the strength of cards among graphs.

If your hole cards are suited you have a 6.5% chance of making a flush if played to the river. This includes the chance of runner runner which you would never play, except as a backdoor. If you have middle connectors your chance of making a straight is 9% if played to the river, but again this figure takes into account runner runner.

The right hand column of graphs shows you how much your hand gains in strength with suited cards. You should take a few minutes to study the graphs. The value of these graphs is not the specific % probabilities as the probabilities include a runner runner. Rather, what you should get from these graphs is the relative strength of connectors to those with gaps, and suited to unsuited.

Even some experts are surprised how much stronger a draw is with three gap suiteds (the graph in the lower right of figure 7.4.c) than connectors (the graph in the upper left).

Suiteds make a big difference

The value of suited versus unsuited increases the chance of you making a hand as much as 5%. That may not seem like much, but it is more than enough for you to play many hands you would otherwise fold. Making the flush is not the only advantage of playing suiteds. You will play some suiteds you would not play if they were not suited, and 2% of the time on the flop will pair both cards. You might play K8s, another hand you would not play if unsuited, and catch a K. Not a superstrong hand, but it could turn out to be the winner. Sometimes, if you have a four flush, you will catch a card on the turn, giving you the possibility of making a straight on the river.

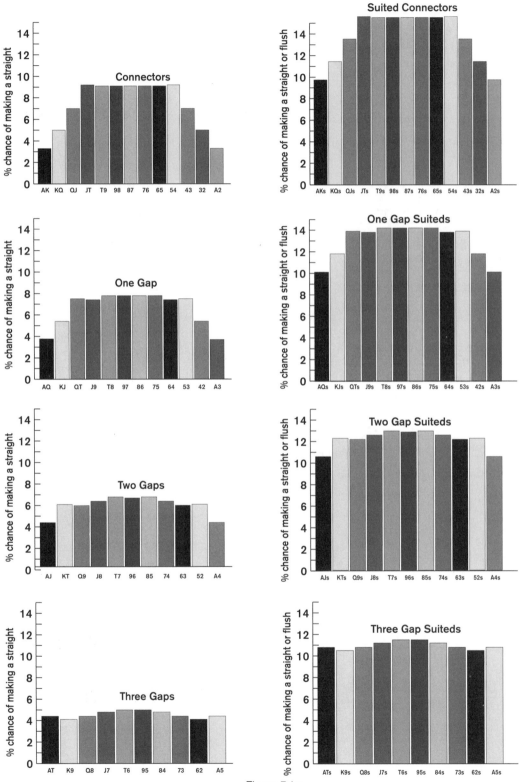

Figure 7.4.c

Preflop numbers

Figures 7.4.d.a-b show how often you will be dealt specific cards and types of hands. These numbers are rounded off to the nearest percent, unless the percentage is less than 0.50%.

Preflop Aces	Probability	
AA	0.45%	Once every 221 hands
AK unsuited	1%	Once every 110.5 hands
AK suited or unsuited	1%	Once every 83 hands
Any Ax unsuited	11%	
AKs	0.03%	Once every 331.5 hands
AQs	0.03%	Once every 331.5 hands
AJs	0.03%	Once every 331.5 hands
Any specific Axs	0.03%	Once every 331.5 hands
Any Axs	4%	Once every 28 hands
If you have an Ace, no other player has an Ace		
Heads up	88%	
6-handed	50%	
10-handed	25%	
No player at the table has an Ace		
Heads up	72%	
6-handed	34%	
10-handed	13%	

Preflop high cards		
KK	0.45%	Once every 221 hands
Any Kx suited or unsuited	15%	
Any Qx suited or unsuited	15%	
Any Kxs	4%	Once every 28 hands
Any Qxs	4%	Once every 28 hands
Any specific Xxs	0.03%	Once every 331.5 hands
At least one face card	42%	
Two cards K or higher	2%	
Two cards Q or higher	5%	
Two cards J or higher	9%	
Two cards T or higher	14%	

Preflop flush		
Two unsuited	76%	
Two suited	24%	

Preflop pairs		
Any specific pair	0.45%	Once every 221 hands
Any pair	6%	Once every 17 hands

Figure 7.4.d.a

Preflop straight draws	Probability	
Connected	16%	
A gap in sequence	15%	
Two gaps in sequence	13%	
Three gaps in sequence	12%	
Connectors		
In the middle	8%	JT, T9, 98, 87, 76, 65, 54
Two from end	2%	QJ, 43
One from end	2%	KQ, 32
At the end	2%	AK, A2
One gap		
In the middle	7%	J9, T8, 97, 86, 75, 64
Two from end	2%	QT, 53
One from end	2%	KJ, 42
At the end	2%	AQ, A3
Two gaps		
In the middle	6%	J8, T7, 96, 85, 74
Two from end	2%	Q9, 63
One from end	2%	KT, 52
At the end	2%	AJ, A4
Three gaps		
In the middle	5%	J7, T6, 95, 84
Two from end	2%	Q8, 73
One from end	2%	K9, 62
At the end	2%	AT, A5
Preflop straight flush draws		
Any suited connectors	4%	Once every 28 hands
Any one gap suiteds	4%	
Any two gap suiteds	3%	
Any three gap suiteds	3%	
Suited connectors		
In the middle	2%	JTs, T9s, 98s, 87s, 76s, 65s, 54s
Two from end	1%	QJs, 43s
One from end	1%	KQs, 32s
At the end	1%	AKs, A2s
One gap suiteds		
In the middle	2%	J9s, T8s, 97s, 86s, 75s, 64s
Two from end	1%	QTs, 53s
One from end	1%	KJs, 42s
At the end	1%	AQs, A3s
Two gap suiteds		
In the middle	2%	J8s, T7s, 96s, 85s, 74s
Two from end	1%	Q9s, 63s
One from end	1%	KTs, 52s
At the end	1%	AJs, A4s
Three gap suiteds		
In the middle	1%	J7s, T6s, 95s, 84s
Two from end	1%	Q8s, 73s
One from end	1%	K9s, 62s
At the end	1%	ATs, A5s

Figure 7.4.d.b

Significance of preflop numbers

It is not important for you to know how often things will happen to you. What is important is what everyone else has. Extremely loose opponents play connectors, one gap cards, two gap cards, and any two suited. They also play A-anything and K-anything. Figure 7.4.e illustrates what would occur on average with every hand at a 10-handed table. Not every hand is average, but this figure is important for you to understand, especially when you are playing at a loose table.

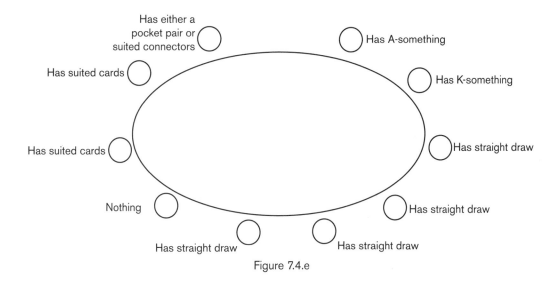

Figure 7.4.e

Ace in the hole

If you have an Ace in the hole, are you ahead? Not as much as you might think. Figure 7.4.f shows you how likely it is for at least one other player to have an Ace when you have one. At a 10-handed table there is a 75% chance someone else has one too.

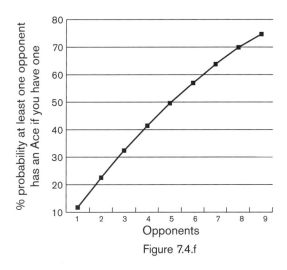

Figure 7.4.f

Preflop summary

Figure 7.4.g summarizes your preflop hands. Over ½ the time you will have something which could make a straight, and about ¼ of the time your cards will be suited. Pocket pairs occur once every 17 hands.

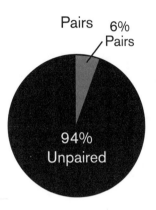

Pairs

6% Pairs

94% Unpaired

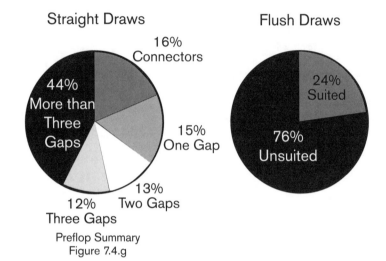

Straight Draws

16% Connectors

15% One Gap

13% Two Gaps

12% Three Gaps

44% More than Three Gaps

Flush Draws

24% Suited

76% Unsuited

Preflop Summary
Figure 7.4.g

The Flop

Pairs, sets, trips	Probability
Flop will contain	
Exactly a pair	17%
Exactly three of a kind	0.24%
If you hold a pair	
You will flop at least a set	12%
If you hold unpaired cards	
You will flop two pair	2%
You will flop trips	1%
You will flop at least a pair	32%
Flushes	
The flop will contain	
Two of one suit; one other	55%
Three of the same suit	5%
Rainbow, none suited	40%
If you have two of a suit you will flop	
Two of your suit	11%
Three of your suit	1%
A four flush or a flush	12%
You will hold two unsuited	70%

The Flop continued

Straights	Probability	Straights continued	Probability
The flop will contain		Two gaps	
Three in sequence	4%	In the middle	1%
Two in sequence interior	33%	Two from end	0.33%
Two in sequence exterior	7%	One from end	0.33%
Any two in sequence	40%	At the end	0.33%
Nothing in sequence	56%	Three gaps	
		In the middle	0.33%
If you hold cards which could form a double inside straight, the flop will be a double inside straight	1%	Two from end	0.33%
		One from end	0.33%
		At the end	0.33%
		Straight flush draws	
You will flop a straight with		All situations have very low probabilities.	
Connectors			
In the middle	1%		
Two from end	0.33%		
One from end	0.33%		
At the end	0.33%		
One gap			
In the middle	1%		
Two from end	0.33%		
One from end	0.33%		
At the end	0.33%		

Pairs

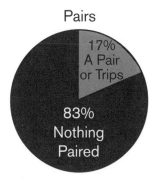

The pie chart on the bottom includes not only the sequenced flop cards, but also the various gaps for straight draws. The point is almost ¾ of the time there will be a possible straight draw on the flop.

Straight Draws

Flush Draws

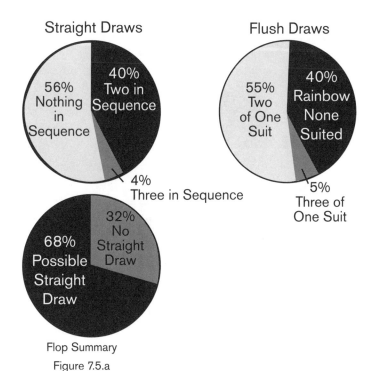

Flop Summary

Figure 7.5.a

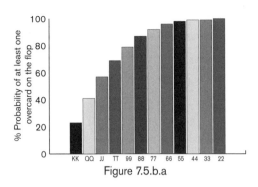

Figure 7.5.b.a

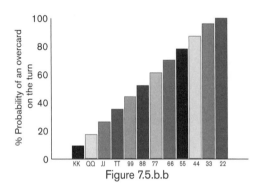

Figure 7.5.b.b

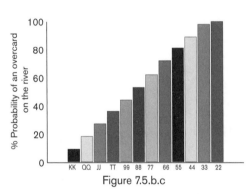

Figure 7.5.b.c

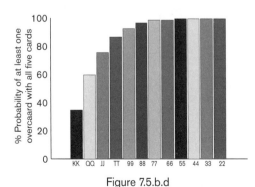

Figure 7.5.b.d

Overcard probabilities

If you have a pocket pair, it is important you know the probability of at least one overcard appearing.

Figures 7.5.b.a-d graph the probability of one or more overcards for the flop, for the turn, for the river, and the overall probability for all five cards. The horizontal axis for all of the graphs indicates pairs but also holds if you have one of those cards with a lower card.

The graphs, especially the flop and all five cards, show important probabilities for overcards.

Let's first focus on 7.5.b.a which shows the probability of at least one overcard on the flop. If you have JJ at least one overcard will occur over ½ the time. With TT there will be at least one overcard about 70% of the time.

With 99 at least one overcard will appear on the flop approximately 80% of the time.

Now look at 7.5.b.d which gives the probability of at least one overcard through the river. If you have JJ at least one overcard will show up by the river over 75% of the time. With TT 85% of the time. And with 99 over 90% of the time.

The exact percentages are not important, but understanding how high the probability an overcard will appear on the board is. Also review how fast the probability increases once you get below JJ. In the Betting Chapter it will be emphasized you must try to eliminate opponents preflop by raising or re-raising with pairs likely to suffer an overcard.

The Gordon Rule

How likely is it your pocket pair is beat preflop? Phil Gordon, a finalist at several World Series of Poker final tables, a multi-million dollar winner, and best-selling poker author, has developed what I call The Gordon Rule. His rule will give you a usable approximation of how likely it is that someone else at the table holds a higher pocket pair than you.

Here's how The Gordon Rule works when you have a pocket pair preflop:

a. Count the number of pocket pairs higher than yours.
b. Count the number of players who are already in the hand or are yet to act.
c. Multiply a by b.
d. Divide c by 2.
e. Change d into a probability by adding a percent sign.

Sounds complicated, but it is very easy. Let's go through two examples.

Example 1. You are directly to the left of the big blind at a 10-handed table with 44. To find the probability someone has a higher pocket pair:

a. Count the number of pocket pairs higher than yours. There are a total of 10 pocket pairs higher than your 44. They are:

55 66 77 88 99 TT JJ QQ KK AA

b. Count the number of players who are in the hand or yet to act. If you are first to the left of the big blind at a 10-handed table, there are 9 players yet to act, two of which are in the blinds.

c. Multiply a times b.

10 hands higher than yours X 9 players yet to act = 90

d. Divide c by 2.

90/2 = 45

e. Change d into a probability by adding a percent sign.

45%

That means The Gordon Rule says there is a 45% chance that someone else at the table has a pocket pair higher than your 44.

Example 2. You are one before the button at a 6-handed table with 88. One person before you bet. All others have folded.

a. Count the number of pocket pairs higher than yours. There are a total of 6 pocket pairs higher than your 88.

b. Count the number of players who are in the hand and yet to act. Include any who have already called or raised before you. In this case we have 4.

The bettor in front of you
The button is yet to act
Both blinds are yet to act

c. Multiply a times b.

   6 hands higher than yours X 4 players yet to act = 24

d. Divide c by 2.

   24/2 = 12

e. Change d into a probability by adding a percent sign.

   12%

The Gordon Rule is simple to use, close to exact, and something you should use every time you have a pocket pair.

If you are interested in the exact numbers, we have developed figure 7.6.a. It shows the probability of another player holding a higher pocket pair, depending on your pair and the number of players.

You hold	Number of opponents left in the hand preflop								
	1	2	3	4	5	6	7	8	9
KK	1%	1%	2%	2%	3%	3%	3%	4%	4%
QQ	1%	2%	3%	4%	5%	6%	7%	8%	9%
JJ	2%	3%	4%	6%	7%	9%	10%	12%	13%
TT	2%	4%	6%	8%	10%	12%	14%	16%	18%
99	3%	5%	7%	10%	12%	15%	17%	20%	22%
88	3%	6%	9%	12%	15%	18%	21%	24%	26%
77	3%	7%	10%	14%	17%	21%	24%	27%	31%
66	4%	8%	12%	16%	20%	24%	27%	31%	35%
55	4%	9%	13%	18%	22%	27%	31%	35%	40%
44	5%	10%	15%	20%	25%	29%	34%	39%	44%
33	5%	11%	16%	22%	27%	32%	38%	43%	49%
22	6%	12%	17%	24%	29%	35%	41%	47%	53%

Figure 7.6.a

Figure 7.6.b shows you the probability of any opponent holding an Ace with a higher kicker, an Ace with the same kicker as you but suited, or a pocket pair. Where the probability is over 50%, the area is filled in. Of particular interest is that when you hold AK under the gun, someone else at a 10-handed table is usually ahead of you before the flop.

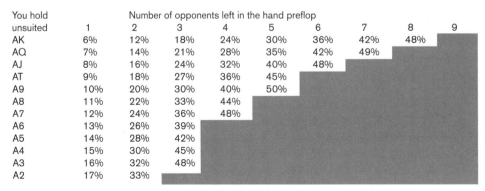

You hold unsuited	Number of opponents left in the hand preflop								
	1	2	3	4	5	6	7	8	9
AK	6%	12%	18%	24%	30%	36%	42%	48%	
AQ	7%	14%	21%	28%	35%	42%	49%		
AJ	8%	16%	24%	32%	40%	48%			
AT	9%	18%	27%	36%	45%				
A9	10%	20%	30%	40%	50%				
A8	11%	22%	33%	44%					
A7	12%	24%	36%	48%					
A6	13%	26%	39%						
A5	14%	28%	42%						
A4	15%	30%	45%						
A3	16%	32%	48%						
A2	17%	33%							

Figure 7.6.b

Postflop

Figure 7.7.a shows the probabilities of making certain hands.

If you have a set on the flop, you have a 1 in 3 chance of getting a boat by the river. If you miss on the turn you still have a 1 in 5 chance of catching on the river. Nothing is "funner" than runner runner. Perhaps, but you only have a 4% chance of catching the last two cards. Never a good play except as a backdoor.

Figure 7.7.c on the next page will turn out to be an extremely useful chart when we get to the Betting Chapter. Here's what the chart does. It converts how many cards are available to complete your hand, called outs, into the minimum number of bets that must be in the limit pot for you to consider continuing to play. You can just skim the figure for now.

The result is the exact number of bets that must be in the pot for a 0 Expected Value, if there were no rake. But there is always a rake, so the rake is then accounted for, resulting in a 0 Expected Value adjusted for the rake. This result is then rounded up to the nearest whole number. **That** whole **number is the minimum bets needed in the pot in order for you to have a positive Expected Value**.

Caution on the river

The more opponents left on the river, especially loose ones, the more careful you must be. Remember, loose players are in for any kind of a draw and some will stay to the river waiting for that inside straight, runner runner flush, or trying to hit that set of ducks.

Figure 7.7.b shows you the minimum possibilities there are to beat you, if all you have is an overpair, even AA. These probabilities don't even take into account an opponent catching a set. And several five-card boards will have multiple possibilities for straights, flushes, or boats. Here's the point. Unless you have the nuts, or a monster hand you don't think can be beat, be extremely cautious on the river.

Last two cards

A set improving to a boat or better

With the turn and river to come	**33%**
A set improving to exactly a boat	
With the turn and river to come	29%
On the turn	13%
On the river	20%
A pair improving to three of a kind or better	
With the turn and river to come	9%
On the turn	4%
On the river	4%

Runner runner

Three suited to make a flush		**4%**
You have three in sequence		
At the end	AKQ or A23	1%
One from end	KQJ or 234	3%
Two or more from end	**such as QJT or 345**	**4%**

Figure 7.7.a

Five cards on the board

Probability of a straight	
that there are at three or more cards which could make a straight	**at least 75%**
Probability of a flush	
that there are three or more flush cards	**at least 37%**
Probability of a full house	
that is a pair, two pair, or trips	**at least 49%**

Figure 7.7.b

	Flop draw for the turn				Turn draw for the river			
Outs or cards available to make your hand	Number of cards left (unknown to you)	Cards left/ Outs	Rake adjustment	Minimum bets needed in the pot to see the turn	Number of cards left (unknown to you)	Cards left/ Outs	Rake adjustment	Minimum bets needed in the pot to see the river
20	47	2.35	2.59	3	46	2.30	2.53	3
19	47	2.47	2.72	3	46	2.42	2.66	3
18	47	2.61	2.87	3	46	2.56	2.81	3
17	47	2.76	3.04	4	46	2.71	2.98	3
16	47	2.94	3.23	4	46	2.88	3.16	4
15	47	3.13	3.45	4	46	3.07	3.37	4
14	47	3.36	3.69	4	46	3.29	3.61	4
13	47	3.62	3.98	4	46	3.54	3.89	4
12	47	3.92	4.31	5	46	3.83	4.22	5
11	47	4.27	4.70	5	46	4.18	4.60	5
10	47	4.70	5.17	6	46	4.60	5.06	6
9	47	5.22	5.74	6	46	5.11	5.62	6
8	47	5.88	6.46	7	46	5.75	6.33	7
7	47	6.71	7.39	8	46	6.57	7.23	8
6	47	7.83	8.62	9	46	7.67	8.43	9
5	47	9.40	10.34	11	46	9.20	10.12	11
4	47	11.75	12.93	13	46	11.50	12.65	13
3	47	15.67	17.23	18	46	15.33	16.87	18
2	47	23.50	25.85	26	46	23.00	25.30	26
1	47	47.00	51.70	52	46	46.00	50.60	51

Outs on flop and turn converted into minimum bets needed in the pot

Figure 7.7.c

	Probability %	Once every so many hands
In five cards		
Your cards and the flop		
Royal flush	0.00015	649,740
Straight flush	0.0015	64,974
Quads	0.024	4,165
Full house	0.1	694
Flush	0.2	505
Straight	0.4	254
Trips	2.1	47
Two pair	4.8	21
A pair	42.3	2
In seven cards		
Your cards and the board through the river		
Royal flush	0.003	33,333
Straight flush	0.031	3,226
Quads	0.17	588
Full house	2.6	38
Flush	3.0	33
Straight	4.6	22
Trips	4.8	20
Two pair	21.8	4
A pair	43.8	2

Figure 7.7.d

Other numbers

Figure 7.7.d includes some interesting and nice to know numbers.

A few notes to the figures on the left. Some numbers may be slightly different than you find in other books, but the operative word is slightly. The reason for the difference is a few hands may be counted twice. A straight and royal flush are special cases of the flush, so they may be included in the count for the flush as well as in their own category. A straight flush is also a straight. Two pair means exactly two pair and not a better hand.

The exact numbers are not nearly as important as you understanding the relative frequency of a specific hand occurring compared to others.

Five card hand frequency

The total number of five card hands possible is 2,598,960. Figure 7.7.d shows how often you will make each type of hand.

	Possible hands	Frequency
Straight flush	40	slight
Quads	624	slight
Full house	3,744	0.14%
Flush	5,108	0.20%
Straight	10,200	0.39%
Set or Trips	54,912	2%
Two pair	123,552	5%
A pair	1,098,240	42%
Nothing	1,302,540	50%
	2,598,960	

Figure 7.7.e

How does this chart help me?

An extremely important point which will be re-emphasized later in the Betting Chapter is to realize how much **pairs dominate play**. Most players, even experienced ones, believe two pair or better win most of the pots. We remember things out of the ordinary such as the two pair, sets, straights, and better, but fail to remember the ordinary pair that won.

What does all this mean? It means **an overpair or top pair with a good kicker (J or higher) will win more hands than it will lose**, even at a 10-handed table. In turn that means when you have an overpair or a pair with a high kicker, you should be aggressive to knock out the draws because in the long run you will win much more than you will lose. The second point is if you don't catch, unless the numbers are right, release immediately. Chapter 9 will explain when the numbers are right.

The last point is not supported by figure 7.7.e, and will be repeated in the Betting Chapter: **when there is heavy betting by someone other than you, the likelihood of your pair holding up decreases**.

This is important when you get to no limit. The high pair does very well winning many small pots in no limit, but if that is all you have, it does poorly in big pots. In no limit tournament play you should not risk all or a large chunk of your chips solely on a high pair.

For the math experts

There will be some math and probability experts who read this chapter and thought we didn't take into account some of the finer points. For example, if you hold JJ does that impact the probability of getting a pair on the flop? Sure it does, since one of the possible pairs has been removed from the deck. When these special events happen, usually the effect is minimal. Instead of confusing the reader with ranges of answers, we used a weighted average, rounded off, or showed the more useful number.

Some may disagree with the Expected Value formula. We chose the most useful method for table play.

A final word

You don't want to be known as a math player. But you must know math to be a player.

Summary

- Probability is the basis for almost everything in this chapter.
- Some hands come up more frequently than others, some less.
- Suited cards close in sequence are more powerful than unsuiteds.
- An Ace in the hole is not as powerful as some players think.
- At a 10-handed table almost all players will have either a good hand or a draw.
- The probability of an overcard on the board is high for medium pocket pairs.
- If there are several loose players on the river, caution.
- A pair will win most of the pots.

Homework

- Know what others will, on average, hold.
- Know your probability of making specific draws.
- Count how often a pair with a Jack or better wins the hand.

CHAPTER 8

Relative Strength

Introduction

Your first two cards actually change in strength depending on the number of opponents who are dealt hands. This has long been known by experts, but on the next few pages we have graphed how a specific hand changes in value depending on the number of your opponents who are dealt hands, not necessarily how many remain in the hand.

As the number of opponents increase, some hands go down in strength, some stay steady, and some actually increase in strength.

What exactly is relative strength?

If the strength of a preflop hand was dependent only on the number of opponents dealt cards, the relative strength graphs in this chapter will show you the probability of a specific hand winning against all others, if played to a showdown.

In the next chapter we will discuss all of the factors, including your number of opponents, which influence whether you play a hand. This Relative Strength Chapter is presented now so you get a feel of how the number of opponents changes the value of various hands. It is also presented as critical for no limit players as they have a special need to understand card strength when playing shorthanded.

How to read the relative strength graphs

There are 169 possible hands. During our initial research we calculated how the relative strength varied from number 1, the best possible hand, down to 169, the worst possible hand, as the number of opponents changes. Although we obtained data on all hands, there are only certain hands worth your time to review. When we drew the graphs for those playable hands we found, as expected, almost all the lines fell in the top 50% and hardly any lines were in the bottom 50%. **What is shown in this chapter is only the top half of the graphs, that is, the top 85 out of 169 hands. The bottom half — the bottom 84 — is left out.**

Each graph in this chapter can be directly compared to other graphs. The vertical scales are the same. When reading the graphs realize the number of opponents means the number of other players receiving cards. It does not mean the number of opponents who elect to stay in the hand.

What conclusions can you draw?

You cannot conclude the hands shown can be played. In fact, later you will find many cannot be played. You cannot say the exact relative strength remains constant depending on how tight or loose the table is, because we have chosen to show you an average limit table. The patterns do hold although the amplitude varies depending on how tight or loose the table is. You can conclude how certain types of hands change in value with the number of opponents. You will see patterns most players are not familiar with. For now, focus on learning the shapes and patterns.

The Swayne relative strength graphs

The results are presented in the following order which will be used throughout the rest of the book whenever many hands are shown:

- Axs, Kxs, Qxs
- Ax, Kx
- Suited connectors, one gap suiteds, two gap suiteds
- Unsuited connectors, one gap unsuiteds
- Pairs

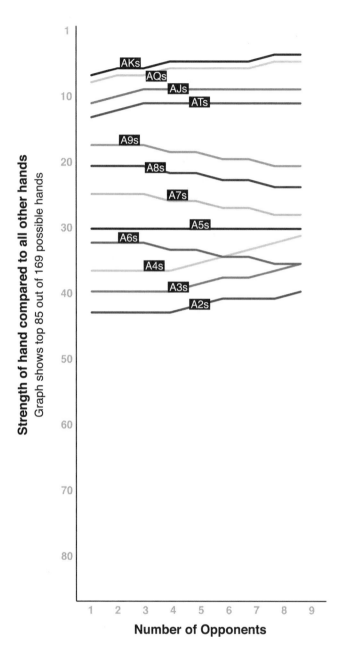

Axs

Strong relative strength cards. You will see how strong they are as we go through other hands.

Note: A2s, A3s, and A4s increase slightly in strength because of the straight possibility.

Kxs

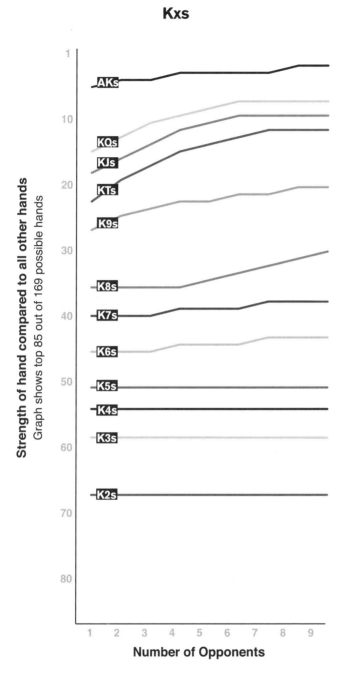

Strength of hand compared to all other hands
Graph shows top 85 out of 169 possible hands

Number of Opponents

Nothing surprising here. Strength of higher Kxs hands increase ever so slightly with the number of opponents.

Qxs

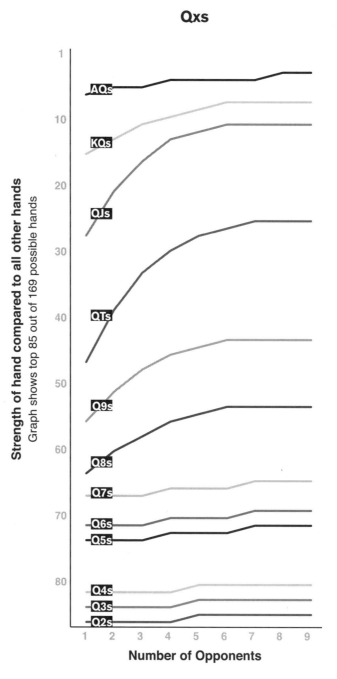

Strength of hand compared to all other hands
Graph shows top 85 out of 169 possible hands

AQs
KQs
QJs
QTs
Q9s
Q8s
Q7s
Q6s
Q5s
Q4s
Q3s
Q2s

Number of Opponents

Notice how the higher Qxs hands increase in strength with more opponents.

Ax

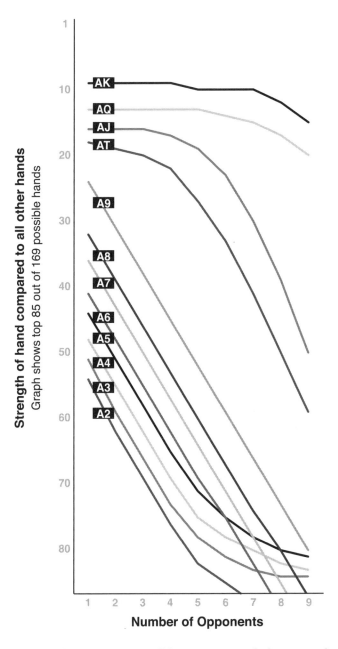

Number of Opponents

This will be surprising to all but experienced players. Ax decreases in strength dramatically with the number of opponents.

The reason for the rate of decrease slowing down for A5, A4, A3, and A2 is again the possibility of making a straight.

Kx

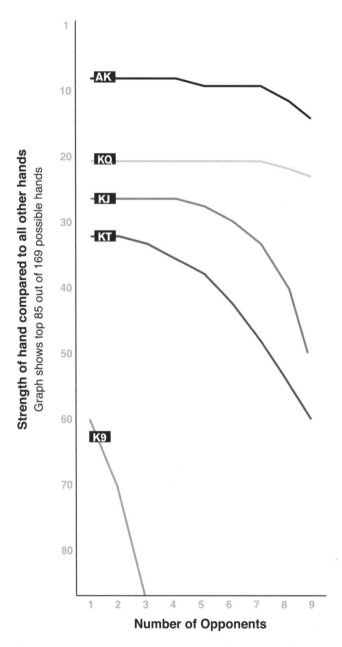

The pattern is similar to Ax, as you would expect, but K9 barely makes the chart.

Suited Connectors

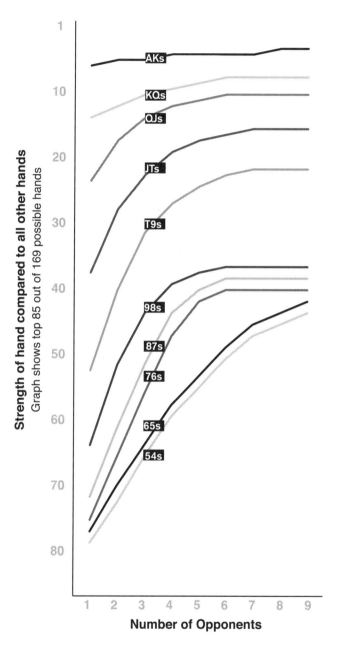

These hands increase dramatically in strength from heads up to a 6-handed table, and then tend to level off.

One Gap Suiteds

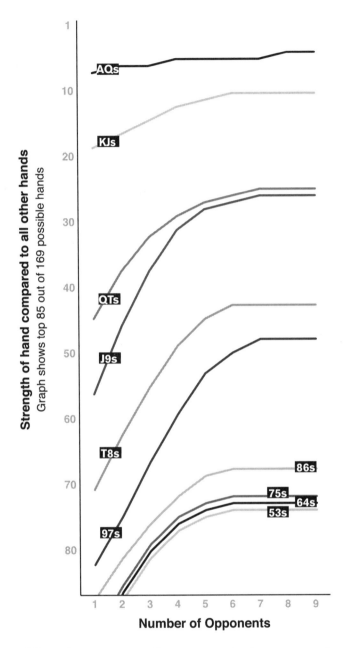

Strength of hand compared to all other hands
Graph shows top 85 out of 169 possible hands

Number of Opponents

These follow the same type of pattern as suited connectors, but obviously not as strong.

Two Gap Suiteds

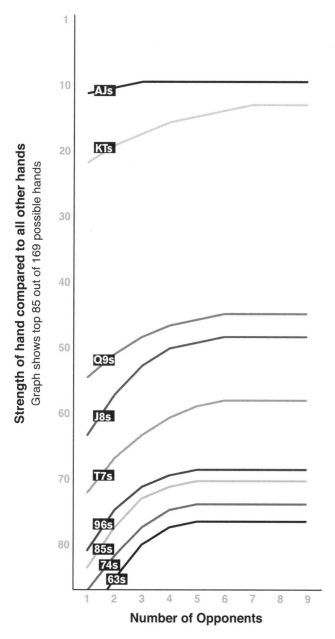

Strength of hand compared to all other hands
Graph shows top 85 out of 169 possible hands

Number of Opponents

AJs
KTs
Q9s
J8s
T7s
96s
85s
74s
63s

Same pattern as suited connectors and one gap suiteds, but not as strong.

Connectors Unsuited

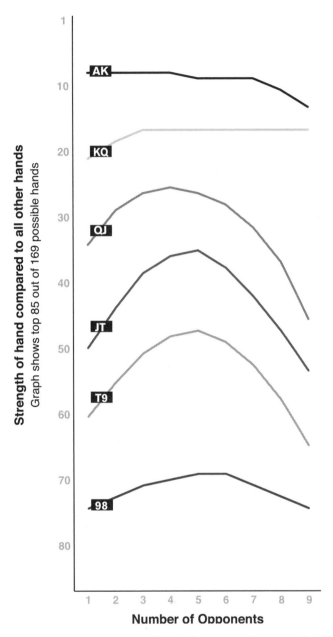

Surprising pattern. An inverted bowl. Notice how 98 barely makes it on the chart. 87 and lower hands don't even come close to the top 50%.

One Gap Unsuited

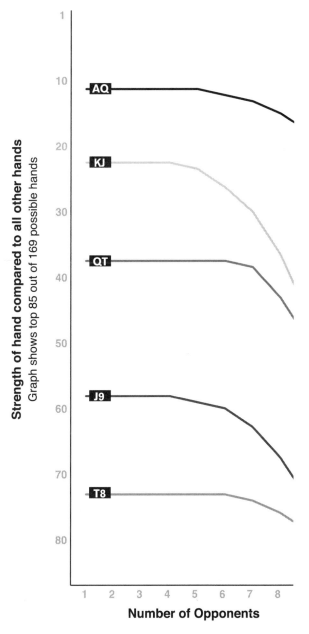

Steady strength with few opponents; strength declines with more opponents.

Pairs

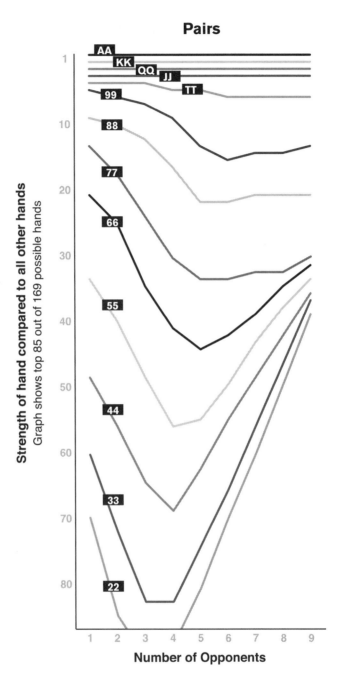

Strength of hand compared to all other hands
Graph shows top 85 out of 169 possible hands

Number of Opponents

These were saved until the end because our reaction was "Wow." A real surprise. A pattern we never expected. It will take a few minutes for the impact of these graphs to sink in.

With the lower pairs notice how relatively strong they are heads up, that they decrease in value with some more opponents, and then increase in value with more opponents.

Why do graphs have different patterns and shapes?

Not sure. Ax graphs make sense. As you can see in the previous chapter's figure 7.4.f, even though a player may hold an Ace, as the number of opponents increase the probability an opponent also has an Ace increases, and so the lower the kicker the lower the strength of the hand should become. It also seems logical that the strength of suited connectors would increase with the number of opponents. But some of the other patterns, especially the lower pairs, do not conform to any theory we have been able to confirm. Just the facts. Jack Webb (younger readers have no idea what this means).

Summary

- The relative strength of your first two cards depends on your number of opponents.
- There are distinctive shapes and patterns for different hand types.
- Some hands decrease in strength with the number of opponents.
- Some hands increase in strength with the number of opponents.
- The graphs for pairs have an unusual pattern.

Homework

- Review all of the relative strength graphs.

Test 2

1. Which of the following hands occur most frequently?
   - ❏ A. AK
   - ❏ B. AKs
   - ❏ C. AA
   - ❏ D. They all occur with the same frequency

2. Which of the following hands occur least frequently?
   - ❏ A. AK
   - ❏ B. AKs
   - ❏ C. AA
   - ❏ D. They all occur with the same frequency

3. How many different ways can QQ be made?
   - ❏ A. 4
   - ❏ B. 6
   - ❏ C. 8
   - ❏ D. 9
   - ❏ E. 12

4. How many different ways can AKs be made?
   - ❏ A. 4
   - ❏ B. 6
   - ❏ C. 8
   - ❏ D. 9
   - ❏ E. 12

5. You will receive a pocket pair about ___ of the time.
   - ❏ A. 2%
   - ❏ B. 6%
   - ❏ C. 15%
   - ❏ D. 24%

6. You will receive suited cards about ___ of the time.
   - ❏ A. 2%
   - ❏ B. 6%
   - ❏ C. 15%
   - ❏ D. 24%

7. You will receive cards that could make a straight, but not suited, about ___ of the time.
   - ❏ A. 11%
   - ❏ B. 21%
   - ❏ C. 31%
   - ❏ D. 41%
   - ❏ E. 51%

8. In poker language we often say the odds are 14:4. This means
   - ❏ A. The event will happen 14 times for every 4 times it won't happen
   - ❏ B. The event won't happen 14 times for every 4 times it will happen
   - ❏ C. Both of the above are usual poker language
   - ❏ D. Neither A or B is correct.

9. The odds are X:Y. To find the right hands side of the odds when drawing in poker, the Y, we must know:
   - ❏ A. How often we will catch
   - ❏ B. How often we won't catch
   - ❏ C. Both of the above
   - ❏ D. None of the above

10. What is the relationship between odds and probability when used in poker?
  - ❏ A. There is no relationship
  - ❏ B. They measure the same thing, but in a different way
  - ❏ C. At times there is a relationship, at other times there is not
  - ❏ D. It is impossible to say

11. If the probability of catching is 50%, this is the same odds as:
  - ❏ A. 2:1
  - ❏ B. 1:2
  - ❏ C. 1:1
  - ❏ D. 1:4
  - ❏ E. None of the above

12. If the probability of catching is 10%, this is the same odds as:
  - ❏ A. 9:1
  - ❏ B. 1:9
  - ❏ C. 10:1
  - ❏ D. 1:10
  - ❏ E. None of the above

13. If the odds are 2 to 1, this is the same as:
  - ❏ A. A chance of 1 out of 2
  - ❏ B. A chance of 2 out of 1
  - ❏ C. A chance of 1 out of 3
  - ❏ D. A chance of 3 out of 1
  - ❏ E. None of the above

14. If the odds are 4:1, this means the same as:
  - ❏ A. It won't happen 4 times for every 1 time it will happen
  - ❏ B. It won't happen 1 time for every 4 times it will happen
  - ❏ C. It won't happen 5 times for every 1 time it will happen
  - ❏ D. It won't happen 1 time for every 5 times it will happen

15. If the odds are 4:1, this means the same as:
  - ❏ A. A 5% probability
  - ❏ B. A 20% probability
  - ❏ C. A 25% probability
  - ❏ D. It can't be determined

16. You have AK. What is the probability that on the flop you will catch exactly one A?
  - ❏ A. 4%
  - ❏ B. 9%
  - ❏ C. 14%
  - ❏ D. 19%

17. You have AK. What is the probability that on the flop you will catch exactly one A or one K?
  - ❏ A. 4%
  - ❏ B. 9%
  - ❏ C. 14%
  - ❏ D. 29%

18. You have AK. What is the probability on the flop you will catch an A or K or better?
  - ❏ A. 22%
  - ❏ B. 27%
  - ❏ C. 33%
  - ❏ D. 48%

19. You have AKs. What is the probability on the flop you will catch an A or K or better or a four flush?
  - ❏ A. 14%
  - ❏ B. 24%
  - ❏ C. 34%
  - ❏ D. 44%
  - ❏ E. 54%

20. You have two suited in your hand. What is the probability of two of your same suit on the flop?
  - ❏ A. 7%
  - ❏ B. 9%
  - ❏ C. 11%
  - ❏ D. 13%
  - ❏ E. 15%

21. You have AKs. What is the approximate probability you will flop a straight?
    ❏ A. less than 1%
    ❏ B. 1%
    ❏ C. 2%
    ❏ D. 3%
    ❏ E. 4%

22. Which occurs most frequently?
    ❏ A. Connectors
    ❏ B. One gap in sequence
    ❏ C. Two gaps in sequence
    ❏ D. Three gaps in sequence
    ❏ E. They all occur with the same frequency

23. In poker language, "pot odds" means:
    ❏ A. The $ in the pot
    ❏ B. The $ in the pot compared to the $ you must bet to stay in the hand
    ❏ C. The $ in the pot per player in the hand
    ❏ D. The $ you could win plus the $ you must put in

24. There is $50 in the pot and you must call $10 to stay in. What is the pot offering you?
    ❏ A. 1:6
    ❏ B. 6:1
    ❏ C. 1:5
    ❏ D. 5:1
    ❏ E. It cannot be determined

25. If the pot size is $30 and you must call $10 to stay in, what are your pot odds?
    ❏ A. 1:3
    ❏ B. 3:1
    ❏ C. 1:4
    ❏ D. 4:1
    ❏ E. None of the above

26. If your pot odds are 3:1 and you must call $10 to stay in, what is the pot size before you bet?
    ❏ A. $20
    ❏ B. $30
    ❏ C. $40
    ❏ D. None of the above

27. If your pot odds are 10:1 and the pot size is $100 before you bet, how much is your bet?
    ❏ A. $10
    ❏ B. $20
    ❏ C. $100
    ❏ D. None of the above

28. If your pot odds are 3:1 and the pot size is $30 before you bet, how much is your bet?
    ❏ A. $10
    ❏ B. $20
    ❏ C. $30
    ❏ D. $40
    ❏ E. None of the above

29. Using pot odds alone, and ignoring implied odds, when should you fold?
    ❏ A. Anytime the pot is offering you more than your odds against
    ❏ B. Anytime the pot is offering you less than your odds against
    ❏ C. When the pot is small
    ❏ D. Two of the above
    ❏ E. None of the above

30. You have a four flush on the flop. What is the probability you will catch a flush on the turn?
    ❏ A. 4%
    ❏ B. 9%
    ❏ C. 14%
    ❏ D. 19%
    ❏ E. 24%

31. You have a four flush on the flop in limit. The pot has 3 bets. Ignoring the rake, how much you already have invested in the pot, implied odds or the amount of future betting, what is your approximate Expected Value if you must make 1 bet to stay in the hand?

❏ A. - ¼ of a bet
❏ B. - ½ of a bet
❏ C. 0
❏ D. + ¼ of a bet
❏ E. + ½ of a bet

32. You have a four flush on the flop in limit. The pot has 4 bets. Ignoring the rake or implied odds, what is your approximate Expected Value if you must make 1 bet to stay in the hand?

❏ A. - ¼ of a bet
❏ B. - ½ of a bet
❏ C. 0
❏ D. + ¼ of a bet
❏ E. + ½ of a bet

33. You have a four flush on the flop in limit. The pot has 6 bets. Ignoring the rake or implied odds, what is your approximate Expected Value if you must make 1 bet to stay in the hand?

❏ A. - 2/3 of a bet
❏ B. - 1/3 of a bet
❏ C. 0
❏ D. + 1/3 of a bet
❏ E. + 2/3 of a bet

34. You have a four flush on the flop in limit. The pot has 7 bets. Ignoring the rake or implied odds, what is your approximate Expected Value if you must make 1 bet to stay in the hand?

❏ A. - 2/3 of a bet
❏ B. - 1/3 of a bet
❏ C. 0
❏ D. + 1/3 of a bet
❏ E. + 1/2 of a bet

35. Ignoring implied odds, when using the concept of Expected Value for a specific draw, which of the following changes to influence our decision?

❏ A. The probability of not catching
❏ B. The probability of catching
❏ C. What we expect our opponents to bet
❏ D. The current size of the pot
❏ E. All of the above influence our decision

36. Which of the following is true?

❏ A. Whenever you have a positive Expected Value that means the same thing as the pot is offering your more than your odds against
❏ B. Whenever you have a positive Expected Value that means the same thing as the pot is offering your less than your odds against
❏ C. Neither is true
❏ D. Both are true

37. What is the relationship between pot odds and Expected Value?

❏ A. They mean the same thing, but expressed in a different way
❏ B. They mean the opposite of each other
❏ C. There is no relationship

38. You have two of the same suit. There are nine opponents dealt cards. What is the probability that someone else also has two of the same suit you hold?
   ❑ A. 50%
   ❑ B. 45%
   ❑ C. 40%
   ❑ D. 35%
   ❑ E. Less than 30%

39. You have two of the same suit. There are seven opponents dealt cards. What is the probability that someone else also has two of the same suit you hold?
   ❑ A. 50%
   ❑ B. 45%
   ❑ C. 40%
   ❑ D. 35%
   ❑ E. Less than 30%

40. You have two of the same suit. There are six opponents dealt cards. What is the probability that someone else also has two of the same suit you hold?
   ❑ A. 15%
   ❑ B. 20%
   ❑ C. 25%
   ❑ D. 30%
   ❑ E. 35%

41. You have two of the same suit and an opponent also has two of the same suit. Both of you catch your flush. If your highest suited card is an 8, what is the probability your opponent has a higher card than you?
   ❑ A. 35%
   ❑ B. 49%
   ❑ C. 62%
   ❑ D. 73%
   ❑ E. 82%

42. You have two of the same suit and an opponent also has two of the same suit. Both of you catch your flush. If your highest suited card is a T, what is the probability your opponent has a higher card than you?
   ❑ A. 35%
   ❑ B. 49%
   ❑ C. 62%
   ❑ D. 73%
   ❑ E. 82%

43. You have two of the same suit and an opponent also has two of the same suit. Both of you catch your flush. If your highest suited card is a J, and there is no higher flush card on the board, what is the probability your opponent has a higher card than you?
   ❑ A. 35%
   ❑ B. 49%
   ❑ C. 62%
   ❑ D. 73%
   ❑ E. 82%

44. You have two of the same suit and an opponent also has two of the same suit. Both of you catch your flush. If your highest suited card is a Q, and there is no higher flush card on the board, what is the probability your opponent has a higher card than you?
   ❑ A. 35%
   ❑ B. 49%
   ❑ C. 62%
   ❑ D. 73%
   ❑ E. 82%

45. You have two of the same suit and an opponent also has two of the same suit. Both of you catch your flush. Which is the lowest card you must hold, assuming there is no higher flush card on the board, in order for you to have about a 50% chance of winning?
❏ A. A
❏ B. K
❏ C. Q
❏ D. J
❏ E. T

46. Which of the following has the highest probability of catching a straight or a flush?
❏ A. T9
❏ B. J9s
❏ C. 76s
❏ D. It can't be determined

47. You will receive at least one Ace in your hand approximately ___ of the time
❏ A. 20%
❏ B. 15%
❏ C. 10%
❏ D. 5%

48. You will receive Axs in your hand approximately ___ of the time
❏ A. 2%
❏ B. 3%
❏ C. 4%
❏ D. 5%
❏ E. 6%

49. You will receive an Ax (unsuited) in your hand approximately ___ of the time
❏ A. 9%
❏ B. 11%
❏ C. 13%
❏ D. 15%
❏ E. 17%

50. If you have an Ace in your hand with nine opponents, what is the probability you are the only one to have an Ace?
❏ A. 25%
❏ B. 30%
❏ C. 35%
❏ D. 40%
❏ E. 45%

51. If you have an Ace in your hand with five opponents, what is the probability you are the only one to have an Ace?
❏ A. 30%
❏ B. 35%
❏ C. 40%
❏ D. 45%
❏ E. 50%

52. In a 10-handed game, what is the probability no one was dealt an Ace?
❏ A. 6%
❏ B. 13%
❏ C. 19%
❏ D. 24%
❏ E. 19%

53. What is the probability you will be dealt two cards Q or higher?
❏ A. 2%
❏ B. 5%
❏ C. 9%
❏ D. 14%
❏ E. None of the above

54. Which of the following starting hands, all of which could form a straight, will you receive most frequently?
❏ A. Connectors
❏ B. A gap in sequence
❏ C. Two gaps in sequence
❏ D. Three gaps in sequence
❏ E. All occur with the same frequency

55. You will receive suited connectors approximately ___ of the time.
- ❏ A. 1%
- ❏ B. 2%
- ❏ C. 3%
- ❏ D. 4%
- ❏ E. None of the above

56. You will receive which of the following most frequently?
- ❏ A. Suited connectors
- ❏ B. Suited with two gaps
- ❏ C. A pocket pair
- ❏ D. All are approximately equal probabilities

57. You will receive suited connectors approximately once every ___ hands.
- ❏ A. 12
- ❏ B. 16
- ❏ C. 20
- ❏ D. 24
- ❏ E. 28

58. At a 10-handed table, on average, approximately how many players will have Ax?
- ❏ A. 1
- ❏ B. 2
- ❏ C. 3
- ❏ D. 4
- ❏ E. 5

59. At a 10-handed table, on average, approximately how many players will have suited cards?
- ❏ A. 1
- ❏ B. 2
- ❏ C. 3
- ❏ D. 4
- ❏ E. 5

60. At a 10-handed table, on average, approximately how many players will have a straight draw?
- ❏ A. 1
- ❏ B. 2
- ❏ C. 3
- ❏ D. 4
- ❏ E. 5

61. At a 10-handed table, on average, approximately how many players will have either a pocket pair or suited connectors?
- ❏ A. 1
- ❏ B. 2
- ❏ C. 3
- ❏ D. 4
- ❏ E. 5

62. If you have an Ace, but not AA, in the hole, what is the probability of another opponent being dealt an A if you have 9 opponents?
- ❏ A. 90%
- ❏ B. 75%
- ❏ C. 60%
- ❏ D. 50%
- ❏ E. 40%

63. What is the probability the flop will contain exactly a pair?
- ❏ A. 7%
- ❏ B. 9%
- ❏ C. 11%
- ❏ D. 13%
- ❏ E. Over 15%

64. What is the probability the flop will have exactly two of a suit?
- ❏ A. 55%
- ❏ B. 50%
- ❏ C. 45%
- ❏ D. 40%
- ❏ E. 35%

65. What is the probability the flop will have all three of the same suit?
   - ❑ A. 1%
   - ❑ B. 2%
   - ❑ C. 3%
   - ❑ D. 4%
   - ❑ E. 5%

66. What is the probability of a rainbow (no two of the same suit) flop?
   - ❑ A. 45%
   - ❑ B. 40%
   - ❑ C. 35%
   - ❑ D. 30%
   - ❑ E. 25%

67. What is the probability the flop will have three in sequence?
   - ❑ A. 4%
   - ❑ B. 5%
   - ❑ C. 6%
   - ❑ D. 7%
   - ❑ E. 8% or higher

68. What is the probability the flop will have at least two in sequence?
   - ❑ A. 34%
   - ❑ B. 38%
   - ❑ C. 44%
   - ❑ D. 48%
   - ❑ E. 54%

69. If you have KK, approximately how often will an A appear on the flop?
   - ❑ A. 12%
   - ❑ B. 24%
   - ❑ C. 32%
   - ❑ D. Above 32%

70. If you have JJ, approximately how often will an A, K or Q appear on the flop?
   - ❑ A. 30%
   - ❑ B. 40%
   - ❑ C. 50%
   - ❑ D. 60%
   - ❑ E. 70%

71. If you have KK, approximately how often will an Ace appear by the river?
   - ❑ A. 17%.
   - ❑ B. 27%
   - ❑ C. 37%
   - ❑ D. 47%
   - ❑ E. 57%

72. If you have JJ, approximately how often will an A, K or Q appear by the river?
   - ❑ A. 65%
   - ❑ B. 70%
   - ❑ C. 75%
   - ❑ D. 82%
   - ❑ E. 88%

73. If you have a set on the flop, you will have a boat or better by the river approximately _____ of the time.
   - ❑ A. 13%
   - ❑ B. 20%
   - ❑ C. 30%
   - ❑ D. 33%
   - ❑ E. 40%

74. You will make runner runner, that is cards on the turn and river to complete either a straight or a flush, approximately ___ of the time.
   - ❑ A. Less than 2%
   - ❑ B. 2%
   - ❑ C. 4%
   - ❑ D. 6%
   - ❑ E. More than 6%

75. All five community cards are on the board. Approximately how often is a flush possible?
    - ❏ A. 67%
    - ❏ B. 57%
    - ❏ C. 47%
    - ❏ D. 37%
    - ❏ E. 27%

76. All five community cards are on the board. Approximately how often is there a pair on the board?
    - ❏ A. 79%
    - ❏ B. 69%
    - ❏ C. 59%
    - ❏ D. 49%
    - ❏ E. 39% or less

77. You are playing limit. You have 3 outs on the turn. Ignoring implied odds, how many bets must be in the pot for you to see the river.
    - ❏ A. 18
    - ❏ B. 16
    - ❏ C. 14
    - ❏ D. 12
    - ❏ E. 10

78. You are playing limit. You have 5 outs on the turn. Ignoring implied odds, how many bets must be in the pot for you to see the river.
    - ❏ A. 17
    - ❏ B. 15
    - ❏ C. 13
    - ❏ D. 11
    - ❏ E. 9

79. You are playing limit. You have 8 outs on the turn. Ignoring implied odds, how many bets must be in the pot for you to see the river.
    - ❏ A. 13
    - ❏ B. 11
    - ❏ C. 9
    - ❏ D. 7
    - ❏ E. It doesn't matter. You should always call with 8 or more outs.

80. You are playing limit. You have 15 outs on the turn. Ignoring implied odds, how many bets must be in the pot for you to see the river.
    - ❏ A. 7
    - ❏ B. 6
    - ❏ C. 5
    - ❏ D. 4
    - ❏ E. It doesn't matter. You should always call with 15 or more outs.

81. Which of these hands does not change in strength depending on how many opponents are dealt cards?
    - ❏ A. ATs
    - ❏ B. A8s
    - ❏ C. A7s
    - ❏ D. A5s
    - ❏ E. None of the above

82. Which of the following hands decreases in strength with more opponents dealt cards?
    - ❏ A. AKs
    - ❏ B. K9s
    - ❏ C. K5s
    - ❏ D. K2s
    - ❏ E. None of the above

83. This is the number of opponents dealt cards you prefer to play A5 against.
   - ❏ A. 1
   - ❏ B. 3
   - ❏ C. 5
   - ❏ D. 7
   - ❏ E. 9

84. Which number of opponents dealt cards is best to play A9 against?
   - ❏ A. 1
   - ❏ B. 3
   - ❏ C. 5
   - ❏ D. 7
   - ❏ E. 9

85. Considering only the number of opponents dealt cards, which number of opponents is best to play 98s against?
   - ❏ A. 1
   - ❏ B. 3
   - ❏ C. 4
   - ❏ D. 5
   - ❏ E. 9

86. Considering only the number of opponents dealt cards, which number of opponents is best to play 54s against?
   - ❏ A. 1
   - ❏ B. 3
   - ❏ C. 5
   - ❏ D. 7
   - ❏ E. 9

87. Considering only the number of opponents dealt cards, which number of opponents is best to play 97s against?
   - ❏ A. 1
   - ❏ B. 2
   - ❏ C. 3
   - ❏ D. 4
   - ❏ E. 5

88. Considering only the number of opponents dealt cards, which number of opponents is best to play JT against?
   - ❏ A. 1
   - ❏ B. 3
   - ❏ C. 5
   - ❏ D. 7
   - ❏ E. 9

89. Considering only the number of opponents dealt cards, which number of opponents is best to play 66 against?
   - ❏ A. 1
   - ❏ B. 3
   - ❏ C. 5
   - ❏ D. 7
   - ❏ E. 9

90. 44 is weakest against which number of opponents dealt cards?
   - ❏ A. 2
   - ❏ B. 4
   - ❏ C. 6
   - ❏ D. 8

91. 44 is strongest against which number of opponents dealt cards?
   - ❏ A. 1
   - ❏ B. 3
   - ❏ C. 5
   - ❏ D. 7
   - ❏ E. 9

92. This pair does not change in strength depending on the number of opponents dealt cards.
   - ❏ A. JJ
   - ❏ B. TT
   - ❏ C. 99
   - ❏ D. Two of the above
   - ❏ E. None of the above

93. This is a pair which is stronger when more opponents are dealt cards than fewer opponents.
   - ❏ A. 22
   - ❏ B. 66
   - ❏ C. 88
   - ❏ D. Two of the above
   - ❏ E. None of the above

94. This is a pair you would always want to play against fewer as opposed to more opponents dealt cards.
   - ❏ A. QQ
   - ❏ B. JJ
   - ❏ C. TT
   - ❏ D. Two of the above
   - ❏ E. None of the above

95. Unless in the blind this is a hand you would never play against four or more opponents.
   - ❏ A. A9
   - ❏ B. K9
   - ❏ C. 22
   - ❏ D. Two of the above
   - ❏ E. None of the above

96. These hands increase in strength with the number of opponents dealt cards.
   - ❏ A. Kx
   - ❏ B. Suited Connectors
   - ❏ C. Pairs
   - ❏ D. Two of the above
   - ❏ E. None of the above

97. This hand decreases slightly in strength against more opponents.
   - ❏ A. QQ
   - ❏ B. JJ
   - ❏ C. TT
   - ❏ D. Two of the above
   - ❏ E. None of the above

See Appendix E for answers

CHAPTER 9

Which Hands to Play

Introducing the seven limit critical factors

Whether or not you decide to play a limit hand depends on seven determining factors.

▶ How loose or tight the table is — The percentage of hands others at the table tend to play.

▶ How passive or aggressive the table is — The amount of calling or raising at your table.

▶ Your card strength — How good your hand is.

▶ Number of opponents — Means just that. The number of other players dealt cards.

▶ Position — Where you are seated relative to the dealer.

▶ The horse — Taking into account where you are seated relative to the last player to act, called the horse, and his playing style.

▶ Pot size — How much money is in the pot.

Protocol

This chapter is long, almost ⅓ of the entire book. Unlike the psych chapters it is based on lots of math, and even drier than the Numbers Chapter. It is not easy. In the introduction you were told this book is for the very serious player. This chapter will test you to see just how serious you are, as it requires becoming proficient with a mathematical approach few players have even contemplated. If you follow it through carefully you will comprehend the concept, but **application takes months of study**. Now you have been warned. Here is the procedure used to see if you play your first two cards.

Part I An Advanced PATL mathematical model will be built. The basic PATL will be expanded using the number of opponents who play in a hand and how much raising or calling occurs.

Part II The strength of all playable, and some not playable, starting hands will be converted into something called the Swayne Win Factor. These Win Factors are the result of over several billion calculations performed on all 169 possible hands. The Win Factor will show you the probability of your preflop cards winning or losing by adjusting for:
1. Your number of opponents. From the graphs you studied in the previous chapter you know how certain hands change in strength depending on how many opponents you have.
2. The degree of table tightness or looseness.

You will find the Win Factors for a hand change with both the number of opponents and how tight/loose the table is. In other words, a hand's Win Factor is not constant. The Win Factor will then be adjusted for the rake.

Part III To see if you can consider playing your first two cards the Win Factor will then be adjusted for your position.

Part IV Then there is an adjustment for how passive or aggressive the table is.

Part V We will then look at the hands you may consider playing.

Part VI The horse will then be factored in.

Part VII Finally, the size of the pot.

Part I – The Advanced PATL Matrix

Working in seven dimensions

Seven determining factors mean we are working with a seven dimensional model. I struggled with how to present seven dimensions to a mostly non-mathematical audience. Here's the approach which avoids the mathematical complexities. First, we will take into account three of the dimensions, but presented in such a way it appears as though it is only two dimensions. Then we will "layer" another dimension on top of what we already have. Then another layer, and another, and finally another, until all seven dimensions have been presented.

Understanding the first step

We are about to build another PATL model. This model will initially focus on the first two of the seven determining factors. Those are:

▸ How loose or tight the table is — The percentage of hands others at the table tend to play.

▸ How passive or aggressive the table is — The amount of calling or raising at your table.

For the first part of the book, you have been using a basic PATL model. You will now be introduced to a mathematically sophisticated Advanced PATL model. As with every model, reality does not always conform exactly to the model. But once you understand the model, you will learn how to use it as the foundation for every preflop decision you make.

Tight or Loose

First, an individual opponent. Take a look at figure 9.1.a.a. This is how to mathematically describe a player using the terms Mega-Tight, Tight, Loose, Very Loose, and Mega-Loose. As you know, a tight player plays few of his hands; a loose player plays a lot of hands. At first, the Tight line looks like it should be more to the right. You will see why it is placed where it is in a few pages.

Now, the table. It has similar mathematical definitions.

How do you tell what kind of table it is? **You count**, yes count, **how many opponents play and fold their preflop hands, and**

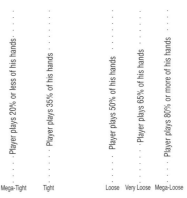

Defining a player's Mega-Tight to Mega-Loose play. Figure 9.1.a.a

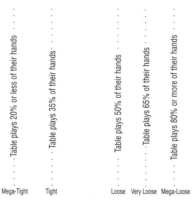

Defining a table's Mega-Tight to
Mega-Loose play.
Figure 9.1.a.b

Defining a player's Very Passive to
Very Aggressive play
Figure 9.1.a.c

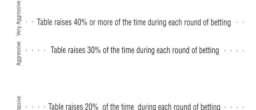

Defining a table's Very Passive to
Very Aggressive play
Figure 9.1.a.d

estimate a percentage. This is done by taking the counted number of hands played by others at the table and dividing them by the total hands dealt to others. You do not include yourself and the hands you play in the count, but do include the blinds played by others.

This can't be a one time count. Players and conditions change. For example, a player goes on tilt, is short stacked, or a new player sits down. Your count needs to be ongoing. After a few months of continuous counting and mentally calculating the percentage of hands played, determining where the table fits will become easier.

Passive or Aggressive

First, let's examine an individual opponent while in a hand. Take a look at figure 9.1.a.c. These are the definitions for Very Passive, Passive, Aggressive, and Very Aggressive. As a general review, you know that a passive player seldom raises; an aggressive player raises a lot.

Now, the table. You will need to know these percentages.

In addition to keeping count for tight/loose, **you must** now also **count and calculate the percentages for the degree of passiveness or aggressiveness of others at your table**.

You must know how mathematically passive/aggressive and tight/loose your table is. Why? Without knowing, you will be guessing and gambling. When you have completed this chapter you will know how the characteristics of the table allow you to use probability, which isn't gambling.

You also need to understand these mathematical definitions may be different from your understanding and past experience of what "tight" or "loose" or what "passive" or "aggressive" mean. Even so, these precise mathematical points will prove profitable for you to use regardless of the traditional use of the terms passive/aggressive or tight/loose.

What is more important, the table or an individual? Preflop, knowing the table is the most important. Postflop, focus on individual opponents.

Building the model

We are now ready to start to build the Advanced PATL model. This model will be in the form of a matrix, similar to the one you already know. Along the vertical axis it will show how passive or aggressive the table is. The horizontal axis will show how tight or loose the table is. See figure 9.1.a.e.

At the intersection of each degree of passive/aggressive and tight/loose there is a plot point, indicated by the heavy circles in figure 9.1.a.f.

Now we remove the lines which showed how passive/aggressive and tight/loose the table might be, leaving just the plot points.

Next all Mega-Tight plot points have been eliminated. You should never be playing in this type of game. As we go through the various plot points you will see that the tighter the game, the fewer hands you can profitably play. Your pots are small. It is almost impossible to stay ahead of the rake at a Mega-Tight table without aggressive bluffing. We have included some calculations later which show the Mega-Tight results, but other than that, Mega-Tight is out.

Very Aggressive tables are wild, expensive, and should be played only once you consider yourself an expert.

When capital letters are used to indicate a type of table, it means that we are referring to a specific plot point. For example, an Aggressive/Loose table means, as is shown in figure 9.1.a.i, we are talking about a table that raises about 30% of the time and opponents who play about 50% of their preflop hands.

Also, when discussing a specific plot point, you will sometimes see a small graph indicating where the plot point lies. An example is shown in figure 9.1.b.

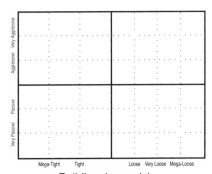

Building the model

Figure 9.1.a.e

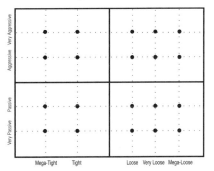

Model with defining lines and plot points

Figure 9.1.a.f

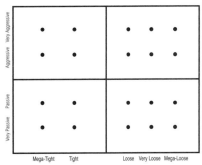

Model with plot points only

Figure 9.1.a.g

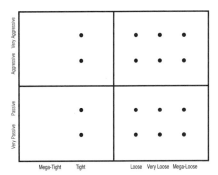

Model with Mega-Tight plot points removed

Figure 9.1.a.h

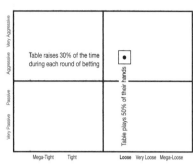

Plot points for an
Aggressive/Loose table
Figure 9.1.a.i

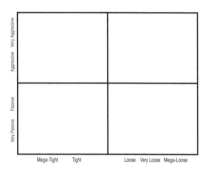

The Advanced PATL matrix
Figure 9.1.a.j

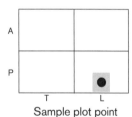

Sample plot point
Figure 9.1.b

Review

Before you continue, make sure you know the mathematical definitions for each of the following in the Advanced PATL Matrix:

- Mega-Tight
- Tight
- Loose
- Very Loose
- Mega-Loose
- Very Passive
- Passive
- Aggressive
- Very Aggressive

From now on when we say a table is Very Aggressive, that will mean the same as the mathematical definition of Very Aggressive, i.e. the table raises 40% or more of the time during each round of betting. Likewise if we say a table is Very Loose, that will mean your opponents play about 65% of their preflop hands. In other words, you will need to know which percentages go with each description.

You must also understand the shorthand that will be used from now on.

Advanced PATL. When capitals are used (capital "A" in Aggressive and capital "L" in Loose) in a sentence, that means we are focusing on that specific plot point. For example, Aggressive with a capital "A" means there is a raise about 30% of the time and Loose with a capital "L" means the table plays about 50% of their preflop hands.

Basic PATL. This is the PATL we have used in previous chapters. When a sentence says you are at an aggressive/loose table (a small "a" for aggressive and a small "l" for loose), that means we are somewhere in the general quadrant for aggressive/loose in the PATL matrix, not at any specific plot point.

Recall from the start of this chapter that there are a total of seven factors which determine limit play.

▶ How loose or tight the table is   The percentage of hands others at the table tend to play.

▸ How passive or aggressive the table is	The amount of calling or raising at your table.
▸ Your card strength	How good your hand is.
▸ Number of opponents	Means just that. The number of other players dealt cards.
▸ Position	Where you are seated relative to the dealer.
▸ The horse	Taking into account where you are seated relative to the last player to act, called the horse, and his playing style.
▸ Pot size	How much money is in the pot.

So far the Advanced PATL matrix only takes into account the first two factors; those are how passive or aggressive the table is and how tight or loose the table is. In the next sections we will focus on the other factors within each quadrant of the Advanced PATL.

Advanced PATL summary
- There are seven factors you must consider before you play a hand.
- There are specific mathematical definitions to define a player's and a table's degree of passiveness and aggressiveness.
- Likewise, specific mathematical definitions are used to define the player's or table's degree of tightness or looseness.
- The PATL matrix takes into account only two of the seven factors.

Homework
- Know all seven factors you must consider before you play a hand.
- Be able to place every table in the Advanced PATL matrix.
- Be able to place every individual in the Advanced PATL matrix.

Part II — Win Factors

Introduction

I usually sit across from Andy, one of our riverboat dealers. Yes, living on the Mississippi, I play on a riverboat. When I fold, which I do about 70% of the time at our Very Passive/Mega-Loose table, Andy will often sneak a peek at my cards and say "Loosen up Charles." Now and then he will say in a carnival barker tone, "You have a 50% chance of winning with those cards. You can either win or you lose, that's 50-50. You had two flush draws, two straight draws, two quad draws."

Andy knows better. When he plays, which he can't do on the boat, he is very selective with the hands he plays. And you must learn to be like Andy.

This is a long portion of a long chapter but by the end of this section you will know what a Win Factor is and under what circumstances a particular hand has a positive Expected Value.

Making your hand or winning with your hand

Many books will tell you what the chances are of you making your hand. But few tell you what your chances are of winning with your hand. And there is a difference. Only when you are drawing to the nuts is your chance of winning the same as the chance of making your hand. In all other cases your chances of winning with your hand are less than just making your hand. For example, you have A♥, K♥; the board through the turn is 5♥, 5♣, T♥, 6♦. You have four hearts and if another heart comes up you have an Ace high heart flush. But, what if your opponent has or is drawing to a boat? Or already has quads? It is obvious your chances of winning the hand are less than just making your hand.

This section will let you know what cards, if played thousands and thousands of times, will have a positive or negative Expected Value; that is, what cards you are likely to win or lose with.

Raw data

We went through every plot point for every hand and arrived with the percentage of time you will win with a particular hand. The result is not just making a hand; it is winning with the hand. These findings depend on how many opponents you have and how tight or loose the table is. Figure 9.2.a has the raw data for

AJ. It is difficult but possible to compare one hand to another, though academics and those who like numbers may find it interesting.

The Swayne Win Factor

To make comparisons easier, all of the raw data for every plot point for every hand — over 7,600 plot points — was converted into a Swayne Win Factor. These Win Factors allow easy comparison of one preflop hand to another and of one plot point to another, depending on how many opponents were dealt cards. In addition, the Win Factors will allow for several adjustments we will make throughout this chapter such as position, how passive/aggressive the table is, and other factors.

A Win Factor of 1.0 means if you play this hand several thousand times, you have a preflop Expected Value of 0. If there were no rake this would be an even bet.

A Win Factor of 1.1 means if you play this hand, you have a positive preflop Expected Value. A good bet. The higher the Win Factor, the higher the Expected Value, and the more you will win.

A Win Factor of 0.9 means you will have a negative preflop Expected Value. A slot machine bet. The lower the Win Factor, the lower your Expected Value, and the more you will lose.

Win Factors are per opponents dealt cards. The best way to understand this statement is with a few examples. A Win Factor of 1.0 does not mean a 50-50 chance of winning unless it is heads up. If you played 10,000 hands with a Win Factor of 1.0 heads up, you should win 5,000 times. If you play 10,000 hands with a Win Factor of 1.0 at a 4-handed table, you should win ¼ of the time, which is 2,500 wins. Against four opponents, that is, 5-handed, a 1.0 Win Factor will have approximately 2,000 wins.

Does the Win Factor remain constant for a particular hand? No. Since the chance of winning varies, so too will the Win Factors. Take a look at figure 9.2.b containing the Win Factors for AJ. Notice how the Win Factors for AJ are extremely low at a Mega-Tight table versus a Mega-Loose table. **The results were counter-intuitive**. Before starting the research we theorized that at a looser table a hand such as AJ would be outdrawn more and therefore have a lower probability of winning. But the facts

AJ

Opponents	Mega-Tight	Tight	Loose	Very Loose	Mega-Loose
1	56	59	61	62	63
2	36	39	42	43	44
3	26	29	32	32	34
4	20	22	25	25	28
5	15	18	20	21	23
6	11	15	16	17	20
7	10	12	14	14	17
8	9	11	12	12	13
9	8	9	10	11	12

Figure 9.2.a

AJ

Opponents	Mega-Tight	Tight	Loose	Very Loose	Mega-Loose
1	1.1	1.2	1.2	1.2	1.3
2	1.1	1.2	1.3	1.3	1.3
3	1.0	1.2	1.3	1.3	1.4
4	1.0	1.1	1.3	1.3	1.4
5	0.9	1.1	1.2	1.3	1.4
6	0.8	1.1	1.1	1.2	1.4
7	0.8	1.0	1.1	1.1	1.4
8	0.8	1.0	1.1	1.1	1.2
9	0.8	0.9	1.0	1.1	1.2

Figure 9.2.b

proved otherwise; that is, the tighter the table, the lower the Win Factors. Also interesting is how this particular hand's Win Factors increase and then decrease with more opponents the looser the table becomes.

At which kind of table and with how many opponents would you prefer to play AJ? Your highest Expected Value is at a Mega-Loose table with 3, 4, 5, 6 or 7 opponents, as all of these plot points have a Win Factor of 1.4. You can see the Win Factors for the same hand change, not only with how many opponents you have, but also how tight/loose your opponents play.

You must learn Win Factors for all table types and any number of opponents. Important point. You cannot control how many opponents are dealt cards. You have almost no control over how tight or loose the table is. You must apply your Win Factor knowledge specifically to the number of opponents and the table tightness or looseness.

In the previous chapter all of the vertical scales were the same, so you could compare the relative strength of each set of hands. Not so with the Win Factor charts. **The vertical scale is adjusted for each hand, which means if you are comparing the Win Factors of one hand to another, you must look at the vertical scale numbers.**

This is the first step to determine what cards you will play. In this section we have come up with a Win Factor for each possible hand you might play and some you may have thought you should play. Again, these Win Factors take into account the strength of your cards, depending on both your number of opponents dealt cards and how tight/loose they play.

Charting the Win Factor

Now let's look at the chart for AJ, which corresponds to the numbers in figure 9.2.c.

So you should only play hands with Win Factors 1.0 or greater? No.

At this point we have not made any adjustments for:

1. The rake and, in some cases, something for the bad beat.
2. Position.
3. Passive/aggressive table.
4. The horse.
5. Pot size.

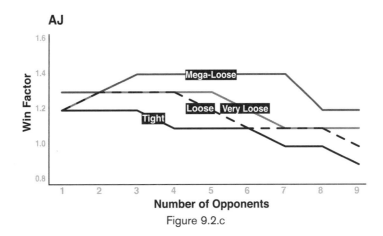

AJ

Figure 9.2.c

Rake adjustment

How do we take into account the rake? Here's how. You will only play hands which have a Win Factor of 1.1 or greater. Even if you are in a tournament where there is no rake, you are going to find the hands which correspond to a Win Factor of 1.1 are so marginal, few players ever play hands with less.

How about position and aggressiveness? What if someone raises? How does the size of the pot figure into all of this? We will show you how to adjust later, but for now you need to understand

**the ONLY hands you will consider playing
are those with a Win Factor of 1.1 or more**.

If faced with both a rake and a collection for the bad beat, you should only consider hands with a Win Factor of 1.2 or better. In tournament situations, in most cases we want to avoid coin flips. Therefore, the rule for tournaments is we only want to consider hands with a Win Factor of at least 1.1. Many players won't play any hand with a Win Factor less than 1.2. Some only play 1.3 or greater.

The next several pages contain the Win Factor calculations and a graph, such as the one at left, for each potentially playable and a few non-playable hands. The non-playables were included only because they include starting hands others recommend, or because too many loose players play A-anything or K-anything. You will also see some hands that no other authors recommend as playable. The calculations include the results for Mega-Tight tables but the graphs do not. You should not be playing in any kind of Mega-Tight game unless you are a true poker expert. When showing the numbers, the shaded portions indicate when you should never consider playing the hand. The comments in the lower left portion of the figures, below the numbers, are only for Mega-Loose 10-handed tables.

All of the Win Factor charts you will find from now on will have a cutoff area shaded at 1.1 and lower to emphasize you should not play any hands below 1.1. If you look at the graph in figure 9.2.d, it is exactly the same as figure 9.2.c except the 1.1 shaded cutoff has been added.

If you only play hands with a Win Factor of 1.1 or higher probability is now on your side. Will you win more money than you lose? Not necessarily. Although which cards to play is the first and most frequent decision you must make, the most money is not made just by playing hands with Win Factors of 1.1 or

AJ

Opponents	Mega-Tight	Tight	Loose	Very Loose	Mega-Loose
1	1.1	1.2	1.2	1.2	1.3
2	1.1	1.2	1.3	1.3	1.3
3	1.0	1.2	1.3	1.3	1.4
4	1.0	1.1	1.3	1.3	1.4
5	0.9	1.1	1.2	1.3	1.4
6	0.8	1.1	1.1	1.2	1.4
7	0.8	1.0	1.1	1.1	1.4
8	0.8	1.0	1.1	1.1	1.2
9	0.8	0.9	1.0	1.1	1.2

A comment will be shown here, below the graph, describing the hand for a 10-handed Mega-Loose table. For example, the comment for AJ would be "Drawing."

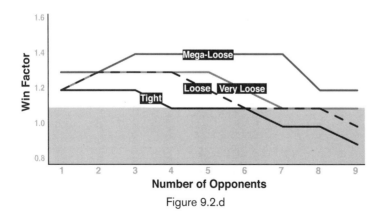

Figure 9.2.d

better. The most money, the most profit, is made with proper and aggressive betting. We'll also get into this later.

Because the term Win Factor will be used extensively from now on, most of the time you will see the initials WF to indicate Win Factor. When more than one WF is meant, the plural of WF will be WFs.

Win Factors compared to relative strength

In the Relative Strength Chapter you learned how the strength of a particular hand relative to all other hands changes depending on the number of opponents. The Win Factors you will now study do not always conform to the opponent graphs because we are now adding a completely new dimension. That dimension is the degree of table tightness or looseness.

You will see some surprises.

Axs

AKs

Opponents	Mega-Tight	Tight	Loose	Very Loose	Mega-Loose
1	1.3	1.3	1.3	1.3	1.3
2	1.4	1.4	1.5	1.5	1.5
3	1.4	1.5	1.6	1.6	1.6
4	1.4	1.6	1.6	1.7	1.7
5	1.4	1.6	1.6	1.7	1.7
6	1.4	1.5	1.7	1.8	1.8
7	1.4	1.5	1.7	1.8	1.8
8	1.3	1.5	1.7	1.8	1.9
9	1.2	1.5	1.7	1.8	1.9

Premium draw.

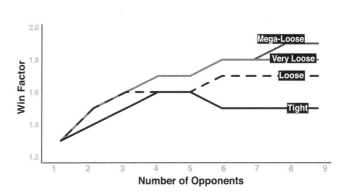

AQs

Opponents	Mega-Tight	Tight	Loose	Very Loose	Mega-Loose
1	1.2	1.3	1.3	1.3	1.3
2	1.3	1.4	1.4	1.4	1.5
3	1.3	1.4	1.5	1.5	1.6
4	1.3	1.4	1.5	1.6	1.6
5	1.3	1.4	1.5	1.6	1.7
6	1.3	1.4	1.5	1.6	1.8
7	1.3	1.4	1.6	1.7	1.8
8	1.3	1.4	1.6	1.7	1.8
9	1.3	1.4	1.6	1.7	1.8

Premium draw.

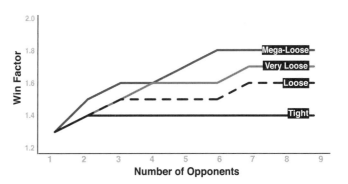

Axs

AJs

Opponents	Mega-Tight	Tight	Loose	Very Loose	Mega-Loose
1	1.2	1.2	1.3	1.3	1.3
2	1.2	1.3	1.4	1.4	1.4
3	1.2	1.3	1.4	1.4	1.5
4	1.2	1.3	1.4	1.5	1.6
5	1.2	1.3	1.4	1.5	1.6
6	1.2	1.3	1.4	1.5	1.6
7	1.2	1.3	1.4	1.5	1.7
8	1.2	1.3	1.4	1.5	1.7
9	1.2	1.3	1.4	1.6	1.7

Strong draw.

ATs

Opponents	Mega-Tight	Tight	Loose	Very Loose	Mega-Loose
1	1.1	1.2	1.2	1.3	1.3
2	1.1	1.2	1.3	1.4	1.4
3	1.1	1.2	1.3	1.4	1.4
4	1.1	1.3	1.4	1.4	1.5
5	1.1	1.3	1.4	1.4	1.5
6	1.1	1.3	1.4	1.4	1.5
7	1.1	1.3	1.4	1.4	1.6
8	1.1	1.3	1.4	1.5	1.6
9	1.1	1.3	1.4	1.5	1.6

Good draw.

A9s

Opponents	Mega-Tight	Tight	Loose	Very Loose	Mega-Loose
1	1.1	1.1	1.2	1.2	1.2
2	1.0	1.1	1.2	1.3	1.3
3	1.0	1.1	1.2	1.3	1.3
4	1.0	1.1	1.2	1.3	1.4
5	1.0	1.1	1.3	1.3	1.4
6	1.0	1.1	1.3	1.3	1.4
7	1.0	1.1	1.3	1.4	1.4
8	1.0	1.2	1.3	1.4	1.4
9	1.0	1.2	1.3	1.4	1.4

Drawing.

Axs

A8s

Opponents	Mega-Tight	Tight	Loose	Very Loose	Mega-Loose
1	1.0	1.1	1.2	1.2	1.2
2	1.0	1.1	1.2	1.2	1.3
3	1.0	1.1	1.2	1.2	1.3
4	1.0	1.1	1.2	1.3	1.3
5	1.0	1.1	1.2	1.3	1.3
6	1.0	1.1	1.2	1.3	1.3
7	1.0	1.1	1.2	1.3	1.4
8	1.0	1.1	1.3	1.3	1.4
9	1.0	1.1	1.3	1.3	1.4

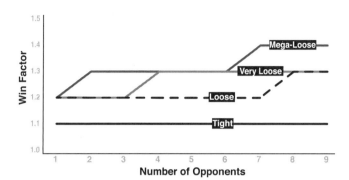

Good draw.

A7s

Opponents	Mega-Tight	Tight	Loose	Very Loose	Mega-Loose
1	1.0	1.1	1.1	1.2	1.2
2	1.0	1.1	1.1	1.2	1.2
3	1.0	1.1	1.1	1.2	1.2
4	1.0	1.1	1.2	1.2	1.3
5	1.0	1.1	1.2	1.2	1.3
6	1.0	1.1	1.2	1.2	1.3
7	1.0	1.1	1.2	1.2	1.3
8	1.0	1.1	1.2	1.3	1.3
9	1.0	1.1	1.2	1.3	1.3

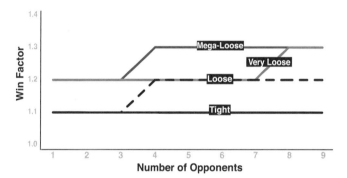

Good draw.

A6s

Opponents	Mega-Tight	Tight	Loose	Very Loose	Mega-Loose
1	1.0	1.1	1.1	1.1	1.2
2	1.0	1.1	1.1	1.1	1.2
3	1.0	1.1	1.1	1.2	1.2
4	1.0	1.1	1.1	1.2	1.2
5	1.0	1.1	1.1	1.2	1.2
6	1.0	1.1	1.1	1.2	1.3
7	1.0	1.1	1.1	1.2	1.3
8	1.0	1.1	1.2	1.2	1.3
9	1.0	1.1	1.2	1.2	1.3

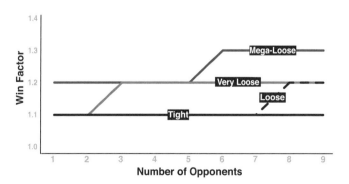

Good draw.

Axs

A5s

Opponents	Mega-Tight	Tight	Loose	Very Loose	Mega-Loose
1	1.0	1.1	1.1	1.1	1.2
2	1.0	1.1	1.1	1.2	1.2
3	1.0	1.1	1.1	1.2	1.2
4	1.1	1.1	1.1	1.2	1.3
5	1.1	1.1	1.1	1.2	1.3
6	1.1	1.1	1.2	1.3	1.3
7	1.1	1.2	1.2	1.3	1.3
8	1.2	1.2	1.3	1.3	1.4
9	1.2	1.3	1.3	1.3	1.4

Good draw.

A4s

Opponents	Mega-Tight	Tight	Loose	Very Loose	Mega-Loose
1	1.0	1.0	1.1	1.1	1.1
2	1.0	1.0	1.1	1.1	1.2
3	1.0	1.0	1.1	1.1	1.2
4	1.0	1.1	1.1	1.2	1.2
5	1.0	1.1	1.1	1.2	1.2
6	1.1	1.1	1.2	1.2	1.3
7	1.1	1.2	1.2	1.3	1.3
8	1.2	1.2	1.3	1.3	1.4
9	1.2	1.2	1.3	1.3	1.4

Good draw.

A3s

Opponents	Mega-Tight	Tight	Loose	Very Loose	Mega-Loose
1	1.0	1.0	1.1	1.1	1.1
2	1.0	1.0	1.1	1.1	1.1
3	1.0	1.0	1.1	1.1	1.2
4	1.0	1.1	1.1	1.2	1.2
5	1.0	1.1	1.1	1.2	1.2
6	1.1	1.1	1.2	1.2	1.3
7	1.1	1.1	1.2	1.2	1.3
8	1.1	1.2	1.2	1.3	1.3
9	1.1	1.2	1.3	1.3	1.3

Good draw.

Axs

A2s

Opponents	Mega-Tight	Tight	Loose	Very Loose	Mega-Loose
1	0.9	1.0	1.1	1.1	1.1
2	0.9	1.0	1.1	1.1	1.1
3	0.9	1.0	1.1	1.1	1.1
4	1.0	1.0	1.1	1.1	1.2
5	1.0	1.0	1.1	1.1	1.2
6	1.0	1.1	1.1	1.1	1.2
7	1.0	1.1	1.1	1.2	1.2
8	1.1	1.2	1.2	1.2	1.3
9	1.1	1.2	1.2	1.2	1.3

Good draw.

Kxs

AKs

Opponents	Mega-Tight	Tight	Loose	Very Loose	Mega-Loose
1	1.3	1.3	1.3	1.3	1.3
2	1.4	1.4	1.5	1.5	1.5
3	1.4	1.5	1.6	1.6	1.6
4	1.4	1.6	1.6	1.7	1.7
5	1.4	1.6	1.6	1.7	1.7
6	1.4	1.5	1.7	1.8	1.8
7	1.4	1.5	1.7	1.8	1.8
8	1.3	1.5	1.7	1.8	1.9
9	1.2	1.5	1.7	1.8	1.9

Premium.

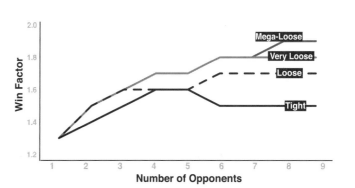

KQs

Opponents	Mega-Tight	Tight	Loose	Very Loose	Mega-Loose
1	1.1	1.2	1.2	1.2	1.2
2	1.1	1.2	1.3	1.3	1.4
3	1.1	1.3	1.4	1.4	1.4
4	1.1	1.3	1.4	1.5	1.6
5	1.1	1.3	1.4	1.5	1.6
6	1.1	1.3	1.4	1.5	1.6
7	1.1	1.4	1.4	1.6	1.7
8	1.1	1.4	1.5	1.6	1.7
9	1.1	1.4	1.5	1.6	1.7

Strong draw.

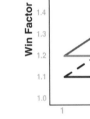

Kxs

KJs

Opponents	Mega-Tight	Tight	Loose	Very Loose	Mega-Loose
1	1.0	1.1	1.2	1.2	1.2
2	1.0	1.1	1.2	1.3	1.3
3	1.0	1.2	1.3	1.3	1.4
4	1.1	1.2	1.3	1.4	1.5
5	1.1	1.3	1.4	1.4	1.5
6	1.1	1.3	1.4	1.5	1.5
7	1.0	1.3	1.4	1.5	1.6
8	1.0	1.3	1.4	1.5	1.6
9	1.0	1.2	1.4	1.5	1.6

Good draw.

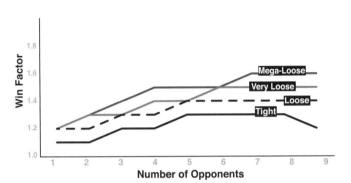

KTs

Opponents	Mega-Tight	Tight	Loose	Very Loose	Mega-Loose
1	1.0	1.1	1.1	1.2	1.2
2	1.0	1.1	1.2	1.2	1.3
3	1.0	1.1	1.2	1.3	1.4
4	1.0	1.2	1.3	1.4	1.4
5	1.0	1.2	1.3	1.4	1.4
6	1.0	1.2	1.3	1.4	1.5
7	1.0	1.2	1.3	1.4	1.5
8	1.0	1.2	1.3	1.4	1.5
9	1.0	1.2	1.4	1.5	1.5

Good draw.

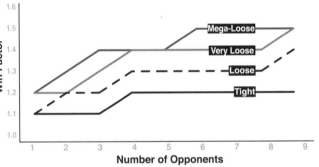

K9s

Opponents	Mega-Tight	Tight	Loose	Very Loose	Mega-Loose
1	0.9	1.0	1.1	1.1	1.2
2	0.9	1.0	1.1	1.2	1.2
3	0.9	1.0	1.1	1.2	1.2
4	1.0	1.1	1.2	1.2	1.3
5	1.0	1.1	1.2	1.3	1.3
6	0.9	1.1	1.2	1.3	1.3
7	0.9	1.1	1.2	1.3	1.4
8	0.9	1.1	1.2	1.3	1.4
9	0.9	1.1	1.3	1.3	1.4

Good draw.

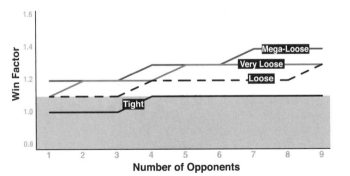

Kxs

K8s

Opponents	Mega-Tight	Tight	Loose	Very Loose	Mega-Loose
1	0.9	1.0	1.1	1.1	1.1
2	0.9	1.0	1.1	1.1	1.1
3	0.9	1.0	1.1	1.1	1.2
4	0.9	1.0	1.1	1.1	1.2
5	0.9	1.0	1.1	1.1	1.2
6	1.0	1.0	1.1	1.2	1.2
7	1.0	1.0	1.1	1.2	1.2
8	1.0	1.0	1.1	1.2	1.3
9	1.0	1.0	1.1	1.2	1.3

Good draw.

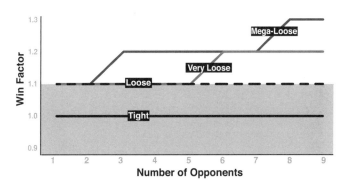

K7s

Opponents	Mega-Tight	Tight	Loose	Very Loose	Mega-Loose
1	0.9	1.0	1.0	1.1	1.1
2	0.9	1.0	1.0	1.1	1.1
3	0.9	1.0	1.0	1.1	1.1
4	0.9	1.0	1.1	1.1	1.2
5	0.9	1.0	1.1	1.1	1.2
6	0.9	1.0	1.1	1.1	1.2
7	0.9	1.0	1.1	1.1	1.2
8	0.9	1.0	1.1	1.2	1.2
9	0.9	1.0	1.1	1.2	1.2

Drawing.

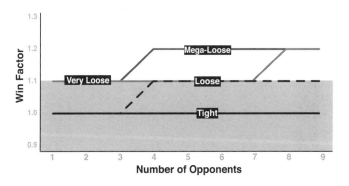

K6s

Opponents	Mega-Tight	Tight	Loose	Very Loose	Mega-Loose
1	0.8	1.0	1.0	1.1	1.1
2	0.8	1.0	1.0	1.1	1.1
3	0.8	1.0	1.0	1.1	1.1
4	0.9	1.0	1.0	1.1	1.1
5	0.9	1.0	1.0	1.1	1.1
6	0.9	1.0	1.1	1.1	1.1
7	0.9	1.0	1.1	1.1	1.1
8	0.9	1.0	1.1	1.1	1.2
9	0.9	1.0	1.1	1.1	1.2

Drawing.

Kxs

K5s

Opponents	Mega-Tight	Tight	Loose	Very Loose	Mega-Loose
1	0.9	0.9	1.0	1.0	1.1
2	0.9	0.9	1.0	1.0	1.1
3	0.9	0.9	1.0	1.0	1.1
4	0.9	0.9	1.0	1.1	1.1
5	0.9	1.0	1.0	1.1	1.1
6	0.9	1.0	1.1	1.1	1.1
7	0.9	1.0	1.1	1.1	1.1
8	0.9	1.0	1.1	1.1	1.2
9	0.9	1.0	1.1	1.1	1.2

Drawing.

K4s

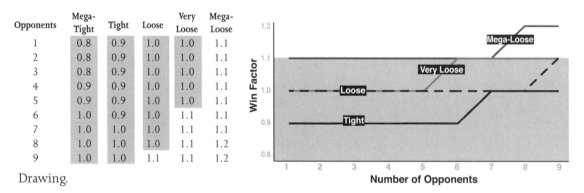

Opponents	Mega-Tight	Tight	Loose	Very Loose	Mega-Loose
1	0.8	0.9	1.0	1.0	1.1
2	0.8	0.9	1.0	1.0	1.1
3	0.8	0.9	1.0	1.0	1.1
4	0.9	0.9	1.0	1.0	1.1
5	0.9	0.9	1.0	1.0	1.1
6	1.0	0.9	1.0	1.1	1.1
7	1.0	1.0	1.0	1.1	1.1
8	1.0	1.0	1.0	1.1	1.2
9	1.0	1.0	1.1	1.1	1.2

Drawing.

K3s

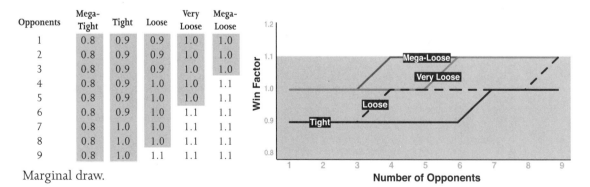

Opponents	Mega-Tight	Tight	Loose	Very Loose	Mega-Loose
1	0.8	0.9	0.9	1.0	1.0
2	0.8	0.9	0.9	1.0	1.0
3	0.8	0.9	0.9	1.0	1.0
4	0.8	0.9	1.0	1.0	1.1
5	0.8	0.9	1.0	1.0	1.1
6	0.8	0.9	1.0	1.1	1.1
7	0.8	1.0	1.0	1.1	1.1
8	0.8	1.0	1.0	1.1	1.1
9	0.8	1.0	1.1	1.1	1.1

Marginal draw.

Kxs

K2s

Opponents	Mega-Tight	Tight	Loose	Very Loose	Mega-Loose
1	0.8	0.9	0.9	1.0	1.0
2	0.8	0.9	0.9	1.0	1.0
3	0.8	0.8	0.9	1.0	1.0
4	0.8	0.9	1.0	1.0	1.0
5	0.8	0.9	1.0	1.0	1.0
6	0.8	0.9	1.0	1.1	1.1
7	0.8	1.0	1.0	1.1	1.1
8	0.8	1.0	1.0	1.1	1.1
9	0.8	1.0	1.1	1.1	1.1

Marginal draw.

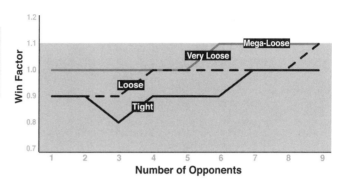

AQs

Opponents	Mega-Tight	Tight	Loose	Very Loose	Mega-Loose
1	1.2	1.3	1.3	1.3	1.3
2	1.3	1.4	1.4	1.4	1.5
3	1.3	1.4	1.5	1.5	1.6
4	1.3	1.4	1.5	1.6	1.6
5	1.3	1.4	1.5	1.6	1.7
6	1.3	1.4	1.5	1.6	1.8
7	1.3	1.4	1.6	1.7	1.8
8	1.3	1.4	1.6	1.7	1.8
9	1.3	1.4	1.6	1.7	1.8

Strong draw.

Qxs

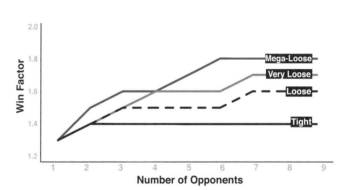

KQs

Opponents	Mega-Tight	Tight	Loose	Very Loose	Mega-Loose
1	1.1	1.2	1.2	1.2	1.2
2	1.1	1.2	1.3	1.3	1.4
3	1.1	1.3	1.4	1.4	1.4
4	1.1	1.3	1.4	1.5	1.6
5	1.1	1.3	1.4	1.5	1.6
6	1.1	1.3	1.4	1.5	1.6
7	1.1	1.4	1.4	1.6	1.7
8	1.1	1.4	1.5	1.6	1.7
9	1.1	1.4	1.5	1.6	1.7

Strong draw.

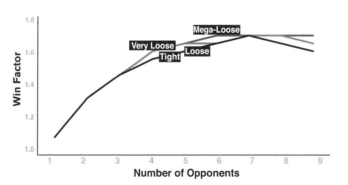

QJs

Opponents	Mega-Tight	Tight	Loose	Very Loose	Mega-Loose
1	1.0	1.0	1.1	1.1	1.2
2	1.0	1.1	1.2	1.2	1.3
3	1.0	1.1	1.2	1.3	1.4
4	1.1	1.2	1.3	1.4	1.4
5	1.1	1.2	1.3	1.4	1.5
6	1.1	1.2	1.3	1.5	1.5
7	1.1	1.2	1.4	1.5	1.5
8	1.1	1.2	1.4	1.5	1.6
9	1.1	1.2	1.4	1.5	1.6

Good draw.

QTs

Opponents	Mega-Tight	Tight	Loose	Very Loose	Mega-Loose
1	0.9	1.0	1.1	1.1	1.1
2	0.9	1.1	1.1	1.2	1.2
3	1.0	1.1	1.2	1.2	1.3
4	1.0	1.1	1.2	1.3	1.4
5	1.0	1.1	1.3	1.3	1.4
6	1.0	1.2	1.3	1.3	1.4
7	1.0	1.2	1.3	1.4	1.4
8	1.0	1.2	1.3	1.4	1.5
9	1.0	1.2	1.3	1.4	1.5

Good draw.

Q9s

Opponents	Mega-Tight	Tight	Loose	Very Loose	Mega-Loose
1	0.9	1.0	1.0	1.1	1.1
2	0.9	1.0	1.1	1.1	1.1
3	0.9	1.0	1.1	1.2	1.2
4	0.9	1.1	1.1	1.2	1.3
5	0.9	1.1	1.1	1.2	1.3
6	0.8	1.1	1.2	1.3	1.3
7	0.8	1.1	1.2	1.3	1.3
8	0.8	1.2	1.2	1.3	1.3
9	0.7	1.2	1.2	1.3	1.3

Good draw.

Qxs

Q8s

Opponents	Mega-Tight	Tight	Loose	Very Loose	Mega-Loose
1	0.8	0.9	1.0	1.0	1.1
2	0.8	0.9	1.0	1.1	1.1
3	0.8	1.0	1.0	1.1	1.1
4	0.9	1.0	1.0	1.1	1.1
5	0.9	1.0	1.1	1.1	1.1
6	0.9	1.0	1.1	1.1	1.2
7	0.9	1.0	1.1	1.1	1.2
8	0.9	1.0	1.1	1.2	1.2
9	0.9	1.0	1.1	1.2	1.2

Drawing.

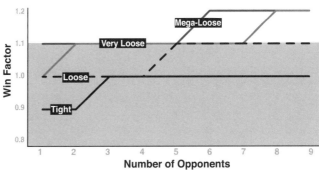

Q7s

Opponents	Mega-Tight	Tight	Loose	Very Loose	Mega-Loose
1	0.8	0.9	0.9	1.0	1.0
2	0.8	0.9	0.9	1.0	1.0
3	0.8	0.9	1.0	1.0	1.0
4	0.8	0.9	1.0	1.0	1.1
5	0.9	0.9	1.0	1.0	1.1
6	0.9	0.9	1.0	1.1	1.1
7	0.9	1.0	1.0	1.1	1.1
8	0.9	1.0	1.1	1.1	1.1
9	0.9	1.0	1.1	1.1	1.1

Marginal draw.

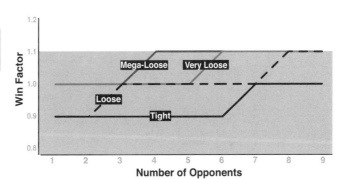

Q6s

Opponents	Mega-Tight	Tight	Loose	Very Loose	Mega-Loose
1	0.8	0.9	0.9	1.0	1.0
2	0.8	0.9	0.9	1.0	1.0
3	0.8	0.9	0.9	1.0	1.0
4	0.9	0.9	1.0	1.0	1.1
5	0.8	0.9	1.0	1.0	1.1
6	0.9	0.9	1.0	1.0	1.1
7	0.9	0.9	1.0	1.0	1.1
8	0.9	0.9	1.0	1.1	1.1
9	0.9	1.0	1.0	1.1	1.1

Marginal draw.

Qxs

Q5s

Opponents	Mega-Tight	Tight	Loose	Very Loose	Mega-Loose
1	0.8	0.8	0.9	1.0	1.0
2	0.8	0.8	0.9	1.0	1.0
3	0.8	0.8	0.9	1.0	1.0
4	0.8	0.9	0.9	1.0	1.0
5	0.8	0.9	1.0	1.0	1.0
6	0.9	0.9	1.0	1.0	1.1
7	0.9	1.0	1.0	1.0	1.1
8	0.9	1.0	1.0	1.1	1.1
9	0.9	1.0	1.0	1.1	1.1

Marginal draw.

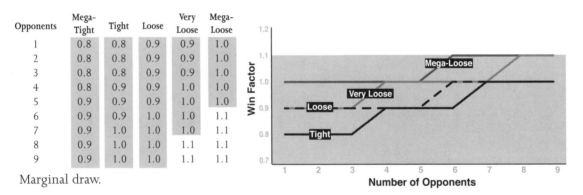

Q4s

Opponents	Mega-Tight	Tight	Loose	Very Loose	Mega-Loose
1	0.8	0.8	0.9	0.9	1.0
2	0.8	0.8	0.9	0.9	1.0
3	0.8	0.8	0.9	0.9	1.0
4	0.8	0.9	0.9	1.0	1.0
5	0.9	0.9	0.9	1.0	1.0
6	0.9	0.9	1.0	1.0	1.1
7	0.9	1.0	1.0	1.0	1.1
8	0.9	1.0	1.0	1.1	1.1
9	0.9	1.0	1.0	1.1	1.1

Marginal draw.

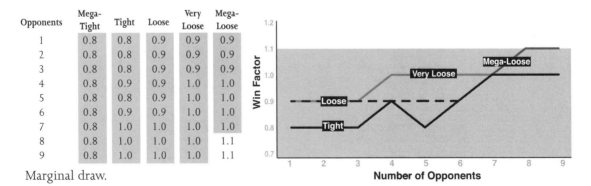

Q3s

Opponents	Mega-Tight	Tight	Loose	Very Loose	Mega-Loose
1	0.8	0.8	0.9	0.9	0.9
2	0.8	0.8	0.9	0.9	0.9
3	0.8	0.8	0.9	0.9	0.9
4	0.8	0.9	0.9	1.0	1.0
5	0.8	0.8	0.9	1.0	1.0
6	0.8	0.9	0.9	1.0	1.0
7	0.8	1.0	1.0	1.0	1.0
8	0.8	1.0	1.0	1.0	1.1
9	0.8	1.0	1.0	1.0	1.1

Marginal draw.

Qxs

Q2s

Opponents	Mega-Tight	Tight	Loose	Very Loose	Mega-Loose
1	0.8	0.8	0.9	0.9	0.9
2	0.8	0.8	0.9	0.9	0.9
3	0.8	0.8	0.8	0.9	0.9
4	0.8	0.8	0.9	0.9	1.0
5	0.8	0.8	0.9	0.9	1.0
6	0.8	0.9	0.9	1.0	1.0
7	0.8	0.9	1.0	1.0	1.0
8	0.8	0.9	1.0	1.0	1.0
9	0.8	1.0	1.0	1.0	1.1

Marginal draw.

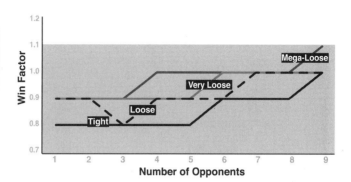

Ax

AK

Opponents	Mega-Tight	Tight	Loose	Very Loose	Mega-Loose
1	1.2	1.3	1.3	1.3	1.3
2	1.3	1.4	1.4	1.4	1.4
3	1.3	1.4	1.4	1.5	1.5
4	1.2	1.4	1.5	1.5	1.6
5	1.1	1.3	1.5	1.5	1.6
6	1.1	1.3	1.5	1.5	1.6
7	1.1	1.2	1.4	1.5	1.6
8	1.1	1.2	1.4	1.4	1.6
9	1.1	1.1	1.3	1.4	1.5

Good draw.

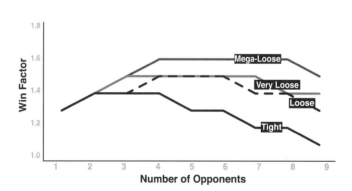

AQ

Opponents	Mega-Tight	Tight	Loose	Very Loose	Mega-Loose
1	1.2	1.2	1.3	1.3	1.3
2	1.2	1.2	1.3	1.4	1.4
3	1.1	1.2	1.3	1.4	1.4
4	1.1	1.2	1.3	1.4	1.5
5	1.1	1.2	1.3	1.4	1.5
6	1.1	1.1	1.3	1.4	1.5
7	1.0	1.1	1.2	1.4	1.4
8	1.0	1.1	1.2	1.4	1.4
9	1.0	1.0	1.1	1.3	1.4

Good draw.

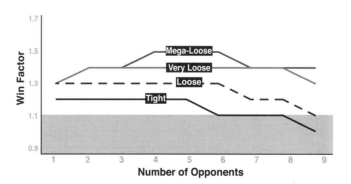

Ax

AJ

Opponents	Mega-Tight	Tight	Loose	Very Loose	Mega-Loose
1	1.1	1.2	1.2	1.2	1.3
2	1.1	1.2	1.3	1.3	1.3
3	1.0	1.2	1.3	1.3	1.4
4	1.0	1.1	1.3	1.3	1.4
5	0.9	1.1	1.2	1.3	1.4
6	0.8	1.1	1.1	1.2	1.4
7	0.8	1.0	1.1	1.1	1.4
8	0.8	1.0	1.1	1.1	1.2
9	0.8	0.9	1.0	1.1	1.2

Drawing.

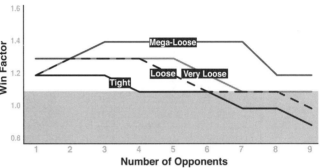

AT

Opponents	Mega-Tight	Tight	Loose	Very Loose	Mega-Loose
1	1.1	1.2	1.2	1.2	1.3
2	1.0	1.1	1.2	1.2	1.3
3	1.0	1.1	1.2	1.2	1.3
4	0.9	1.1	1.2	1.2	1.3
5	0.8	1.0	1.1	1.2	1.3
6	0.7	0.9	1.1	1.1	1.3
7	0.6	0.9	1.0	1.1	1.2
8	0.6	0.8	1.0	1.1	1.2
9	0.6	0.8	1.0	1.1	1.2

Drawing.

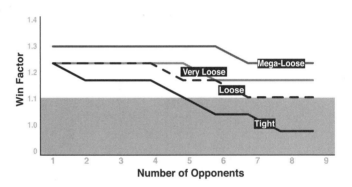

A9

Opponents	Mega-Tight	Tight	Loose	Very Loose	Mega-Loose
1	1.0	1.1	1.1	1.2	1.2
2	0.9	1.0	1.1	1.2	1.2
3	0.8	1.0	1.1	1.1	1.2
4	0.8	1.0	1.0	1.1	1.2
5	0.7	0.8	1.0	1.1	1.1
6	0.7	0.8	1.0	1.1	1.1
7	0.7	0.8	0.9	1.0	1.0
8	0.7	0.7	0.8	0.9	1.0
9	0.7	0.7	0.8	0.9	1.0

Not playable.

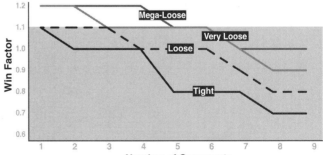

A8

Opponents	Mega-Tight	Tight	Loose	Very Loose	Mega-Loose
1	1.0	1.1	1.1	1.1	1.2
2	0.9	1.0	1.1	1.1	1.2
3	0.8	1.0	1.0	1.1	1.1
4	0.8	0.9	1.0	1.1	1.1
5	0.7	0.8	0.9	1.0	1.1
6	0.7	0.8	0.9	1.0	1.1
7	0.7	0.8	0.8	0.9	1.0
8	0.7	0.7	0.8	0.9	1.0
9	0.7	0.7	0.8	0.8	0.9

Not playable.

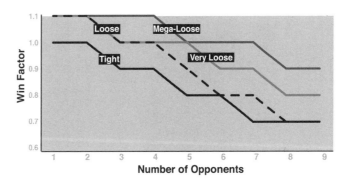

A7

Opponents	Mega-Tight	Tight	Loose	Very Loose	Mega-Loose
1	1.0	1.0	1.1	1.1	1.1
2	0.8	1.0	1.1	1.1	1.1
3	0.8	0.9	1.0	1.0	1.1
4	0.8	0.9	1.0	1.0	1.1
5	0.7	0.8	0.9	1.0	1.0
6	0.7	0.8	0.8	0.9	1.0
7	0.7	0.7	0.8	0.9	1.0
8	0.7	0.7	0.7	0.8	0.9
9	0.7	0.7	0.7	0.8	0.9

Not playable.

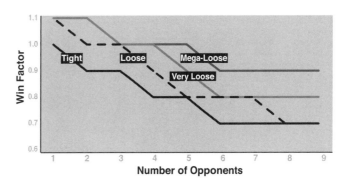

A6

Opponents	Mega-Tight	Tight	Loose	Very Loose	Mega-Loose
1	0.9	1.0	1.1	1.1	1.1
2	0.8	0.9	1.0	1.1	1.1
3	0.8	0.9	1.0	1.0	1.0
4	0.7	0.8	0.9	1.0	1.0
5	0.7	0.8	0.8	0.9	1.0
6	0.7	0.7	0.8	0.8	0.9
7	0.7	0.7	0.8	0.8	0.9
8	0.7	0.7	0.7	0.8	0.9
9	0.7	0.7	0.7	0.8	0.9

Not playable.

A5

Opponents	Mega-Tight	Tight	Loose	Very Loose	Mega-Loose
1	0.9	1.0	1.1	1.1	1.1
2	0.9	0.9	1.0	1.1	1.1
3	0.8	0.9	1.0	1.0	1.1
4	0.8	0.9	1.0	1.0	1.1
5	0.8	0.8	0.9	1.0	1.0
6	0.8	0.8	0.9	0.9	1.0
7	0.7	0.8	0.9	0.9	1.0
8	0.7	0.8	0.9	0.9	0.9
9	0.7	0.8	0.9	0.9	0.9

Not playable.

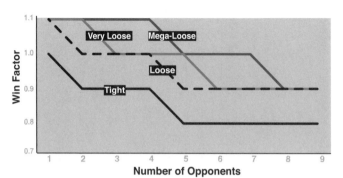

A4

Opponents	Mega-Tight	Tight	Loose	Very Loose	Mega-Loose
1	0.9	1.0	1.0	1.1	1.1
2	0.8	0.9	1.0	1.0	1.1
3	0.8	0.9	1.0	1.0	1.0
4	0.8	0.9	0.9	1.0	1.0
5	0.8	0.8	0.9	0.9	1.0
6	0.8	0.8	0.8	0.9	1.0
7	0.7	0.8	0.8	0.9	1.0
8	0.7	0.8	0.8	0.9	0.9
9	0.7	0.8	0.8	0.9	0.9

Not playable.

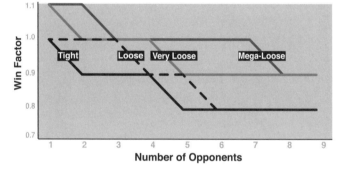

A3

Opponents	Mega-Tight	Tight	Loose	Very Loose	Mega-Loose
1	0.9	1.0	1.0	1.1	1.1
2	0.8	0.9	1.0	1.0	1.0
3	0.8	0.8	0.9	1.0	1.0
4	0.7	0.8	0.9	0.9	1.0
5	0.7	0.8	0.8	0.9	1.0
6	0.7	0.8	0.8	0.9	0.9
7	0.7	0.8	0.8	0.9	0.9
8	0.7	0.8	0.8	0.9	0.9
9	0.7	0.8	0.8	0.8	0.9

Not playable.

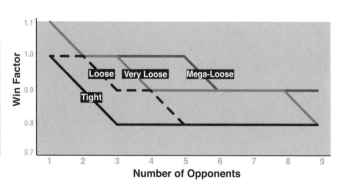

Ax

A2

Opponents	Mega-Tight	Tight	Loose	Very Loose	Mega-Loose
1	0.9	1.0	1.0	1.0	1.1
2	0.8	0.9	0.9	1.0	1.0
3	0.8	0.8	0.9	0.9	1.0
4	0.7	0.8	0.9	0.9	1.0
5	0.7	0.7	0.8	0.8	0.9
6	0.7	0.7	0.8	0.8	0.9
7	0.7	0.7	0.8	0.8	0.9
8	0.7	0.7	0.8	0.8	0.9
9	0.7	0.7	0.8	0.8	0.9

Not playable.

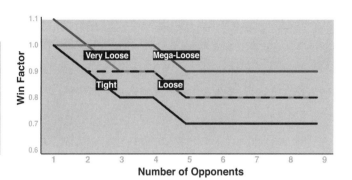

Kx

AK

Opponents	Mega-Tight	Tight	Loose	Very Loose	Mega-Loose
1	1.2	1.3	1.3	1.3	1.3
2	1.3	1.4	1.4	1.4	1.4
3	1.3	1.4	1.4	1.5	1.5
4	1.2	1.4	1.5	1.5	1.6
5	1.1	1.3	1.5	1.5	1.6
6	1.1	1.3	1.5	1.5	1.6
7	1.1	1.2	1.4	1.5	1.6
8	1.1	1.2	1.4	1.4	1.6
9	1.1	1.1	1.3	1.4	1.5

Good draw.

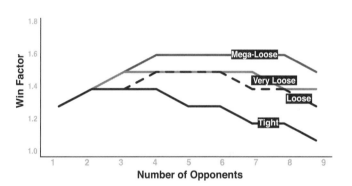

KQ

Opponents	Mega-Tight	Tight	Loose	Very Loose	Mega-Loose
1	1.0	1.1	1.2	1.2	1.2
2	1.0	1.1	1.2	1.2	1.3
3	1.0	1.1	1.2	1.3	1.3
4	1.0	1.1	1.2	1.3	1.4
5	1.0	1.1	1.2	1.3	1.4
6	1.0	1.1	1.2	1.3	1.4
7	1.0	1.1	1.2	1.3	1.4
8	1.0	1.0	1.2	1.3	1.4
9	1.0	1.0	1.1	1.3	1.4

Good draw.

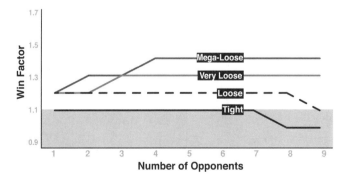

Kx

KJ

Opponents	Mega-Tight	Tight	Loose	Very Loose	Mega-Loose
1	1.0	1.1	1.1	1.2	1.2
2	0.9	1.1	1.1	1.2	1.2
3	0.9	1.1	1.2	1.2	1.3
4	0.9	1.1	1.2	1.2	1.3
5	0.8	1.0	1.1	1.2	1.3
6	0.8	1.0	1.1	1.2	1.3
7	0.7	1.0	1.1	1.2	1.3
8	0.7	0.9	1.1	1.2	1.3
9	0.7	0.9	1.0	1.1	1.2

Drawing.

KT

Opponents	Mega-Tight	Tight	Loose	Very Loose	Mega-Loose
1	0.9	1.0	1.1	1.2	1.2
2	0.9	1.0	1.1	1.2	1.2
3	0.8	1.0	1.1	1.2	1.2
4	0.8	1.0	1.1	1.2	1.2
5	0.7	1.0	1.1	1.1	1.2
6	0.7	0.9	1.1	1.1	1.2
7	0.6	0.9	1.0	1.1	1.2
8	0.6	0.8	1.0	1.1	1.2
9	0.6	0.8	0.9	1.1	1.2

Drawing.

K9

Opponents	Mega-Tight	Tight	Loose	Very Loose	Mega-Loose
1	0.9	1.0	1.0	1.1	1.1
2	0.8	0.9	1.0	1.1	1.1
3	0.8	0.9	1.0	1.1	1.1
4	0.7	0.9	1.0	1.1	1.1
5	0.7	0.8	0.9	1.0	1.1
6	0.7	0.8	0.9	1.0	1.1
7	0.7	0.8	0.9	1.0	1.0
8	0.7	0.7	0.8	0.9	1.0
9	0.7	0.7	0.8	0.9	0.9

Not playable.

Suited Connectors

AKs

Opponents	Mega-Tight	Tight	Loose	Very Loose	Mega-Loose
1	1.3	1.3	1.3	1.3	1.3
2	1.4	1.4	1.5	1.5	1.5
3	1.4	1.5	1.6	1.6	1.6
4	1.4	1.6	1.6	1.7	1.7
5	1.4	1.6	1.6	1.7	1.7
6	1.4	1.5	1.7	1.8	1.8
7	1.4	1.5	1.7	1.8	1.8
8	1.3	1.5	1.7	1.8	1.9
9	1.2	1.5	1.7	1.8	1.9

Premium draw.

KQs

Opponents	Mega-Tight	Tight	Loose	Very Loose	Mega-Loose
1	1.1	1.2	1.2	1.2	1.2
2	1.1	1.2	1.3	1.3	1.4
3	1.1	1.3	1.4	1.4	1.4
4	1.1	1.3	1.4	1.5	1.6
5	1.1	1.3	1.4	1.5	1.6
6	1.1	1.3	1.4	1.5	1.6
7	1.1	1.4	1.4	1.6	1.7
8	1.1	1.4	1.5	1.6	1.7
9	1.1	1.4	1.5	1.6	1.7

Strong draw.

QJs

Opponents	Mega-Tight	Tight	Loose	Very Loose	Mega-Loose
1	1.0	1.0	1.1	1.1	1.2
2	1.0	1.1	1.2	1.2	1.3
3	1.0	1.1	1.2	1.3	1.4
4	1.1	1.2	1.3	1.4	1.4
5	1.1	1.2	1.3	1.4	1.5
6	1.1	1.2	1.3	1.5	1.5
7	1.1	1.2	1.4	1.5	1.5
8	1.1	1.2	1.4	1.5	1.6
9	1.1	1.2	1.4	1.5	1.6

Good draw.

Suited Connectors

JTs

Opponents	Mega-Tight	Tight	Loose	Very Loose	Mega-Loose
1	0.9	1.0	1.0	1.1	1.1
2	0.9	1.0	1.1	1.1	1.2
3	0.9	1.0	1.2	1.2	1.3
4	1.0	1.0	1.2	1.3	1.4
5	1.0	1.1	1.3	1.3	1.4
6	1.0	1.1	1.3	1.3	1.4
7	1.0	1.1	1.3	1.4	1.4
8	1.0	1.2	1.3	1.4	1.5
9	1.1	1.2	1.3	1.4	1.5

Good draw.

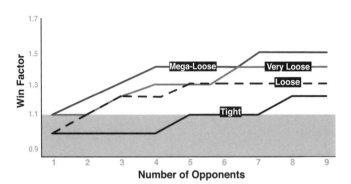

T9s

Opponents	Mega-Tight	Tight	Loose	Very Loose	Mega-Loose
1	0.8	0.9	1.0	1.0	1.0
2	0.8	1.0	1.0	1.1	1.1
3	0.9	1.0	1.1	1.1	1.2
4	0.9	1.1	1.1	1.2	1.2
5	1.0	1.1	1.1	1.2	1.3
6	1.0	1.1	1.1	1.3	1.3
7	1.0	1.1	1.2	1.3	1.3
8	1.1	1.1	1.2	1.3	1.4
9	1.1	1.2	1.3	1.3	1.4

Good draw.

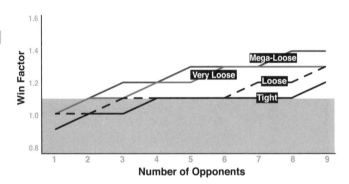

98s

Opponents	Mega-Tight	Tight	Loose	Very Loose	Mega-Loose
1	0.8	0.8	0.9	0.9	1.0
2	0.8	0.9	0.9	1.0	1.0
3	0.9	1.0	1.0	1.0	1.1
4	0.9	1.0	1.1	1.1	1.2
5	1.0	1.0	1.1	1.1	1.2
6	1.1	1.1	1.1	1.1	1.2
7	1.1	1.1	1.1	1.1	1.2
8	1.1	1.1	1.2	1.2	1.3
9	1.1	1.1	1.2	1.2	1.3

Good draw.

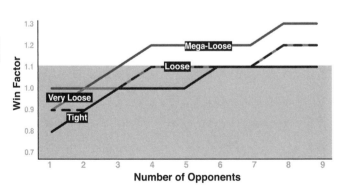

Suited connectors

87s

Opponents	Mega-Tight	Tight	Loose	Very Loose	Mega-Loose
1	0.8	0.8	0.9	0.9	0.9
2	0.8	0.9	0.9	0.9	1.0
3	0.9	0.9	1.0	1.0	1.0
4	1.0	1.0	1.0	1.1	1.1
5	1.0	1.0	1.0	1.1	1.1
6	1.0	1.1	1.1	1.1	1.1
7	1.0	1.1	1.1	1.1	1.2
8	1.1	1.1	1.2	1.2	1.2
9	1.1	1.1	1.2	1.2	1.2

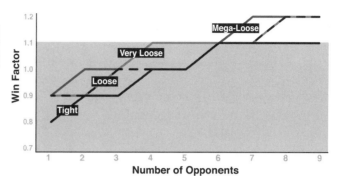

Drawing.

76s

Opponents	Mega-Tight	Tight	Loose	Very Loose	Mega-Loose
1	0.8	0.8	0.8	0.9	0.9
2	0.8	0.8	0.9	0.9	0.9
3	0.9	0.9	0.9	1.0	1.0
4	1.0	1.0	1.0	1.0	1.0
5	1.0	1.0	1.0	1.0	1.0
6	1.1	1.1	1.1	1.1	1.1
7	1.1	1.1	1.1	1.1	1.1
8	1.1	1.1	1.2	1.2	1.2
9	1.1	1.1	1.2	1.2	1.2

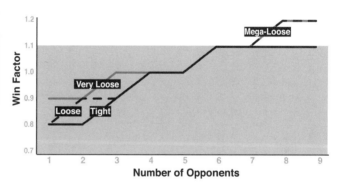

Drawing.

65s

Opponents	Mega-Tight	Tight	Loose	Very Loose	Mega-Loose
1	0.7	0.8	0.8	0.8	0.8
2	0.8	0.8	0.9	0.9	0.9
3	0.9	0.9	0.9	0.9	0.9
4	1.0	1.0	1.0	1.0	1.0
5	1.0	1.0	1.0	1.0	1.0
6	1.2	1.1	1.1	1.1	1.1
7	1.2	1.2	1.1	1.1	1.1
8	1.2	1.2	1.2	1.2	1.2
9	1.2	1.2	1.2	1.2	1.2

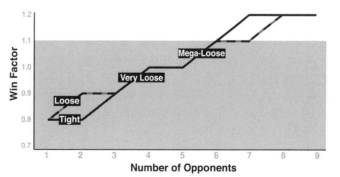

Drawing.

Suited connectors

54s

Opponents	Mega-Tight	Tight	Loose	Very Loose	Mega-Loose
1	0.7	0.8	0.8	0.8	0.8
2	0.8	0.8	0.8	0.8	0.8
3	0.9	0.9	0.9	0.9	0.9
4	1.0	1.0	0.9	1.0	1.0
5	1.0	1.0	1.0	1.0	1.0
6	1.1	1.1	1.1	1.1	1.1
7	1.2	1.2	1.1	1.1	1.1
8	1.2	1.2	1.2	1.2	1.2
9	1.2	1.2	1.2	1.2	1.2

Drawing.

43s

Opponents	Mega-Tight	Tight	Loose	Very Loose	Mega-Loose
1	0.7	0.7	0.7	0.7	0.8
2	0.8	0.8	0.8	0.8	0.8
3	0.8	0.8	0.8	0.8	0.8
4	0.9	0.9	0.9	0.9	0.9
5	1.0	1.0	0.9	0.9	0.9
6	1.1	1.0	1.0	1.0	1.0
7	1.1	1.1	1.0	1.0	1.0
8	1.1	1.1	1.1	1.1	1.0
9	1.1	1.1	1.1	1.1	1.1

Drawing.

One gap suiteds

AQs

Opponents	Mega-Tight	Tight	Loose	Very Loose	Mega-Loose
1	1.2	1.3	1.3	1.3	1.3
2	1.3	1.4	1.4	1.4	1.5
3	1.3	1.4	1.5	1.5	1.6
4	1.3	1.4	1.5	1.6	1.6
5	1.3	1.4	1.5	1.6	1.7
6	1.3	1.4	1.5	1.6	1.8
7	1.3	1.4	1.6	1.7	1.8
8	1.3	1.4	1.6	1.7	1.8
9	1.3	1.4	1.6	1.7	1.8

Premium draw.

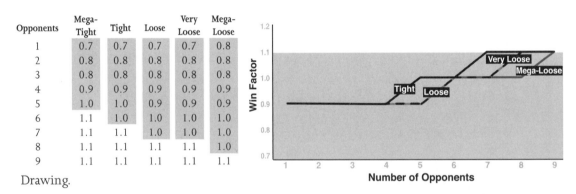

One gap suiteds

KJs

Opponents	Mega-Tight	Tight	Loose	Very Loose	Mega-Loose
1	1.0	1.1	1.2	1.2	1.2
2	1.0	1.1	1.2	1.3	1.3
3	1.0	1.2	1.3	1.3	1.4
4	1.1	1.2	1.3	1.4	1.5
5	1.1	1.3	1.4	1.4	1.5
6	1.1	1.3	1.4	1.5	1.5
7	1.0	1.3	1.4	1.5	1.6
8	1.0	1.3	1.4	1.5	1.6
9	1.0	1.2	1.4	1.5	1.6

Good draw.

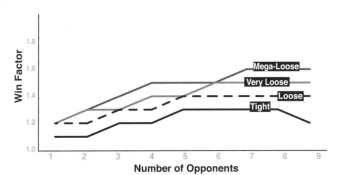

QTs

Opponents	Mega-Tight	Tight	Loose	Very Loose	Mega-Loose
1	0.9	1.0	1.1	1.1	1.1
2	0.9	1.1	1.1	1.2	1.2
3	1.0	1.1	1.2	1.2	1.3
4	1.0	1.1	1.2	1.3	1.4
5	1.0	1.1	1.3	1.3	1.4
6	1.0	1.2	1.3	1.3	1.4
7	1.0	1.2	1.3	1.4	1.4
8	1.0	1.2	1.3	1.4	1.5
9	1.0	1.2	1.3	1.4	1.5

Good draw.

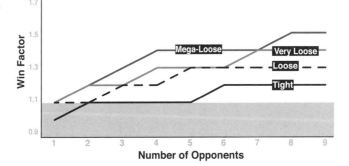

J9s

Opponents	Mega-Tight	Tight	Loose	Very Loose	Mega-Loose
1	0.8	0.9	1.0	1.0	1.1
2	0.9	1.0	1.0	1.1	1.1
3	0.9	1.0	1.1	1.1	1.2
4	0.9	1.0	1.1	1.2	1.2
5	1.0	1.0	1.1	1.2	1.3
6	1.0	1.1	1.2	1.3	1.3
7	1.0	1.1	1.2	1.3	1.3
8	0.9	1.1	1.2	1.3	1.4
9	0.9	1.1	1.2	1.3	1.4

Good draw.

One gap suiteds

T8s

Opponents	Mega-Tight	Tight	Loose	Very Loose	Mega-Loose
1	0.8	0.9	0.9	1.0	1.0
2	0.8	0.9	1.0	1.0	1.1
3	0.8	0.9	1.0	1.0	1.1
4	0.9	1.0	1.1	1.1	1.2
5	1.0	1.0	1.1	1.1	1.2
6	1.0	1.1	1.1	1.1	1.2
7	1.0	1.1	1.1	1.1	1.2
8	1.0	1.1	1.2	1.2	1.3
9	1.0	1.1	1.2	1.2	1.3

Good draw.

97s

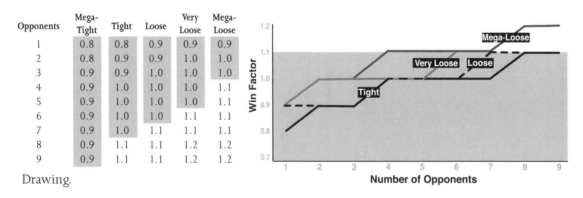

Opponents	Mega-Tight	Tight	Loose	Very Loose	Mega-Loose
1	0.8	0.8	0.9	0.9	0.9
2	0.8	0.9	0.9	1.0	1.0
3	0.9	0.9	1.0	1.0	1.0
4	0.9	1.0	1.0	1.0	1.1
5	0.9	1.0	1.0	1.0	1.1
6	0.9	1.0	1.0	1.1	1.1
7	0.9	1.0	1.1	1.1	1.1
8	0.9	1.1	1.1	1.2	1.2
9	0.9	1.1	1.1	1.2	1.2

Drawing.

86s

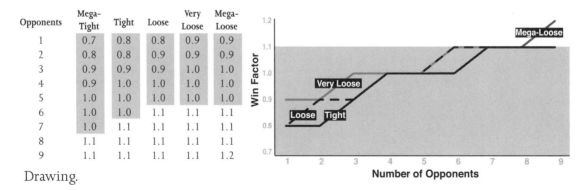

Opponents	Mega-Tight	Tight	Loose	Very Loose	Mega-Loose
1	0.7	0.8	0.8	0.9	0.9
2	0.8	0.8	0.9	0.9	0.9
3	0.9	0.9	0.9	1.0	1.0
4	0.9	1.0	1.0	1.0	1.0
5	1.0	1.0	1.0	1.0	1.0
6	1.0	1.0	1.1	1.1	1.1
7	1.0	1.1	1.1	1.1	1.1
8	1.1	1.1	1.1	1.1	1.1
9	1.1	1.1	1.1	1.1	1.2

Drawing.

One gap suiteds

75s

Opponents	Mega-Tight	Tight	Loose	Very Loose	Mega-Loose
1	0.7	0.8	0.8	0.8	0.8
2	0.8	0.8	0.8	0.9	0.9
3	0.9	0.9	0.9	0.9	0.9
4	0.9	0.9	0.9	1.0	1.0
5	1.0	1.0	1.0	1.0	1.0
6	1.1	1.1	1.1	1.1	1.1
7	1.1	1.1	1.1	1.1	1.1
8	1.1	1.1	1.1	1.1	1.1
9	1.1	1.1	1.1	1.1	1.1

Marginal draw.

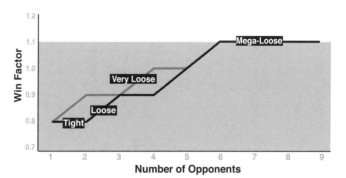

64s

Opponents	Mega-Tight	Tight	Loose	Very Loose	Mega-Loose
1	0.7	0.7	0.8	0.8	0.8
2	0.8	0.8	0.8	0.8	0.8
3	0.8	0.9	0.9	0.9	0.9
4	1.0	1.0	1.0	0.9	0.9
5	1.0	1.0	1.0	1.0	1.0
6	1.0	1.0	1.0	1.0	1.0
7	1.0	1.0	1.0	1.0	1.0
8	1.1	1.1	1.1	1.1	1.1
9	1.1	1.1	1.1	1.1	1.1

Marginal draw.

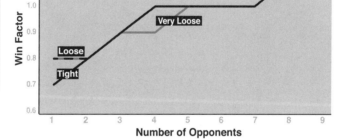

53s

Opponents	Mega-Tight	Tight	Loose	Very Loose	Mega-Loose
1	0.7	0.7	0.8	0.8	0.8
2	0.8	0.8	0.8	0.8	0.8
3	0.8	0.8	0.8	0.8	0.8
4	1.0	0.9	0.9	0.9	0.9
5	1.0	1.0	1.0	1.0	1.0
6	1.1	1.1	1.0	1.0	1.0
7	1.1	1.1	1.1	1.1	1.0
8	1.1	1.1	1.1	1.1	1.1
9	1.1	1.1	1.1	1.1	1.1

Marginal draw.

Two gap suiteds

AJs

Opponents	Mega-Tight	Tight	Loose	Very Loose	Mega-Loose
1	1.2	1.2	1.3	1.3	1.3
2	1.2	1.3	1.4	1.4	1.4
3	1.2	1.3	1.4	1.4	1.5
4	1.2	1.3	1.4	1.5	1.6
5	1.2	1.3	1.4	1.5	1.6
6	1.2	1.3	1.4	1.5	1.6
7	1.2	1.3	1.4	1.5	1.7
8	1.2	1.3	1.4	1.5	1.7
9	1.2	1.3	1.4	1.6	1.7

Strong draw.

KTs

Opponents	Mega-Tight	Tight	Loose	Very Loose	Mega-Loose
1	1.0	1.1	1.1	1.2	1.2
2	1.0	1.1	1.2	1.2	1.3
3	1.0	1.1	1.2	1.3	1.4
4	1.0	1.2	1.3	1.4	1.4
5	1.0	1.2	1.3	1.4	1.4
6	1.0	1.2	1.3	1.4	1.5
7	1.0	1.2	1.3	1.4	1.5
8	1.0	1.2	1.3	1.4	1.5
9	1.0	1.2	1.4	1.5	1.5

Good draw.

Q9s

Opponents	Mega-Tight	Tight	Loose	Very Loose	Mega-Loose
1	0.9	1.0	1.0	1.1	1.1
2	0.9	1.0	1.1	1.1	1.1
3	0.9	1.0	1.1	1.2	1.2
4	0.9	1.1	1.1	1.2	1.3
5	0.9	1.1	1.1	1.2	1.3
6	0.8	1.1	1.2	1.3	1.3
7	0.8	1.1	1.2	1.3	1.3
8	0.8	1.2	1.2	1.3	1.3
9	0.7	1.2	1.2	1.3	1.3

Good draw.

Two gap suiteds

J8s

Opponents	Mega-Tight	Tight	Loose	Very Loose	Mega-Loose
1	0.8	0.9	1.0	1.0	1.0
2	0.8	0.9	1.0	1.0	1.1
3	0.8	0.9	1.0	1.0	1.1
4	0.8	1.0	1.0	1.1	1.1
5	0.9	1.0	1.0	1.1	1.1
6	0.9	1.0	1.1	1.1	1.2
7	0.9	1.0	1.1	1.1	1.2
8	0.9	1.0	1.1	1.1	1.2
9	0.9	1.0	1.1	1.1	1.2

Drawing.

T7s

Opponents	Mega-Tight	Tight	Loose	Very Loose	Mega-Loose
1	0.8	0.8	0.9	0.9	1.0
2	0.8	0.9	0.9	1.0	1.0
3	0.8	0.9	1.0	1.0	1.0
4	0.9	0.9	1.0	1.0	1.1
5	0.8	1.0	1.0	1.1	1.1
6	0.8	1.0	1.0	1.1	1.1
7	0.9	1.0	1.0	1.1	1.1
8	0.9	1.0	1.0	1.1	1.2
9	0.9	1.0	1.0	1.1	1.2

Drawing.

96s

Opponents	Mega-Tight	Tight	Loose	Very Loose	Mega-Loose
1	0.7	0.8	0.9	0.9	0.9
2	0.8	0.8	0.9	0.9	0.9
3	0.8	0.8	0.9	0.9	1.0
4	0.9	0.9	0.9	1.0	1.0
5	0.9	0.9	1.0	1.0	1.0
6	1.0	1.0	1.0	1.0	1.1
7	1.0	1.0	1.0	1.0	1.1
8	1.0	1.0	1.1	1.1	1.1
9	1.0	1.0	1.1	1.1	1.1

Marginal draw.

Two gap suiteds

85s

Opponents	Mega-Tight	Tight	Loose	Very Loose	Mega-Loose
1	0.7	0.8	0.8	0.8	0.9
2	0.8	0.8	0.8	0.8	0.9
3	0.8	0.8	0.8	0.9	0.9
4	0.9	0.9	0.9	0.9	1.0
5	0.9	1.0	1.0	1.0	1.0
6	0.9	1.0	1.0	1.0	1.0
7	0.9	1.0	1.0	1.0	1.0
8	1.0	1.0	1.1	1.1	1.1
9	1.0	1.1	1.1	1.1	1.1

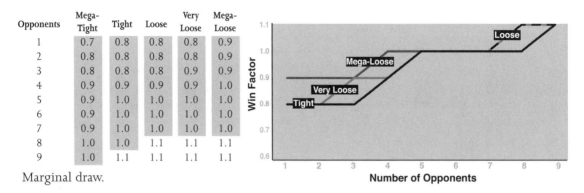

Marginal draw.

74s

Opponents	Mega-Tight	Tight	Loose	Very Loose	Mega-Loose
1	0.7	0.7	0.8	0.8	0.8
2	0.8	0.8	0.8	0.8	0.8
3	0.8	0.8	0.8	0.8	0.8
4	0.9	0.9	0.9	0.9	0.9
5	0.9	0.9	0.9	0.9	0.9
6	1.0	1.0	1.0	0.9	0.9
7	1.0	1.0	1.0	1.0	1.0
8	1.0	1.0	1.0	1.0	1.0
9	1.0	1.0	1.0	1.0	1.1

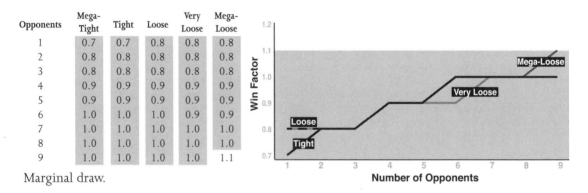

Marginal draw.

63s

Opponents	Mega-Tight	Tight	Loose	Very Loose	Mega-Loose
1	0.7	0.7	0.7	0.8	0.8
2	0.8	0.8	0.8	0.8	0.8
3	0.8	0.8	0.8	0.8	0.8
4	0.9	0.9	0.9	0.9	0.9
5	1.0	0.9	0.9	0.9	0.9
6	1.0	1.0	0.9	0.9	0.9
7	1.0	1.0	1.0	1.0	1.0
8	1.0	1.0	1.0	1.0	1.0
9	1.0	1.0	1.0	1.0	1.0

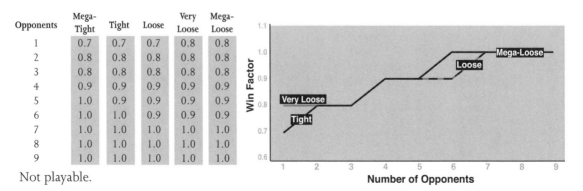

Not playable.

Three gap suiteds

ATs

Opponents	Mega-Tight	Tight	Loose	Very Loose	Mega-Loose
1	1.1	1.2	1.2	1.3	1.3
2	1.1	1.2	1.3	1.4	1.4
3	1.1	1.2	1.3	1.4	1.4
4	1.1	1.3	1.4	1.4	1.5
5	1.1	1.3	1.4	1.4	1.5
6	1.1	1.3	1.4	1.4	1.5
7	1.1	1.3	1.4	1.4	1.6
8	1.1	1.3	1.4	1.5	1.6
9	1.1	1.3	1.4	1.5	1.6

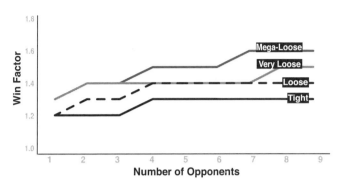

Good draw.

K9s

Opponents	Mega-Tight	Tight	Loose	Very Loose	Mega-Loose
1	0.9	1.0	1.1	1.1	1.2
2	0.9	1.0	1.1	1.2	1.2
3	0.9	1.0	1.1	1.2	1.2
4	1.0	1.1	1.2	1.2	1.3
5	1.0	1.1	1.2	1.3	1.3
6	0.9	1.1	1.2	1.3	1.3
7	0.9	1.1	1.2	1.3	1.4
8	0.9	1.1	1.2	1.3	1.4
9	0.9	1.1	1.3	1.3	1.4

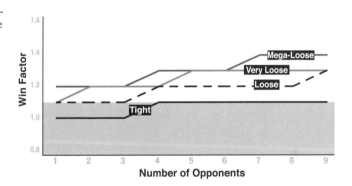

Good draw.

Q8s

Opponents	Mega-Tight	Tight	Loose	Very Loose	Mega-Loose
1	0.8	0.9	1.0	1.0	1.1
2	0.8	0.9	1.0	1.1	1.1
3	0.8	1.0	1.0	1.1	1.1
4	0.9	1.0	1.0	1.1	1.1
5	0.9	1.0	1.1	1.1	1.1
6	0.9	1.0	1.1	1.1	1.2
7	0.9	1.0	1.1	1.1	1.2
8	0.9	1.0	1.1	1.2	1.2
9	0.9	1.0	1.1	1.2	1.2

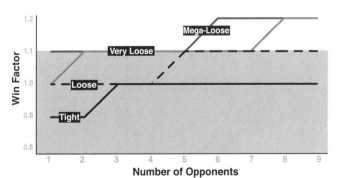

Drawing.

Three gap suiteds

J7s

Opponents	Mega-Tight	Tight	Loose	Very Loose	Mega-Loose
1	0.8	0.9	0.9	1.0	1.0
2	0.8	0.9	0.9	1.0	1.0
3	0.8	0.9	0.9	1.0	1.0
4	0.8	0.9	1.0	1.0	1.1
5	0.8	0.9	1.0	1.0	1.1
6	0.8	0.9	1.0	1.1	1.1
7	0.8	1.0	1.0	1.1	1.1
8	0.8	1.0	1.0	1.1	1.1
9	0.9	1.0	1.0	1.1	1.1

Marginal draw.

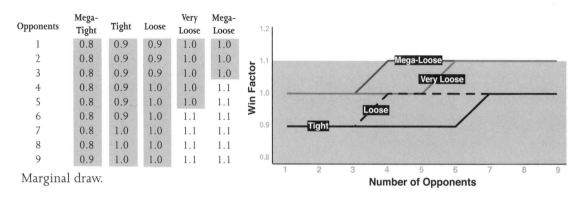

Connectors unsuited

AK

Opponents	Mega-Tight	Tight	Loose	Very Loose	Mega-Loose
1	1.2	1.3	1.3	1.3	1.3
2	1.3	1.4	1.4	1.4	1.4
3	1.3	1.4	1.4	1.5	1.5
4	1.2	1.4	1.5	1.5	1.6
5	1.1	1.3	1.5	1.5	1.6
6	1.1	1.3	1.5	1.5	1.6
7	1.1	1.2	1.4	1.5	1.6
8	1.1	1.2	1.4	1.4	1.6
9	1.1	1.1	1.3	1.4	1.5

Good drawing.

KQ

Opponents	Mega-Tight	Tight	Loose	Very Loose	Mega-Loose
1	1.0	1.1	1.2	1.2	1.2
2	1.0	1.1	1.2	1.2	1.3
3	1.0	1.1	1.2	1.3	1.3
4	1.0	1.1	1.2	1.3	1.4
5	1.0	1.1	1.2	1.3	1.4
6	1.0	1.1	1.2	1.3	1.4
7	1.0	1.1	1.2	1.3	1.4
8	1.0	1.0	1.2	1.3	1.4
9	1.0	1.0	1.1	1.3	1.4

Good drawing.

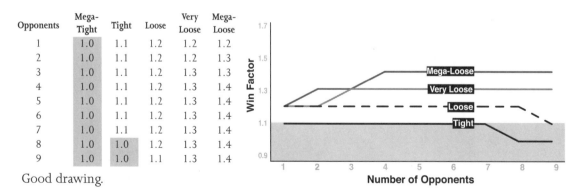

Connectors unsuited

QJ

Opponents	Mega-Tight	Tight	Loose	Very Loose	Mega-Loose
1	0.9	1.0	1.1	1.1	1.1
2	0.9	1.0	1.1	1.1	1.2
3	0.9	1.0	1.1	1.2	1.2
4	0.8	1.0	1.1	1.2	1.3
5	0.7	1.0	1.1	1.2	1.3
6	0.7	1.0	1.1	1.2	1.3
7	0.7	1.0	1.1	1.2	1.3
8	0.7	0.8	1.1	1.2	1.3
9	0.7	0.8	1.0	1.1	1.2

Drawing.

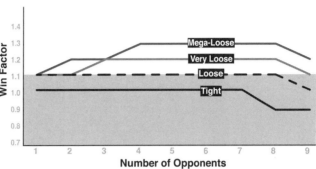

JT

Opponents	Mega-Tight	Tight	Loose	Very Loose	Mega-Loose
1	0.8	0.9	1.0	1.0	1.1
2	0.8	0.9	1.0	1.1	1.1
3	0.8	0.9	1.0	1.1	1.2
4	0.8	0.9	1.1	1.1	1.2
5	0.8	0.9	1.1	1.1	1.2
6	0.8	0.9	1.1	1.1	1.2
7	0.7	0.9	1.0	1.1	1.2
8	0.7	0.9	1.0	1.1	1.2
9	0.7	0.9	1.0	1.1	1.2

Drawing.

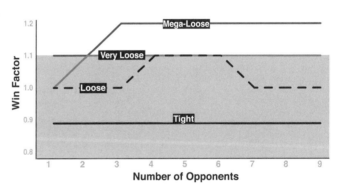

T9

Opponents	Mega-Tight	Tight	Loose	Very Loose	Mega-Loose
1	0.8	0.8	0.9	1.0	1.0
2	0.8	0.8	0.9	1.0	1.0
3	0.8	0.8	0.9	1.0	1.0
4	0.8	0.9	0.9	1.0	1.0
5	0.8	0.8	0.9	1.0	1.0
6	0.7	0.8	0.9	1.0	1.0
7	0.7	0.9	0.9	1.0	1.0
8	0.7	0.9	0.9	1.0	1.0
9	0.7	0.9	0.9	1.0	1.0

Not playable.

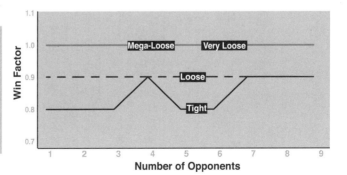

Connectors unsuited

98

Opponents	Mega-Tight	Tight	Loose	Very Loose	Mega-Loose
1	0.8	0.8	0.9	0.9	0.9
2	0.8	0.8	0.9	0.9	0.9
3	0.8	0.8	0.9	0.9	0.9
4	0.8	0.8	0.9	0.9	1.0
5	0.8	0.8	0.9	0.9	1.0
6	0.8	0.8	0.9	0.9	1.0
7	0.8	0.8	0.9	0.9	1.0
8	0.8	0.8	0.9	0.9	1.0
9	0.8	0.8	0.8	0.9	1.0

Not playable.

One gap unsuited

AQ

Opponents	Mega-Tight	Tight	Loose	Very Loose	Mega-Loose
1	1.2	1.2	1.3	1.3	1.3
2	1.2	1.2	1.3	1.4	1.4
3	1.1	1.2	1.3	1.4	1.4
4	1.1	1.2	1.3	1.4	1.5
5	1.1	1.2	1.3	1.4	1.5
6	1.1	1.1	1.3	1.4	1.5
7	1.0	1.1	1.2	1.4	1.4
8	1.0	1.1	1.2	1.4	1.4
9	1.0	1.0	1.1	1.3	1.4

Good drawing.

KJ

Opponents	Mega-Tight	Tight	Loose	Very Loose	Mega-Loose
1	1.0	1.1	1.1	1.2	1.2
2	0.9	1.1	1.1	1.2	1.2
3	0.9	1.1	1.2	1.2	1.3
4	0.9	1.1	1.2	1.2	1.3
5	0.8	1.0	1.1	1.2	1.3
6	0.8	1.0	1.1	1.2	1.3
7	0.7	1.0	1.1	1.2	1.3
8	0.7	0.9	1.1	1.2	1.3
9	0.7	0.9	1.0	1.1	1.2

Drawing.

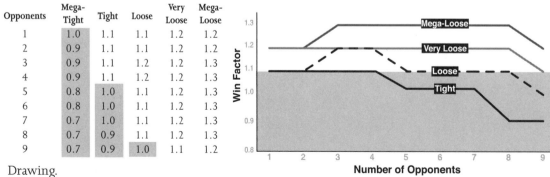

One gap unsuited

QT

Opponents	Mega-Tight	Tight	Loose	Very Loose	Mega-Loose
1	0.9	0.9	1.0	1.1	1.1
2	0.8	0.9	1.0	1.1	1.1
3	0.8	0.9	1.0	1.1	1.2
4	0.8	0.9	1.0	1.1	1.2
5	0.7	0.9	1.0	1.1	1.2
6	0.7	0.9	1.0	1.1	1.2
7	0.6	0.9	1.0	1.1	1.2
8	0.6	0.8	1.0	1.1	1.2
9	0.6	0.8	1.0	1.1	1.2

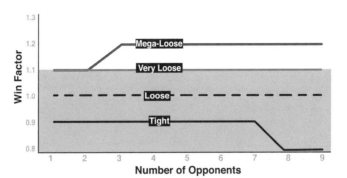

Drawing.

J9

Opponents	Mega-Tight	Tight	Loose	Very Loose	Mega-Loose
1	0.8	0.9	0.9	1.0	1.0
2	0.8	0.8	0.9	1.0	1.0
3	0.8	0.8	0.9	1.0	1.0
4	0.7	0.8	0.9	1.0	1.0
5	0.7	0.8	0.9	1.0	1.0
6	0.7	0.8	0.9	1.0	1.0
7	0.7	0.7	0.9	1.0	1.0
8	0.7	0.7	0.9	0.9	1.0
9	0.7	0.7	0.8	0.9	1.0

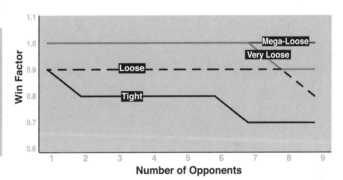

Not playable.

T8

Opponents	Mega-Tight	Tight	Loose	Very Loose	Mega-Loose
1	0.7	0.8	0.8	0.9	0.9
2	0.7	0.8	0.8	0.9	0.9
3	0.7	0.8	0.8	0.9	1.0
4	0.7	0.8	0.8	0.9	1.0
5	0.7	0.8	0.8	0.9	1.0
6	0.7	0.8	0.8	0.9	1.0
7	0.7	0.8	0.8	0.9	1.0
8	0.7	0.8	0.8	0.9	1.0
9	0.7	0.8	0.8	0.9	1.0

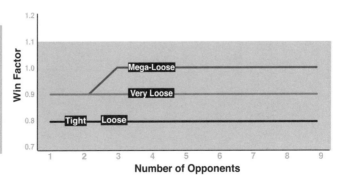

Not playable.

Two gaps unsuited

AJ

Opponents	Mega-Tight	Tight	Loose	Very Loose	Mega-Loose
1	1.1	1.2	1.2	1.2	1.3
2	1.1	1.2	1.3	1.3	1.3
3	1.0	1.2	1.3	1.3	1.4
4	1.0	1.1	1.3	1.3	1.4
5	0.9	1.1	1.2	1.3	1.4
6	0.8	1.1	1.1	1.2	1.4
7	0.8	1.0	1.1	1.1	1.4
8	0.8	1.0	1.1	1.1	1.2
9	0.8	0.9	1.0	1.1	1.2

Drawing.

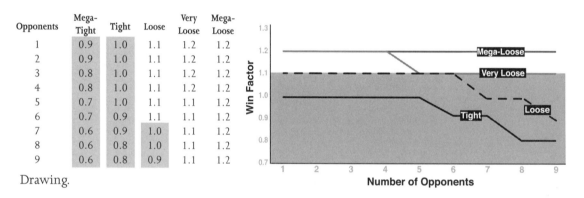

KT

Opponents	Mega-Tight	Tight	Loose	Very Loose	Mega-Loose
1	0.9	1.0	1.1	1.2	1.2
2	0.9	1.0	1.1	1.2	1.2
3	0.8	1.0	1.1	1.2	1.2
4	0.8	1.0	1.1	1.2	1.2
5	0.7	1.0	1.1	1.1	1.2
6	0.7	0.9	1.1	1.1	1.2
7	0.6	0.9	1.0	1.1	1.2
8	0.6	0.8	1.0	1.1	1.2
9	0.6	0.8	0.9	1.1	1.2

Drawing.

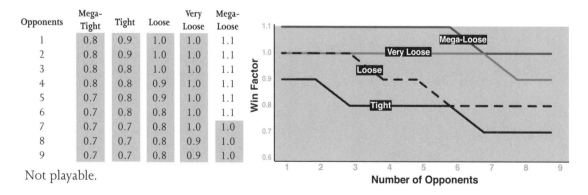

Q9

Opponents	Mega-Tight	Tight	Loose	Very Loose	Mega-Loose
1	0.8	0.9	1.0	1.0	1.1
2	0.8	0.9	1.0	1.0	1.1
3	0.8	0.8	1.0	1.0	1.1
4	0.8	0.8	0.9	1.0	1.1
5	0.7	0.8	0.9	1.0	1.1
6	0.7	0.8	0.8	1.0	1.1
7	0.7	0.7	0.8	1.0	1.0
8	0.7	0.7	0.8	0.9	1.0
9	0.7	0.7	0.8	0.9	1.0

Not playable.

Pairs

AA

Opponents	Mega-Tight	Tight	Loose	Very Loose	Mega-Loose
1	1.7	1.7	1.7	1.7	1.7
2	2.2	2.2	2.2	2.2	2.2
3	2.5	2.5	2.5	2.5	2.5
4	2.7	2.7	2.7	2.8	2.8
5	2.8	2.8	2.8	2.9	2.9
6	2.8	2.9	2.9	2.9	3.0
7	2.8	3.0	3.0	3.0	3.0
8	2.8	2.9	2.9	3.0	3.0
9	2.8	2.8	2.8	2.9	3.0

Monster.

KK

Opponents	Mega-Tight	Tight	Loose	Very Loose	Mega-Loose
1	1.6	1.6	1.6	1.6	1.6
2	1.9	2.0	2.0	2.0	2.0
3	2.1	2.2	2.2	2.2	2.3
4	2.2	2.3	2.4	2.4	2.4
5	2.3	2.3	2.4	2.5	2.5
6	2.3	2.3	2.4	2.5	2.5
7	2.3	2.3	2.4	2.5	2.5
8	2.2	2.3	2.3	2.4	2.5
9	2.0	2.2	2.3	2.4	2.5

Monster.

QQ

Opponents	Mega-Tight	Tight	Loose	Very Loose	Mega-Loose
1	1.4	1.5	1.5	1.6	1.6
2	1.7	1.7	1.8	1.9	1.9
3	1.7	1.9	2.0	2.0	2.0
4	1.8	2.0	2.0	2.1	2.2
5	1.8	1.9	2.0	2.1	2.2
6	1.8	1.9	2.0	2.1	2.2
7	1.8	1.9	2.0	2.1	2.2
8	1.7	1.9	2.0	2.1	2.1
9	1.7	1.9	2.0	2.1	2.1

Premium.

Pairs

JJ

Opponents	Mega-Tight	Tight	Loose	Very Loose	Mega-Loose
1	1.3	1.4	1.5	1.5	1.5
2	1.4	1.6	1.7	1.7	1.8
3	1.5	1.6	1.8	1.8	1.9
4	1.5	1.7	1.8	1.9	1.9
5	1.5	1.7	1.7	1.8	1.9
6	1.5	1.7	1.7	1.8	1.9
7	1.5	1.6	1.7	1.8	1.8
8	1.5	1.6	1.7	1.7	1.8
9	1.5	1.6	1.7	1.7	1.8

Premium.

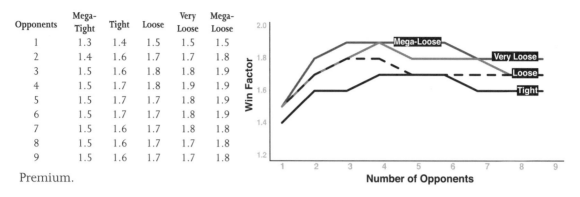

TT

Opponents	Mega-Tight	Tight	Loose	Very Loose	Mega-Loose
1	1.3	1.3	1.4	1.4	1.5
2	1.3	1.4	1.6	1.6	1.7
3	1.3	1.4	1.6	1.6	1.7
4	1.3	1.5	1.6	1.6	1.7
5	1.3	1.5	1.6	1.6	1.7
6	1.3	1.5	1.5	1.5	1.7
7	1.4	1.4	1.5	1.5	1.6
8	1.4	1.4	1.5	1.5	1.6
9	1.3	1.4	1.5	1.5	1.6

Strong.

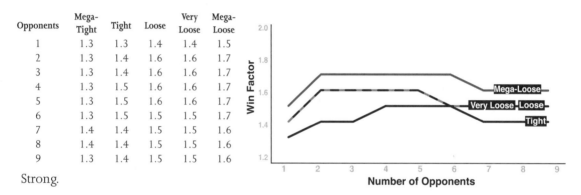

99

Opponents	Mega-Tight	Tight	Loose	Very Loose	Mega-Loose
1	1.2	1.3	1.3	1.4	1.4
2	1.2	1.3	1.4	1.5	1.5
3	1.2	1.3	1.4	1.5	1.6
4	1.2	1.3	1.4	1.5	1.6
5	1.2	1.3	1.4	1.4	1.5
6	1.2	1.3	1.4	1.4	1.5
7	1.2	1.3	1.4	1.4	1.5
8	1.2	1.4	1.4	1.4	1.5
9	1.2	1.4	1.4	1.4	1.5

Good draw.

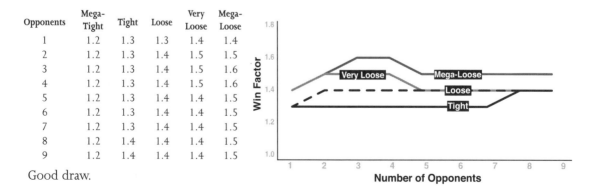

Pairs

88

Opponents	Mega-Tight	Tight	Loose	Very Loose	Mega-Loose
1	1.1	1.2	1.3	1.3	1.3
2	1.1	1.2	1.3	1.4	1.4
3	1.1	1.2	1.3	1.4	1.4
4	1.1	1.2	1.3	1.4	1.4
5	1.1	1.2	1.3	1.4	1.4
6	1.2	1.2	1.3	1.4	1.4
7	1.2	1.3	1.3	1.4	1.4
8	1.2	1.3	1.3	1.4	1.4
9	1.2	1.3	1.3	1.4	1.4

Good draw.

77

Opponents	Mega-Tight	Tight	Loose	Very Loose	Mega-Loose
1	1.0	1.1	1.2	1.3	1.3
2	1.0	1.1	1.2	1.3	1.3
3	1.0	1.1	1.2	1.3	1.3
4	1.1	1.1	1.2	1.3	1.3
5	1.1	1.1	1.2	1.3	1.3
6	1.1	1.2	1.2	1.3	1.3
7	1.1	1.2	1.2	1.3	1.3
8	1.1	1.3	1.3	1.3	1.3
9	1.2	1.3	1.3	1.3	1.3

Good draw.

66

Opponents	Mega-Tight	Tight	Loose	Very Loose	Mega-Loose
1	1.0	1.1	1.1	1.2	1.2
2	1.0	1.1	1.1	1.2	1.2
3	1.0	1.1	1.1	1.2	1.2
4	1.0	1.1	1.1	1.2	1.2
5	1.1	1.1	1.1	1.2	1.2
6	1.1	1.2	1.2	1.2	1.2
7	1.2	1.2	1.2	1.2	1.2
8	1.2	1.3	1.3	1.3	1.3
9	1.2	1.3	1.3	1.3	1.3

Good draw.

55

Opponents	Mega-Tight	Tight	Loose	Very Loose	Mega-Loose
1	1.0	1.0	1.1	1.1	1.1
2	1.0	1.0	1.1	1.1	1.1
3	1.0	1.0	1.1	1.1	1.1
4	1.0	1.0	1.1	1.1	1.1
5	1.1	1.1	1.1	1.1	1.1
6	1.1	1.1	1.1	1.1	1.1
7	1.2	1.2	1.2	1.1	1.2
8	1.3	1.3	1.3	1.2	1.2
9	1.3	1.3	1.3	1.3	1.3

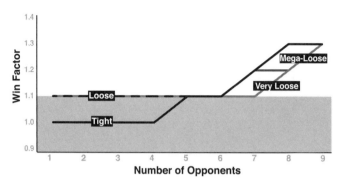

Good draw.

44

Opponents	Mega-Tight	Tight	Loose	Very Loose	Mega-Loose
1	0.9	1.0	1.0	1.0	1.1
2	0.9	1.0	1.0	1.0	1.1
3	0.9	1.0	1.0	1.0	1.1
4	1.0	1.0	1.0	1.0	1.1
5	1.0	1.0	1.0	1.0	1.1
6	1.1	1.1	1.1	1.1	1.1
7	1.1	1.2	1.2	1.1	1.1
8	1.3	1.3	1.3	1.2	1.2
9	1.3	1.3	1.3	1.3	1.3

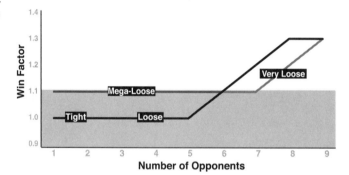

Good draw.

Pairs

33

Opponents	Mega-Tight	Tight	Loose	Very Loose	Mega-Loose
1	0.9	0.9	0.9	0.9	1.0
2	0.9	0.9	1.0	1.0	1.0
3	0.9	1.0	1.0	1.0	1.0
4	1.0	1.0	1.0	1.0	1.0
5	1.0	1.0	1.0	1.0	1.0
6	1.1	1.1	1.1	1.1	1.1
7	1.1	1.1	1.1	1.1	1.1
8	1.3	1.3	1.3	1.2	1.2
9	1.3	1.3	1.3	1.3	1.3

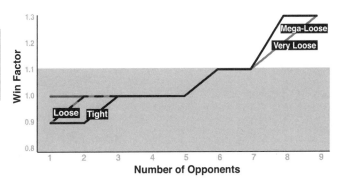

Good draw.

22

Opponents	Mega-Tight	Tight	Loose	Very Loose	Mega-Loose
1	0.9	0.9	0.9	0.9	0.9
2	0.9	0.9	0.9	0.9	0.9
3	0.9	0.9	0.9	0.9	0.9
4	0.9	0.9	0.9	0.9	0.9
5	1.0	1.0	1.0	1.0	1.0
6	1.1	1.1	1.1	1.1	1.1
7	1.1	1.1	1.1	1.1	1.1
8	1.3	1.3	1.2	1.2	1.2
9	1.3	1.3	1.3	1.3	1.3

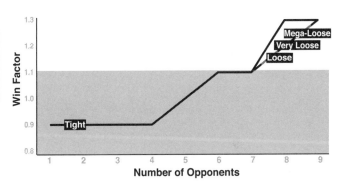

Good draw.

Extremely marginal draws

How could any sane author tell you there are times when you can play "Bozo" hands such as 74s, K3s, K2s and Q7s and lower? Admittedly these hands are only slightly better than a coin flip, but that's what the research shows. In a few pages you will see how infrequently these hands may be played.

Win Factors do not include ties

The Win Factor represents the relative probability of a hand winning. It does not include the probability of a tie. If ties were included, there are some hands where the Win Factors would be increased by 0.1.

Win Factor summary

- There is a difference between making your hand and winning the hand.
- Win Factors have been developed for all starting hands.
- Win Factors take into account how tight/loose the table is and your number of opponents.
- An adjustment for the rake brings the minimum playable Win Factor to 1.1.
- The charts show how the same hand's Win Factors change depending on how tight/loose the table is and how many opponents are dealt cards.

Homework

- Learn every Win Factor for every hand. No small task.

Part III — Win Factor adjustments for position

Hold'em is position

Hold'em is a game of position. Hold'em is just like real estate. Location, location, location. All the experts emphasize the importance of position in hold'em. Negreanu's words are best: "**Position is power.**" Position can do the work betting does. You may get some free cards. Good position gives you the most information; it allows you to control the hand and the size of the pot. In no limit, the player who controls the pot size is the one who can manipulate equity with his bets. When you are in early position it is like running up a down escalator; late position is as easy as using an elevator.

The earlier your position, the fewer hands you may play. The later, the more.

A few of the finer points.

> The power of position increases as the number of players in the hand dwindles.

> Position is worth more at a tight table than a loose one. "**I'd rather have position than cards**," says Charlie Kline. He is right, especially at a tight table with few opponents. Position without card strength isn't worth nearly as much at a loose table.

> Position is strongest during the early rounds of betting and loses some, but certainly not all, power on the turn and river. On the river, if out of position, especially in no limit, generally you are better off check-calling than betting out. We'll get into more depth on this topic in the Betting Chapter.

This section makes adjustments for position in conjunction with tightness/looseness; then, in the next portion we factor in aggressiveness. To facilitate the corrections, only WFs are used. We could have shown all the individual hands but that is very cumbersome; so WFs are used for now, but later in this chapter we will turn the WFs back into specific hands.

It is not necessary that you thoroughly study the charts presented in this section. They are included so you understand how we arrived at the hands you may consider playing. Later in this chapter we have published the hands for 6- and 10-handed tables. If you usually play at a different size table, you may use the figures presented in this section to derive your own set of WFs using this section as a guide.

Playable Win Factors, 10-handed adjusted for the number of opponents, tight/loose, rake and position.

Tight table (Opponents play 35% of their hands)

Button	Seat 9	Seat 8	Seat 7	Seat 6	Seat 5	Seat 4	Seat 3	Big blind	Small blind
1.8+	1.8+	1.8+	1.8+	1.8+	1.8+	1.8+	1.8+		1.8+
1.7	1.7	1.7	1.7	1.7	1.7	1.7	1.7		1.7
1.6	1.6	1.6	1.6	1.6	1.6	1.6	1.6		1.6
1.5	1.5	1.5	1.5	1.5	1.5	1.5	1.5		1.5
1.4	1.4	1.4	1.4	1.4	1.4				1.4
1.3	1.3	1.3	1.3						1.3
1.2	1.2	1.2	1.2						1.2
1.1	1.1								1.1

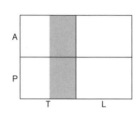

Loose table (Opponents play 50% of their hands)

Button	Seat 9	Seat 8	Seat 7	Seat 6	Seat 5	Seat 4	Seat 3	Big blind	Small blind
1.8+	1.8+	1.8+	1.8+	1.8+	1.8+	1.8+	1.8+		1.8+
1.7	1.7	1.7	1.7	1.7	1.7	1.7	1.7		1.7
1.6	1.6	1.6	1.6	1.6	1.6	1.6	1.6		1.6
1.5	1.5	1.5	1.5	1.5	1.5	1.5	1.5		1.5
1.4	1.4	1.4	1.4	1.4	1.4	1.4	1.4		1.4
1.3	1.3	1.3	1.3	1.3	1.3				1.3
1.2	1.2	1.2	1.2						1.2
1.1	1.1								1.1

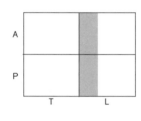

Very Loose table (Opponents play 65% of their hands)

Button	Seat 9	Seat 8	Seat 7	Seat 6	Seat 5	Seat 4	Seat 3	Big blind	Small blind
1.8+	1.8+	1.8+	1.8+	1.8+	1.8+	1.8+	1.8+		1.8+
1.7	1.7	1.7	1.7	1.7	1.7	1.7	1.7		1.7
1.6	1.6	1.6	1.6	1.6	1.6	1.6	1.6		1.6
1.5	1.5	1.5	1.5	1.5	1.5	1.5	1.5		1.5
1.4	1.4	1.4	1.4	1.4	1.4	1.4	1.4		1.4
1.3	1.3	1.3	1.3	1.3	1.3				1.3
1.2	1.2	1.2	1.2						1.2
1.1	1.1	1.1	1.1						1.1

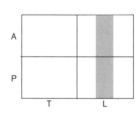

Mega-Loose table (Opponents play 80% of their hands)

Button	Seat 9	Seat 8	Seat 7	Seat 6	Seat 5	Seat 4	Seat 3	Big blind	Small blind
1.8+	1.8+	1.8+	1.8+	1.8+	1.8+	1.8+	1.8+		1.8+
1.7	1.7	1.7	1.7	1.7	1.7	1.7	1.7		1.7
1.6	1.6	1.6	1.6	1.6	1.6	1.6	1.6		1.6
1.5	1.5	1.5	1.5	1.5	1.5	1.5	1.5		1.5
1.4	1.4	1.4	1.4	1.4	1.4	1.4	1.4		1.4
1.3	1.3	1.3	1.3	1.3	1.3	1.3	1.3		1.3
1.2	1.2	1.2	1.2	1.2	1.2	1.2	1.2		1.2
1.1	1.1	1.1	1.1	1.1	1.1	1.1	1.1		1.1

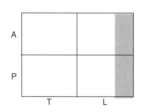

Figure 9.3.a

Playable Win Factors, 6-handed, adjusted for the number of opponents, tight/loose, rake and position.

Tight table (Opponents play 35% of their hands)

Button	Seat 5	Seat 4	Seat 3	Big blind	Small blind
1.8+	1.8+	1.8+	1.8+		1.8+
1.7	1.7	1.7	1.7		1.7
1.6	1.6	1.6	1.6		1.6
1.5	1.5	1.5			1.5
1.4	1.4	1.4			1.4
1.3	1.3	1.3			1.3
1.2	1.2				1.2
1.1	1.1				1.1

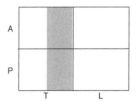

Loose table (Opponents play 50% of their hands)

Button	Seat 5	Seat 4	Seat 3	Big blind	Small blind
1.8+	1.8+	1.8+	1.8+		1.8+
1.7	1.7	1.7	1.7		1.7
1.6	1.6	1.6	1.6		1.6
1.5	1.5	1.5	1.5		1.5
1.4	1.4	1.4			1.4
1.3	1.3	1.3			1.3
1.2	1.2				1.2
1.1	1.1				1.1

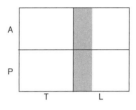

Very loose table (Opponents play 65% of their hands)

Button	Seat 5	Seat 4	Seat 3	Big blind	Small blind
1.8+	1.8+	1.8+	1.8+		1.8+
1.7	1.7	1.7	1.7		1.7
1.6	1.6	1.6	1.6		1.6
1.5	1.5	1.5	1.5		1.5
1.4	1.4	1.4	1.4		1.4
1.3	1.3	1.3	1.3		1.3
1.2	1.2				1.2
1.1	1.1				1.1

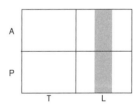

Mega-Loose table (Opponents play 80% of their hands)

Button	Seat 5	Seat 4	Seat 3	Big blind	Small blind
1.8+	1.8+	1.8+	1.8+		1.8+
1.7	1.7	1.7	1.7		1.7
1.6	1.6	1.6	1.6		1.6
1.5	1.5	1.5	1.5		1.5
1.4	1.4	1.4	1.4		1.4
1.3	1.3	1.3	1.3		1.3
1.2	1.2	1.2	1.2		1.2
1.1	1.1	1.1	1.1		1.1

Figure 9.3.b

Figures 9.3.a and 9.3.b show position adjustments for a 10-handed game and a 6-handed game respectively. As you would expect, the earlier your position, the fewer hands you may play, and conversely, the later your position, the more hands you may play.

Position summary

• Position is more important than card strength.
• The earlier your position, the fewer hands you may play; the later, the more.
• At this point hands have been turned into WFs. Adjustments have been made for the number of opponents, how tight or loose the table is, and for position.

Homework

• Review 9.3.a-b to see how position affects the playable WFs.

Part IV — Win Factor adjustments for passive/aggressive

Passive/aggressive adjustments

The more aggressive the table, the fewer hands you may play. More passive means more playable hands.

Figures 9.4.a.a-d are 10-handed tables, from Tight through Mega-Loose, with the appropriate adjustments for aggressiveness. Figures 9.4.b.a-d are 6-handed tables, from Tight through Mega-Loose, with adjustments for aggressiveness.

The figures on the next few pages represent the WFs of hands after taking into account the following criteria:

▸ How loose or tight the table is	The percentage of hands others at the table tend to play.
▸ How passive or aggressive the table is	The amount of calling or raising at your table.
▸ Your card strength	How good your hand is.
▸ Number of opponents	Means just that. The number of other players dealt cards.
▸ Position	Where you are seated relative to the dealer.
▸ The horse	Taking into account where you are seated relative to the last player to act, called the horse, and his playing style.
▸ Pot size	How much money is in the pot.

Playable Win Factors, 10-handed, adjusted for the number of opponents, tight/loose, rake, position, and passive/aggressive

Tight table (Opponents play 35% of their hands) **Very Aggressive**

Button	Seat 9	Seat 8	Seat 7	Seat 6	Seat 5	Seat 4	Seat 3	Big blind	Small blind
1.8+	1.8+	1.8+	1.8+	1.8+	1.8+	1.8+	1.8+		1.8+
1.7	1.7	1.7	1.7						1.7
1.6	1.6								1.6
1.5	1.5								1.5

A / P / T / L

Tight table (Opponents play 35% of their hands) **Aggressive**

Button	Seat 9	Seat 8	Seat 7	Seat 6	Seat 5	Seat 4	Seat 3	Big blind	Small blind
1.8+	1.8+	1.8+	1.8+	1.8+	1.8+	1.8+	1.8+		1.8+
1.7	1.7	1.7	1.7	1.7	1.7	1.7	1.7		1.7
1.6	1.6	1.6	1.6	1.6	1.6				1.6
1.5	1.5	1.5	1.5						1.5
1.4	1.4	1.4	1.4						1.4
1.3	1.3								1.3

A / P / T / L

Tight table (Opponents play 35% of their hands) **Passive**

Button	Seat 9	Seat 8	Seat 7	Seat 6	Seat 5	Seat 4	Seat 3	Big blind	Small blind
1.8+	1.8+	1.8+	1.8+	1.8+	1.8+	1.8+	1.8+		1.8+
1.7	1.7	1.7	1.7	1.7	1.7	1.7	1.7		1.7
1.6	1.6	1.6	1.6	1.6	1.6	1.6	1.6		1.6
1.5	1.5	1.5	1.5	1.5	1.5				1.5
1.4	1.4	1.4	1.4						1.4
1.3	1.3	1.3	1.3						1.3
1.2	1.2								1.2

A / P / T / L

Tight table (Opponents play 35% of their hands) **Very Passive**

Button	Seat 9	Seat 8	Seat 7	Seat 6	Seat 5	Seat 4	Seat 3	Big blind	Small blind
1.8+	1.8+	1.8+	1.8+	1.8+	1.8+	1.8+	1.8+		1.8+
1.7	1.7	1.7	1.7	1.7	1.7	1.7	1.7		1.7
1.6	1.6	1.6	1.6	1.6	1.6	1.6	1.6		1.6
1.5	1.5	1.5	1.5	1.5	1.5	1.5	1.5		1.5
1.4	1.4	1.4	1.4	1.4	1.4				1.4
1.3	1.3	1.3	1.3						1.3
1.2	1.2	1.2	1.2						1.2
1.1	1.1								1.1

A / P / T / L

Figure 9.4.a.a

Playable Win Factors, 10-handed adjusted for the number of opponents, tight/loose, rake, position, and passive/aggressive

Loose table (Opponents play 50% of their hands)   **Very Aggressive**

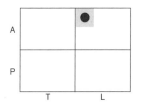

Button	Seat 9	Seat 8	Seat 7	Seat 6	Seat 5	Seat 4	Seat 3	Big blind	Small blind
1.8+	1.8+	1.8+	1.8+	1.8+	1.8+	1.8+	1.8+		1.8+
1.7	1.7	1.7	1.7	1.7	1.7	1.7	1.7		1.7
1.6	1.6	1.6	1.6	1.6	1.6				1.6
1.5	1.5	1.5	1.5						1.5
1.4	1.4								1.4

Loose table (Opponents play 50% of their hands)   **Aggressive**

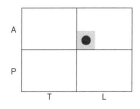

Button	Seat 9	Seat 8	Seat 7	Seat 6	Seat 5	Seat 4	Seat 3	Big blind	Small blind
1.8+	1.8+	1.8+	1.8+	1.8+	1.8+	1.8+	1.8+		1.8+
1.7	1.7	1.7	1.7	1.7	1.7	1.7	1.7		1.7
1.6	1.6	1.6	1.6	1.6	1.6	1.6	1.6		1.6
1.5	1.5	1.5	1.5	1.5	1.5				1.5
1.4	1.4	1.4	1.4						1.4
1.3	1.3								1.3

Loose table (Opponents play 50% of their hands)   **Passive**

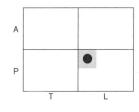

Button	Seat 9	Seat 8	Seat 7	Seat 6	Seat 5	Seat 4	Seat 3	Big blind	Small blind
1.8+	1.8+	1.8+	1.8+	1.8+	1.8+	1.8+	1.8+		1.8+
1.7	1.7	1.7	1.7	1.7	1.7	1.7	1.7		1.7
1.6	1.6	1.6	1.6	1.6	1.6	1.6	1.6		1.6
1.5	1.5	1.5	1.5	1.5	1.5	1.5	1.5		1.5
1.4	1.4	1.4	1.4	1.4	1.4				1.4
1.3	1.3	1.3	1.3						1.3
1.2	1.2								1.2

Loose table (Opponents play 50% of their hands)   **Very Passive**

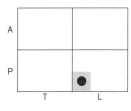

Button	Seat 9	Seat 8	Seat 7	Seat 6	Seat 5	Seat 4	Seat 3	Big blind	Small blind
1.8+	1.8+	1.8+	1.8+	1.8+	1.8+	1.8+	1.8+		1.8+
1.7	1.7	1.7	1.7	1.7	1.7	1.7	1.7		1.7
1.6	1.6	1.6	1.6	1.6	1.6	1.6	1.6		1.6
1.5	1.5	1.5	1.5	1.5	1.5	1.5	1.5		1.5
1.4	1.4	1.4	1.4	1.4	1.4	1.4	1.4		1.4
1.3	1.3	1.3	1.3	1.3	1.3				1.3
1.2	1.2	1.2	1.2						1.2
1.1	1.1								1.1

Figure 9.4.a.b

Playable Win Factors, 10-handed, adjusted for the number of opponents, tight/loose, rake, position, and passive/aggressive

Very Loose table (Opponents play 65% of their hands) — **Very Aggressive**

Button	Seat 9	Seat 8	Seat 7	Seat 6	Seat 5	Seat 4	Seat 3	Big blind	Small blind
1.8+	1.8+	1.8+	1.8+	1.8+	1.8+	1.8+	1.8+		1.8+
1.7	1.7	1.7	1.7	1.7	1.7	1.7	1.7		1.7
1.6	1.6	1.6	1.6	1.6	1.6				1.6
1.5	1.5	1.5	1.5						1.5
1.4	1.4	1.4	1.4						1.4

A / P , T / L

Very Loose table (Opponents play 65% of their hands) — **Aggressive**

Button	Seat 9	Seat 8	Seat 7	Seat 6	Seat 5	Seat 4	Seat 3	Big blind	Small blind
1.8+	1.8+	1.8+	1.8+	1.8+	1.8+	1.8+	1.8+		1.8+
1.7	1.7	1.7	1.7	1.7	1.7	1.7	1.7		1.7
1.6	1.6	1.6	1.6	1.6	1.6	1.6	1.6		1.6
1.5	1.5	1.5	1.5	1.5	1.5				1.5
1.4	1.4	1.4	1.4						1.4
1.3	1.3	1.3	1.3						1.3

A / P , T / L

Very Loose table (Opponents play 65% of their hands) — **Passive**

Button	Seat 9	Seat 8	Seat 7	Seat 6	Seat 5	Seat 4	Seat 3	Big blind	Small blind
1.8+	1.8+	1.8+	1.8+	1.8+	1.8+	1.8+	1.8+		1.8+
1.7	1.7	1.7	1.7	1.7	1.7	1.7	1.7		1.7
1.6	1.6	1.6	1.6	1.6	1.6	1.6	1.6		1.6
1.5	1.5	1.5	1.5	1.5	1.5	1.5	1.5		1.5
1.4	1.4	1.4	1.4	1.4	1.4				1.4
1.3	1.3	1.3	1.3						1.3
1.2	1.2	1.2	1.2						1.2

A / P , T / L

Very Loose table (Opponents play 65% of their hands) — **Very Passive**

Button	Seat 9	Seat 8	Seat 7	Seat 6	Seat 5	Seat 4	Seat 3	Big blind	Small blind
1.8+	1.8+	1.8+	1.8+	1.8+	1.8+	1.8+	1.8+		1.8+
1.7	1.7	1.7	1.7	1.7	1.7	1.7	1.7		1.7
1.6	1.6	1.6	1.6	1.6	1.6	1.6	1.6		1.6
1.5	1.5	1.5	1.5	1.5	1.5	1.5	1.5		1.5
1.4	1.4	1.4	1.4	1.4	1.4	1.4	1.4		1.4
1.3	1.3	1.3	1.3	1.3	1.3				1.3
1.2	1.2	1.2	1.2						1.2
1.1	1.1	1.1	1.1						1.1

A / P , T / L

Figure 9.4.a.c

Playable Win Factors, 10-handed, adjusted for the number of opponents, tight/loose, rake, position, and passive/aggressive

Mega-Loose table (Opponents play 80% of their hands) — **Very Aggressive**

Button	Seat 9	Seat 8	Seat 7	Seat 6	Seat 5	Seat 4	Seat 3	Big blind	Small blind
1.8+	1.8+	1.8+	1.8+	1.8+	1.8+	1.8+	1.8+		1.8+
1.7	1.7	1.7	1.7	1.7	1.7	1.7	1.7		1.7
1.6	1.6	1.6	1.6	1.6	1.6	1.6	1.6		1.6
1.5	1.5	1.5	1.5	1.5	1.5	1.5	1.5		1.5
1.4	1.4	1.4	1.4	1.4	1.4	1.4	1.4		1.4

Mega-Loose table (Opponents play 80% of their hands) — **Aggressive**

Button	Seat 9	Seat 8	Seat 7	Seat 6	Seat 5	Seat 4	Seat 3	Big blind	Small blind
1.8+	1.8+	1.8+	1.8+	1.8+	1.8+	1.8+	1.8+		1.8+
1.7	1.7	1.7	1.7	1.7	1.7	1.7	1.7		1.7
1.6	1.6	1.6	1.6	1.6	1.6	1.6	1.6		1.6
1.5	1.5	1.5	1.5	1.5	1.5	1.5	1.5		1.5
1.4	1.4	1.4	1.4	1.4	1.4	1.4	1.4		1.4
1.3	1.3	1.3	1.3	1.3	1.3	1.3	1.3		1.3

Mega-Loose table (Opponents play 80% of their hands) — **Passive**

Button	Seat 9	Seat 8	Seat 7	Seat 6	Seat 5	Seat 4	Seat 3	Big blind	Small blind
1.8+	1.8+	1.8+	1.8+	1.8+	1.8+	1.8+	1.8+		1.8+
1.7	1.7	1.7	1.7	1.7	1.7	1.7	1.7		1.7
1.6	1.6	1.6	1.6	1.6	1.6	1.6	1.6		1.6
1.5	1.5	1.5	1.5	1.5	1.5	1.5	1.5		1.5
1.4	1.4	1.4	1.4	1.4	1.4	1.4	1.4		1.4
1.3	1.3	1.3	1.3	1.3	1.3	1.3	1.3		1.3
1.2	1.2	1.2	1.2	1.2	1.2	1.2	1.2		1.2

Mega-Loose table (Opponents play 80% of their hands) — **Very Passive**

Button	Seat 9	Seat 8	Seat 7	Seat 6	Seat 5	Seat 4	Seat 3	Big blind	Small blind
1.8+	1.8+	1.8+	1.8+	1.8+	1.8+	1.8+	1.8+		1.8+
1.7	1.7	1.7	1.7	1.7	1.7	1.7	1.7		1.7
1.6	1.6	1.6	1.6	1.6	1.6	1.6	1.6		1.6
1.5	1.5	1.5	1.5	1.5	1.5	1.5	1.5		1.5
1.4	1.4	1.4	1.4	1.4	1.4	1.4	1.4		1.4
1.3	1.3	1.3	1.3	1.3	1.3	1.3	1.3		1.3
1.2	1.2	1.2	1.2	1.2	1.2	1.2	1.2		1.2
1.1	1.1	1.1	1.1	1.1	1.1	1.1	1.1		1.1

Figure 9.4.a.d

Playable Win Factors, 6-handed, adjusted for the number of opponents, tight/loose, rake, position, and passive/aggressive

Tight table (Opponents play 35% of their hands) **Very Aggressive**

Button	Seat 5	Seat 4	Seat 3	Big blind	Small blind
1.8+	1.8+	1.8+	1.8+		1.8+
1.7	1.7	1.7			1.7
1.6	1.6	1.6			1.6
1.5	1.5				1.5
1.4	1.4				1.4

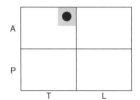

Tight table (Opponents play 35% of their hands) **Aggressive**

Button	Seat 5	Seat 4	Seat 3	Big blind	Small blind
1.8+	1.8+	1.8+	1.8+		1.8+
1.7	1.7	1.7	1.7		1.7
1.6	1.6	1.6			1.6
1.5	1.5	1.5			1.5
1.4	1.4				1.4
1.3	1.3				1.3

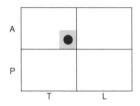

Tight table (Opponents play 35% of their hands) **Passive**

Button	Seat 5	Seat 4	Seat 3	Big blind	Small blind
1.8+	1.8+	1.8+	1.8+		1.8+
1.7	1.7	1.7	1.7		1.7
1.6	1.6	1.6	1.6		1.6
1.5	1.5	1.5			1.5
1.4	1.4	1.4			1.4
1.3	1.3				1.3
1.2	1.2				1.2

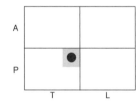

Tight table (Opponents play 35% of their hands) **Very Passive**

Button	Seat 5	Seat 4	Seat 3	Big blind	Small blind
1.8+	1.8+	1.8+	1.8+		1.8+
1.7	1.7	1.7	1.7		1.7
1.6	1.6	1.6	1.6		1.6
1.5	1.5	1.5			1.5
1.4	1.4	1.4			1.4
1.3	1.3	1.3			1.3
1.2	1.2				1.2
1.1	1.1				1.1

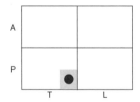

Figure 9.4.b.a

Playable Win Factors, 6-handed, adjusted for the number of opponents, tight/loose, rake, position, and passive/aggressive

Loose table (Opponents play 50% of their hands) **Very Aggressive**

Button	Seat 5	Seat 4	Seat 3	Big blind	Small blind
1.8+	1.8+	1.8+	1.8+		1.8+
1.7	1.7	1.7			1.7
1.6	1.6	1.6			1.6
1.5	1.5				1.5
1.4	1.4				1.4

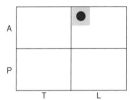

Loose table (Opponents play 50% of their hands) **Aggressive**

Button	Seat 5	Seat 4	Seat 3	Big blind	Small blind
1.8+	1.8+	1.8+	1.8+		1.8+
1.7	1.7	1.7	1.7		1.7
1.6	1.6	1.6			1.6
1.5	1.5	1.5			1.5
1.4	1.4				1.4
1.3	1.3				1.3

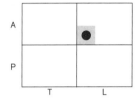

Loose table (Opponents play 50% of their hands) **Passive**

Button	Seat 5	Seat 4	Seat 3	Big blind	Small blind
1.8+	1.8+	1.8+	1.8+		1.8+
1.7	1.7	1.7	1.7		1.7
1.6	1.6	1.6	1.6		1.6
1.5	1.5	1.5	1.5		1.5
1.4	1.4	1.4			1.4
1.3	1.3	1.3			1.3
1.2	1.2				1.2

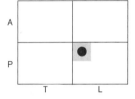

Loose table (Opponents play 50% of their hands) **Very Passive**

Button	Seat 5	Seat 4	Seat 3	Big blind	Small blind
1.8+	1.8+	1.8+	1.8+		1.8+
1.7	1.7	1.7	1.7		1.7
1.6	1.6	1.6	1.6		1.6
1.5	1.5	1.5	1.5		1.5
1.4	1.4	1.4			1.4
1.3	1.3	1.3			1.3
1.2	1.2				1.2
1.1	1.1				1.1

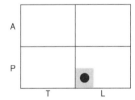

Figure 9.4.b.b

Playable Win Factors, 6-handed, adjusted for the number of opponents, tight/loose, rake, position, and passive/aggressive

Very Loose table (Opponents play 65% of their hands) **Very Aggressive**

Button	Seat 5	Seat 4	Seat 3	Big blind	Small blind
1.8+	1.8+	1.8+	1.8+		1.8+
1.7	1.7	1.7	1.7		1.7
1.6	1.6	1.6	1.6		1.6
1.5	1.5				1.5
1.4	1.4				1.4

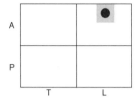

Very Loose table (Opponents play 65% of their hands) **Aggressive**

Button	Seat 5	Seat 4	Seat 3	Big blind	Small blind
1.8+	1.8+	1.8+	1.8+		1.8+
1.7	1.7	1.7	1.7		1.7
1.6	1.6	1.6	1.6		1.6
1.5	1.5	1.5	1.5		1.5
1.4	1.4				1.4
1.3	1.3				1.3

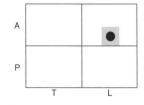

Very Loose table (Opponents play 65% of their hands) **Passive**

Button	Seat 5	Seat 4	Seat 3	Big blind	Small blind
1.8+	1.8+	1.8+	1.8+		1.8+
1.7	1.7	1.7	1.7		1.7
1.6	1.6	1.6	1.6		1.6
1.5	1.5	1.5	1.5		1.5
1.4	1.4	1.4	1.4		1.4
1.3	1.3	1.3	1.3		1.3
1.2	1.2				1.2

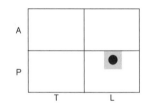

Very Loose table (Opponents play 65% of their hands) **Very Passive**

Button	Seat 5	Seat 4	Seat 3	Big blind	Small blind
1.8+	1.8+	1.8+	1.8+		1.8+
1.7	1.7	1.7	1.7		1.7
1.6	1.6	1.6	1.6		1.6
1.5	1.5	1.5	1.5		1.5
1.4	1.4	1.4	1.4		1.4
1.3	1.3	1.3	1.3		1.3
1.2	1.2				1.2
1.1	1.1				1.1

Figure 9.4.b.c

Playable Win Factors, 6-handed, adjusted for the number of opponents, tight/loose, rake, position, and passive/aggressive

Mega-Loose table (Opponents play 80% of their hands) **Very Aggressive**

Button	Seat 5	Seat 4	Seat 3	Big blind	Small blind
1.8+	1.8+	1.8+	1.8+		1.8+
1.7	1.7	1.7	1.7		1.7
1.6	1.6	1.6	1.6		1.6
1.5	1.5	1.5	1.5		1.5
1.4	1.4	1.4	1.4		1.4

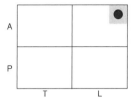

Mega-Loose table (Opponents play 80% of their hands) **Aggressive**

Button	Seat 5	Seat 4	Seat 3	Big blind	Small blind
1.8+	1.8+	1.8+	1.8+		1.8+
1.7	1.7	1.7	1.7		1.7
1.6	1.6	1.6	1.6		1.6
1.5	1.5	1.5	1.5		1.5
1.4	1.4	1.4	1.4		1.4
1.3	1.3	1.3	1.3		1.3

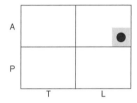

Mega-Loose table (Opponents play 80% of their hands) **Passive**

Button	Seat 5	Seat 4	Seat 3	Big blind	Small blind
1.8+	1.8+	1.8+	1.8+		1.8+
1.7	1.7	1.7	1.7		1.7
1.6	1.6	1.6	1.6		1.6
1.5	1.5	1.5	1.5		1.5
1.4	1.4	1.4	1.4		1.4
1.3	1.3	1.3	1.3		1.3
1.2	1.2	1.2	1.2		1.2

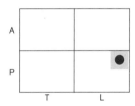

Mega-Loose table (Opponents play 80% of their hands)**Very Passive**

Button	Seat 5	Seat 4	Seat 3	Big blind	Small blind
1.8+	1.8+	1.8+	1.8+		1.8+
1.7	1.7	1.7	1.7		1.7
1.6	1.6	1.6	1.6		1.6
1.5	1.5	1.5	1.5		1.5
1.4	1.4	1.4	1.4		1.4
1.3	1.3	1.3	1.3		1.3
1.2	1.2	1.2	1.2		1.2
1.1	1.1	1.1	1.1		1.1

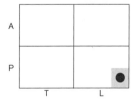

Figure 9.4.b.d

Developing your own models

Some experts feel some of the models presented are too liberal, while others say they're too conservative. I suggest you learn and use these models until you have worked your way to expert status. Then, using WFs, other dimensions, and your natural style of play, create your own models.

Passive/aggressive summary

• The more passive the table, the more hands you can play. As table aggressiveness increases, the number of playable hands decreases.
• The figures in this section now represent WFs for hands that have met all criteria for playing except final adjustments for the horse and pot size.

Homework

• Review how the WFs are adjusted for passive/aggressive.

Part V — Hands you may consider playing

Finally, some answers, almost

On the next several pages you will find all the hands you could play, although in the final portions of this chapter we will discuss two final adjustments — one for the horse and the other for the size of the pot. The charts you will see take into account the strength of the cards, the number of opponents, tight/loose, dealer position, and passive/aggressive. Each page represents the same plot points as were derived in Part IV of this chapter, but now we have converted everything into specific hands. You will find which hands, using the proper portion of the hand pyramid, go with which seats, and the appropriate Win Factors. Also included is how often you must fold. Included in this section are the results for both 10-handed and 6-handed games.

Favorite hands

You are about to see specific recommended hands. These hands are for the beginner through intermediate player. Until you have completed your 250,000 hands, you should not widen your range of playable hands. Until you are a poker expert, we recommend you follow the results in this chapter. Follow the numbers. Play the numbers — the right numbers.

Some expert players play hands such as A9, K9, J9, T9, 98, Q9, J8, T8, 87, 76, 65, 54, and worse. In almost every case these hands have a WF of less than 1.1. Understand that the professional may not be concerned about what he has, but what his opponent *doesn't* have. Experts are confident they can outplay opponents postflop, can read an opponent, or get away when they are beat.

You will find AK is not recommended in a few special situations. This is heresy in the poker world, but the beginner and intermediate must adhere to the numbers. You will seldom see an advanced player fold AK preflop.

Order of presentation

10-handed tables are presented first in the order shown in figure 9.5.a.a, starting with Very Aggressive/Tight, continuing with the various Very Loose tables, and finally Mega-Loose. Then 6-handed tables are shown in the same order. Recall from the previous section that preflop position means nothing at a Mega-Loose

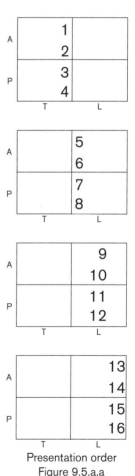

Presentation order
Figure 9.5.a.a

table, but becomes more important the tighter the table. The hands you may play are shown by seat position with both the hand pyramid and the WFs.

Folding versus playing

From the previous sections, you know the relationship between the table type and the number of hands you may play. The looser the table, the more hands; the tighter, the less hands. The more passive the table, the more hands; the more aggressive, the fewer hands. Combining these concepts means you will be playing very few hands at a Very Aggressive/Tight type table and the most at a Very Passive/Mega-Loose type table.

Figure 9.5.a.b shows the frequency of preflop folding depending on the exact type of table.

Figure 9.5.a.c shows how often you may play preflop. The results are as you would expect. The fewest hands will be played at the Very Aggressive/Tight table and the most are played at a Very Passive/Mega-Loose table

Figure 9.5.b is shown over the next several pages. You will see the hands you may play depending on the table's exact location in the Advanced PATL. We have calculated how often you may consider playing a hand and how often you must fold and presented the results in a pie chart. You will be folding a lot, probably a lot more than you are used to. If the pie chart indicates you will only be playing 10% of your hands that means, on average, that in one hour at a casino you will only be playing three hands. **Folding so much requires a high degree of discipline and patience** and does take a lot of the fun out of playing. You can actually go hours without playing a hand. But that's the price of profitability.

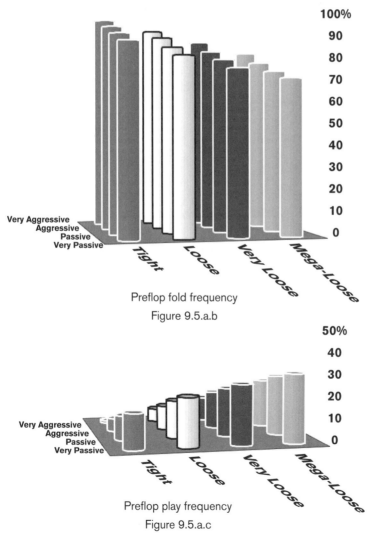

Preflop fold frequency
Figure 9.5.a.b

Preflop play frequency
Figure 9.5.a.c

Tight tables. 10-handed. Hands you may play.

Very Aggressive/Tight table. 10-handed. Hands you may play.

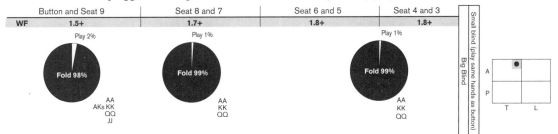

Aggressive/Tight table. 10-handed. Hands you may play.

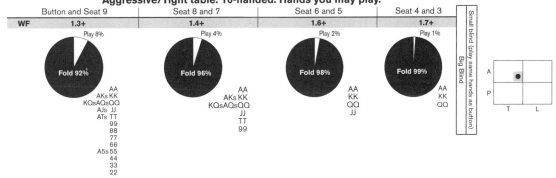

Passive/Tight table. 10-handed. Hands you may play.

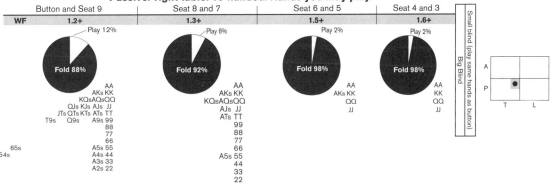

Very Passive/Tight table. 10-handed. Hands you may play.

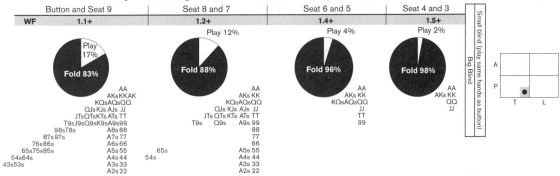

Figure 9.5.b

Loose tables. 10-handed. Hands you may play.

Very Aggressive/Loose table. 10-handed. Hands you may play.

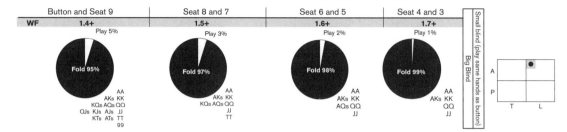

	Button and Seat 9	Seat 8 and 7	Seat 6 and 5	Seat 4 and 3
WF	1.4+	1.5+	1.6+	1.7+

Play 5% — Fold 95%
AA
AKs KK
KQs AQs QQ
QJs KJs AJs JJ
KTs ATs TT
99

Play 3% — Fold 97%
AA
AKs KK
KQs AQs QQ
JJ
TT

Play 2% — Fold 98%
AA
AKs KK
AQs QQ
JJ

Play 1% — Fold 99%
AA
AKs KK
QQ
JJ

Small blind (play same hands as button) / Big Blind — A / P — T / L

Aggressive/Loose table. 10-handed. Hands you may play.

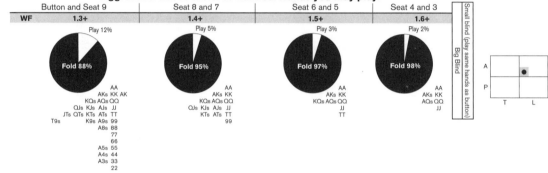

	Button and Seat 9	Seat 8 and 7	Seat 6 and 5	Seat 4 and 3
WF	1.3+	1.4+	1.5+	1.6+

Play 12% — Fold 88%
AA
AKs KK AK
KQs AQs QQ
QJs KJs AJs JJ
JTs QTs KTs ATs TT
T9s K9s A9s 99
A8s 88
77
66
A5s 55
A4s 44
A3s 33
22

Play 5% — Fold 95%
AA
AKs KK
KQs AQs QQ
QJs KJs AJs JJ
KTs ATs TT
99

Play 3% — Fold 97%
AA
AKs KK
KQs AQs QQ
JJ
TT

Play 2% — Fold 98%
AA
AKs KK
AQs QQ
JJ

Small blind (play same hands as button) / Big Blind — A / P — T / L

Passive/Loose table. 10-handed. Hands you may play.

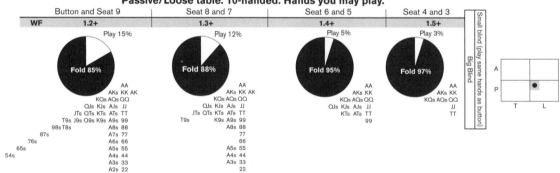

	Button and Seat 9	Seat 8 and 7	Seat 6 and 5	Seat 4 and 3
WF	1.2+	1.3+	1.4+	1.5+

Play 15% — Fold 85%
AA
AKs KK AK
KQs AQs QQ
QJs KJs AJs JJ
JTs QTs KTs ATs TT
T9s J9s Q9s K9s A9s 99
98s T8s A8s 88
87s A7s 77
76s A6s 66
65s A5s 55
54s A4s 44
A3s 33
A2s 22

Play 12% — Fold 88%
AA
AKs KK AK
KQs AQs QQ
QJs KJs AJs JJ
JTs QTs KTs ATs TT
T9s K9s A9s 99
A8s 88
77
66
A5s 55
A4s 44
A3s 33
22

Play 5% — Fold 95%
AA
AKs KK
KQs AQs QQ
QJs KJs AJs JJ
KTs ATs TT
99

Play 3% — Fold 97%
AA
AKs KK
KQs AQs QQ
JJ
TT

Small blind (play same hands as button) / Big Blind — A / P — T / L

Very Passive/Loose table. 10-handed. Hands you may play.

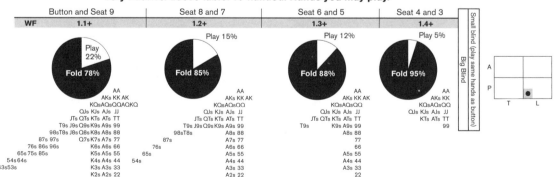

	Button and Seat 9	Seat 8 and 7	Seat 6 and 5	Seat 4 and 3
WF	1.1+	1.2+	1.3+	1.4+

Play 22% — Fold 78%
AA
AKs KK AK
KQs AQs QQ AQ KQ
QJs KJs AJs JJ
JTs QTs KTs ATs TT
T9s J9s Q9s K9s A9s 99
98s T8s J8s Q8s K8s A8s 88
87s 97s Q7s K7s A7s 77
76s 86s 96s K6s A6s 66
65s 75s 85s K5s A5s 55
54s 64s K4s A4s 44
43s 53s K3s A3s 33
K2s A2s 22

Play 15% — Fold 85%
AA
AKs KK AK
KQs AQs QQ
QJs KJs AJs JJ
JTs QTs KTs ATs TT
T9s J9s Q9s K9s A9s 99
98s T8s A8s 88
87s A7s 77
76s A6s 66
65s A5s 55
54s A4s 44
A3s 33
A2s 22

Play 12% — Fold 88%
AA
AKs KK AK
KQs AQs QQ
QJs KJs AJs JJ
JTs QTs KTs ATs TT
T9s K9s A9s 99
A8s 88
77
66
A5s 55
A4s 44
A3s 33
22

Play 5% — Fold 95%
AA
AKs KK
KQs AQs QQ
QJs KJs AJs JJ
KTs ATs TT
99

Small blind (play same hands as button) / Big Blind — A / P — T / L

Very Loose tables. 10-handed. Hands you may play.

Very Aggressive/Very Loose table. 10-handed. Hands you may play.

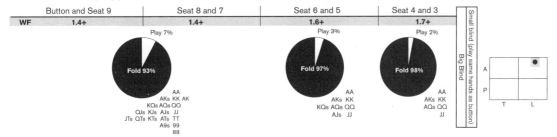

	Button and Seat 9	Seat 8 and 7	Seat 6 and 5	Seat 4 and 3	
WF	1.4+	1.4+	1.6+	1.7+	Small blind (play same hands as button)

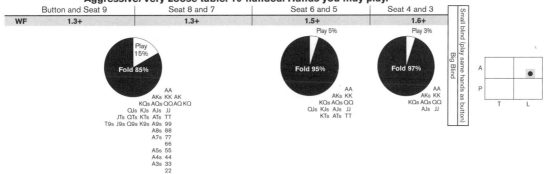

Play 7%
Fold 93%

AA
AKs KK AK
KQs AQs QQ
QJs KJs AJs JJ
JTs QTs KTs ATs TT
A9s 99
88

Play 3%
Fold 97%

AA
AKs KK
KQs AQs QQ
AJs JJ

Play 2%
Fold 98%

AA
AKs KK
AQs QQ
JJ

Aggressive/Very Loose table. 10-handed. Hands you may play.

	Button and Seat 9	Seat 8 and 7	Seat 6 and 5	Seat 4 and 3	
WF	1.3+	1.3+	1.5+	1.6+	Small blind (play same hands as button)

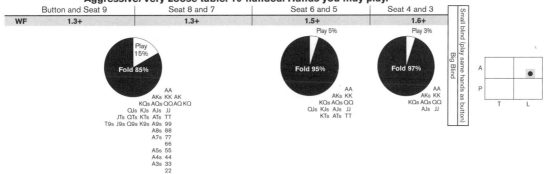

Play 15%
Fold 85%

AA
AKs KK AK
KQs AQs QQ AQ KQ
QJs KJs AJs JJ
JTs QTs KTs ATs TT
T9s J9s Q9s K9s A9s 99
A8s 88
A7s 77
66
A5s 55
A4s 44
A3s 33
22

Play 5%
Fold 95%

AA
AKs KK
KQs AQs QQ
QJs KJs AJs JJ
KTs ATs TT

Play 3%
Fold 97%

AA
AKs KK
KQs AQs QQ
AJs JJ

Passive/Very Loose table. 10-handed. Hands you may play.

	Button and Seat 9	Seat 8 and 7	Seat 6 and 5	Seat 4 and 3	
WF	1.2+	1.2+	1.4+	1.5+	Small blind (play same hands as button)

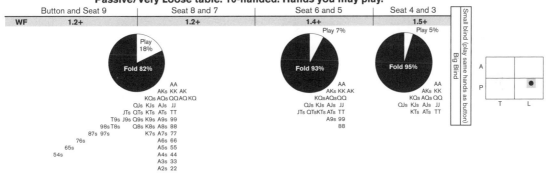

Play 18%
Fold 82%

AA
AKs KK AK
KQs AQs QQ AQ KQ
QJs KJs AJs JJ
JTs QTs KTs ATs TT
T9s J9s Q9s K9s A9s 99
98s T8s Q8s K8s A8s 88
87s 97s K7s A7s 77
A6s 66
A5s 55
A4s 44
A3s 33
A2s 22
76s
65s
54s

Play 7%
Fold 93%

AA
AKs KK AK
KQs AQs QQ
QJs KJs AJs JJ
JTs QTs KTs ATs TT
A9s 99
88

Play 5%
Fold 95%

AA
AKs KK
KQs AQs QQ
QJs KJs AJs JJ
KTs ATs TT

Very Passive/Very Loose table. 10-handed. Hands you may play.

	Button and Seat 9	Seat 8 and 7	Seat 6 and 5	Seat 4 and 3	
WF	1.1+	1.1+	1.3+	1.4+	Small blind (play same hands as button)

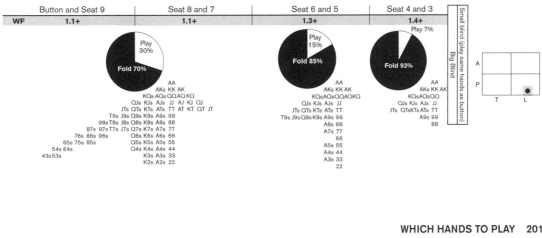

Play 30%
Fold 70%

AA
AKs KK AK
KQs AQs QQ AQ KQ
QJs KJs AJs JJ AJ KJ QJ
JTs QTs KTs ATs TT AT KT QT JT
T9s J9s Q9s K9s A9s 99
98s T8s J8s Q8s K8s A8s 88
87s 97s T7s J7s Q7s K7s A7s 77
76s 86s 96s Q6s K6s A6s 66
65s 75s 85s Q5s K5s A5s 55
54s 64s Q4s K4s A4s 44
43s 53s K3s A3s 33
K2s A2s 22

Play 15%
Fold 85%

AA
AKs KK AK
KQs AQs QQ AQ KQ
QJs KJs AJs JJ
JTs QTs KTs ATs TT
T9s J9s Q9s K9s A9s 99
A8s 88
A7s 77
66
A5s 55
A4s 44
A3s 33
22

Play 7%
Fold 93%

AA
AKs KK AK
KQs AQs QQ
QJs KJs AJs JJ
JTs QTs KTs ATs TT
A9s 99
88

Mega-Loose tables. 10-handed. Hands you may play.

Very Aggressive/Mega-Loose table. 10-handed. Hands you may play.

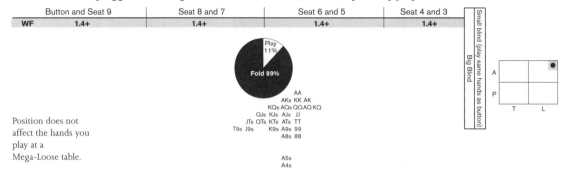

	Button and Seat 9	Seat 8 and 7	Seat 6 and 5	Seat 4 and 3	Small blind (play same hands as button)
WF	1.4+	1.4+	1.4+	1.4+	Big Blind

Position does not affect the hands you play at a Mega-Loose table.

Play 11%
Fold 89%

```
                AA
            AKs KK AK
        KQs AQs QQ AQ KQ
      QJs KJs AJs JJ
   JTs QTs KTs ATs TT
T9s J9s     K9s A9s 99
            A8s 88

            A5s
            A4s
```

A
P
T   L

Aggressive/Mega-Loose table. 10-handed. Hands you may play.

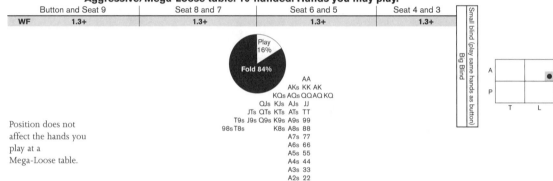

	Button and Seat 9	Seat 8 and 7	Seat 6 and 5	Seat 4 and 3	Small blind (play same hands as button)
WF	1.3+	1.3+	1.3+	1.3+	Big Blind

Position does not affect the hands you play at a Mega-Loose table.

Play 16%
Fold 84%

```
                AA
            AKs KK AK
        KQs AQs QQ AQ KQ
      QJs KJs AJs JJ
   JTs QTs KTs ATs TT
T9s J9s Q9s K9s A9s 99
98s T8s     K8s A8s 88
            A7s 77
            A6s 66
            A5s 55
            A4s 44
            A3s 33
            A2s 22
```

A
P
T   L

Passive/Mega-Loose table. 10-handed. Hands you may play.

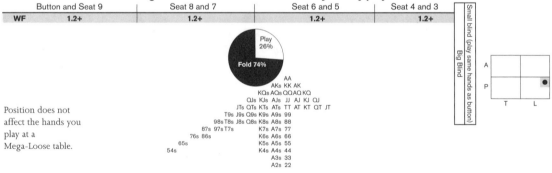

	Button and Seat 9	Seat 8 and 7	Seat 6 and 5	Seat 4 and 3	Small blind (play same hands as button)
WF	1.2+	1.2+	1.2+	1.2+	Big Blind

Position does not affect the hands you play at a Mega-Loose table.

Play 26%
Fold 74%

```
                    AA
                AKs KK AK
            KQs AQs QQ AQ KQ
        QJs KJs AJs JJ AJ KJ QJ
     JTs QTs KTs ATs TT AT KT QT JT
   T9s J9s Q9s K9s A9s 99
 98s T8s Q8s K8s A8s 88
87s 97s T7s     K7s A7s 77
 76s 86s         K6s A6s 66
            K5s A5s 55
     65s    K4s A4s 44
   54s          A3s 33
                A2s 22
```

A
P
T   L

Very Passive/Mega-Loose table. 10-handed. Hands you may play.

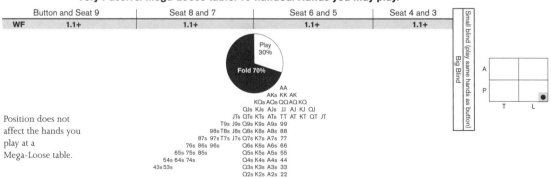

	Button and Seat 9	Seat 8 and 7	Seat 6 and 5	Seat 4 and 3	Small blind (play same hands as button)
WF	1.1+	1.1+	1.1+	1.1+	Big Blind

Position does not affect the hands you play at a Mega-Loose table.

Play 30%
Fold 70%

```
                        AA
                    AKs KK AK
                KQs AQs QQ AQ KQ
            QJs KJs AJs JJ AJ KJ QJ
         JTs QTs KTs ATs TT AT KT QT JT
       T9s J9s Q9s K9s A9s 99
     98s T8s J8s Q8s K8s A8s 88
    87s 97s T7s J7s Q7s K7s A7s 77
   76s 86s 96s   Q6s K6s A6s 66
            Q5s K5s A5s 55
    65s 75s 85s  Q4s K4s A4s 44
   54s 64s 74s   Q3s K3s A3s 33
 43s 53s         Q2s K2s A2s 22
```

A
P
T   L

Tight tables. 6-handed. Hands you may play.

Very Aggressive/Tight table. 6-handed. Hands you may play.

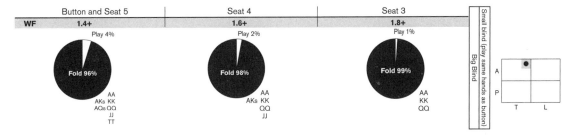

Very Aggressive/Tight table. 6-handed. Hands you may play.

Aggressive/Tight table. 6-handed. Hands you may play.

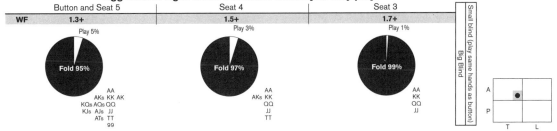

Passive/Tight table. 6-handed. Hands you may play

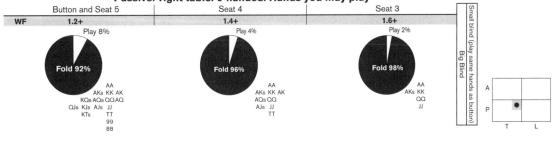

Very Passive/Tight table. 6-handed. Hands you may play.

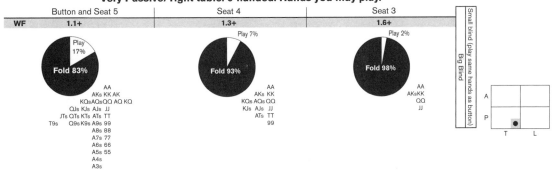

Loose tables. 6-handed. Hands you may play.

Very Aggressive/Loose table. 6-handed. Hands you may play.

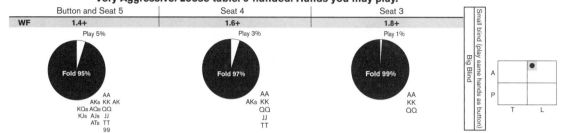

	Button and Seat 5	Seat 4	Seat 3	
WF	1.4+	1.6+	1.8+	
	Play 5%	Play 3%	Play 1%	
	Fold 95%	Fold 97%	Fold 99%	
	AA AKs KK AK KQs AQs QQ KJs AJs JJ ATs TT 99	AA AKs KK QQ JJ TT	AA KK QQ	

Aggressive/Loose table. 6-handed. Hands you may play.

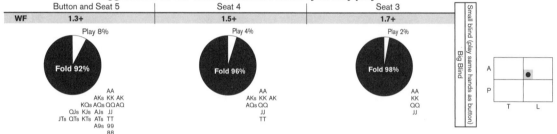

	Button and Seat 5	Seat 4	Seat 3	
WF	1.3+	1.5+	1.7+	
	Play 8%	Play 4%	Play 2%	
	Fold 92%	Fold 96%	Fold 98%	
	AA AKs KK AK KQs AQs QQ AQ QJs KJs AJs JJ JTs QTs KTs ATs TT A9s 99 88	AA AKs KK AK AQs QQ JJ TT	AA KK QQ JJ	

Passive/Loose table. 6-handed. Hands you may play.

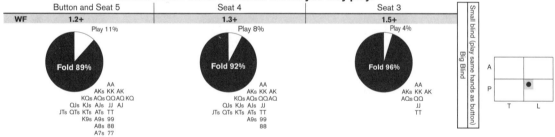

	Button and Seat 5	Seat 4	Seat 3	
WF	1.2+	1.3+	1.5+	
	Play 11%	Play 8%	Play 4%	
	Fold 89%	Fold 92%	Fold 96%	
	AA AKs KK AK KQs AQs QQ AQ KQ QJs KJs AJs JJ AJ JTs QTs KTs ATs TT K9s A9s 99 A8s 88 A7s 77	AA AKs KK AK KQs AQs QQ AQ QJs KJs AJs JJ JTs QTs KTs ATs TT A9s 99 88	AA AKs KK AK AQs QQ JJ TT	

Very Passive/Loose table. 6-handed. Hands you may play.

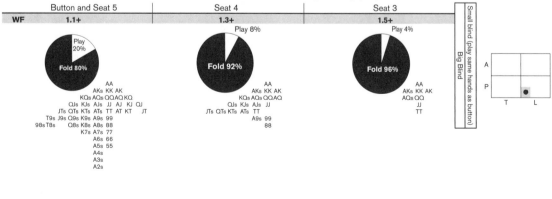

	Button and Seat 5	Seat 4	Seat 3	
WF	1.1+	1.3+	1.5+	
	Play 20%	Play 8%	Play 4%	
	Fold 80%	Fold 92%	Fold 96%	
	AA AKs KK AK KQs AQs QQ AQ KQ QJs KJs AJs JJ AJ KJ QJ JTs QTs KTs ATs TT AT KT JT T9s J9s Q9s K9s A9s 99 98s T8s Q8s K8s A8s 88 K7s A7s 77 A6s 66 A5s 55 A4s A3s A2s	AA AKs KK AK KQs AQs QQ AQ QJs KJs AJs JJ JTs QTs KTs ATs TT A9s 99 88	AA AKs KK AK AQs QQ JJ TT	

Very Loose tables. 6-handed. Hands you may play.

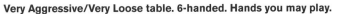

Very Aggressive/Very Loose table. 6-handed. Hands you may play.

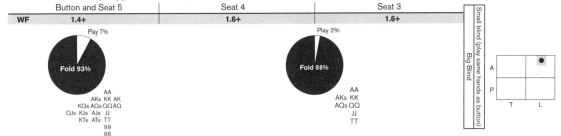

	Button and Seat 5	Seat 4	Seat 3	
WF	1.4+	1.6+	1.6+	

Play 7%

Fold 93%

AA
AKs KK AK
KQs AQs QQ AQ
QJs KJs AJs JJ
KTs ATs TT
99
88

Play 2%

Fold 98%

AA
AKs KK
AQs QQ
JJ
TT

Small blind (play same hands as button)

Big Blind

A

P

T   L

Aggressive/Very Loose table. 6-handed. Hands you may play.

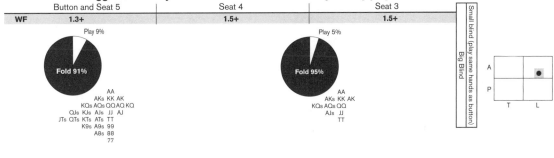

	Button and Seat 5	Seat 4	Seat 3	
WF	1.3+	1.5+	1.5+	

Play 9%

Fold 91%

AA
AKs KK AK
KQs AQs QQ AQ KQ
QJs KJs AJs JJ AJ
JTs QTs KTs ATs TT
K9s A9s 99
A8s 88
77

Play 5%

Fold 95%

AA
AKs KK AK
KQs AQs QQ
AJs JJ
TT

Small blind (play same hands as button)

Big Blind

A

P

T   L

Passive/Very Loose table. 6-handed. Hands you may play.

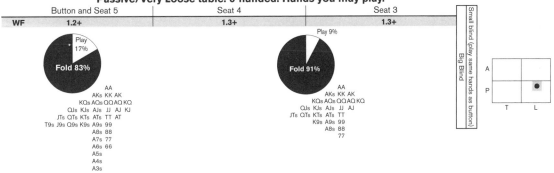

	Button and Seat 5	Seat 4	Seat 3	
WF	1.2+	1.3+	1.3+	

Play 17%

Fold 83%

AA
AKs KK AK
KQs AQs QQ AQ KQ
QJs KJs AJs JJ AJ KJ
JTs QTs KTs ATs TT AT
T9s J9s Q9s K9s A9s 99
A8s 88
A7s 77
A6s 66
A5s
A4s
A3s

Play 9%

Fold 91%

AA
AKs KK AK
KQs AQs QQ AQ KQ
QJs KJs AJs JJ AJ
JTs QTs KTs ATs TT
K9s A9s 99
A8s 88
77

Small blind (play same hands as button)

Big Blind

A

P

T   L

Very Passive/Very Loose table. 6-handed. Hands you may play.

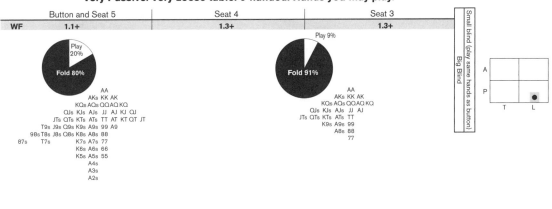

	Button and Seat 5	Seat 4	Seat 3	
WF	1.1+	1.3+	1.3+	

Play 20%

Fold 80%

AA
AKs KK AK
KQs AQs QQ AQ KQ
QJs KJs AJs JJ AJ KJ QJ
JTs QTs KTs ATs TT AT KT QT JT
T9s J9s Q9s K9s A9s 99 A9
98s T8s J8s Q8s K8s A8s 88
87s T7s K7s A7s 77
K6s A6s 66
K5s A5s 55
A4s
A3s
A2s

Play 9%

Fold 91%

AA
AKs KK AK
KQs AQs QQ AQ KQ
QJs KJs AJs JJ AJ
JTs QTs KTs ATs TT
K9s A9s 99
A8s 88
77

Small blind (play same hands as button)

Big Blind

A

P

T   L

Mega-Loose tables. 6-handed. Hands you may play.

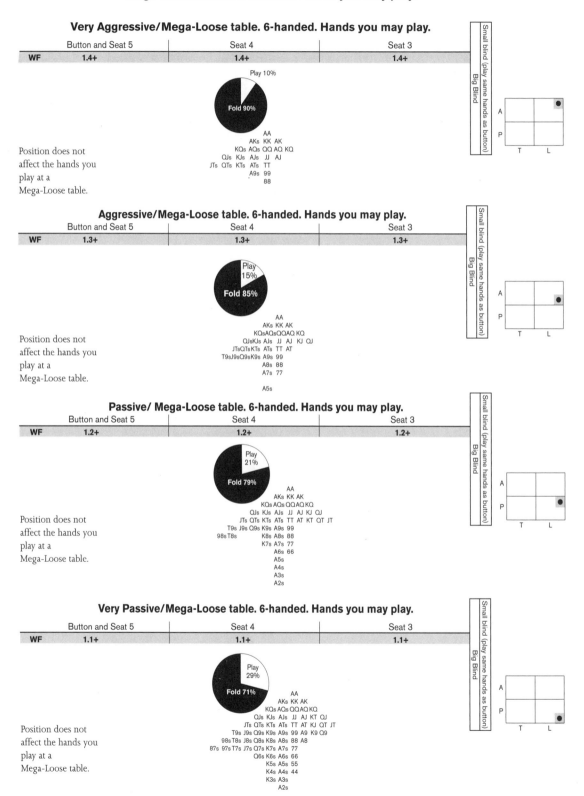

Very Aggressive/Mega-Loose table. 6-handed. Hands you may play.

	Button and Seat 5	Seat 4	Seat 3	
WF	1.4+	1.4+	1.4+	

Small blind (play same hands as button)

Big Blind

Play 10%

Fold 90%

AA
AKs KK AK
KQs AQs QQ AQ KQ
QJs KJs AJs JJ AJ
JTs QTs KTs ATs TT
A9s 99
88

Position does not
affect the hands you
play at a
Mega-Loose table.

A
P
T L

Aggressive/Mega-Loose table. 6-handed. Hands you may play.

	Button and Seat 5	Seat 4	Seat 3	
WF	1.3+	1.3+	1.3+	

Small blind (play same hands as button)

Big Blind

Play 15%

Fold 85%

AA
AKs KK AK
KQs AQs QQ AQ KQ
QJs KJs AJs JJ AJ KJ QJ
JTs QTs KTs ATs TT AT
T9s J9s Q9s K9s A9s 99
A8s 88
A7s 77

A5s

Position does not
affect the hands you
play at a
Mega-Loose table.

A
P
T L

Passive/ Mega-Loose table. 6-handed. Hands you may play.

	Button and Seat 5	Seat 4	Seat 3	
WF	1.2+	1.2+	1.2+	

Small blind (play same hands as button)

Big Blind

Play 21%

Fold 79%

AA
AKs KK AK
KQs AQs QQ AQ KQ
QJs KJs AJs JJ AJ KJ QJ
JTs QTs KTs ATs TT AT KT QT JT
T9s J9s Q9s K9s A9s 99
98s T8s K8s A8s 88
K7s A7s 77
A6s 66
A5s
A4s
A3s
A2s

Position does not
affect the hands you
play at a
Mega-Loose table.

A
P
T L

Very Passive/Mega-Loose table. 6-handed. Hands you may play.

	Button and Seat 5	Seat 4	Seat 3	
WF	1.1+	1.1+	1.1+	

Small blind (play same hands as button)

Big Blind

Play 29%

Fold 71%

AA
AKs KK AK
KQs AQs QQ AQ KQ
QJs KJs AJs JJ AJ KT QJ
JTs QTs KTs ATs TT AT KJ QT JT
T9s J9s Q9s K9s A9s 99 A9 K9 Q9
98s T8s J8s Q8s K8s A8s 88 A8
87s 97s T7s J7s Q7s K7s A7s 77
Q6s K6s A6s 66
K5s A5s 55
K4s A4s 44
K3s A3s
A2s

Position does not
affect the hands you
play at a
Mega-Loose table.

A
P
T L

Review of card strength versus opponents

In the Relative Strength Chapter you were exposed to the concept that card strength varies according to how many opponents are dealt cards.

As an example, the hands in figure 9.5.c all have a WF of 1.1 or greater for the same Mega-Loose plot point in the Advanced PATL. We have bolded the hands which remain constant regardless of the number of opponents dealt cards. Examine these charts carefully. You could construct similar comparisons for any consistent plot point and come to these same important conclusions.

1. **Lower, suited cards are only playable against many opponents**.
2. **Higher, unsuited cards are stronger against fewer opponents**.

10-handed

```
                        AA
                     AKsKKAK
                  KQsAQsQQAQKQ
               QJs KJs AJs  JJ  AJ  KT  QJ
             JTs QTs KTs ATs  TT  AT  KJ  QT  JT
             T9s J9sQ9sK9sA9s 99
          98sT8sJ8sQ8sK8sA8s 88
      87s 97sT7sJ7sQ7sK7sA7s 77
   76s 86s 96s    Q6sK6sA6s 66
   65s75s 85s     Q5sK5sA5s 55
54s64s74s         Q4sK4sA4s 44
43s53s            Q3sK3s A3s 33
                  Q2sK2s A2s 22
```

6-handed

```
                        AA
                     AKsKKAK
                  KQsAQsQQAQKQ
               QJs KJs AJs  JJ  AJ  KT  QJ
             JTs QTs KTs ATs  TT  AT  KJ  QT  JT
             T9s J9sQ9sK9sA9s 99
          98sT8sJ8sQ8sK8sA8s 88
      87s 97sT7sJ7sQ7sK7sA7s 77
                  Q6sK6sA6s 66
                     K5sA5s 55
                     K4sA4s 44
                  K3s A3s
                  A2s
```

3-handed

```
                        AA
                     AKsKKAK
                  KQsAQsQQAQKQ
               QJs KJs AJs  JJ  AJ  KJ  QJ
             JTs QTs KTs ATs  TT  AT  KT  QT  JT
             T9s J9sQ9sK9sA9s 99   A9  K9
          T8s J8sQ8sK8sA8s 88   A8  K8
                  K7sA7s 77   A7  K7
                  K6sA6s 66   A6
                  K5sA5s 55   A5
                  K4sA4s 44   A4
                     A3s
                     A2s
```

Figure 9.5.c

An interim model

To learn how to use the WFs for every situation takes months. The model below was developed only because we understand the desire of students to play now. In addition, many students will, during their learning period, play several tables on the internet simultaneously. Even when some mastery of the WFs is gained, it is extremely difficult when playing three or more tables at the same time to immediately analyze exactly where an individual table fits in the Advanced PATL. Therefore, until you can pinpoint every table with the proper Advanced PATL plot point and instantly know which hands to play, figure 9.5.d presents an interim set of hands you may play. **This is not a substitute for knowing thoroughly every hand for every plot point shown on the previous pages.**

This model teaches the value of position and the relationship between position and the number of playable hands. It illustrates how card strength changes with the number of opponents. On a 10-handed table, notice how few hands are playable in seats 3 and 4, how big unsuiteds are not playable in early position, and how cards you may never have played before can be played on the button. For the 6-handed table, low suited connectors are worthless, and on the button, unlike on a 10-handed table, you can play A9, A8, K9, and Q9. This model does not take into account the horse, which will be discussed in the next section. This model is not nearly as precise as playing the hands shown on the previous pages. Using 9.5.d will not yield 1.5 big bets per hour, but it does yield a positive Expected Value.

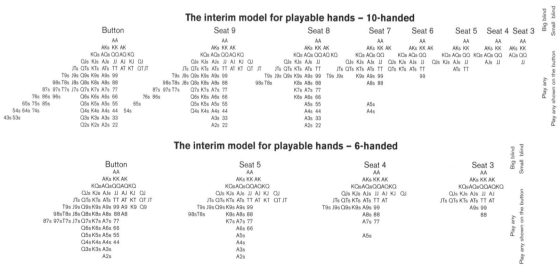

Figure 9.5.d

Mega-Tight

```
                AA
            AKs KK AK
        KQs AQs QQ AQ KQ
    QJs KJs AJs JJ AJ KJ QJ
JTs QTs KTs ATs TT AT KT QT JT
T9s J9s Q9s K9s A9s 99 A9 K9 Q9
            A8s 88
            A7s 77
```

Tight

```
                AA
            AKs KK AK
        KQs AQs QQ AQ KQ
    QJs KJs AJs JJ AJ KJ QJ
JTs QTs KTs ATs TT AT KT QT JT
T9s J9s Q9s K9s A9s 99 A9 K9 Q9 J9 T9
98s T8s J8s Q8s K8s A8s 88 A8              98
87s 97s T7s J7s Q7s K7s A7s 77                      87
76s 86s 96s              A6s 66
65s 75s 85s              A5s 55
54s 64s 74s              A4s 44
                         A3s 33
                         A2s 22
```

Hands you play

```
                AA
            AKs KK AK
        KQs AQs QQ AQ KQ
    QJs KJs AJs JJ AJ KJ QJ
JTs QTs KTs ATs TT AT KT QT JT
T9s J9s Q9s K9s A9s 99
98s T8s J8s Q8s K8s A8s 88
87s 97s T7s J7s Q7s K7s A7s 77
76s 86s 96s     Q6s K6s A6s 66
65s 75s 85s     Q5s K5s A5s 55
54s 64s 74s     Q4s K4s A4s 44
43s 53s         Q3s K3s A3s 33
                Q2s K2s A2s 22
```

Loose

```
                AA
            AKs KK AK
        KQs AQs QQ AQ KQ
    QJs KJs AJs JJ AJ KJ QJ
JTs QTs KTs ATs TT AT KT QT JT
T9s J9s Q9s K9s A9s 99 A9 K9 Q9 J9 T9
98s T8s J8s Q8s K8s A8s 88 A8 K8        98
87s 97s              K7s A7s 77 A7 K7        87
76s 86s              K6s A6s 66 A6 K6        76
65s 75s              K5s A5s 55 A5 K5        65
54s 64s              K4s A4s 44 A4 K4        54
43s 53s              K3s A3s 33 A3 K3
                     K2s A2s 22 A2 K2
```

Very Loose

```
                AA
            AKs KK AK
        KQs AQs QQ AQ KQ
    QJs KJs AJs JJ AJ KJ QJ
JTs QTs KTs ATs TT AT KT QT JT
T9s J9s Q9s K9s A9s 99 A9 K9 Q9 J9 T9
98s T8s J8s Q8s K8s A8s 88 A8 K8 J8 T8 98
87s 97s T7s J7s Q7s K7s A7s 77 A7 K7 T7 97 87
76s 86s 96s              A6s 66 A6 K6    96 86 76
65s 75s 85s              A5s 55 A5 K5    85 75 65
54s 64s 74s              A4s 44 A4 K4    74 64 54
43s 53s 63s              A3s 33 A3 K3    63 53 43
32s 42s 52s              A2s 22 A2 K2          32
```

Mega-Loose

```
                AA
            AKs KK AK
        KQs AQs QQ AQ KQ
    QJs KJs AJs JJ AJ KJ QJ
JTs QTs KTs ATs TT AT KT QT JT
T9s J9s Q9s K9s A9s 99 A9 K9 Q9 J9 T9
98s T8s J8s Q8s K8s A8s 88 A8 K8 Q8 J8 T8 98
87s 97s T7s J7s Q7s K7s A7s 77 A7 K7    J7 T7 97 87
76s 86s 96s T6s J6s Q6s K6s A6s 66 A6 K6 T6 96 86 76
65s 75s 85s 95s T5s J5s Q5s K5s A5s 55 A5 K5 95 85 75 65
54s 64s 74s 84s 94s T4s J4s Q4s K4s A4s 44 A4 K4 84 74 64 54
43s 53s 63s 73s 83s 93s T3s J3s Q3s K3s A3s 33 A3 K3 73 63 53 43
32s 42s 52s 62s 72s 82s 92s T2s J2s Q2s K2s A2s 22 A2 K2 62 52 42 32
```

Figure 9.5.e

Range of your opponents' hands

Remember back in Chapter 3 when we introduced you to reading the hands of your opponents? A broad statement was made which said a tight plays fewer and stronger hands than a loose. Then, using the basic PATL, we showed you some of the hands that each would play. Now that you understand the Advanced PATL we are ready to take this concept to a higher level. In figure 9.5.e you can see the probable distribution of starting hands a player could play depending on his degree of tightness or looseness.

We see how tight a Mega-Tight really is, and how loose a Mega-Loose is. The Mega-Loose is really playing almost any two cards. He does play any two suited and any cards which could possibly make a straight. At the other end of the spectrum is the Mega-Tight who plays only high cards. This entire figure is worth your while to study. You will still continue to count how many hands an opponent plays to determine how tight or loose he is. But now, every time a player shows his cards, you will be able to confirm your counts so you may place an opponent in the Advanced PATL, and possibly make minor adjustments.

You will find some players are even more tight than a Mega-Tight, and other Mega-Tights will not play hands such as K9 and Q9 but will play most, if not all, pairs. Others may have favorite hands they like to play. So, while figure 9.5.e is useful, it is not exact.

Most important is to see how an opponent plays specific cards based on position and the other determining factors.

As you review the hands played by the Tight in figure 9.5.e, it appears as though you play more hands than the Tight. This is an illusion. As you'll recall, the unsuited hands occur much more frequently than the suiteds. You will actually play slightly fewer hands than the Tight. For example, the Tight will play T9 but you will not. And you know there are times you can play Q6s and lower, 53s, and a few other hands most Tights would consider to be trash.

Professionals will not only be playing the same hands you will, but often will also play those of the Loose as well.

Summary

- WFs have been converted into specific hands.
- Potentially playable hands are shown using both the hand pyramid and WFs.
- The charts take into account all of the seven determining factors except the horse and pot size.
- Until you have mastered the charts, an interim model of playable hands has been provided.
- Do not widen your range of hands until you have played 250,000 hands.

Homework

- Learn every hand you can consider playing for every situation.

Part VI — Horse adjustments

The horse

Up until now Win Factors have been used primarily as an adjustment for the preflop table. Now we will introduce you to the horse, and you will find you will use a preflop WF adjustment for individual players. The horse is the last opponent to have acted. All but the most advanced players fail to make any adjustment for the horse. The advanced player considers the following:

1. What kind of player the horse is.
2. The horse's position.
3. Where the horse is seated relative to where the advanced player is seated.

The basic horse adjustment

The horse is the last player to have bet or raised. The horse is sometimes referred to as "in the lead." Several experts tell you to "tighten up" when faced with a bet or raise. Translating "tighten up" into the context of this book means you must increase your WF requirements to adjust for the horse. Until you are an experienced player you will use a basic adjustment. You will place the horse in the PATL and then make a specific WF adjustment to the hands you will play. This basic adjustment takes into account what kind of player the horse is, but does not take into account the horse's position or where the horse is seated relative to you. You will see, as you probably expect, you must make more adjustments for tight horses and less for loose horses.

Shorthand: If a figure indicates "WF + 1" that means you must increase your WF by 0.1; the decimal point is ignored. If the horse bets, figure 9.6.a shows the WF adjustments. For example, if you were in seat 7 at a Very Passive/Very Loose 10-handed table, figure 9.6.a.c says you should call with a WF of 1.1 or greater. But before you have a chance to act, a passive/tight bets. Per 9.6.a you must now increase your WF requirement +2, which means you now need a WF of 1.3 or better to call.

A horse does not always stay the horse, of course. If a player is the first to bet he is the horse. If someone calls he is now the horse. If another player then raises, that raiser is the horse. If another player re-raises, that player is now the horse. Whoever calls the re-raise is now the horse. In a single round of betting the horse will start off to be one player, then become another, and so on. You may recall the concept that it takes a stronger hand to

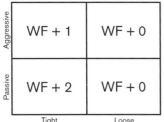

	Tight	Loose
Aggressive	WF + 1	WF + 0
Passive	WF + 2	WF + 0

WF adjustment when the
horse bets
Figure 9.6.a

	Tight	Loose
Aggressive	WF + 2	WF + 0
Passive	WF + 3	WF + 1

WF adjustment when the
horse raises
Figure 9.6.b

call a bet or raise than to make one. You can see that is true now, and can see the adjustments you must make, for all except the aggressive/loose raiser.

If the horse raises you must increase your WFs as shown in 9.6.b. For example, if you were in seat 7 at the same Very Passive/Very Loose 10-handed table as the example above, if a passive/tight raises you must increase your WF requirements +3; to stay in you must now have a WF of 1.4 or better.

If the horse re-raises, you must increase your WFs as shown in 9.6.c.

	Tight	Loose
Aggressive	WF + 3	WF + 0
Passive	WF + 4	WF + 2

WF adjustment when the
horse re-raises
Figure 9.6.c

Advanced adjustments for the horse

These WF adjustments will take into account the horse's position and where the horse is seated relative to you. These changes, on top of the basic adjustment, are for advanced players only. The reason for suggesting only experienced players use these techniques is the complexity of being able to move mentally from one WF chart to another, and then to another. But, as before, you will use WFs. You may find once you have made both the basic and advanced adjustments, you have run out of hands to play. So be it; although you should stay in any hand if your WF is 1.8 or better. These next two factors recognize it does take a stronger hand to call a raise than to make a raise, and in many cases you must fold.

First, you will use the basic adjustment just discussed.

To adjust for the horse's position, use the increases in WFs shown in figure 9.6.d.

Last, in addition to both the basic adjustment and factoring in the horse's position, use figure 9.6.e to factor in where the horse is seated relative to you.

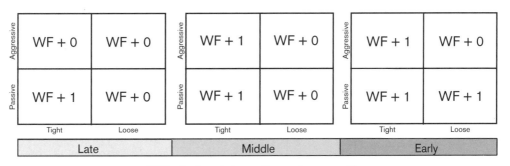

WF adjustment depending on horse position
Figure 9.6.d

	Aggressive	WF + 1	WF + 0			Aggressive	WF + 0	WF + 0

	Tight	Loose
If horse is on your left	**Your seat**	**If horse is on your right**

WF adjustment depending where the horse is sitting relative to you

Figure 9.6.e

Difficulty in adjustment

Until you have a great feel for all of the WFs, it is not easy to make even basic horse adjustments (Oh Willlberrr). The only way you can is to take a few minutes each day to start to learn the WF numbers. Difficult? Yes. Impossible? Not for the world class player.

When to disregard the horse adjustments

As with many things in life, there are exceptions to the rule. Those exceptions occur when you don't have, or don't expect to have, a certain minimum number of callers. These exceptions will be defined in the next section.

Horse summary

- The original horse may not be, and is usually not, the final horse.
- The horse is the last opponent to have acted.
- Adjusting your WFs for the horse allows you to play as an advanced player.
- Tight horses require the most adjustments; loose horses the least.
- There are specific adjustments made when the horse bets, raises, or re-raises.
- Being able to make horse adjustments takes time.

Homework

- Learn and use the basic horse adjustment.
- Then learn and use the advanced horse adjustments.
- Construct 300 scenarios for specific hands, opponents, and other various conditions with horses in different PATL quadrants and determine both the WF you must use and identify the specific hands you could play.

Part VII — Pot size

Introduction
You must take into account the pot size before you stay in any hand.

Preflop pot size
You will not be using WFs after the flop. Postflop you are going to have to know a few numbers. But not preflop. That's because, although we haven't discussed it, the WFs actually indirectly take into account the money which should be in the pot. No need to go into a lengthy mathematical explanation, but the size of the pot depends on whether your table is passive or aggressive which, in turn, gives an indication as to the size of the pot. However, this relationship is not exact. For almost all preflop situations, if you have the correct WF, you are going to stay in the hand regardless of the pot size. The only time you will fold is when the money in the pot, relative to your WF, is too small. WFs are derived from probability; the lower your WF the lower your probability of winning. Yes, you will have a positive Expected Value with a low WF, but you won't catch often, and when you do you want a good size pot. Small limit pots are not worth seeing with a low WF. Even if everyone hasn't acted, if you know how your table usually plays, you can usually predict how many will call preflop. I recommend you fold, unless you have, or anticipate, at least the following number of callers:

> WF of 1.3 needs 3 other callers.
> WF of 1.2 needs 4 other callers.
> WF of 1.1 needs 5 other callers.

Most advanced players disregard these recommendations and see the flop.

Postflop pot size
Everything in this chapter up until now has been concerned with your hand preflop. But for the next few pages we will focus on postflop pot size because:

> **once the flop is shown, the size of the pot will be the primary determining factor in whether you continue to play a hand.**

Postflop you can forget about WFs. You will have to know some numbers, but you will not have to do much math. We have done most of it for you. We use probability and the size of the pot to determine whether or not to consider making a call or bet.

Using the concept of Expected Value, you know you will bet, call or raise anytime you are in positive Expected Value territory because over the long term you will win money.

You also know anytime you are in negative Expected Value territory you will fold because over the long term you will lose money. We will discuss later what you will do if you imply — that is, estimate — there will be enough bets to push your hand into positive Expected Value.

Calculating the minimum pot size

We need to find the minimum size of the pot needed for you to even consider betting. The pot size will be converted into bets. That way you won't have to learn numbers for a specific game or convert small bets into big bets.

Here's the procedure used. First, we need to calculate the probability of you making your hand. Then we must multiply that probability by the size of the pot. If your bet is less than the expected win, you may consider betting. Why don't we just say bet? Because the numbers presented later only take into account making your hand, not winning your hand. If your bet is more than the expected win, you never bet, because over the long term you will certainly lose money.

This was explained in the Numbers Chapter, but because it is so important, it is worth a review. On the flop you will know 5 cards, the 2 in your hand and the 3 on the board. There are 52 cards in the deck, so drawing on the turn there are 47 (52 − 5 = 47) unknown cards. After the turn you know 6 out of the 52 so drawing on the river there are 46 unknown cards. "Outs" is poker parlance for the number of cards left in the deck which will make a hand. We then take the number of outs and divide that number by the number of unknown cards left. For example, suppose you have AK and you didn't hit a A or K on the flop.

To make top pair with top kicker you can get any one of 6 cards — any of the 3 remaining Aces or any of the 3 remaining Kings — on the turn. You have 6 outs to make top pair. There are 47 unknown cards on the turn.

6/47 (12.76%) is the probability of you making top pair on the turn.

Suppose you missed on the turn. You still have 6 outs to make your hand. There are now 46 unknown cards.

6/46 (13.04%) is the probability of you making top pair on the river.

These probabilities must now be converted into how many bets must be in the pot for you to consider betting. Back in the Numbers Chapter, figure 7.6.b showed how we converted the number of outs into the bets needed. Now we are going to apply those calculations to obtain minimum bets needed in the pot for specific draws.

Numbers you need to know
Figure 9.7.a, the Truth Drawing Numbers, shows the important results of Expected Value calculations including an adjustment for the rake. The far left column shows your drawing situations. The middle column describes the hand, or hands, you would make with the right card. **The right hand column has the minimum number of bets that must be in the pot in order for you to consider calling to see the next card**. If you have these draws on the flop, figure 9.7.a does not take into account that you can see two more cards. In limit you should make your postflop drawing decisions on a card-by-card basis. In a few cases where there is a one-bet difference between the flop and turn, the more conservative number is used. In limit, you are never pot committed. You are only committed to the Truth Drawing Numbers.

Truth Drawing Numbers
Minimum bets needed in the pot when drawing

What you have on either the flop or turn	Drawing to make	Minimum bets in the pot to see the next card
Four flush and open-ended straight	Flush or straight	4
Four flush with double inside straight draw	Flush or straight	4
Four flush with two overcards	Flush or high pair	4
Open-ended straight with two overcards	Straight or high pair	4
Four flush and inside straight draw	Flush or straight	5
Four flush with A or face overcard	Flush or high pair	5
Open-ended straight with A or face overcard	Straight or high pair	5
Double inside straight draw with A or face overcard	Straight or high pair	5
Inside straight draw with two overcards	Straight or high pair	6
Four flush	**Flush**	**6**
Open-ended straight	**Straight**	**7**
Inside straight draw with Ace or face overcard	Straight or high pair	8
Three of a kind	Full house or quads	8
No hole card paired, such as AK	**High pair**	**9**
One hole card paired	**Two pair or three of a kind**	**11**
Inside straight draw	**Straight**	**13**
Two pair	Full house	13
Pocket pair	**Three of a kind**	**26**

Figure 9.7.a

The **situations in bold** and the **minimum number of bets in bold** are those you need to memorize. You will run into those situations often. **The Truth Drawing Numbers are the most important numbers you must know in limit when drawing postflop.**

Examples

For example, you have AK. You are 3rd to act. You raised. Everyone except the little and big blinds folded. They both called. At this point there are 6 small bets in the pot. The flop comes and you miss. The small blind checks; the big blind bets. Should you call? There are 7 small bets in the pot. Look at the Truth Drawing Numbers. They say there must be at least 8 bets in the pot for you to consider calling. There are only 7. You must fold.

Another example. Again you have AK. You are 3rd to act. You raised on the button. You have three callers, including both blinds. At this point there are 8 small bets in the pot. The flop comes and you miss. The bettor to your right bets. Should you call? Now there are 8 small bets in the pot. The Truth Drawing Numbers say there must be at least 8 bets in the pot for you to consider calling. There are, so you might call. You call if you believe you would have the best hand with an A or K on the turn. If your judgment about having the winning hand with top pair is correct, the probabilities are in your favor.

Again you have AK. You are 3rd to act. You raised in late position. You have four callers, including both blinds. At this point there are 10 small bets in the pot. The flop comes and you miss. Everyone checks, and you check. On the turn you miss again. Everyone checks except the bettor to your right, who now bets. Should you call? If you haven't played a lot, when you look at the Truth Drawing Numbers, you might conclude you should. There are 10 small bets in the pot, but now if you call you must call with a big bet. The 10 small bets are the equivalent of 5 big bets. The Truth Drawing Numbers say there must be at least 8 bets for you to call, and there are not that many big bets in the pot, so you must fold.

Deducting bad outs

There are times when you cannot use the situations and results shown in the Truth Drawing Numbers, figure 9.7.a. They occur when one of the cards you need will probably help an opponent beat you. Suppose your hole cards are the 5♥ and the 5♣. The flop does not show a pair, you miss, and there are two spades showing. Betting is sufficient that if you used the Truth Drawing Numbers, you would call. But one of the two cards you need to make a set is the 5♠ which could easily give an opponent a flush. Instead of having two cards to make a winnable set, you really only have one, the 5♦. How do you adjust? The best, but not easiest, solution is to memorize the outs and bet chart shown in figure 7.6.c. Or, if you can do a little math in your head, you can get a close solution quickly. Here's how. Divide the number of outs into 50. Then round up whatever you get. The answer will either be the same as, or a very close approximation to, the correct Truth Drawing Number. As an example, suppose you have 8 outs. 50/8 = 6.25, rounded up is 7 bets, which is exactly what appears in the Truth Drawing Numbers, figure 9.7.a. Beginners should use this approximation before staying in a hand with a draw.

When playing pot limit, which is a variation of limit but allows you to bet up to the amount in the pot, the Truth Drawing Numbers mean nothing. You must still take into account the size of the pot, but it is more complicated because you have to take your number of outs, divide that by the number of unknown cards left, and multiply that result by the amount in the pot. If you have difficulty dividing by the number of unknown cards, divide by 50, as that will be a close approximation. As always, if the result is a positive Expected Value, you stay in. If not, fold.

How do the Truth Drawing Numbers relate to pot odds?

It is the same thing if pot odds are used correctly. The Truth Drawing Numbers are easier to use.

What about implied odds?

"Implied odds" is poker language used to describe what will probably be the size of the pot during this round of betting, or the next round or the round after that, compared to how much you think you will have to bet to stay in the hand. **When we use the concept of implied odds we are not looking at the immediate round of betting, rather we forecast our total investment throughout the entire hand and compare that to our total possible return on that investment**. It is a guess. But if you know your opponents, it is an educated guess. Here's why some players guess. When it is the player's turn to act, he realizes he should theoretically not call, because he knows the Truth Drawing Numbers, or "pot odds," but he believes other players who have not yet acted will bet and make the pot size big enough that it will be correct to call.

To help determine the implied bets during the current betting round, always glance at all players' fingers, especially the opponents to your left, to see who has their cards off the table, indicating a fold; calling chips in their hands, indicating a call; or two bets, signaling a raise.

Example. You have AK; seems like you are getting that hand a lot. You raised preflop. There are two callers and the small blind folded. There are now 7 small bets in the pot. The flop comes and you miss. The big blind bets. At this point there are 8 bets in the pot. The Truth Drawing Numbers say there must be 9 bets for you to call. But you know the player behind you is loose and likes to be in every pot. You believe, that is you "imply," he will call, bringing the total number of bets to 9. If the bets are 9 the Truth Drawing Numbers say it is correct to call. You "implied" he would bet. That's what the term "implied odds" means.

When the flop comes, being able to predict the minimum size of the pot on the river is not an easy skill to master. In fact, many experienced players do not think that far ahead in a hand.

Do the minimum number of bets in the Truth Drawing Numbers take into account implied odds?

No. If you believe the pot size will be a certain amount after you act, you may use that "implied" number of bets in the pot to determine if you stay in the hand.

Do not underestimate how valuable, especially in big pots, using implied odds is. A common situation is at a loose table, when there was a raise preflop with many callers and you have a medium or low pocket pair, but didn't catch on the flop. If you used the Truth Drawing Numbers alone, that is there must be 26 small bets in the pot for you to call, in most cases you would fold. But, if you know your opponents well, and predict there will be at least 26 small bets on the turn, you should pay one more small bet to see if you catch. A similar situation arises when you have hit less than top pair on the flop. The Truth Drawing Numbers indicate there should be 10 small bets in the pot for you to see the turn trying to catch two pair or trips. However, if you believe there will be 10 bets after you see the turn card, you should stay in for one bet.

If you are a beginner, forget implied odds for now. If you are an advanced beginner, it is not recommended you think of implied odds beyond the current round of betting until you know your opponents well enough to project the amount of betting which will go on in future rounds of betting. If you are an experienced player, but are not experienced when the flop comes at forecasting the minimum size of the final pot, you must learn this skill. Don't use implied odds unless, while on the flop, you can estimate the final size of the pot within 3 big bets 80% of the time. World class players can, on the flop, closely predict the final size of most pots.

Keeping track of the number of bets

The easiest way to keep track of the number of bets in the pot is with your chips. Keep a few chips aside which will be used to stack as the bets are made; in other words you will never use these chips to bet, only to know how many bets are in the pot. We'll call this your keeping track of bets stack. For each bet made put a chip on your bets stack. Now you will know how many bets have been made just by looking at your stack. When you get to the turn just take the stack and divide it in half as you are going from small bets to big bets on the turn. If you have memorized the Truth Drawing Numbers in figure 9.7.a, all you have to do is compare your draw to the size of your stack. If the stack is lower than the bets shown in the Truth Drawing Numbers, you must fold. If your stack is equal to or greater than the Truth Drawing Numbers, you should stay in the hand if you believe your draw, if made, will be the winner.

Even if you don't use this stack method of keeping track of the number of bets in the pot, you must always know, and you need to know without pausing to count the pot or ask the dealer, as this will be a tell that you are on a draw, how much is in the pot.

Another easy method is just to listen carefully as the dealer will announce how many players are in the hand. For example preflop the dealer says, "Eight players," and there have not been any raises, there are eight bets in the pot. If everyone had called a raise there would be 16 bets in the pot.

The beginner

"I'm a beginner. All this material is too complicated for me. I want to play in a home game next week. Can't you simplify all of this?" What is presented here is not a substitute for determining which hands you may play. It is intended for those true beginners who need some guidelines. You will not always be playing the hands you should, but using these benchmarks should keep you out of trouble.

Beginner Level I – The Rule of 100

Use these values, the same as you would for blackjack, for your cards

> An Ace will have a value of 11.
>
> A King, Queen, Jack or Ten will be 10.
>
> Use the number that appears on lower cards.

Multiply and add

> Multiply your two cards together. An Ace and a 7 would be $(11 \times 7) = 77$.
>
> Add 30 if they are suited.
>
> Add 30 if they are paired.
>
> Add 60 if they are both paired and suited. Anytime you add 60, you need to understand the cards better. Stay at this Beginner Level I for at least another month.

If no one has raised, and your total is 100 or higher, play the cards. If not, fold.

> KT (10×10) = 100. Play.
>
> A7s $(11 \times 7) + 30$ = 107. Play.
>
> 77 $(7 \times 7) + 30$ = 79. Fold.

If anyone has raised, only play a top ten hand. See figure 10.8.d for the top ten hands.

Beginner Level II – Position adjustment

Adjust the numbers above and play fewer hands in early position, more in later position, as shown in figure 9.7.b.a

95	100	105
Late	Middle	Early

Figure 9.7.b.a

Beginner Level III – Position and tight or loose table adjustment

You should know by now a tight table does not see the flop often, and a loose table sees a lot of flops. If less than ½ the players see the flop we will call this a tight table. If ½ or more see the flop this will be a loose table.

Figure 9.7.b.b

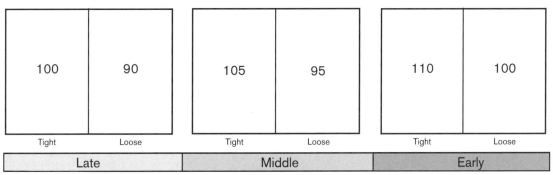

Figure 9.7.b.c

Figure 9.7.b.c indicates at a loose table, in early position, your cards need to total at least 100, at a tight table, 110. Then, in middle position at a loose table, your cards must total 95, and so on.

The beginner playing no limit

Some of this will be reinforced in a later chapter, however it is included here as many beginners will only read these few pages.

If you are a beginner playing no limit, your only chance of winning is to do all of the following:

1. Play lion or lamb poker. That means you either raise or you get out. And you should be folding at least 80% of the time.
2. You want the hand to be over either preflop or on the flop. The reason you do not want to have the hand get to the turn and river is that the better players will know how to outplay you. Do not try to build the pot, no matter how good you think your hand is. You want to get the hand over fast.
3. The way you attempt to get the hand is to raise enough preflop or on the flop to get everyone to fold.
4. Since your objective is to get everyone to fold as fast as possible you should follow these beginner lion or lamb

rules. All of these rules apply only if you decide to stay in a hand.

a. Preflop a lion

    (1)   If you are the first to bet, you will raise 5 times the big blind.

    (2)   If a player in front of you calls, and you want everyone to fold, raise 7 times the big blind.

    (3)   If a player in front of you bets or raises and you have a hand you want to play, re-raise him the size of the pot.

    (4)   If a player in front of you bets or raises and you have a hand you want to play, if you are going to have to use up ⅓ or more of your chips anyway, go all in.

b. Flop a lion

    (1)   If you missed the flop, only have one remaining opponent, are the first to bet, and bet strong preflop, you will take one stab at the pot by betting the full size of the pot. Other than this one bluff, you will not bluff at any other time.

    (2)   If you missed and someone bets in front of you, you will not chase with two overcards trying to catch top pair, nor will you chase with an inside straight draw. You will chase and call, for anything less than a pot size bet, an open-ended straight or a four flush draw.

    (3)   If you think your hand is the best and someone else bets, raise the full size of the pot.

c. Turn and river a lamb

    (1)   If you are unfortunate enough to get to the turn or river, play passive, even if you have what you think is a good hand. You are Little Red Riding Hood in with the wolf.

    (2)   Do not be concerned with extracting more money from your opponents if you have a good hand. Be happy if you win what's in the middle.

    (3)   With heavy betting, top pair is not often the best hand. If betting is light, you may check and call. If the betting is heavy and all you have is top pair, you should consider folding.

    (4)   If you believe you have the best hand, only bet ½ the pot.

Summary

- Pot size must be taken into account before you stay in a hand.
- Preflop WFs take into account the size of the pot except when the pot is very small.
- Postflop, the size of the pot will be the primary determining factor whether you continue to play a hand.
- There is a minimum number of bets that must be in the pot before you consider betting.
- The Truth Drawing Numbers tell you what to do on a draw.
- If one of your outs can possibly give an opponent a better hand, you cannot use the Truth Drawing Numbers without making an adjustment.
- If there are a certain number of minimum bets in the pot, you will stay in if you believe your hand or made draw will be the winner.
- Implying how many bets will be in the pot is important as it allows you to stay in large pots.
- Use your chips or find another method to keep track of the number of bets in the pot.
- Beginners may use some guidelines to help them stay out of too much trouble.
- Beginners playing no limit must play lion or lamb poker.

Homework

- Memorize and use the Truth Drawing Numbers.
- Create 100 situations when you must deduct bad outs and show exactly how you would make the adjustments.
- Imply the size of each betting round for every hand you play or watch from now on.
- On the flop imply the total size of the pot at the end of the hand for all hands you play or watch.

1. You are playing limit at a 6-handed Aggressive/ Loose table and seated on the button. Which of the following hands are mathematically correct to play?
   - ❏ A. KQ
   - ❏ B. 77
   - ❏ C. A7s
   - ❏ D. QJs
   - ❏ E. None are playable

2. You are playing limit at a 6-handed Very Passive/ Loose table and seated #3. Which of the following hands are mathematically correct to play?
   - ❏ A. 99
   - ❏ B. KQs
   - ❏ C. AJs
   - ❏ D. Two of the above
   - ❏ E. None are playable

3. You are playing limit at a 6-handed Very Aggressive/ Mega-Loose table and seated on the button. Which of the following hands are mathematically correct to play?
   - ❏ A. AK
   - ❏ B. A9s
   - ❏ C. 77
   - ❏ D. Two of the above
   - ❏ E. None are playable

4. You are playing limit at a 6-handed Aggressive/ Mega-Loose table and seated #4. Which of the following hands are mathematically correct to play?
   - ❏ A. A5s
   - ❏ B. KT
   - ❏ C. AT
   - ❏ D. Two of the above
   - ❏ E. None are playable

5. You are playing limit at a 6-handed Passive/Mega-Loose table and seated #5. Which of the following hands are mathematically correct to play?
   - ❏ A. T8s
   - ❏ B. A9
   - ❏ C. A2s
   - ❏ D. Two of the above
   - ❏ E. None are playable

6. You are playing limit at a 6-handed Passive/Mega-Loose table and seated at the small blind. Which of the following hands are mathematically correct to play?
   - ❏ A. T8s
   - ❏ B. A9
   - ❏ C. A2s
   - ❏ D. Two of the above
   - ❏ E. None are playable

7. You are playing limit at a 6-handed Very Aggressive/ Very Loose table and seated on the button. Which of the following hands are mathematically correct to play?
   - ❏ A. 77
   - ❏ B. AJ
   - ❏ C. QTs
   - ❏ D. All are playable
   - ❏ E. None are playable

8. You are playing limit at a 6-handed Very Aggressive/Very Loose table and seated #5. Which of the following hands are mathematically correct to play?
   - ❏ A. 77
   - ❏ B. AJ
   - ❏ C. QTs
   - ❏ D. All are playable
   - ❏ E. None are playable

9. You are playing limit at a 6-handed Very Aggressive/Very Loose table and seated #3. Which of the following hands are mathematically correct to play?
   - ❏ A. 88
   - ❏ B. KQ
   - ❏ C. QJs
   - ❏ D. Two of the above
   - ❏ E. None are playable

10. You are playing limit at a 6-handed Passive/Very Loose table and seated on the button. Which of the following hands are mathematically correct to play?
   - ❏ A. 55
   - ❏ B. A2s
   - ❏ C. KJ
   - ❏ D. Two of the above
   - ❏ E. All are playable

11. You are playing limit at a 6-handed Very Passive/ Very Loose table and seated on the button. Which of the following hands are mathematically correct to play?
   - ❏ A. JT
   - ❏ B. T7s
   - ❏ C. 87s
   - ❏ D. All are playable
   - ❏ E. None are playable

12. You are playing limit at a 6-handed Very Passive/ Very Loose table and seated #3. Which of the following hands are mathematically correct to play?
   - ❏ A. JT
   - ❏ B. T7s
   - ❏ C. 87s
   - ❏ D. All are playable
   - ❏ E. None are playable

13. You are playing limit at a 6-handed Very Aggressive/Loose table and seated #4. Which of the following hands are mathematically correct to play?
   - ❏ A. JTs
   - ❏ B. K7s
   - ❏ C. AQ
   - ❏ D. Two of the above
   - ❏ E. None are playable

14. You are playing limit at a 6-handed Very Aggressive/Loose table and seated #3. Which of the following hands are mathematically correct to play?
   - ❏ A. 99
   - ❏ B. KJs
   - ❏ C. AQ
   - ❏ D. Two of the above
   - ❏ E. None are playable

15. You are playing limit at a 6-handed Aggressive/ Loose table and seated #3. Which of the following hands are mathematically correct to play?
   - ❏ A. 99
   - ❏ B. KJs
   - ❏ C. AQ
   - ❏ D. All are playable
   - ❏ E. None are playable

16. You are playing limit at a 6-handed Passive/ Loose table and seated on the button. Which of the following hands are mathematically correct to play?
   - ❏ A. AT
   - ❏ B. KJ
   - ❏ C. 77
   - ❏ D. All are playable
   - ❏ E. None are playable

17. You are playing limit at a 6-handed Passive/ Loose table and seated #5. Which of the following hands are mathematically correct to play?
   - ❏ A. AT
   - ❏ B. KJ
   - ❏ C. 77
   - ❏ D. All are playable
   - ❏ E. None are playable

18. You are playing limit at a 6-handed Very Aggressive/Tight table and seated #3. Which of the following hands are mathematically correct to play?
   - ❏ A. AK
   - ❏ B. 99
   - ❏ C. KQs
   - ❏ D. All are playable
   - ❏ E. None are playable

19. You are playing limit at a 6-handed Aggressive/ Tight table and seated on the button. Which of the following hands are mathematically correct to play?
   - ❏ A. QJs
   - ❏ B. AK
   - ❏ C. 88
   - ❏ D. All are playable
   - ❏ E. Two are playable

20. You are playing limit at a 6-handed Aggressive/ Tight table and seated #3. Which of the following hands are mathematically correct to play?
   - ❏ A. QJs
   - ❏ B. AK
   - ❏ C. 88
   - ❏ D. All are playable
   - ❏ E. None are playable

21. You are playing limit at a 6-handed Very Passive/ Tight table and seated #4. Which of the following hands are mathematically correct to play?
   - ❏ A. T9s
   - ❏ B. A3s
   - ❏ C. 55
   - ❏ D. All are playable
   - ❏ E. None are playable

22. You are playing limit at a 6-handed Very Passive/ Tight table and seated #4. Which of the following hands are mathematically correct to play?
   - ❏ A. KJ
   - ❏ B. A3s
   - ❏ C. 44
   - ❏ D. All are playable
   - ❏ E. None are playable

23. You are playing limit at a 6-handed Very Passive/Tight table and seated #3. Which of the following hands are mathematically correct to play?

❏ A. KJ
❏ B. A3s
❏ C. 44
❏ D. All are playable
❏ E. None are playable

24. You are playing limit at a 6-handed Passive/Tight table and seated #4. Which of the following hands are mathematically correct to play?

❏ A. 77
❏ B. AJ
❏ C. KTs
❏ D. All are playable
❏ E. None are playable

25. You are playing limit at a 6-handed Passive/Tight table and seated #3. Which of the following hands are mathematically correct to play?

❏ A. AQ
❏ B. 99
❏ C. KQs
❏ D. All are playable
❏ E. None are playable

26. You are playing limit at a 10-handed Very Passive/Mega-Loose table and seated #3. Which of the following hands are mathematically correct to play?

❏ A. JT
❏ B. 54s
❏ C. 86s
❏ D. All are playable
❏ E. None are playable

27. You are playing limit at a 10-handed Very Passive/Mega-Loose table and seated on the button. Which of the following hands are mathematically correct to play?

❏ A. A9
❏ B. 53s
❏ C. 63s
❏ D. All are playable
❏ E. None are playable

28. You are playing limit at a 10-handed Very Passive/Mega-Loose table and seated #8. Which of the following hands are mathematically correct to play?

❏ A. A9
❏ B. 53s
❏ C. 63s
❏ D. All are playable
❏ E. None are playable

29. You are playing limit at a 10-handed Passive/Mega-Loose table and seated on the button. Which of the following hands are mathematically correct to play?

❏ A. 43s
❏ B. JT
❏ C. A9
❏ D. All are playable
❏ E. Two are playable

30. You are playing limit at a 10-handed Passive/Mega-Loose table and seated #7. Which of the following hands are mathematically correct to play?

❏ A. 54s
❏ B. QT
❏ C. 22
❏ D. All are playable
❏ E. None are playable

31. You are playing limit at a 10-handed Passive/ Mega-Loose table and seated #9. Which of the following hands are mathematically correct to play?
- ❑ A. 54s
- ❑ B. A9
- ❑ C. 63s
- ❑ D. All are playable
- ❑ E. None are playable

32. You are playing limit at a 10-handed Passive/ Mega-Loose table and seated #7. Which of the following hands are mathematically correct to play?
- ❑ A. 54s
- ❑ B. A9
- ❑ C. 63s
- ❑ D. All are playable
- ❑ E. None are playable

33. You are playing limit at a 10-handed Very Passive/ Mega-Loose table and seated #3. Which of the following hands are mathematically correct to play?
- ❑ A. 74s
- ❑ B. Q2s
- ❑ C. 22
- ❑ D. All are playable
- ❑ E. None are playable

34. You are playing limit at a 10-handed Very Passive/ Mega-Loose table and seated on the button. Which of the following hands are mathematically correct to play?
- ❑ A. 63s
- ❑ B. A9
- ❑ C. Q2s
- ❑ D. All are playable
- ❑ E. None are playable

35. You are playing limit at a 10-handed Very Passive/ Mega-Loose table and seated #5. Which of the following hands are mathematically correct to play?
- ❑ A. 63s
- ❑ B. A9
- ❑ C. Q2s
- ❑ D. All are playable
- ❑ E. None are playable

36. You are playing limit at a 10-handed Very Passive/ Mega-Loose table and seated #9. Which of the following hands are mathematically correct to play?
- ❑ A. 74s
- ❑ B. K2s
- ❑ C. A9
- ❑ D. All are playable
- ❑ E. Two are playable

37. You are playing limit at a 10-handed Very Aggressive/Very Loose table and seated on the button. Which of the following hands are mathematically correct to play?
- ❑ A. 74s
- ❑ B. K2s
- ❑ C. A9
- ❑ D. All are playable
- ❑ E. None are playable

38. You are playing limit at a 10-handed Very Aggressive/Very Loose table and seated #5. Which of the following hands are mathematically correct to play?
- ❑ A. 74s
- ❑ B. K2s
- ❑ C. A9
- ❑ D. All are playable
- ❑ E. None are playable

39. You are playing limit at a 10-handed Aggressive/ Very Loose table and seated #7. Which of the following hands are mathematically correct to play?

   ❑ A. T9s
   ❑ B. A3s
   ❑ C. KQ
   ❑ D. All are playable
   ❑ E. None are playable

40. You are playing limit at a 10-handed Aggressive/ Very Loose table. Which of the following are NOT ever mathematically correct to play?

   ❑ A. A6s
   ❑ B. A2s
   ❑ C. A7s
   ❑ D. Two of the above
   ❑ E. None of the above

41. You are playing limit at a 10-handed Passive/Very Loose table and seated #4. Which of the following hands are mathematically correct to play?

   ❑ A. 99
   ❑ B. AK
   ❑ C. QTs
   ❑ D. None are playable
   ❑ E. All are playable

42. You are playing limit at a 10-handed Very Passive/ Very Loose table and seated #6. Which of the following hands are mathematically correct to play?

   ❑ A. 99
   ❑ B. AK
   ❑ C. QJs
   ❑ D. None are playable
   ❑ E. All are playable

43. You are playing limit at a 10-handed Very Passive/ Very Loose table and seated #7. Which of the following hands are mathematically correct to play?

   ❑ A. 64s
   ❑ B. K2s
   ❑ C. JT
   ❑ D. None are playable
   ❑ E. All are playable

44. You are playing limit at a 10-handed Very Aggressive/Loose table and seated on the button. Which of the following hands are mathematically correct to play?

   ❑ A. 77
   ❑ B. A8s
   ❑ C. AK
   ❑ D. None are playable
   ❑ E. All are playable

45. You are playing limit at a 10-handed Very Aggressive/Loose table and seated #4. Which of the following hands are mathematically correct to play?

   ❑ A. TT
   ❑ B. QJs
   ❑ C. AQs
   ❑ D. None are playable
   ❑ E. All are playable

46. You are playing limit at a 10-handed Aggressive/ Loose table seated and on the button. Which of the following hands are mathematically correct to play?

   ❑ A. A9s
   ❑ B. 88
   ❑ C. AK
   ❑ D. None are playable
   ❑ E. All are playable

47. You are playing limit at a 10-handed Aggressive/ Loose table and seated #6. Which of the following hands are mathematically correct to play?
   - ❏ A. 99
   - ❏ B. JTs
   - ❏ C. AK
   - ❏ D. None are playable
   - ❏ E. All are playable

48. You are playing limit at a 10-handed Passive/ Loose table and seated on the button. Which of the following hands are mathematically correct to play?
   - ❏ A. 22
   - ❏ B. J8s
   - ❏ C. AQ
   - ❏ D. None are playable
   - ❏ E. All are playable

49. You are playing limit at a 10-handed Passive/ Loose table and seated #8. Which of the following hands are mathematically correct to play?
   - ❏ A. A2s
   - ❏ B. A7s
   - ❏ C. AK
   - ❏ D. None are playable
   - ❏ E. All are playable

50. You are playing limit at a 10-handed Passive/ Loose table and seated #4. Which of the following hands are mathematically correct to play?
   - ❏ A. AJs
   - ❏ B. AK
   - ❏ C. TT
   - ❏ D. None are playable
   - ❏ E. All are playable

51. You are playing limit at a 10-handed Very Passive/ Loose table and seated #9. Which of the following hands are mathematically correct to play?
   - ❏ A. AJ
   - ❏ B. J7s
   - ❏ C. Q6s
   - ❏ D. None are playable
   - ❏ E. All are playable

52. You are playing limit at a 10-handed Very Passive/ Loose table and seated #7. Which of the following hands are mathematically correct to play?
   - ❏ A. 54s
   - ❏ B. K9s
   - ❏ C. AK
   - ❏ D. None are playable
   - ❏ E. All are playable

53. You are playing limit at a 10-handed Very Aggressive/Tight table and seated on the button. Which of the following hands are mathematically correct to play?
   - ❏ A. TT
   - ❏ B. KQs
   - ❏ C. AQs
   - ❏ D. None are playable
   - ❏ E. All are playable

54. You are playing limit at a 10-handed Aggressive/ Tight table and seated on the button. Which of the following hands are mathematically correct to play?
   - ❏ A. A9s
   - ❏ B. QJs
   - ❏ C. AK
   - ❏ D. None are playable
   - ❏ E. All are playable

55. You are playing limit at a 10-handed Passive/ Tight table and seated on the button. Which of the following hands are mathematically correct to play?
❏ A. A2s
❏ B. 65s
❏ C. Q9s
❏ D. None are playable
❏ E. All are playable

56. You are playing limit at a 10-handed Passive/Tight table and seated #7. Which of the following hands are mathematically correct to play?
❏ A. A5s
❏ B. 87s
❏ C. AK
❏ D. None are playable
❏ E. All are playable

57. You are playing limit at a 10-handed Passive/Tight table and seated #6. Which of the following hands are mathematically correct to play?
❏ A. TT
❏ B. AJs
❏ C. AK
❏ D. None are playable
❏ E. Two are playable

58. You are playing limit at a 10-handed Very Passive/ Tight table and seated on the button. Which of the following hands are mathematically correct to play?
❏ A. A8s
❏ B. KQ
❏ C. 53s
❏ D. None are playable
❏ E. Two are playable

59. You are playing limit at a 10-handed Very Passive/ Tight table and seated #7. Which of the following hands are mathematically correct to play?
❏ A. A8s
❏ B. KQ
❏ C. 54s
❏ D. None are playable
❏ E. All are playable

60. You are playing limit at a 10-handed Very Passive/ Tight table and seated #3. Which of the following hands are mathematically correct to play?
❏ A. AQs
❏ B. AK
❏ C. TT
❏ D. None are playable
❏ E. All are playable

61. Lower suited cards would be best played against this number of opponents dealt cards.
❏ A. 2
❏ B. 4
❏ C. 7
❏ D. 8

62. Higher unsuited cards would be best played against this number of opponents dealt cards.
❏ A. 2
❏ B. 4
❏ C. 7
❏ D. 8

63. This type of player will play Q9.
❏ A. Tight
❏ B. Loose
❏ C. Very Loose
❏ D. Mega-Loose
❏ E. More than one of the above

64. This type of player will play T6s.
- ❏ A. Tight
- ❏ B. Loose
- ❏ C. Very Loose
- ❏ D. Mega-Loose
- ❏ E. More than one of the above

65. This type of player will play 32.
- ❏ A. Tight
- ❏ B. Loose
- ❏ C. Very Loose
- ❏ D. Mega-Loose
- ❏ E. More than one of the above

66. You will play more hands than the _____ and less hands than the _____.
- ❏ A. Mega-Tight; Tight
- ❏ B. Loose; Very Loose
- ❏ C. Loose; Tight
- ❏ D. Very Loose; Tight

67. If the last person to bet is a passive/tight, how much of an adjustment do you need to make to your preflop WF?
- ❏ A. 0
- ❏ B. +1
- ❏ C. +2
- ❏ D. +3

68. If the last person to bet is a passive/loose, how much of an adjustment do you need to make to your preflop WF?
- ❏ A. 0
- ❏ B. +1
- ❏ C. +2
- ❏ D. +3

69. If the last person to raise is an aggressive/tight, how much of an adjustment do you need to make to your preflop WF?
- ❏ A. 0
- ❏ B. +1
- ❏ C. +2
- ❏ D. +3

70. In limit on the flop or turn, if you have a draw to both a four flush and an inside straight, what must be the minimum number of bets in the pot to see the next card?
- ❏ A. 5
- ❏ B. 6
- ❏ C. 7
- ❏ D. 8
- ❏ E. 9

71. In limit on the flop or turn, if you have a draw to a four flush, what must be the minimum number of bets in the pot to see the next card?
- ❏ A. 5
- ❏ B. 6
- ❏ C. 7
- ❏ D. 8
- ❏ E. 9

72. In limit on the flop or turn, if you have a draw with no hole card paired, such as AK, what must be the minimum number of bets in the pot to see the next card?
- ❏ A. 7
- ❏ B. 9
- ❏ C. 10
- ❏ D. 11
- ❏ E. 13

73. In limit on the flop or turn, if you have a draw to an inside straight, what must be the minimum number of bets in the pot to see the next card?

❑ A. 7
❑ B. 8
❑ C. 10
❑ D. 11
❑ E. 13

74. When we forecast our total investment through out the entire hand and compare that to our total possible return on that investment, in poker language this is known as:

❑ A. Odds
❑ B. Pot Odds
❑ C. Implied Odds
❑ D. Expected Value
❑ E. None of the above

See Appendix E for answers

CHAPTER 10

Betting

Knowing how and when to bet allows you to win the most.

Reward and punishment

Aggression is rewarded
Hold'em is made for aggression. Miller, Sklansky, and Malmuth in their *Small Stakes Hold'em* say it best, "Raising when you should call can cost you a bet. **Calling when you should raise**, however, **can cost you a whole pot**." Unless you are out of position or have nothing but a marginal draw, bet heavy or fold. Miller has two more great points:

1. "The larger the pot the more risks you should be willing to take to win it," and
2. "**Save pots, not bets**."

Aggression is selective and targeted and therefore requires more skill. By selective and targeted we mean you do not play a hand unless the WF is right. You do not stay in a hand unless the numbers are right or you have position. But a**s long as you are in, get in with both feet**. Very Aggressive players in the Advanced PATL live by the phrase, "If it's worth a call, it's worth a raise." Paraphrasing Sklansky, almost all aggressives agree with, "Any hand good enough to call a raise with, is worth a re-raise."

Anytime you believe you have the best hand there is no question of being as aggressive as possible. As long as you remain in the hand, the more different draws available to hurt you, the more aggressive you must be. When playing high limit or at a tight table, add deception to your aggression.

You don't always have to be the aggressor
To be a long term winner, as long as you are in the hand, you want aggressive betting. But you do not need to be the aggressor if there are aggressives yet to act. If others won't be aggressive, and you are still willing to call, then don't limp, get aggressive.

Aggressiveness and the number of opponents
Aggressiveness has different implications depending on how many opponents are dealt cards. If you have few opponents, aggressive betting can win often, even if you miss. If you have several opponents aggressive betting pays off with bigger pots when you catch.

Calling is punished
Callers do not win the most in hold'em. Callers lose. Anyone who consistently calls demonstrates weakness. **Callers can only win if they have the best hand**. Unless they are a passive/tight, they are telling everyone else they are on a draw or don't have much. The aggressive will use the caller as a punching bag by betting, raising, and re-raising. **Passive calling costs you money.**

Checking and calling is punished more
If there is anything an expert player pounds more than a caller, it is the player who checked and called.

Taking the lead is rewarded
When you are the lead bettor or raiser, the horse, you tend to control the hand. If you have position and you are both the lead bettor and raiser, you control both the size of the pot and the play of passive opponents. Another benefit of taking the lead at a tight table is if you have missed, since you have been representing a big hand all along, you are in good shape if you find yourself at the river and the only way you can win is to bluff. You don't have to have the best hand to win; all you have to do is make them fold.

What the best players do, in this order

1. Fold. They fold most of their hands.
2. Raise or bet. If they are in a hand, they are in aggressively.
3. Call. They seldom call.

What happens if your personality isn't aggressive or you don't enjoy taking the lead?

Play tighter; play higher WFs than recommended. But when you do come into a hand, force yourself to be aggressive and take the lead. If you can't bring yourself to do this, hold'em is not the game for you. You may win the oft quoted grinder, that is, passive/tight, average of one big bet per hour, but you will never have the winnings you could.

General comments

Table or individual PATL

Recognizing when to focus on the table PATL versus an individual's PATL is the first step in betting. Preflop focus should be on the table's PATL. Postflop, you must switch to where your remaining opponents fall in their individual PATL. Figure 10.1 shows the relative importance.

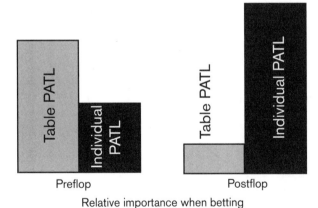

Relative importance when betting

Figure 10.1

Chips speak

A call says you are on a draw. A raise says you have a good hand. A check-raise or re-raise says you have the best hand. A check-raise can be used if you need to slow down an aggressive/loose.

Asking what he has

The way you ask what someone has is to **raise or re-raise preflop or on the flop when bets are small**. Better to find out now and fold, than to stay in when the bets are big. This is a play you should use often. It saves you bets. Suppose you have TT. A Jack flops along with lower rags. A player in early position bets. You should raise. If any bettor other than an aggressive/loose calls — letting you know he probably has a Jack, with not a very good kicker — you are likely dead. If he had a Jack with an Ace, King, or Queen, he would have re-raised. If he bets on the turn, you would fold. Some players would have called on the flop, and then called all the way to the river. Those players would have spent 2½ big bets to find out they lost the hand. You spent 2 small bets — that is the same as 1 big bet — to find out you should fold. Of course, your aggressive opponent could have been bluffing, but unless he is an experienced player, he would not bet out on the turn.

Opponents who fold to aggressive play

In limit, if your objective is to get an opponent to fold, see figure 10.2. Where an opponent falls within the PATL has a lot to do with the betting rounds during which they can be intimidated. In no limit, more opponents fold on the flop against aggressive play and fewer fold on the turn than figure 10.2 indicates.

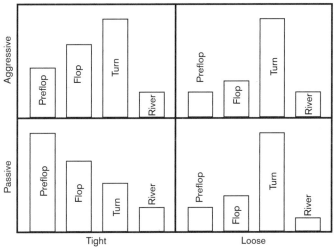

Folding frequency in limit with aggressive play
Figure 10.2

	Tight	Loose
Aggressive	Will run over opponents	Will run over opponents
Passive	Will not run over opponents	Will not run over opponents

Figure 10.3

Running over opponents

Many expert players play the people, not the cards. These experts will identify the loose player who stays with draws and other marginal hands, and aggressively push them out of pots. The cards these experts hold have almost no effect on how they bet. If you find yourself in a game against one of these players, you either have to put your Very Aggressive hat on, wait until you have a very good hand to play — one with an appropriate high WF — or move to another table.

Building the limit pot

There are a few schools of thought for building the pot when you think you have the best hand.

1. Play straightforward and do not slowplay. Bet out. Raise. This works best when you are playing loose players. When you have a made hand you punish drawers by betting and raising. This is repeated until it appears you are beat, either by a card on the board or by heavy betting — especially from multiple opponents.

2. Check-raise on the flop. This works well at a loose table with its typically large number of callers, but has the disadvantage of everyone checking or folding on the turn. Another disadvantage is that with many callers who believe they are now pot committed, as you will have at a loose table, you run a greater risk of being outdrawn.

3. Slowplay on the flop and then raise or check-raise on the turn. This works best when aggressives are still in the hand.

Most players check and call when on a draw. **If you are on a draw, you should aggressively build the pot preflop and on the flop, especially with many callers**. Now when we combine the concept of punishing drawers when you have a made hand along with building the pot aggressively when you are on a draw, you will find yourself in big pots on the turn. On the turn, if you still have the best hand you will continue aggressively; if still on a draw, check and call.

Buying the button

Heavy betting is recommended in late position. There are two major reasons for this aggression. First, you are building the pot if you win. As mentioned previously, you have better information the later your position. The best position to be in is on the button, as you will have the most information possible and be in control of the pot. Unless you are already the button this is the second major reason for raising in late position. If those after you fold, you now have the button. You have bought the button.

When you are raised

Your opponent has announced he thinks he has the best hand or a draw to the best hand. Before you get into a "raisefest," use your boardology and your knowledge of where he fits in the PATL to figure out what range of hands he probably has. A raise from a passive means something. A raise from an aggressive may not mean anything.

	Tight	Loose
Aggressive	Can't tell if raise means anything	Raise means nothing
Passive	Raise really means something	Raise means something

Figure 10.4

When you check-raise

The advantages of check-raising are to:

1. Build the pot.
2. Have checkers and drawers fold.
3. Get the calling tights to check in the next betting round.
4. Trap the aggressives.
5. Neutralize your early or middle position.

The problem with a check-raising is that when everyone else checks, you have given a free card. A check-raise attempt should only be made if there are aggressives left to act; forget the check-raise with only passives in the hand. Another problem with a check-raise is that you can no longer hide in the weeds; everyone will assume you have a strong hand. If the board contains a pair, do not check-raise unless the pair helped you. Never check-raise unless the flop helped you. Only check-raise with a draw if that draw is both on the flop and to the nuts. In general, straightforward play works best on the turn and river. However, if you are ahead, down to aggressive opponents, and early to bet, a check-raise will work on the turn.

You are check-raised

When someone check-raises you, unless you have a great hand, you are probably beat, and should fold. Even the aggressive/loose won't usually check-raise unless he hits; he just bets out or raises, trying to push everyone out. The aggressive/tight who missed will check-raise if he smells weakness.

Overcall

A player bets. Someone raises. It comes to you. If you call this raise use both the horse adjustments and your horse sense. Unless both opponents are aggressive/loose, you must believe your hand or draw is not just equal to, but better than the hand of the opponent who called the raise.

Beware boards with high cards

There are certain boards which are so dangerous, that unless they help you, extreme caution, and usually folding, is in order.
1. All high cards with one card paired or the board shows a high pair.
2. A three or four flush.
3. Three or more high cards in sequence or with a one-gap sequence.

You have a good hand but there's heavy betting by two or more opponents

A good hand isn't good enough, unless the bettors are aggressive/loose. Stay in only if the number of bets in the pot justifies your draw — the Truth Drawing Number.

Betting patterns and callers

Postflop you will continue to be aggressive with premium draws. The tighter the table, the more callers you will need to stay on a medium draw; the looser, the fewer callers are needed.

Bluffing

Only attempt a bluff against good players and then only when you have been setting it up throughout the entire hand, or a scare card hits on the turn or river.

In low limit with a full table, generally the best hand wins. In high limit, as the table becomes smaller, bluffing is used more. If it is down to five-or-fewer-handed, aggressive bluffing becomes the norm.

Figure 10.5

In limit, you want to build the pot on a draw early in the hand; the flop is a perfect time to do so. Even though this is a semi-bluff, generally you should raise or re-raise on the flop with three or more in the hand.

We will discuss bluffing more in the next chapter.

The continuation bet

A favorite play by an aggressive is the continuation bet. He raised during the previous betting round; the herd thinned down to one or two callers. No matter what appears on the board, if he is first to act, he bets, representing a strong hand, hoping everyone will fold. Continuation bets work best against one, at most two, remaining tight opponents. A continuation bet is more common in limit as smart players in no limit will carefully read the board before they automatically bet. If you are heads up against a professional in no limit, and he was the preflop raiser and is the first to act on the flop, he will almost always continuation bet, regardless of the board. If you are the aggressor with position in a limit game, use the continuation bet liberally. A tight who led the betting previously and bets out against three or more opponents has something; this is not a continuation bet.

Pot equity

Pot equity is a term which has too many different meanings. Some players say pot equity when they really mean pot odds or Expected Value. Others use pot equity to express a player's share of the pot. Some say it is how much investment a player has in a pot. We will define pot equity as a method of comparing a player's share of the current round of betting to the probability of that player making a hand.

There are three steps for using this concept of pot equity:

First, a player estimates how much he must put in — that is his share — during the current betting round and compares that to what he thinks his opponents will put in — that is their share. He then calculates his share compared to the total and arrives at a percentage.

Second, he calculates the probability of making his hand.

Third, he compares the percentage of money he is putting into this betting round to the probability of him making his hand. If his percentage is greater than his probability, he folds. If his percentage is less than his probability, he calls, or may raise. The easiest way to understand this concept is with examples.

Example 1

Limit. The flop comes. A player has an open-ended straight. He is last to act. Three players bet in front of him.

With this example our player knows how much he must put in during the current betting round compared to what his opponents put in. He then calculates his percentage compared to the total. The other players have put in 3 bets. Our player must put in 1 bet. So our player is putting ¼ or 25% of the bets during this betting round.

Our player knows, because he read the Numbers Chapter, his chance of catching a straight if played to the river is 31%.

He then compares the percentage of money he is putting into this betting round, 25%, to the probability he will get a straight if played to the river, 31%. When his percentage contribution, in this case 25%, is less than his probability, 31%, he stays in. In this example he would at least call, but more than likely raise.

Example 2

Limit. The flop comes. A player has an open-ended straight. He is last to act. One opponent bets in front of him.

The other player has put in 1 bet. Our player must put in 1 bet. So our player is putting in ½ of the bets or 50% of the bets during this betting round.

The probability of catching a straight if played to the river is 31%.

His percentage contribution is 50% and that is more than his probability of 31%. He would fold.

With both of these examples, we assumed the flop was on the board, and used the probability of catching if we played to the river. A player on the flop using the concept of pot equity might very well use the probability of catching on the turn, not the probability of seeing two more cards to make his decision. And if the turn card has been shown, he must use the probability of catching on the river.

Pot equity in no limit

Pot equity in no limit uses the same principles. The difference is — and it is a big difference — unless you are the last to act, or know the opponents left to act are passive, you don't know how much it will cost you to stay in the hand.

Turn equity

When you hear "turn equity" this means the player is taking into account only the probability of winning by seeing just the next card, and comparing that to the percentage of money he must put in to see the next card. Although the term "turn equity" may not be used much, this type of thinking occurs in no limit on the turn with one card to come, or on the flop when the player knows if he doesn't catch on the turn, one opponent will bet heavy and push him out before he can see the river. He uses the pot equity concept to determine if he will stay in to see the next card.

Which is better, pot equity or Expected Value?

You can see both pot equity and Expected Value use probability. Pot equity focuses on the percentage of the player's current bet and does not take into account how much is already in the pot. Expected Value does. The concept of pot equity can be used for raising, but as an overall strategy, you are better off always using Expected Value.

More general comments

Your betting pattern with a draw

As we will repeat often, with a draw you make the most in limit by getting money in the pot during the first two betting rounds. In a few pages you will find specific times to call or raise depending on whether the table is loose or tight, your position, and the number of opponents. Early position is difficult, as you do not want to get re-raised and then isolated, and therefore you won't be building the pot often in early position. An exception is if you are in the blind preflop with many callers and catch, then raising to build the pot is a good play. On the flop, in middle or late position, continue to build the pot with a raise as long as pot equity says to do so. If in late position, on the turn you will take the free card, call if the Truth Drawing Numbers are right. If you miss and there are only a few tight opponents remaining, you may continue to bet to set up a bluff on the river.

When the board pairs
When the board pairs with anything TT or lower and you are the first to act, a bluff is in order if there are only tights remaining. If you are in the blind and the board shows a low pair, bet.

Steals
Let's assume you have the reputation of an aggressive bettor who, when he stays in a hand, has good cards. You will go for steals during any betting round if:

1. No remaining opponent is the kind who will call you just to see what you have.
2. You are down to one or two tight opponents.
3. The pot is small with only tight opponents. Small pots are much easier to steal than big ones. Tight opponents understand the numbers and will usually let a small pot go.
4. You smell weakness and you are the first to act. This is one of the few times early position is an advantage. Try for a steal with a bet. The turn is the best round for this play.

	Tight	Loose
Aggressive	One or two opponents; go for the steal	No steal attempt
Passive	One or two opponents; go for the steal	No steal attempt

When to go for a steal on any betting round
Figure 10.6

When you have a boat or better
Raise and re-raise unless you have the nuts in which case you may slowplay until the turn. If there is heavy betting from another opponent, beware of the bigger boat. Quads are rare. Unless you are against a heavy betting passive/tight, ignore the possibility.

Betting yourself out of a pot
Does aggressive play always pay off? This next concept may take a few minutes to understand. It says you can build the pot so high that smart players will stay in the hand with a draw they would have folded if the pot was small. Figure 10.7.a shows who knows the numbers and who doesn't.

If an opponent understands the numbers, he will stay in with a draw when his Expected Value is positive. Here is the conclusion. If you are down to one or two opponents who know the numbers, especially aggressive/tights, you should not always continue to raise and re-raise if you can see a draw on the board that could beat you. See figures 10.7.a-b.

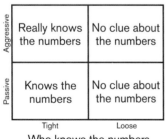

	Tight	Loose
Aggressive	Really knows the numbers	No clue about the numbers
Passive	Knows the numbers	No clue about the numbers

Who knows the numbers
Figure 10.7.a

Betting yourself into a pot

If you can bet yourself out of a pot, you can also bet yourself into a pot. You're at a passive/loose table in late position with a small pair. You raise preflop, a value bet if you hit, the big blind re-raises, and everyone calls. On the flop you miss but there is an early bettor and several callers. When it gets to you there are 26 small bets in the pot. Following the Truth Drawing Numbers, you call. If the pot was less, you would have folded on the flop. You might have called anyway if you implied enough bets on the turn. Obviously, if you hit on the turn you will probably win. When this happens you have actually bet yourself into a pot.

	Tight	Loose
Aggressive	Can easily bet yourself out of a pot	Cannot bet yourself out of a pot
Passive	Could bet yourself out of a pot	Cannot bet yourself out of a pot

Betting yourself out of a pot

Figure 10.7.b

Fold when beat

No matter how much you have put in the pot, if you know you are beat, fold as early as possible. The only exception is pre-river if you are on a monster draw and the Truth Drawing Numbers say it is correct to stay in.

Preflop

Attack, attack, always attack loose players, or fold

You must only bet preflop hands with the proper WFs. When you are in a hand, in middle or late position with loose players, aggressive play will win you the most money. Some aggressive players will raise preflop with a playable WF in any position, as they understand they have a positive Expected Value and that when they hit, this is their way to build the pot.

If you are this type of aggressive player you should know when you should definitely not raise, even with a playable WF. That exception is in early position at a loose table with a WF of 1.3 or less; here you should only call to see the flop. In all other cases, preflop raising will allow you to value bet or protect your hand by thinning the herd.

If you are trying to eliminate players by raising when bets are small, understand that loose players who have already put in one bet will put in another bet. Raising will not thin the loose herd, but will build the pot.

Anytime you are not sure whether to call or fold preflop, fold.

Get rid of the blinds

Regardless of the type of table, if you are staying in the hand in late position with a WF of 1.3 or better, raise to get rid of the trash hands in the blinds. Every hand, even a random one, has at least a 32% chance of hitting something on the flop. Two blinds means a 54% chance of one or both of them catching. Force the blinds to pay to play.

Preflop limit betting models

Great chess players have all their various opening moves mapped out and modeled, regardless of who makes the first move. Preflop is your chess opening move. We are going to look at two possible limit betting models. After you understand how they were built, you should create your own depending on how liberal or conservative you prefer to play. The left hand side of figures 10.8.a and 10.8.b will show you potential betting models using Win Factors. They show a basic betting play, what to do when faced with a raise, or faced with calling 2 bets, all depending on the number of actual or implied callers. You should carefully study the left hand side of both of these figures as one is very liberal with betting and the other is more conservative. **These models are for limit play only**.

When a phrase such as "3+ callers" is used, this means you take the stated action when you know or imply there will be 3 or more callers. If you do not believe you will have at least 3 callers, you fold. Similarly, the phrase "4- callers" means you take the stated action if you have or imply 4 or fewer callers.

On the right hand side of 10.8.a we have shown the hands which are played according to this model for both a 10-handed and 6-handed Mega-Loose table, while 10.8.b shows Very Loose tables. The hands in bold correspond to the WFs shown. If you find the action stated too conservative or liberal for your taste, you must build your own preflop betting model. If you do, you should use a similar pattern shown in figures 10.8.a or 10.8.b. Specifically, your model should meet the following criteria:

1. Use Win Factors to build your model. The hands corresponding to the WFs are found in Part II of Chapter 9. Remember, WFs change depending on the degree of tightness or looseness and how many opponents are dealt

cards. For example, the hands shown on the right hand side of figures 10.8.a-b correspond to the exact same WFs at Mega-Loose and Very Loose tables; the only difference is the number of opponents dealt cards. If you carefully compare the right hand columns you may be surprised to see how the number of opponents influences which hands you can play.

2. The lower your WF, the more callers you must have. This makes sense, as the lower your WF, the lower your probability of winning, and so when you do catch — which won't be often with a low WF — you want it to pay.

3. In addition, you need more callers if faced with or anticipating a raise; and even more with a 2-bet situation.

Expert limit players tend to be more aggressive than these models indicate.

As you learn the WFs you will be able to adapt a model to any table, regardless of how many are in the game, or how tight or loose the table is. You will mentally be able to construct a WF chart for the number of opponents, such as the 10-handed table shown in figure 10.8.c, adjust for how tight or loose the table is, and then convert the WFs into specific hands. The concept is simple; the execution is not easy.

How does this preflop betting model relate to the horse?

This model does not take into account the horse. As you become more experienced and know where each opponent falls in the PATL, you will be able to modify your betting based the horse.

Preflop guidelines. Mega Loose table.

	Basic play	Faced with or imply a raise	Faced with or imply 2 bets	Win Factor	These hands correspond to Win Factors for a 10-handed Mega-Loose table.	These hands correspond to Win Factors for a 6-handed Mega-Loose table.
Fold	Never	Never	Never	1.8+	AA AKs KK AQs QQ JJ	AA KK QQ JJ
Call	Never	Never	Never			
Raise	Always	Always	Always			
Fold	Never	Never	Never	1.7	AA AKs KK KQs AQs QQ AJs JJ	AA AKs KK AQs QQ JJ TT
Call	Never	Never	Never			
Raise	Always	Always	Always			
Fold	Never	Never	Never	1.6	AA AKs KK KQs AQs QQ QJs KJs AJs JJ ATs TT	AA AKs KK AK KQs AQs QQ AJs JJ TT
Call	Never	Heads up	2 callers			
Raise	Always	2+ callers	3+ callers			
Fold	Never	Heads up	2 - callers	1.5	AA AKs KK AK KQs AQs QQ QJs KJs AJs JJ JTs QTs KTs ATs TT 99	AA AKs KK AK KQs AQs QQ AQ QJs KJs AJs JJ ATs TT 99
Call	Heads up	2 callers	3 callers			
Raise	2+ callers	3+ callers	4+ callers			
Fold	Heads up	2 - callers	3 - callers	1.4	AA AKs KK AK KQs AQs QQ AQ KQ QJs KJs AJs JJ JTs QTs KTs ATs TT T9s J9s K9s A9s 99 A8s 88	AA AKs KK AK KQs AQs QQ AQ KQ QJs KJs AJs JJ AJ JTs QTs KTs ATs TT A9s 99 88
Call	2 callers	3 callers	4 callers			
Raise	3+ callers	4+ callers	5+ callers		A5s A4s	
Fold	2 - callers	3 - callers	4 - callers	1.3	AA AKs KK AK KQs AQs QQ AQ KQ QJs KJs AJs JJ JTs QTs KTs ATs TT T9s J9s Q9s K9s A9s 99 98s T8s K8s A8s 88 A7s 77 A6s 66 A5s 55 A4s 44 A3s 33 A2s 22	AA AKs KK AK KQs AQs QQ AQ KQ QJs KJs AJs JJ AJ QJ JTs QTs KTs ATs TT AT KJ T9s J9s Q9s K9s A9s 99 K8s A8s 88 A7s 77 A5s
Call	3 callers	4 callers	5 callers			
Raise	4+ callers	5+ callers	6+ callers			
Fold	3 - callers	4 - callers	5 - callers	1.2	AA AKs KK AK KQs AQs QQ AQ KQ QJs KJs AJs JJ AJ KJ QJ JTs QTs KTs ATs TT AT KT QT JT T9s J9s Q9s K9s A9s 99 98s T8s J8s Q8s K8s A8s 88 87s 97s T7s K7s A7s 77 76s 86s K6s A6s 66 65s K5s A5s 55 54s K4s A4s 44 A3s 33 A2s 22	AA AKs KK AK KQs AQs QQ AQ KQ QJs KJs AJs JJ AJ KJ QJ JTs QTs KTs ATs TT AT KT QT JT T9s J9s Q9s K9s A9s 99 98s T8s K8s A8s 88 K7s A7s 77 A6s 66 A5s A4s A3s A2s
Call	4 callers	5 callers	6 callers			
Raise	5+ callers	6+ callers	7+ callers			
Fold	4 - callers	5 - callers	6 - callers	1.1	AA AKs KK AK KQs AQs QQ AQ KQ QJs KJs AJs JJ AJ KT QJ JTs QTs KTs ATs TT AT KJ QT JT T9s J9s Q9s K9s A9s 99 98s T8s J8s Q8s K8s A8s 88 87s 97s T7s J7s Q7s K7s A7s 77 76s 86s 96s Q6s K6s A6s 66 65s 75s 85s Q5s K5s A5s 55 54s 64s 74s Q4s K4s A4s 44 43s 53s Q3s K3s A3s 33 Q2s K2s A2s 22	AA AKs KK AK KQs AQs QQ AQ KQ QJs KJs AJs JJ AJ KJ QJ JTs QTs KTs ATs TT AT KT QT JT T9s J9s Q9s K9s A9s 99 A9 KT Q9 98s T8s J8s Q8s K8s A8s 88 A8 K9 87s 97s T7s J7s Q7s K7s A7s 77 Q6s K6s A6s 66 K5s A5s 55 K4s A4s 44 K3s A3s A2s
Call	5 callers	6 callers	7 callers			
Raise	6+ callers	7+ callers	8+ callers			

Figure 10.8.a

	Basic play	Faced with or imply a raise	Faced with or imply 2 bets	Win Factor	These hands correspond to Win Factors for a 10-handed Very Loose table.	These hands correspond to Win Factors for a 6-handed Very Loose table.
Fold	Never	Never	Never	1.9+	AA KK QQ	AA KK QQ
Call	Never	Never	Never			
Raise	Always	Always	Always			
Fold	Never	Never	Never	1.8	AA / **AKs** KK / QQ	AA / KK / QQ / **JJ**
Call	Never	Never	Never			
Raise	Always	Always	Always			
Fold	Never	Never	Never	1.7	AA / AKs KK / **AQs** QQ / **JJ**	AA / **AKs** KK / QQ / JJ
Call	Never	2 callers	3 callers			
Raise	2+ callers	3+ callers	4+ callers			
Fold	Never	2 - callers	3 - callers	1.6	AA / AKs KK / **KQs** AQs QQ / **AJs** JJ	AA / AKs KK / **AQs** QQ / JJ / **TT**
Call	2 callers	3 callers	4 callers			
Raise	3+ callers	4+ callers	5+ callers			
Fold	2 - callers	3 - callers	4 - callers	1.5	AA / AKs KK / KQs AQs QQ / **QJs KJs** AJs JJ / **KTs ATs TT**	AA / AKs KK **AK** / **KQs** AQs QQ / **AJs** JJ / TT
Call	3 callers	4 callers	5 callers			
Raise	4+ callers	5+ callers	6+ callers			
Fold	3 - callers	4 - callers	5 - callers	1.4	AA / AKs KK **AK** / KQs AQs QQ / QJs KJs AJs JJ / **JTs QTs** KTs ATs TT / **A9s 99** / **88**	AA / AKs KK AK / KQs AQs QQ **AQ** / QJs KJs AJs JJ / **KTs ATs** TT / **99** / **88**
Call	4 callers	5 callers	6 callers			
Raise	5+ callers	6+ callers	7+ callers			
Fold	4 - callers	5 - callers	6 - callers	1.3	AA / AKs KK AK / KQs AQs QQ **AQ KQ** / QJs KJs AJs JJ / JTs QTs KTs ATs TT / **T9s J9s Q9s K9s** A9s 99 / **A8s 88** / **A7s 77** / **66** / **A5s 55** / **A4s 44** / **A3s 33** / **22**	AA / AKs KK AK / KQs AQs QQ AQ **KQ** / QJs KJs AJs JJ **AJ** / **JTs QTs** KTs ATs TT / **K9s A9s** 99 / **A8s 88** / **77**
Call	5 callers	6 callers	7 callers			
Raise	6+ callers	7+ callers	8+ callers			
Fold	5 - callers	6 - callers	7 - callers	1.2	AA / AKs KK AK / KQs AQs QQ AQ KQ / QJs KJs AJs JJ / JTs QTs KTs ATs TT / T9s J9s Q9s K9s A9s 99 / **98s T8s** Q8s K8s A8s 88 / **87s 97s K7s** A7s 77 / **76s** A6s 66 / **65s** A5s 55 / **54s** A4s 44 / A3s 33 / **A2s** 22	AA / AKs KK AK / KQs AQs QQ AQ KQ / QJs KJs AJs JJ AJ **KJ QJ** / **JTs QTs** KTs ATs TT **AT** / **T9s J9s Q9s K9s** A9s 99 / A8s 88 / **A7s 77** / **A6s 66** / **A5s** / **A4s** / **A3s**
Call	6 callers	7 callers	8 callers			
Raise	7+ callers	8+ callers	9 callers			

Figure 10.8.b

Preflop betting – Win Factors – Summary Model – 10-handed

Monster	Tight	Loose	Very Loose	Mega-Loose
AA	2.8	2.8	2.9	3.0
KK	2.2	2.3	2.4	2.5
Premium				
QQ	1.9	2.0	2.1	2.1
AKs	1.5	1.7	1.8	1.9
JJ	1.6	1.7	1.7	1.8
Strong				
AQs	1.4	1.6	1.7	1.8
AJs	1.3	1.4	1.6	1.7
KQs	1.4	1.5	1.6	1.7
TT	1.4	1.5	1.5	1.6
Good drawing				
ATs	1.3	1.4	1.5	1.6
A9s	1.2	1.3	1.4	1.4
KJs	1.2	1.4	1.5	1.6
KTs	1.2	1.4	1.5	1.5
K9s	1.1	1.3	1.3	1.4
K8s	1.0	1.1	1.2	1.3
QJs	1.2	1.4	1.5	1.6
QTs	1.2	1.3	1.4	1.5
Q9s	1.2	1.2	1.3	1.3
AK	1.1	1.3	1.4	1.5
AQ	1.0	1.1	1.3	1.4
KQ	1.0	1.1	1.3	1.4
JTs	1.2	1.3	1.4	1.5
T9s	1.2	1.3	1.3	1.4
98s	1.1	1.2	1.2	1.3
J9s	1.1	1.2	1.3	1.4
T8s	1.1	1.2	1.2	1.3
99	1.4	1.4	1.4	1.5
88	1.3	1.3	1.4	1.4
77	1.3	1.3	1.3	1.3
66	1.3	1.3	1.3	1.3
55	1.3	1.3	1.3	1.3
44	1.3	1.3	1.3	1.3
33	1.3	1.3	1.3	1.3
22	1.3	1.3	1.3	1.3
A8s	1.1	1.3	1.3	1.4
A7s	1.1	1.2	1.3	1.3
A6s	1.1	1.2	1.2	1.3

Good drawing (continued)	Tight	Loose	Very Loose	Mega-Loose
A4s	1.2	1.3	1.3	1.4
A3s	1.2	1.3	1.3	1.3
A2s	1.2	1.2	1.2	1.3
Drawing				
87s	1.1	1.2	1.2	1.2
76s	1.1	1.2	1.2	1.2
65s	1.2	1.2	1.2	1.2
54s	1.2	1.2	1.2	1.2
43s	1.2	1.2	1.1	1.1
97s	1.1	1.1	1.2	1.2
86s	1.1	1.1	1.1	1.2
K7s	1.0	1.1	1.2	1.2
K6s	1.0	1.1	1.1	1.2
K5s	1.0	1.1	1.1	1.2
K4s	1.0	1.1	1.1	1.2
Q8s	1.0	1.1	1.2	1.2
AJ	0.9	1.0	1.1	1.2
AT	0.8	1.0	1.1	1.2
KJ	0.9	1.0	1.1	1.2
QJ	0.8	1.0	1.1	1.2
JT	0.9	1.0	1.1	1.2
KT	0.8	0.9	1.1	1.2
QT	0.8	1.0	1.1	1.2
J8s	1.0	1.1	1.1	1.2
T7s	1.0	1.0	1.1	1.2
Marginal draw				
75s	1.1	1.1	1.1	1.1
64s	1.1	1.1	1.1	1.1
53s	1.1	1.1	1.1	1.1
K3s	1.0	1.1	1.1	1.1
K2s	1.0	1.1	1.1	1.1
Q7s	1.0	1.1	1.1	1.1
Q6s	1.0	1.0	1.1	1.1
Q5s	1.0	1.0	1.1	1.1
Q4s	1.0	1.0	1.1	1.1
Q3s	1.0	1.0	1.0	1.1
Q2s	1.0	1.0	1.0	1.1
96s	1.0	1.1	1.1	1.1
85s	1.1	1.1	1.1	1.1
74s	1.0	1.0	1.0	1.1
J7s	1.0	1.0	1.1	1.1

Preflop Betting – Win Factors

Figure 10.8.c

Figure 10.8.d is interesting, although not definitive. The top 40 hands are shown for 10-handed games, depending on how tight or loose the table is, along with their Win Factors, but does not take into account all of the determining factors.

Strength of preflop hands depending on table type

	Tight		Loose		Very Loose		Mega-Loose	
1	AA	2.8	AA	2.8	AA	2.9	AA	3.0
2	KK	2.2	KK	2.4	KK	2.4	KK	2.5
3	QQ	1.9	QQ	2.0	QQ	2.1	QQ	2.1
4	JJ	1.6	JJ	1.7	AKs	1.8	AKs	1.9
5	AKs	1.5	AKs	1.7	AQs	1.7	AQs	1.8
6	AQs	1.4	AQs	1.6	JJ	1.7	JJ	1.8
7	KQs	1.4	KQs	1.5	AJs	1.6	AJs	1.7
8	TT	1.4	TT	1.5	KQs	1.6	KQs	1.7
9	99	1.4	AJs	1.4	TT	1.5	TT	1.6
10	AJs	1.3	ATs	1.4	ATs	1.5	ATs	1.6
11	ATs	1.3	KJs	1.4	KJs	1.5	KJs	1.6
12	88	1.3	KTs	1.4	KTs	1.5	QJs	1.6
13	77	1.3	QJs	1.4	QJs	1.5	KTs	1.5
14	66	1.3	99	1.4	A9s	1.4	AK	1.5
15	55	1.3	A9s	1.3	QTs	1.4	QTs	1.5
16	44	1.3	A8s	1.3	AK	1.4	JTs	1.5
17	33	1.3	K9s	1.3	JTs	1.4	99	1.5
18	22	1.3	QTs	1.3	99	1.4	A9s	1.4
19	A5s	1.3	AK	1.3	88	1.4	A8s	1.4
20	A9s	1.2	JTs	1.3	AQ	1.3	K9s	1.4
21	KJs	1.2	T9s	1.3	K9s	1.3	AQ	1.4
22	KTs	1.2	88	1.3	Q9s	1.3	KQ	1.4
23	QJs	1.2	77	1.3	KQ	1.3	J9s	1.4
24	QTs	1.2	66	1.3	T9s	1.3	T9s	1.4
25	Q9s	1.2	55	1.3	J9s	1.3	88	1.4
26	JTs	1.2	44	1.3	77	1.3	A5s	1.4
27	T9s	1.2	33	1.3	66	1.3	A4s	1.4
28	A4s	1.2	22	1.3	55	1.3	K8s	1.3
29	A3s	1.2	A5s	1.3	44	1.3	Q9s	1.3
30	A2s	1.2	A4s	1.3	33	1.3	98s	1.3
31	65s	1.2	A3s	1.3	22	1.3	T8s	1.3
32	54s	1.2	Q9s	1.2	A8s	1.3	77	1.3
33	AK	1.1	98s	1.2	A7s	1.3	66	1.3
34	98s	1.1	J9s	1.2	A5s	1.3	55	1.3
35	J9s	1.1	T8s	1.2	A4s	1.3	44	1.3
36	T8s	1.1	A7s	1.2	A3s	1.3	33	1.3
37	A8s	1.1	A6s	1.2	A2s	1.2	22	1.3
38	A7s	1.1	A2s	1.2	K8s	1.2	A7s	1.3
39	A6s	1.1	87s	1.2	98s	1.2	A3s	1.3
40	87s	1.1	76s	1.2	87s	1.2	A2s	1.3

Figure 10.8.d

```
                 AA
            AKs KK AK
          KQs AQs QQ
        QJs KJs AJs  JJ
      JTs QTs KTs ATs  TT
    T9s J9s Q9s  A9s 99
  98s             A8s 88
                  A7s 77
                      66
                  A5s 55
                  A4s 44
                  A3s 33
                  A2s 22
```

The core 35 for 10-handed

Figure 10.8.e

	Tight	Loose
Aggressive	Possible to get these players to fold so you can isolate	Difficult to get these players to fold so you can isolate
Passive	Easy to get these players to fold so you can isolate	Difficult to get these players to fold so you can isolate

Figure 10.9

The core 35 for 10-handed

Figure 10.8.2 is important, especially when you sit down at a table and you know nothing about your opponents. It shows the 35 hands which appear in all of the top 40 hands regardless of how tight or loose the table is. These results should come as a surprise to many. The only unsuited hand is AK. Even though AQ, KQ, and AJ do not make the cut, I will often play these hands against new opponents if I am convinced that the table is not tight. Although this model is for a 10-handed table, you may construct a similar model for any number of opponents.

Isolation

Isolation means you use aggressive play to try to get rid of all but one opponent as soon as possible so you can have a showdown on the river. If you have high cards or a high pair, you prefer isolation, especially at a 10-handed table. If you have late position against all but aggressive/loose players, a raise may accomplish isolation. If one player has raised and no one has yet called, a re-raise will almost always result in isolation.

Very low WF hands prefer multi-way pots

Marginal drawing cards have a low WF. With a low WF it's better to have many opponents preflop, because if you catch — which won't be often — you want a big pot. Many advanced players who limp in to a multi-way pot in early position will not hesitate to re-raise if given the opportunity.

Raising from the blinds or early position

When you raise from early position you represent that you have extremely strong cards, although you really may just be trying to build the preflop pot with a draw. That's good at a tight table as most others will fold. If you are on a draw, this play tends to immediately neutralize your poor position. As long as you remain in the hand, you are committed to representing a strong hand; if you show weakness, you can count on being pounded by an aggressive. If you actually have a hand it is difficult to build the pot when you raise preflop from early position, as you will most likely just be called in later betting rounds.

If you want to build the pot at a loose table, check-raise from early position preflop or on the flop when there are still lots of opponents in the hand.

Defending your blind

Defending is usually a bad play. If you are the big blind and the small blind stays in, fold unless you have a pair. You want to defend your blind heads up, as one-on-one is more about betting than cards. Place the raiser in his PATL. If he is passive, fold. Fold unless he is an aggressive and you hold a pocket pair. If you hold a 22, A-anything, or K-anything, then re-raise. Unless you are re-raised you are probably ahead, at least until the flop. Look back at figure 7.13. Preflop a pair is favored and, since 50% of hands end up with nothing, an A or K is also favored. On the flop if you have a pair, any pair, or an A in the hole, continue to bet aggressively. Also note that you should defend your blind more in a short-handed game.

Stealing the blinds

You are in late position preflop with no callers. You raise and hope the blinds fold. That's stealing the blinds. It is really stealing if you raised with a monster such as 72. WFs mean nothing when you are trying to steal the blinds. You are more concerned with what those in the blinds don't have than what you have. Since they will have random hands, unless you meet resistance, you are generally in good shape.

	Tight	Loose
Aggressive	Four or fewer opponents to your left remaining	No steal attempt, even with only blinds remaining
Passive	Four or fewer opponents to your left remaining	No steal attempt, even with only blinds remaining

When to attempt to steal blinds
Figure 10.10

Stealing the blinds is worthwhile. In no limit tournaments, it is extremely important. Unfortunately, experienced players will know what you are trying. But tight players, even though they know what you are doing, will tend to fold much more than loose ones. Therefore, if you are the first to enter the pot, raise in late position if the remaining players to your left are tight players.

You will be ahead if you are successful with 58% of your limit blind steals.

The first to bet wins

Figure 10.11 shows you the degree of deception you should use based on your position. The closer you are to the big blind, the less you are fooling anyone when you attempt a blind steal — except the passive/loose, and they won't know enough not to defend their blind and call a raise. The further away from the button, the better your chance of deceiving your remaining opponents, even the tight ones. When the table shows weakness on the flop or postflop by checking to you, and you have position, bet even if you missed.

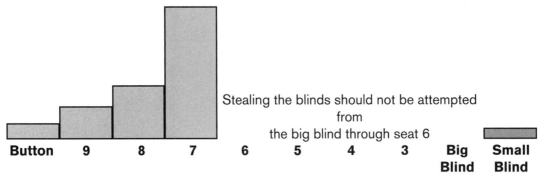

Stealing the blinds should not be attempted from the big blind through seat 6

| Button | 9 | 8 | 7 | 6 | 5 | 4 | 3 | Big Blind | Small Blind |

How much you are deceiving your experienced opponents when you attempt to steal the blinds

Figure 10.11

Regardless, you have to find out if your blinds will fold when raised. One sign is to watch what your blind opponents do preflop when raised from your right with no previous callers. This clue may be helpful, but at your first opportunity try to steal the blinds yourself. You need to find out who won't be bluffed with an attempted blind steal. If you get a re-raise from an aggressive player that probably doesn't mean the re-raiser has better cards. It more likely means he is an experienced player who isn't going to let you steal his blind. Too bad this time, but it is good information for the future.

Although this next sentence should be obvious, surprisingly it isn't to some of my students. You do not want to try to steal the blinds if there was a caller earlier preflop. Anyone who has called in front of you thinks their hand is worth a call. Even though the blinds may fold, the initial caller probably won't. If you raised with a WF of less than 1.1, you are now stuck in a hand hoping for a flop that probability says won't be there. If you find that your blinds fold, and continue to fold, you may now start attempting to steal the blinds from a further away position, to see if those players fold too. As seen in figure 10.11, at a 10-handed table a blind steal attempt from seat 7 or 8 is fairly well disguised.

Stealing posts

A final word on stealing. When a player posts, or, even better, when several players post, if you are the first to enter the pot, raise, even if you have nothing, and go for the steal, regardless of your position.

Recall that in limit you need to steal the blinds 58% of the time to be profitable. With someone posting you only need to be right 45% of the time; two posts 37%; three posts 31%. Attempting to steal the posts and blinds is a worthwhile play.

Checking in the dark when on the big blind
With several loose callers in the hand, when you are the big blind, do not even look at your cards preflop. If the small blind is out, check in the dark. If you hit, make it a check-raise.

Flop
After you see the flop, your checking, betting, or folding is primarily determined by:
1. The Truth Drawing Numbers.
2. Your ability to read your opponents and their hands. Reading the horse.
3. The postflop betting recommendations in figure 10.12. Note how the recommendations differ for tight opponents, shown on the left hand side, versus loose opponents, shown on the right.

Whether you hit or miss on the flop
Figure 10.12 shows how to bet if you hit. What happens if you missed on the flop? Prepare to fold with the first bet at a tight table. At a loose table you will not always fold. Keeping the lead helps if you are going to continue in the hand with either a bluff or some sort of draw. Checking and calling is the worst play as it tells everyone your hand is weak; you missed and are now drawing. Figure 10.12 also gives betting recommendations when the flop doesn't help you. In almost all cases, unless you are at a tight table, you should fold. The terms used in this figure under "You completely miss" are:

A "ragged" board doesn't help you, but it may not have helped anyone else either. There is not a two flush; no two or three in sequence; no Ace or King on the board.

"Something" on the flop means something that may help an opponent. Two in sequence, a two flush, or a low pair qualify as something on the board.

"Dangerous" would include a three flush, three in sequence, three that could easily make a straight, a high pair, or all high cards. Unless you have a hot hand, or a great draw, taking into account the Truth Drawing Numbers, you need to be prepared to fold.

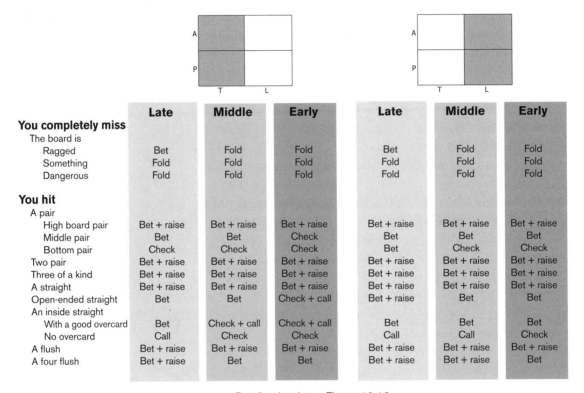

	Late	Middle	Early	Late	Middle	Early
You completely miss						
The board is						
Ragged	Bet	Fold	Fold	Bet	Fold	Fold
Something	Fold	Fold	Fold	Fold	Fold	Fold
Dangerous	Fold	Fold	Fold	Fold	Fold	Fold
You hit						
A pair						
High board pair	Bet + raise	Bet + raise	Bet + raise	Bet + raise	Bet + raise	Bet + raise
Middle pair	Bet	Bet	Check	Bet	Bet	Bet
Bottom pair	Check	Check	Check	Bet	Check	Check
Two pair	Bet + raise	Bet + raise	Bet + raise	Bet + raise	Bet + raise	Bet + raise
Three of a kind	Bet + raise	Bet + raise	Bet + raise	Bet + raise	Bet + raise	Bet + raise
A straight	Bet + raise	Bet + raise	Bet + raise	Bet + raise	Bet + raise	Bet + raise
Open-ended straight	Bet	Bet	Check + call	Bet + raise	Bet	Bet
An inside straight						
With a good overcard	Bet	Check + call	Check + call	Bet	Bet	Bet
No overcard	Call	Check	Check	Call	Call	Check
A flush	Bet + raise	Bet + raise	Bet + raise	Bet + raise	Bet + raise	Bet + raise
A four flush	Bet + raise	Bet	Bet	Bet + raise	Bet + raise	Bet

Postflop betting – Figure 10.12

Checking to the preflop raiser

If you catch, even second high pair, do not check; bet out to see where you are. You may win the pot with your bet.

If you are ahead on the flop

Figure 10.13 tells us that on the flop 71% of the hand has been played. Yes, this is obvious but the obvious is often overlooked. Whoever is ahead on the flop is the clear favorite to win the hand. If that's you, in limit you should build the pot and bet as though the pot is yours.

First at a tight table

If you are the first to bet preflop at a tight table with a WF of 1.3+, raise.

Flop a monster

When you flop a monster, slowplay by checking and calling until the turn, hoping an opponent catches something, or perhaps inducing a bet from an aggressive who smells weakness.

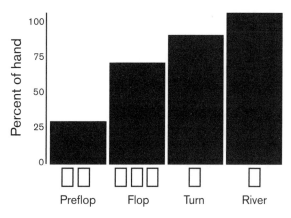

Figure 10.13

You have top pair or pocket overpair on the flop

Remember top pair with an Ace through face kicker wins more often than it loses. The pots will not be nearly as big as when sets compete with straights or better; nevertheless, they win the majority of pots. But you should not slowplay. The more opponents you have, especially loose ones, and the longer they stay in the hand, the more likely it is that someone will outdraw you. Bet extremely aggressively to thin the herd. You want to make it expensive for someone with drawing cards to stay in. If you have AQ you always prefer the flop to be Q high. Top pair with an A kicker is better than an A hitting, as an opponent could have AK. As a side note, if you have a pocket overpair, look at your hole cards after the flop, right before you bet. Hand readers will not put you on a wired pair.

You have second high pair on the flop with no other draw

If first to act, bet. Do not check, regardless of position. If there is an A or K on the board, and someone bets first, fold. If there is no A or K on the board, raise or re-raise now while the bets are small to find out if you are beat.

Overcards

Per the Truth Drawing Numbers there must be 9 bets in the pot for you to see the turn if you have nothing but overcards. There is a special situation where you only need 8 bets to continue. This infrequent occurrence is when you have two suited overcards, one of which is an Ace, the flop has nothing closer than a three gap sequence, and is a rainbow with one of your suit.

You flop two pair, one of which is the high board pair

This is a good, but not great, hand. Bet hard or, if in early position, check-raise.

You flop two pair without the high board pair

Bet extremely hard. You are vulnerable to someone who has a higher pair if the board pairs. Your three pair won't be worth much.

You flop trips; no straight or flush likely

Slowplay, but make sure everyone puts in at least one bet on the flop. Raise or check-raise on the turn. If you get re-raised, just continue to call with less than an A or K kicker.

You flop trips; straight or flush draw on the board

Bet. Raise. Make it expensive for drawers to stay in.

You flop a set, top card or middle card; no straight likely; no two or three flush on the board

Slowplay but make sure everyone puts one bet in the pot on the flop. Raise or check-raise on the turn.

You flop a set, bottom board card

No slowplay. Go aggressive.

You flop a set; straight or flush draw on the board

Bet out. Raise. Make it expensive for drawers to see cards. Back off if flush or straight card comes on turn or river.

You flop a straight; no flush possibility

If you have the high end, slowplay. If you have anything other than the high end, bet out.

You flop a straight; a two flush on the board

Bet hard. Force the flush drawers to pay.

You flop a straight; a three flush on the board

Bet hard now to see who has the flush or is on a draw. If you are raised by a passive player, he has the flush, and you should fold. If you are called, either no one has the flush yet or they have a small flush. Be aware, some players slowplay a strong flopped flush.

You flop a flush but your pocket high card isn't very good

Go aggressive and try to get everyone out. Back off and possibly fold if another of that suit appears on the board.

You flop the nut flush

Slowplay. Let others catch up. As bait for the hand readers look at your hole cards to indicate you are not sure if you have one of the flush cards. If the board pairs on the turn, change tactics and bet hard.

You flop a boat, low three of a kind

Bet.

You flop a boat, high three of a kind

Slowplay. Bet or check-raise on the turn.

You flop a good draw

With a four flush, open-ended straight, or double inside straight draw, always bet if there are only tights left. Always bet, raise and re-raise if there are several others who will call, regardless of the types of players. Check and call with few players as long as the Truth Drawing Numbers are correct.

Going for a free card

It is really a ½ price card. Here's why. You raise on the flop in late position and hope everyone checks to you in the next round so you can check if you don't hit. You paid a small bet for the raise instead of having to call a big bet on the turn. You save ½ a big bet. When do you go for a free card? It depends on three things:

1. Your position.
2. Where your opponents are in their individual PATL.
3. The strength of your draw.

If you are ahead with less than a monster, never allow a free card; bet. If you are in late position with any kind of draw, likewise do not allow a free card. The only time you will allow a free card is when you have nothing. In Chapter 2 the free card play was recommended against only loose players. However, now we take into account the strength of your draw in figures 10.14.a-b.

Figure 10.14.a shows when to go for a free card if you have a strong draw, such as the nut flush draw or an open-ended straight at the upper end.

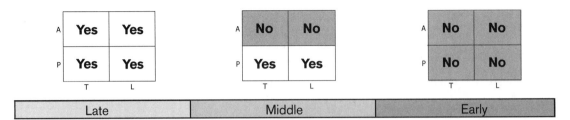

When to go for a free card with a strong draw
Figure 10.14.a

Figure 10.14.b shows when to go for a free card with a weak draw, such as a low flush or stright draw.

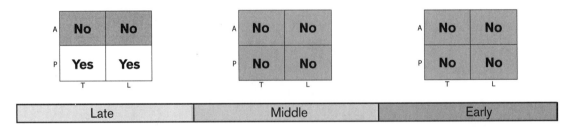

When to go for a free card with a weak draw
Figure 10.14.b

Who has a pair?

Anytime there are three or more players on the flop probability says one of them has at least a pair. Recall from figure 7.3 that any unpaired hole cards have a 32% chance of catching at least one pair on the flop. From figure 7.5.a you also know any player has a 6% probability of having a pocket pair. Therefore, on the flop an individual player has a 38% chance of having at least a pair. Two players and there is a 3 in 5 chance someone has at least a pair. Three and there is over a 3 in 4 chance at least one has a pair. If you are one of the players and you don't have a pair, the chance of someone else having a pair is increased.

Checking in the dark on the flop

If you are the first to act on the flop, on a draw with several in the hand, a check in the dark will partially neutralize your poor position, especially when you hit and end up check-raising.

Dangerous flops

When high cards flop

Not good unless the flop hits you. One, sometimes several, of the players in the hand will have something to go with the high cards. As stated earlier, QJ and JT are hazardous at any kind of table with many callers.

When the board pairs

Someone could have a boat. If heavy betting has been going on prior to the board pairing, the boat is much more likely, especially if a high card pairs. The two low pair you got with the big blind, and have been betting and raising with, just went down the drain. The term is "counterfeited." Your straight or flush draw is probably worthless.

When a three flush appears on the flop

In a 10-handed game at least two hands will usually be suited. Remember that 24% of all hands are suited, and many loose opponents will stay with any two suited. If a passive/loose leads the betting on a three flush, you should assume he already has the flush.

When cards flop in sequence or close sequence

At a 10-handed table, on average, preflop, at least four players will have a straight draw. At a loose table this flop is a red flag. The higher the cards, the greater the risk.

Both a two or three flush and cards in sequence or near sequence

A high pair at a loose table is not as strong when double draws flop, especially with several loose callers.

Flop bottom pair

Usually worthless. But if the Truth Drawing Numbers are right, don't check; bet out or call to see the turn for one bet.

You can't win except with runner runner

Recall from the Numbers Chapter your chance of a runner runner is a terrible 4%. Fold. The only rare exception is if you have both a backdoor straight and flush draw. Now your chance of catching is theoretically increased. If one of your draws is to the nuts and there are at least 14 bets in the pot, you may see the turn for one bet.

Turn/river

The turn

Bets go from small to big. This is the most difficult betting round in high limit and no limit. If you are up against aggressives it will also be expensive.

Not sure to check or bet

If you can't decide between betting or checking on the turn, bet.

A check on the turn

When a passive opponent checks on the turn it means he is on a draw or has less than the high pair. It is a sign of weakness. Attack.

When the board pairs on the river

If the pair is J or higher, and you only have a pair less than the river card, check and call.

When only one card can make a straight

If that card is a J or higher, back off. Check and call.

When connectors could make a straight

Put your opponents in their PATL. Who would stay in with high or low connectors? Who would stay in with high or low suited connectors?

When one gap cards could make a straight

Again, put opponents in their PATL and judge who would play the cards.

When a four flush appears

If you don't have one and you are down to one opponent, on average there is a 39% chance he has the flush; two opponents, a 63% chance; three or more, you are probably dead. If someone else bets and another player calls, or worse, raises, you know to fold.

Anytime there is heavy betting and you have less than a top dog hand

Fold.

Anytime you smell weakness and you have nothing

If everyone checked on the flop, many times the first who bets on the turn wins. When you smell weakness, bet out against tights on the turn and river. Bet out against passive/loose players on the turn; the turn is when you can intimidate a passive/loose player. Check or fold against loose players on the river.

Anytime you smell weakness and you have 2nd or 3rd pair

Bet out, raise against tights. If the board shows an A or K, it is all right to raise against loose players for information. If the board shows anything lower than the A or K, raise on the turn; call on the river. If the herd thinned out to two or fewer callers on the river, bet out or call.

You have top pair with a good kicker or an overpair; flush or straight draw on the board

On the turn bet hard, raise. Check and call on the river.

You have top pair with a good kicker or an overpair; nothing else apparent on the board

Bet; raise; re-raise.

You have top pair with less than a good kicker

Bet out on the turn; fold to a raise; check and call on the river.

You have trips; flush or straight draw on the board

Bet hard on the turn; call if re-raised. If then re-raised, check and call on the river; otherwise bet.

You have a set; nothing else apparent on the board

Bet hard; raise; re-raise.

You have a set; higher set or flush or straight possibility on the board

Bet hard on the turn; call on the river.

You have the low end straight; nothing else apparent on the board

Bet on the turn; call on the river.

You have the low end straight; flush or higher straight draw possible

On the turn bet out, raise. On the river, call.

You have the high end straight; nothing apparent on the board

Both turn and river, bet out, raise, re-raise.

The board has three of your suit and you have a low flush

On the turn bet out and raise. On the river, call.

The board has three of your suit; you have a low flush; the board is paired

If the board pairs on the turn; bet, call, raise. If the board pairs on the river, call.

The board has three of your suit; you have one of the two highest cards to make your flush

Bet extremely hard, there is only one higher flush card available and that hand would have to be suited. If raised, re-raise.

The board has four of your suit; you have a low flush; nothing else apparent on the board

Bet hard on the turn; fold on a raise. Check and call on the river; fold on a raise.

The board has four of your suit; you have a flush with the second highest flush card; nothing else apparent on the board

Bet hard; there is only one card that can beat you. Call if re-raised.

The river

You are either in or out. This is the easiest betting round. Bet out or raise if you believe you have the best hand. Do not bet out against a loose player with a scare card on the river, rather, check and call. Do not check-raise unless there are still many opponents, and then only if you are sure someone will bet.

In limit, if you are last to act heads up with less than a strong hand, generally there is no reason to bet. If you have your opponent beat he will fold and you will not win any more. If he caught the winner on the river, he will be waiting to check-raise.

Big pot on the river

In limit, call if you have any chance, even a small one, of winning. You don't have to be right often to make this a profitable play. In figure 10.15 notice with a pot that has 8 bets, you only have to win 1 out of 9 hands for the call to be profitable.

Bets in the pot on the river	How often you must be right to call
5	1/6
6	1/7
7	1/8
8	1/9
9	1/10
10	1/11

Figure 10.15

When should you not call on the river if you don't have much? If an aggressive player bets and you have as little as a low pair, you should call. However, there are times you should not call. If a passive/tight bets out, fold. If a player bets, then another calls, unless that caller is an aggressive/loose he certainly has something and you are better off folding.

If you plan to call on the river

If you are first to bet on the river, and you plan to call if someone bets, see if you can win the pot by betting out.

The final bet heads up

If you are first to act, your lone loose opponent has called all the way to the river and the only way he could beat you is with that river straight or flush card, do not bet out. Check and call. If you bet and he missed he will fold and you have made nothing extra. If you bet and he raises you will call, and if he did hit, you will have lost an extra big bet.

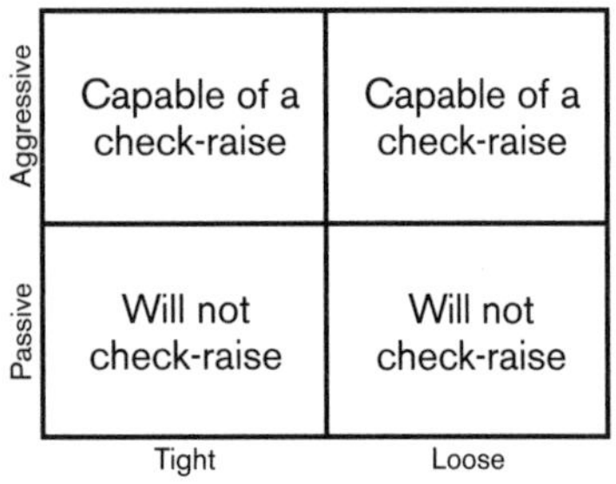

	Tight	Loose
Aggressive	Capable of a check-raise	Capable of a check-raise
Passive	Will not check-raise	Will not check-raise

Opponents who might check-raise

Figure 10.16

Opponents who might-check raise

If you are the last to act, your opponent has checked to you and the only way he could win is with the river card, use figure 10.16 to determine if the player is likely to check-raise if he hit.

The boardology warning

Before you bet heavily on the turn or river with a set or anything less, you must see if there is a straight draw on the board. Likewise, on the river, and sometimes on the turn, before you get in a raisefest with a full house, make sure there is not another higher full house possibility. Although rare, look for the straight flush or quads. As mentioned many times, flush draws are easy to see; straight draws are easy to miss.

Everyone agrees with the above, but too many get caught up in the moment, forget their boardology, and fail to carefully read the board. Don't you be one of them. Taking your time to see what can beat you does not cost you anything. Being on automatic aggressive pilot does.

The check-raise

I like to check-raise if I am in early position in a multi-way pot with aggressives left to act. If I check against only one smart opponent or only passive/tights left to act, I will miss a bet.

The no limit value bet

We are about to get to no limit. If you have the best hand and need to extract a few more chips, bet between 25% and 75% of the pot. The 25% would be used if you feel your opponent has a weak hand; go with the 75% if you think he has a strong hand.

A defensive bet

In no limit, when you are the first to act on the turn or river and you intend to call an opponent's bet, a play used by many professionals is to bet out a smaller amount than they think their opponent would bet if they just checked. When the first to act on the turn or river bets out, that indicates he has something strong, even though he may only have a marginal hand, such as second high pair. More than likely the opponent will just call, as opposed to reraising. The defensive bet saves the difference between what was bet and what the opponent would have bet if you had checked. The risk is, of course, that your opponent may reraise.

A final word on position

When you don't have it, passive play is usually best. Certainly in no limit, particularly tournaments, when you are out of position, let others do the betting and keep the pot as small as you can. When you have position, you are in control, and may make the pots larger than you would if out of position. When you've got it, use it.

Bankroll needed

When playing limit, you will need to have a bankroll sufficient to cover the inevitable negative variance, that is losses, that will occur. The bankroll needed depends on how passive or aggressive the type of table you usually play. In figure 10.17 you will see multiples of the big blind which are the suggested bankroll needed. For example if you play at a Very Aggressive table you should have 600 times the big blind, 500 times the big blind for an Aggressive table, and so on. At a $5/$10 Very Aggressive table you should have a bankroll of $6,000.

Aggressive	600
	500
Passive	400
	300

Multiple of the Big Blind needed
Figure 10.17

The no limit exception

After all of the discussion and aggressive examples, there is one major time when it doesn't pay to be aggressive. When? In a no limit tournament where the blinds go up slowly and everyone starts off with deep stacks. If these conditions exist, you are going to find that the path the best players in the world use to make it to the money and the final table is not one of aggression, and that a lot of this, and some other chapters, is thrown out the window. We'll discuss this approach in the next chapter.

You are almost ready

After you pass the final exam, you are ready to start playing for money you care about.

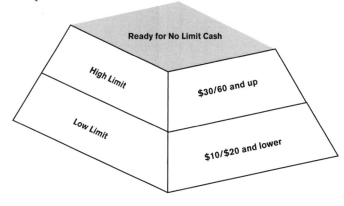

Summary

- **Betting is where the money is made**.
- Hold'em rewards the leader and the aggressor.
- Hold'em punishes the follower and the caller.
- Limit drawing hands should aggressively build the pot preflop and on the flop, especially with many callers.
- Individual PATLs are most important postflop.
- Raise when bets are small to find out how strong other hands are.
- The turn is where most players will fold when faced with aggressive play.
- When in late position preflop, but not on the button, a raise may allow you to buy the button.
- When you are check-raised, unless you have a great hand, you are probably beat.
- You can't bluff bad players.
- Aggressive/tights often use the continuation bet, regardless of whether they hit or not.
- Preflop, the higher your WF, the more aggressive you should play.
- Your position both preflop and postflop will impact your betting.
- How tight or loose the table or opponents are will impact your betting.
- Isolate when you have high cards or a high pair.
- Stealing blinds is profitable.
- If you are ahead on the flop, you are favored to win.
- If you are ahead, bet like the pot is yours.
- If three players see the flop, on average at least one should have a pair or better.
- If you have any chance to win a medium or large pot on the river, call.
- You can actually play so aggressively that you bet yourself out of a pot or into a pot.
- Fold as soon as you know you are beat.
- Boardology will let you know you may be beat. Save your bets.
- You will not use aggression much in certain no limit tournaments.

Homework

- Learn and use the preflop betting numbers in figure 10.8.
- Learn and use the postflop betting patterns in figure 10.12.

CHAPTER 11

No Limit

Introduction

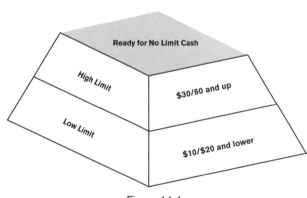

Figure 11.1.a

Warning. **Before you can become good at no limit, you must become great at limit**. If you skimmed the first ten chapters or immediately flipped to this chapter you will lose a ton of money unless you first become great, not just good, at limit. As shown in figure 11.1.a, mastering limit is the least expensive way to become good at no limit, as it provides the most solid foundation possible. You should not move from high limit to no limit until you are consistently winning an average of at least 1.5 big bets per hour.

This chapter is designed to build on your expertise in limit, make you into a good no limit player, and then let you know what it takes to become world class. Anyone can become great at limit by following the first ten chapters. It is a matter of math knowledge and psych skills, all of which can be learned. Yes, it takes a lot of study, but practice — doing and learning, learning and doing — can make anyone a great limit player. The more effort made in limit, the more success.

Not exactly so with no limit. Cash no limit, although more difficult than high limit, will use the same style of play as limit. But **not every player can make the transition from great limit player to great no limit tournament player.** The game and styles of play are different and a much higher level is needed just to be good. The concept shown in figure 11.1.b, although shown at the start of the book, is important to repeat. As you climb the pyramid, the more difficult the play.

You will be shown what is needed, and the tactics can be learned. This chapter will teach you how to be good. But, a certain type of personality is necessary to become great. You either have it or you don't. We'll discuss this at the end of this chapter.

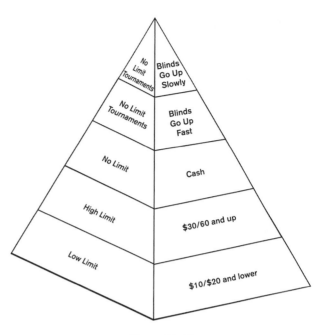

Figure 11.1.b

Here's how this chapter is organized. First, we will go through each of the previous chapters and point out what parts of those chapters are needed or not needed with no limit. From this review you will understand a lot of why the games are different. But just to make sure you know, we will then discuss the important differences. Next, tactics will be revealed which will make you a good player. Last, a discussion to let you know if you have what it takes to become world class in no limit.

The first ten chapters

Introducing the tortoise strategy. Up until now we have emphasized a hare strategy. Be aggressive/tight. Be fast when in a hand. And we will find the hare will still win in many no limit games. But, later in this chapter we will discuss the tortoise method of play. It is used primarily in no limit tournaments when two conditions are met: the blinds go up slowly *and* everyone starts off with a deep stack of chips, as much as 250 times the first big blind. The next several pages will focus entirely on the hare strategy. When we get to the tortoise, you will find it is not an easy concept to grasp, as it will throw out much of what we have already learned about the hare.

If limit is a step to no limit, some parts of the step are more important, some less, and some don't apply at all. This section will comment on portions of the first ten chapters so you know what's important and what's not. To preclude too many no limit phrases, you can just add "to no limit" or "in no limit" at the end of almost every sentence.

Chapter 1 – Introduction
- Poker cannot become golf balls still applies.
- Math knowledge and psych skills are needed; however, as figure 1.1 indicates, psych skills dominate.
- The degree of difficulty with each betting round applies.

Chapter 2 – The Swayne PATL Matrix
- You need to know the basic PATL matrix.
- Loose players still make the most mistakes.
- The players are called the same names.
- How chips are stacked still gives a clue as to how tight or loose the player is, although almost everyone's chips will be stacked in specific incremental amounts.
- There are fewer loose players in no limit; however, many of the best are loose.
- You may not have a choice, but you should still avoid tables where everyone is aggressive/tight.
- Choosing your seat is even more important; however, when you play in a tournament, your seat will be randomly assigned.
- The cost to stay in the hand is much higher.
- The pot size fluctuates substantially more.
- Your bankroll swing is much greater in no limit than limit.
- Despite what you see on TV, there are few bad beats, although you will remember the expensive ones for a long time.
- Position is huge.
- Bluffing occurs more frequently but not by the best players unless it is to steal a small pot.
- Reading hands is extremely important.
- The variance of preflop pot size is more pronounced.
- The number of hands you will play, because of the quality of competition, will generally be fewer.
- No limit games can be noisy, even if the quality of play is high.

- Wins are less a function of where an opponent falls in the PATL than other factors.

the leading bettor will not always
 table.

osition and reading other
his PATL.

ou will find loose players,
straightforward play.

old.

 draws; they are high cards

gh cards and pairs; they are

ot apply.

done less.

re cards on the river; you do
rds.

d Their Hands
y important to the no limit

plays what depending on their
ng hands are played less to the
 pairs or with a bluff tend to

osition shown in figure 3.27
nds shown do not.
- Putting each opponent on a hand is much more important but is also more difficult than in limit, as you will run into many aggressive/tight players.
- Your no tell routine is extremely important.

Chapter 4 – Deception
- Deception is much more important.
- Few no limit players will play bad cards to establish a loose image.

Chapter 5 – Boardology
- Used extensively on the flop; many players take several seconds to study the flop.

Chapter 6 – Playing the Blinds
- Chapter 6 is written for limit players. Playing the blinds in no limit is different, as players defend their blinds more when playing shorthanded or when raised from late position.

Chapter 7 – The Numbers Chapter
- Probability will be extremely important in no limit, more than most players understand.
- With all respect to Mr. Brunson, playing a rush should not be attempted in any kind of game.
- The hand frequencies are exactly the same, as are all the numbers in Chapter 7.
- The outs chart, figure 7.11, means nothing in no limit. You will have to understand and use both probability and Expected Value, especially when you bet to make it too expensive for an opponent on a draw to call.

Chapter 8 – Relative Strength
- All the graphs are much more important for you to know, especially the fewer opponents you have.

Chapter 9 – Which Hands to Play
- The seven determining factors are important; however, because of the aggressive nature of most no limit cash players, they are more difficult to apply.
- Placing a table in the Advanced PATL is of roughly equal importance.
- Placing each opponent in their Advanced PATL is much more important.
- Win Factors are of similar importance.
- Hands you may consider playing are very important; however, unless in a tournament, because of the quality of the table, you will seldom be playing a hand with a WF of less than 1.3.
- Pot size is much more important.
- Implied odds take on a dominant role.

- The Truth Drawing Numbers, so important in limit, mean nothing in no limit.
- The method of keeping track of the number of bets means nothing.

Chapter 10 – Betting
- Aggression is much more important in several, but not all, situations.
- Calling in cash games is punished more but also rewarded more in certain tournament games.
- The individual PATL is more important than the table PATL.
- Chips speak louder.
- The concept of asking what another player has with an early raise still works in no limit, but is much more dangerous than in limit both because it is too expensive and you are subject to a re-raise.
- The concept of folding to aggressive play is much more important; however, the frequencies in figure 10.2 mean nothing in no limit.
- Running over opponents is more prevalent in cash no limit and for small pots in tournaments.
- When you are check-raised in no limit, you don't know if you are beat or are being bluffed. Knowing where your opponent falls in his PATL helps you decide.
- The continuation bet is a favorite play among some no limit players.
- You will not have a betting pattern with a draw. You will be introduced to random deception shortly, so no one will be able to tell if you are on a draw or have a made hand.
- Stealing preflop with position is much more prevalent.
- Fold when you are beat.
- If you have anything, raise to get the blinds to fold.
- The betting charts, figure 10.8, do not apply, although the concept of betting harder with position, or against loose opponents or both, does apply.
- Isolation will occur much more frequently.
- You will seldom get a chance to play a low WF hand, as multi-way pots with position are infrequent.
- Defending a blind is more frequent.
- Stealing blinds is much more frequent.

- If you are ahead on the flop, unless you have the nuts, get opponents out.
- The comments throughout the Betting Chapter on specific types of hands may apply, although as you will see shortly, more raising than calling will occur.
- The principle of betting hard to get draws to fold is much more important.
- The free card play is useless.

What is extremely important?

Even though the previous section discussed each of these, here is a review of what is extremely important for no limit.

- Psych skills.
- Choosing your table.
- Choosing your seat.
- The cost to stay in a hand.
- Position.
- Most winning hands are not made draws; they are high cards and pairs.
- Most big pots are not a high pair; they are made draws.
- Fewer see the flop.
- Fewer showdowns.
- The Reading Opponents and Their Hands Chapter.
- Putting each opponent on a hand.
- No tell routine.
- Deception.
- Taking your time to read the board, primarily on the flop.
- Probability.
- The Numbers Chapter.
- The graphs in the Relative Strength Chapter.
- The seven determining factors, even though they are more difficult to apply.
- Placing each opponent in the Advanced PATL.
- Win Factors.
- Hands you may consider playing are important for cash no limit, but are looser for some tournaments.
- Pot size.
- Implied odds, although more difficult to determine, become huge.
- Aggression.

- Betting harder with position.
- Isolation.
- Defending blinds.
- Stealing blinds.
- Betting hard to get draws to fold.

A word on the extremely important

- **Aggression rules** except in certain tournament situations.
- If your hand is not good enough to raise with, unless you have a draw that will bust an opponent, fold.
- Position is used aggressively.
- Isolation occurs much more frequently. Many hands are down to two players before the turn. Avoid being all in unless you have isolation and the hand.
- In cash games pairs, even second high pair, win more small pots than draws.
- There is more raising and folding before the turn; not nearly as many callers as there are in limit.
- Lots of bluffing in late position trying to steal the blinds.
- Because of the quality of opponents, advanced deception is necessary.
- Check-raising, although not a frequent play, definitely neutralizes poor position.
- Players who have learned how to play on the internet rely on betting patterns not tells. Shortly we will discuss how to deceive with your betting patterns. Players who have learned how to play against people rely on a traditional mix of tells and betting patterns.
- Knowing where each opponent lies **exactly** in the Advanced PATL helps you decide what to do.
- Putting each opponent on a hand, or at least a range of hands, although much more difficult to do than with limit, becomes extremely important.
- Knowing an opponent's betting patterns is a top priority. You must watch every hand played by every opponent carefully.
- Your no tell routine is mandatory, especially when against traditional, non-internet players.

What's different?

- **The rules for various forms of no limit dictate the type of play required.**
- This is a game dominated by one of two strategies.
  1. Stay out of most small pots, unless it is obvious that a bet will pick it up, and win a few big ones.
  2. Used in certain tournaments by the majority of better players who are excellent hand readers: The tortoise strategy; slowly but steadily increase your chip stack. Pick up several small pots via aggressive betting with position. Win big pots by building pots when you have a good hand or staying in when you can imply positive Expected Value.
- Several advanced players will see many flops cheaply then use their experience to outplay the less experienced.
- Successful, less experienced players rely on heavy betting, as much as four times the pot preflop or on the flop, putting pressure on the more experienced.
- More hands are won when no one calls a raise.
- You can control the Expected Value of drawing hands with your bet.
- You will have to defend your blinds more aggressively when someone is attempting a steal.
- A good hand should get as much value as possible.
- **The first aggressor, especially when shorthanded or heads up, puts pressure on his opponents and wins more than his fair share of the pots**.
- The player who acts after a raiser will usually either re-raise, trying to isolate the raiser, or fold.
- The flop is where the bets and plays are made.
- **The pot grows geometrically** especially when you arrive at the turn.
- The turn is by far the most difficult to play as it requires the most difficult decisions.
- Fewer hands played per hour. Sometimes you can have a birthday waiting.
- If an aggressive/loose has the lead and position, he will continue to bet as though he has the best hand.
- Lots of heads up play postflop.
- Many players use all ins when they don't want a call, sometimes on a semi-bluff.

- If a tight player bets, as opposed to going all in, it is usually because he wants to be called or is looking for information.
- In tournaments especially you will find:
  Lots of blind stealing by the better players.
  Less skill in later rounds; more luck.
  More bluffing toward the end.
  Although they will be educated guesses, you will have to guess a lot.
  Many more preflop all ins.
  Anything can happen.
  At times you must gamble.
- Range of hands.

This discussion on the range of hands will be difficult for many to accept, at least until they use it. Up until now everything we have learned, and everything you should have been practicing, emphasized sophisticated mathematical models to determine your starting hands.

Forget all of it. Well, almost all.

At times no limit allows you to play all of the hands we showed for a Very Passive/Mega-Loose 10-handed table, that is all of the hands shown in figure 11.2. Experts may play an even wider range of hands.

Why? Because when you catch with what many opponents would consider to be a trash hand your implied odds are astronomical. With the hidden straight don't be surprised to take all of the chips of an opponent who flopped a set.

```
                              AA
                         AKs KK AK
                     KQs AQs QQ AQ KQ
                 QJs KJs AJs  JJ  AJ KT QJ
             JTs QTs KTs ATs  TT  AT KJ QT JT
          T9s J9s Q9s K9s A9s  99
       98s T8s J8s Q8s K8s A8s  88
    87s 97s T7s J7s Q7s K7s A7s  77
 76s 86s 96s           Q6s K6s A6s  66
65s 75s 85s            Q5s K5s A5s  55
54s 64s 74s            Q4s K4s A4s  44
43s 53s                Q3s K3s A3s  33
                       Q2s K2s A2s  22
```

Possible cash and tournament no
limit playable hands
Figure 11.2

Position in no limit

Position is still power, but the WFs, by position, are not exactly the same. The reasons are that there will be fewer opponents staying in a hand than in limit, and the high implied odds just discussed.

With any of these hands you could come in for a traditional raise of 3 to 4 times the big blind, or call a raise of that amount. You will come in for 2.5 times the big blind if you are using the tortoise strategy, which will be discussed shortly. Certainly you may attempt to get everyone to fold preflop with a higher raise with AA or KK, and that higher raise should let everyone know what you have and force the tight players to fold.

If you are out of position preflop you may be re-raised often and have to dump your hand before seeing the flop. Low WF hands do not hit often and you must not risk any significant portion of your chips to call a re-raise with a low WF hand. It will happen often against aggressives, and though this folding on a re-raise will be difficult to accept, you must do it. If the table is aggressive, just as in limit, in no limit you will not play a low WF hand out of position.

The true advantage of postflop position in no limit is the risk/reward relationship, and it is magnified exponentially. With position your risk goes way down and your potential reward goes way up. In limit, out of position, risk is limited to a fixed increment of bets. Loss is limited. In no limit, when an opponent has top pair, often he will risk all of his chips and you, with position, get to play the hand on your terms. Either take him down or muck.

High pairs

What if you have high pair or an overpair on the flop? Try to take down the pot immediately. If you don't, this next thought will go against much of what we have learned so far. In no limit it is important to understand that a high pair or an overpair, although fast betting hands in limit, must be played passively postflop. They are good for winning small pots but tend to lose more big no limit pots than they win.

How about the unsuited high cards on the right side of the pyramid? Your opponents are playing those cards too, as well as high pairs. On the flop, unless you catch an open-ended straight, a straight, trips, or two pair, passive play is best. Folding on the flop will be much more common than in limit.

Introducing three more critical factors

These are three additional dimensions to the seven you already know from limit.

▶ Unlimited betting	Anyone can bet any amount at any time.
▶ Stack size	How many chips you have compared to both the cost per orbit and to opponents' stacks.
▶ The type of no limit game	Cash or tournament.

Let's discuss each.

▸ Unlimited Betting

No limit is dangerous and exciting. You can lose everything on one pot. But you can win a ton too. Some general principles:

- In a cash game, you do not want anyone to call when you go all in, in most situations.
- In a tournament, you should not go all in unless you have the winner or are short stacked and must gamble.
- Against a loose player, get your chips in slowly. Extract as much as you can.
- Against a tight player, get your chips in fast. Be satisfied with winning the pot now.
- Aggressive no limit play requires much more skill than limit.
- Deception is so much more important in no limit.
- Check-raising is an excellent tactic in cash games.
- Seldom are more than three players in a hand.
- Getting to see a lot of flops cheaply is a tactic used by many.
- You can use Expected Value to make it too expensive for an opponent to draw.

Although several figures in this chapter show a small PATL, they show the location within the Advanced PATL with either a ●, which indicates where some successful players fall, or a ★ indicating where most successful players fit. Important to note, **these placements** do not indicate the WFs played as they do with limit, rather they **indicate the style of play used**. Review **figure 3.7 for the aggressive/loose style**.

▸ Stack size

This new critical dimension has two components, but for the most part, one only applies in tournaments; you can always re-buy at a cash game. One part of this new dimension is your stack size compared to the cost to play an orbit. The other is your stack size compared to those of your remaining opponents.

Stack size compared to the cost per orbit

An orbit is one revolution around the table. Cost per orbit is how much a player must spend to play an orbit, assuming he does not play a hand. It includes the sum of one revolution of both blinds and, where applicable, antes. When play includes antes the result is a dramatically higher cost per orbit. How big your stack size is compared to the cost per orbit determines your style of play. Cutoff numbers are shown for a 10-handed table. You may use higher cutoff numbers than shown but definitely not lower. As the number of opponents decrease, since you will be paying for the blinds more frequently than with a full table, the cutoffs must be increased.

10+ times the cost/orbit

From your study of the Which Hands to Play Chapter, you should have deduced that even at aggressive tables you should get a playable hand 10% to 20% of the time, regardless of position. If you are at a full 10-handed table that means once every orbit you will get one or two playable hands; every orbit will cost a minimum of a big blind and a small blind. If your stack size is ten times or more the sum of the blinds and antes, you will get more than enough playable hands over the next several hours, and theoretically should win more than your share. Traditional aggressive/tight play is best.

5–9 times the cost/orbit

You are a little more desperate at this point, but not yet completely desperate. Your play will shift towards loose and you will be playing more hands than the WFs would suggest.

4 or less times the cost/orbit

Desperation is close and the fewer orbits you can cover, the more desperate play must become. You must make a stand, otherwise you will be eaten up by the orbit cost. The longer you wait for a premium hand the greater the chance that when you get it, you won't have enough to make it worthwhile even if you win. Very Aggressive/ Mega-Loose is your only chance of survival. Wait until you can be the first to bet with any hand with a WF of 1.0 or better and go all in.

Figure 11.3 summarizes, depending on your orbit coverage, the style of play required.

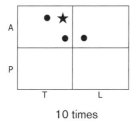

10 times

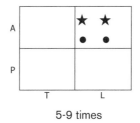

5-9 times

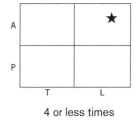

4 or less times

Stack size compared to cost/orbit
Figure 11.3

Stack size compared to other players
Big stack
The chip leader can muscle the table or use more traditional aggressive/tight play. The big stack has the ability to control the table; however, figure 11.4 shows how most winners play. As opposed to bullying the table, they select the best targets. They use their stack for a series of small aggressive wins from middle or late position and wait for strong hands to win good sized pots. Unless they have the cards and position, they avoid multi-way pots with too much chance of being outdrawn, and huge pots where they could lose a good portion of their stack. They also avoid those with big stacks who could take a good chunk of their chips, and small stacks too, preferring not to let them double up on him, unless they perceive weaknesses, in which case they will bully the small stack.

Middle stack
Middle stack play requires aggressive/tight to aggressive/loose play. Middle stacks should be focused on bullying the smaller stacks. As the middle stack becomes shorter it forces the player to be more aggressive/loose and to selectively gamble. Although he prefers not going up against a big stack, he realizes the best play is to start to turn the game into one betting round. He waits until he is first to act preflop and has something, then goes all in.

Short stack

Anything less than four times the orbit coverage or five times the average pot is short stacked. The smart player has no choice and shifts his play to the upper right hand portion of the PATL. He cannot wait; he makes preflop moves. He tries to wait until he is first to act with a reasonable hand and goes all in. If he is the second to enter a pot, and has something slightly better than reasonable, he may gamble and go all in.

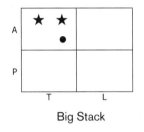

Big Stack

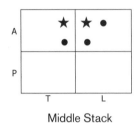

Middle Stack

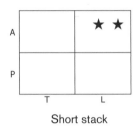

Short stack

Stack size compared to others
Figure 11.4

Stack size and the number of hands played

The general rule you should use is as your stack size goes up, play fewer and only the strongest hands. As your stack size goes down, play more and weaker hands.

Stack size and betting

If you have a deep stack and have a good hand, you are in better shape than the draw you are up against. If you are the deep stack with a good made hand, you have enough chips to continually extract more value during each betting round against a draw. Nothing new with that. But now we are about to go through a strange concept. If you have a short stack and have a good draw, you are often in better shape than the deep stack who already has a good hand. If you have a short stack with a good draw, get your money in the middle. You put pressure on your opponent with the deep stack. Calling with a short stack, hoping to complete a good draw, is not the best play.

If you and your opponents have deep stacks, and you believe your starting hand is the strongest, you may increase your preflop raise. When everyone in the hand has a deep stack, preflop play is loose, and a higher raise will usually result in the same number of callers as your normal raise would.

▶ The type of no limit game

Cash game
- You may buy as many chips as you want anytime.
- The blinds remain fixed as long as you play.
- Characterized by the strategy of picking up a few small pots with position and waiting to win a few big ones.
- Easy to bet enough to make draws unprofitable.
- Few all ins.
- Successful players use a similar style to the limit players as shown in 11.5.a.

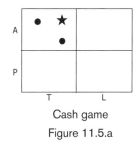

Cash game
Figure 11.5.a

Low stakes; no limit
- Buy in is for a predetermined maximum amount.
- Characterized by a strategy of trying to win big pots.
- More preflop aggressive betting with more all ins than with a cash game.
- Difficult to bet enough to make draws unprofitable.
- More luck, less skill than cash games.
- Successful players use a more aggressive/loose style than cash game winners. See 11.5.b.

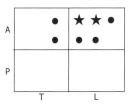

Low limit; no limit
Figure 11.5.b

Once you are an expert in high limit, the amounts of cash in no limit should not bother you. When you are finished both this chapter and your 250,000 hands, you can move immediately into cash no limit.

A brief word on pot limit

Pot limit, that is when you are allowed to bet as much as is in the pot but no more, is more difficult than limit and is a logical experience step towards no limit tournaments. The reason we don't include a thorough discussion and suggest practice is, with the exception of online and some major poker centers, it is difficult to find games with several different opponents with different abilities. Generally you will find the same opponents, and all are good to great players. Playing in that environment only helps to a degree.

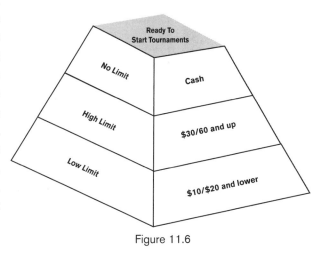

Figure 11.6

The rules of the tournament

One facet of the rules is blinds and antes go up as the tournament progresses. This one difference has a dramatic effect on play and the types of players who win tournaments. Many of the best cash game players have a difficult time winning tournaments. The style that wins in limit and the no limit cash game, that is aggressive/tight, and the one they are accustomed to playing, is appropriate only during some phases of tournaments and is not a winning strategy as you get closer to the final table. As the blinds go up, and depending on how fast they go up, a player must shift his style of play. One factor is the same regardless of the rate of blind increase; as the blinds become bigger, more attempts are made to steal the blinds with position.

When blinds go up fast

When blinds go up fast, every 30 minutes or more frequently, winning players cannot play aggressive/tight. They are forced into the loose portion of the PATL. They no longer have the luxury of waiting for better hands with good position. Luck plays a big part when the blinds go up fast. The style of play required is shown in figure 11.7, depending on the phase of the tournament.

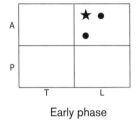

Early phase

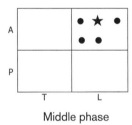

Middle phase
When blinds go up fast
Figure 11.7

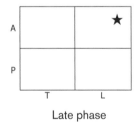

Late phase

When blinds go up slowly

When the blinds go up slowly, every one or two hours, better players can play as aggressive/tights, picking up small, uncontested pots with aggressive betting when they have position, and a few big ones when they hit. The luck factor is diminished. Bluffing, especially during the early rounds, is minimal. After the early phase, there is a fork in the road. Either the player is a hare or a tortoise. We'll discuss hare play first as it is the one attempted by many players. After a review of this fast play, we will look at tortoise, or small bet poker (also known as small ball) as an entirely separate section. You will see why shortly.

When blinds go up slowly – hare play

Hare play is aggressive play. Any hare who has made it to the final table is now playing in the upper right hand of the PATL. During the early rounds the best play is shown on the far left in figure 11.8, and this is where the converted limit or good cash no limit player shines. It is his comfort zone. As play moves towards the middle, and the prize money is within sight, most players tend to tighten up trying to make the cutoff; however, the hare starts to make a shift towards a looser style. Their play is to steal chips from those who are tightening up. Almost every hare who has made it to the final table is now playing Very Aggressive, and has made the shift to much looser play. If you take a look at the tournament hare winners you will see they all, at the time of the final table, fall somewhere in the upper right PATL.

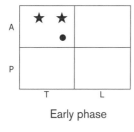 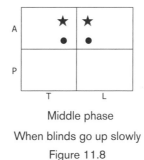 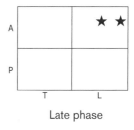

Early phase   Middle phase   Late phase

When blinds go up slowly

Figure 11.8

By now you recognize what happens to the hare style of play throughout a tournament. Early, unless the blinds are increasing rapidly, aggressive/tight is best. As it progresses and gets closer to the prize money aggressive/loose takes over. At the end everyone is at the same place, Very Aggressive/Loose or Very Aggressive/Mega-Loose.

After you finish this chapter, you are ready to start no limit tournaments. Focus first on tournaments when blinds go up fast and learn how to change your style of play as needed.

You will find hare play where blinds go up slowly has an advantage only if all players start off with a relatively low stack of chips compared to the initial blind. After you finish this chapter, and in particular the next section, which will explain an entirely different, but more successful method of tournament play, you are then ready to graduate to professional no limit tournaments.

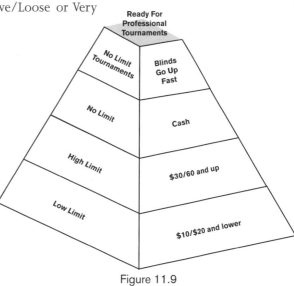

Figure 11.9

The tortoise strategy

This concept is so different, we have devoted an entire section to what it is and how to do it.

Slow and steady wins the race. Two small steps forward, one step back. Sometimes a big one forward. No big steps back. I must credit much of this to Mr. Daniel Negreanu. What you are about to read is a blend of his brilliant small ball concept, also known as small bet poker, and my tortoise play. Daniel is the master. If you want to find out exactly how he plays small ball, go to *PokerVT. com*.

This method of play works best under two conditions:

1. The blinds go up slowly. No more than once every hour, preferably slower.
2. Everyone starts off with a deep stack of chips. An example of a deep stack would be when a player starts off with a stack of chips 250 times the initial big blind.

This is not an advanced method of play, it is an extremely advanced method. Remember what we said about you becoming great at limit play before you could become good at no limit? Another caveat. Before you can become a successful tortoise, you must become a great hare in limit and a good hare in no limit. Tortoise play takes an extreme amount of discipline and experience, requires great hand reading know-how, and superior postflop decision making.

Tortoise philosophy

- Small steps forward. **Slowly increase your stack without taking a big risk**.
- Small steps forward. Based on **winning the blinds, antes, and small pots**, with an occasional big step forward for a big pot with a strong hand.
- No big steps back. **Protect your chip stack**. Do not risk more than 10% of your chips preflop and, unless you believe your hand is the winner, avoid risking 20% postflop. Later in this chapter I will show you there are times you will have better than a 50-50 chance to win with a draw, and if you were playing a cash game you would go all in; but in a tournament, especially in the early and middle stages, defending your chip stack is more important than winning a big pot. So even if

you have a draw with tons of outs you will not risk your tournament life with a draw. Definitely avoid coin flips in big pots, even when in your favor.

- Small steps forward. Unless you have a monster, you want to win the pot as soon as possible. With the cards you will play, monsters are generally straights and flushes.
- Small steps forward. **Go after small pots** aggressively with position. You stay away from big ones unless you know you can win. The only time you play a big pot is with the best hand.
- You cannot be a successful tortoise without superior hand reading skills. With position against a lone opponent you don't even have to look at your cards. If you think he has a weak hand, raise him out.
- Sometimes a big step forward. **The hands the tortoise wants are the lower WF hands** you would generally just stay in the hand with. The big step forward comes when the lower WF suiteds hit a straight or flush, especially the hidden straight. Remember the Boardology Chapter when we discussed the hidden straight? Even good players miss seeing it. Negreanu likens it to putting a small worm at the end of a pole and realizing, every now and then, you will catch a big fish. Yes, you will lose a lot of small worms along the way, but those worms didn't cost you much. The payoff is with the big fish.
- One step back. With position **control the pot size and keep it small** so when you miss, which will be often, you will not lose much. When out of position it is difficult to control the size of the pot.
- Small steps forward. **Position is extremely important**. Build the pot with position when you have a strong hand.
- Sometimes a big step forward. Tortoise passive/loose also pays off when you actually do have a strong hand as you will get more callers, perhaps raisers, as opponents assume you are playing what they would consider a trash hand.
- No big steps back. **All in does not fit in the tortoise's shell**.

General preflop tortoise tactics

- Play passive/loose until the flop. You will see lots of flops with this style of play. With position you should call a normal raise with a low WF hand, even if you only have a few opponents.
- Playable hands, with position, go all the way down to a 1.1

WF for a Mega-Loose table. Yes, even with only one opponent at a tight table you would stay in with 53s.

- You will get re-raised a lot preflop and will be forced to fold a lot on those re-raises.
- You want to get to the flop on the cheap so you can outplay your opponents after the flop.
- The non-suited portion for the hands of a Mega-Loose table, the right hand side of the hand pyramid, should be played passively. This even includes AK unsuited. You may raise with position preflop with A-face trying to win the pot immediately. But if you miss, you must be prepared to release. Any A-face will generally pay off best for small pots, but, unless you catch a straight, will not win big pots. The rest of the unsuited hands on the right side of the hand pyramid, unless the straight is caught, play even worse. Opponents who play the right hand side of the pyramid, especially A-face, can't release when they catch a piece. In big pots you must release if you don't catch big.
- Be cheap with your raises.
- Minimize losses. See the flop cheaply. If you are the first to enter, bet enough to get trash hands to fold. Instead of 3 or 4 times the big blind, 2½ times the big blind should do the trick. If someone else has already bet enough to get trash to fold and you can get in cheap with a playable hand, you call.
- Play passively preflop. With JJ or QQ check and call to the flop. Call with AA and KK. If re-raised with your AA or KK, you re-raise with the objective of taking the pot right there.
- Low WF hands are best played when your opponent has a deep stack. You are looking to catch and hurt the big stack with a low WF hand. Avoid small stacks with a low WF hand.
- Raise with position to steal a pot. Against callers, bet 1.5-2 times the pot.

General postflop tortoise tactics
- Postflop play depends on:

  The flop. The more sequenced or flushed, the more passive/tight you must be.

  Where the opponent falls in the Advanced PATL. The tighter your opponent, unless you are going to bluff, the more passive/tight you must be.

Your hand reading skills.

Your chip stack. The greater your chip stack, the more passive/tight you should be. If your stack is down, the more aggressive/loose your play.

Position. If you have it, play aggressive/loose, especially with few passives remaining.

Your experience and ability to make difficult decisions, especially on the turn.

- Anytime an opponent calls postflop, he is telling you he has something.
- When a tight player goes all in, regardless of the betting round, you should usually fold.

Specific flop tortoise tactics

- Remember the numbers. If you have one opponent who has unpaired cards he only has a 32% chance of getting a pair or better on the flop. Even if you don't catch on the flop probability says he missed too. If you have position you are in the driver's seat. Use it.
- Passively check when you are on a draw. Get to the turn on the cheap.
- If you can win the pot on the flop, get aggressive and try to take it. Check on the flop if you have the winner and the board doesn't look dangerous.
- Tortoise play does not include the limit tactic of betting aggressively on the flop to find out where you are at, as you want to keep the size of the pot small. A tortoise will passively check, or check-call, and rely on his hand reading.
- Always attempt to control the size of the pot, trying to keep the pot small unless you have a winner. Easiest to accomplish when you have position. Keep your bets to the pot size or less. ½ the pot on the flop is fine.
- However, if you think he missed the flop, you can sometimes put on your hare suit and bet 50%–80% of the pot. Try to win it now.
- A big plus of playing low WF hands in no limit is the same as when playing any low WF hand; that is, they are easy to release if you don't catch.

- Although this goes against all hare and traditional thought, a tortoise believes **it is all right to give a free card**. If you get outdrawn and play to the river, at least you get the information.

Specific turn tortoise tactics

- The turn is the most difficult to play because as the pot size gets bigger, you could easily reach the 20% of chip stack threshold. You must fold on the turn if you are risking more than 20% of your stack with anything other than a very strong hand.
- Unless you have the hand, continue to control the size of the pot or fold. On the turn 60% of the pot is fine.

Specific river tortoise tactics

- The tortoise tries to get to the river on the cheap by passively checking and calling.
- River play is straightforward. Without the best hand do not bet out of position on the river; rather, check and call.

Tortoise calls

- Call minimum re-raises.
- If you have second highest possible pair, against tights either call or fold.
- Call if your opponent is short stacked. The shorter his stack, the more range of hands he will play, including a WF of 1.0 or even lower. If his stack size is less than 4 times his cost per orbit, call with any mediocre hand.
- As stated previously, check and call on the river when out of position.

Tortoise raises

Generally, raises are meant to get opponents to fold.

- When do you vary your bet and raise sizes? The answer is almost never, because when you do, you are giving away information to perceptive opponents. But, when you are up against a lone opponent or just the blinds, and you are trying to steal the pot, you may vary your bets. The two criteria to consider are the experience level of your opponent and how tight/loose he plays.

The more experienced a lone opponent, the more you should raise preflop to get him to fold. Instead of 2.5 times the big blind, you may raise 4 or 5 times the big blind. Postflop, against an experienced lone opponent, a bet of 50% to 75% of the pot will, in many cases, cause him to fold. Against an inexperienced player, your usual tortoise raise preflop of 2.5 times the big blind is appropriate. Postflop, against the inexperienced player, try to steal the pot on the cheap with a bet of 33% to 50% of the pot.

How tight or loose your lone opponent plays is the second factor. Preflop, the tighter he is the more you raise. Against a Tight you would raise 4 times the big blind. Against a Mega-Tight you will raise 5 times the big blind. With any kind of loose player preflop you will raise your usual 2.5 times the big blind and rely on your postflop skills to win the pot. Postflop, switch tactics. If the tight opponent called you preflop, that tells you he has something. Unless you believe you are ahead, you must now focus on keeping the pot small. If you are going to stay in the hand either check and call or, if you do raise, keep it in the range of 33% to 50% of the pot. On the flop, you will bet more against the loose than against the tight. A stab of 50% to 75% of the pot will often take the pot right there.

What happens when the tactics conflict? For example, postflop we know we should bet and raise more against the experienced player and less against the tight player. As often is the case we could be up against an experienced tight postflop. Do we bet 33% to 50% of the pot or 50% to 75% of the pot? If we were in a cash game, we would take the aggressive approach and bet 50% to 75% of the pot. But in a tournament, using the small ball thought process, we want to minimize our losses; therefore we take the conservative approach and bet 33% to 50% of the pot.

- Position. Raise one or two callers if you have late position. With three or more callers fold if you have nothing, or see the flop cheaply if you have something. Out of position, be passive/tight. In position, be aggressive/loose.
- To get a raiser to fold with a mediocre hand or a pure bluff, which you would only do against an aggressive/loose when you are deep stacked, re-raise 4-5 times the initial raise.

When your stack size starts to go down

- If your stack size gets close to 10 times the cost per orbit, continue to play passive/loose preflop. See as many flops as you can by calling with all the playable no limit hands.
- Once your stack size gets to 9 times the cost per orbit, throw off your tortoise shell and put on your hare suit. Aggressive/tight. If you are fortunate enough to win a big pot and your stack becomes deep again, go find your shell and put it back on, i.e. passive/tight preflop out of position, passive/loose with position.
- When your chip stack is low — 4 times or less the cost per orbit — you must be an extreme aggressive/loose. If your stack is below 10 bets, and you are first to act preflop, go all in with any WF of 1.0 or greater.

Tortoise conclusion

- Remember in Chapter 3 when we said it was impossible to read the hand of an aggressive/loose? The tortoise is even more difficult. We are going to show you some PATL figures, and as you will see, a tortoise can be in different areas depending on several factors. That's because, even though we will review each as a specific factor, many of them are intermingled with others. This is a several-dimension method of thinking which I have not been able to put into three, much less two, dimensional form. Even though the overall picture is complicated, let's see where the tortoise may fall in the PATL.

Figure 11.10.a shows where the tortoise is depending the stage of the tournament.

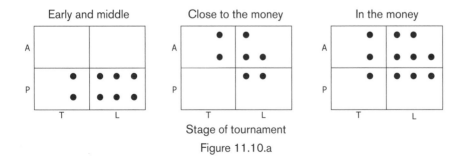

Figure 11.10.a

11.10.b illustrates where he might be depending on the betting round.

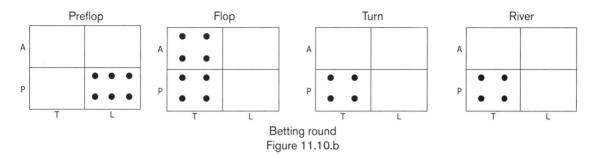

Betting round
Figure 11.10.b

11.10.c shows how he will play according to his position.

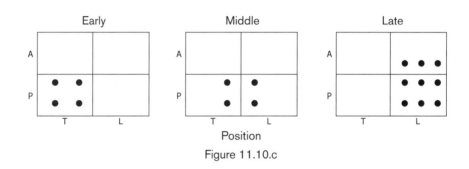

Position
Figure 11.10.c

The style also changes depending on how much he must bet, as shown in 11.10.d.

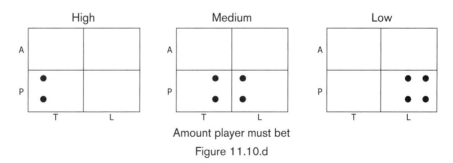

Amount player must bet
Figure 11.10.d

And 11.10.e shows adjustments based on the strength of his opponents.

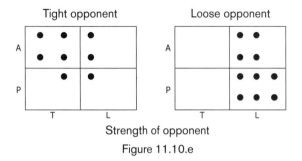

Strength of opponent

Figure 11.10.e

Figure 11.10.f shows adjustments in the tortoise's style of play based on the size of his chip stack. He would play just the opposite if he had a deep stack and his opponent was on a short stack.

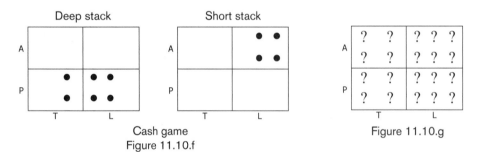

Cash game

Figure 11.10.f

Figure 11.10.g

Finally, 11.10.g illustrates how the tortoise moves all over the PATL depending on position, the betting round, how difficult the opponents in the hand are, how much he must bet, his chip stack, his opponents' stacks, and the stage of the tournament. He could be anywhere at almost anytime. Notice that the hand strength is not a factor.

A final word on tortoise play

Remember when we said some great no limit cash players do not make a successful transition to tournament play? The reason is they cannot shift gears and become looser. The same thing actually happens in reverse. Some professionals become so good at small ball that when they go back to playing cash games, they forget that aggressive/tight is the best style for that type of game. They try to use the tortoise strategy in cash no limit and find it doesn't work as well as traditional aggressive/tight.

Now that you understand the specialized form of tortoise play, and how it compares to hare play, we will go back to a more general discussion.

Tactics

Checking and calling

Check only if you:

>   Are trying to trap
>   Have nothing and decide not to bluff
>   Are on a draw and decide not to semi-bluff

Call only if you are:

>   Last to act
>   On a draw
>   Laying a trap

Swayne deceptive betting

Betting patterns are used to read hands; you must adopt a pattern impossible to read. You will use your cards to tell you what to do. You may choose different amounts than those presented, but whatever amounts you choose should not vary except when taking into account the quality of the opponent. You may add another layer of deception by betting more against solid players and less against those who are not. Less experienced players should use multiples at, close to, or even higher than the high end shown; more advanced players tend to use bets closer to the low end. Expert players tend to disregard this technique and rely on their ability to read their opponents to decide how much to bet.

Preflop

Let's assume preflop that you will use your right hand card to tell you what to do. If you are going to be the first to act and raise, you will use a multiple of the big blind. Tight players tend to bet 2.5-3 times the big blind. Less experienced players should bet more to keep the tight players from seeing the flop cheaply, where these better players (the tights) could use their skill to

If your right hand card is

Multiply the big blind by

	♣	♦	♥	♠
Low end	1	1.5	2	2.5
High end	2	3	4	5

Figure 11.11.a

If your right hand card is

% of pot to bet for info, value, or bluff

	♣	♦	♥	♠
Low end	20%	30%	40%	50%
High end	50%	100%	150%	200%

Figure 11.11.b

If the middle card on the flop is

% of pot to bet for info, value, or bluff

	♣	♦	♥	♠
Low end	20%	30%	40%	50%
High end	50%	100%	150%	200%

Figure 11.11.c

outfox a less experienced player. Use figure 11.11.a as a guide to determine how much you will raise. Both a low end and a high end are shown. Choose either or something in between. Note the suits are in alphabetical order from left to right.

If you are not the first to act preflop, and you are bluffing, betting for value, or looking for information (which is also known as a probe bet), use your right card to determine how much to bet as shown in figure 11.11.b. Again, less experienced players would use somewhere close to the high end, or even more than the percentages shown. Experts who do not use this method generally bet ⅓, ½, or ¾ of the pot.

Postflop

Unless you are checking on the flop, use the suit of the card in the middle of the board to determine your bet, as in the Deception Chapter. On the turn use the suit of the turn card. It will be the same percentage of the pot you used when not the first to act preflop. Better players tend to bet anywhere from ⅓ to ¾ of the pot depending on whether they are value betting or looking for information. You will use figure 11.11.c whether you are bluffing, looking for information, or value betting.

Of course, you should round off your bets as opposed to betting exactly 30% of the pot, but with this deception method no one will ever be able to read your betting pattern. The only times you will deviate with a higher amount are when you are heads up against a tight opponent or do not want any callers.

Changing the numbers and percentages

You may change the numbers and percentages used in 11.11.a-c depending on your stack size, how tight your opponents are, and some other factors that will be introduced shortly. When you do change one of the numbers or percentages, you should change all of them, otherwise a superior opponent who pays attention to betting patterns will be able to read your bets. You may also adopt an easier deception method by using the color of the card to indicate a simpler multiple. You want to confuse your opponents, not yourself.

Neutralizing poor position

In no limit there are two fundamental ways to neutralize your poor position, both of which involve some risk. You are already familiar with the first method, check-raising. The defensive bet is another. Here you call on the flop and bet out on the turn. Most opponents will assume you have something when you bet and will just call, or even better, fold. The result is that you control the size of the pot on the turn, and usually avoid an opponent bluff on the river. This play does not work well in limit. A defensive bet can also be used on the river when you plan on calling anyway. If you lose you generally save the difference between what you bet and the amount the opponent would have bet if you checked.

Few opponents on the flop

Often you face only two opponents or are heads up on the flop. Remember your math from The Numbers Chapter. Unpaired hole cards have a 32% chance of making at least a pair on the flop and any opponent has a 6% chance of having a pocket pair. Therefore, any player has a 38% chance of having a pair when the flop comes. If you are heads up and you have a pair, even if it is not top pair, this is a strong hand; you are the statistical favorite. If you have a pair against only two opponents, you are, theoretically, ahead.

Anytime you hit two pair or better from your unpaired hole cards, this is a huge hand against few opponents. You must bet enough to get draws to fold. A pot size bet will get most draws to fold, unless the opponent still has a positive Expected Value or is thinking in terms of implied odds.

Using Expected Value when on a draw

Every great player constantly uses pot odds, that is, Expected Value, in no limit. Positive Expected Value is good. When you are on a draw you want positive Expected Value. Negative Expected Value is bad. Stay away. When your opponent is on a draw you can use the amount you bet to put him into negative Expected Value territory.

Using Expected Value for seeing one more card when you are drawing

Here we are going to use Expected Value when you are on a draw, whether you are on the flop or the turn. When we discuss Expected Value in no limit we will ignore the rake, as in some tournament games it doesn't exist and in cash games it is usually a small amount relative to the pot.

The same warning that was discussed in limit about just making your hand versus winning the hand applies here, but to an even greater extent as the pots are much bigger. Before using Expected Value you must be convinced that making your hand will win the pot. As always, your out count must eliminate bad outs — those that could help your opponent more than you — and avoid double-counting the same card as two outs.

% probability of catching the next card	Outs
42.6	20
40.4	19
38.3	18
36.2	17
34.0	16
31.9	15
29.8	14
27.7	13
25.5	12
23.4	11
21.3	10
19.1	9
17.0	8
14.9	7
12.8	6
10.6	5
8.5	4
6.4	3
4.3	2
2.1	1

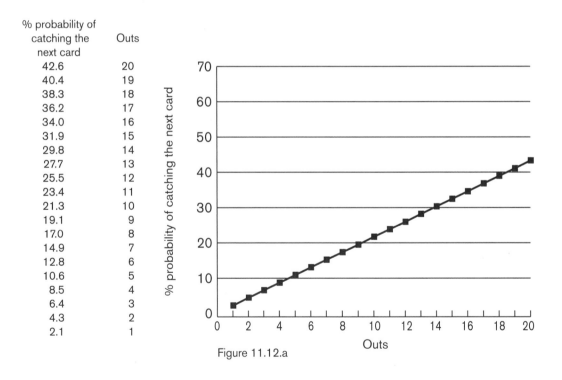

Figure 11.12.a

Take a look at the numbers and the accompanying graph in figure 11.12.a. The horizontal axis shows how many outs you have; the vertical axis is your probability of catching.

The numbers shown are for drawing to the turn and although the numbers for drawing to the river are slightly different, we will use the turn numbers, as they are more conservative.

When you are the last to act and on a draw, before you call a bet to see the next card, here's what you need to do:

1. Determine how many outs you have.
2. From 11.12.a, find out your probability of catching.
3. Calculate your probability of not catching.
4. See how much is in the pot.
5. Determine your Expected Value. If positive, stay in with either a call or a raise; if negative, fold.

Let's go through some examples.

Example 1

The flop and turn are on the board. You are on the button. The first player bet, the second called, and you must decide whether to call to see the river. You have the nut flush draw with, of course, an Ace overcard. You believe if you either hit your flush, or pair your Ace, your hand will be the winner. The pot is $2,000. To call will cost you $200. Do you stay in the hand? Time for some mental math.

1. How many outs do you have? 9 flush cards plus 3 cards to pair the Ace gives you 12 outs.
2. What is your probability of catching? From 11.12.a your probability of catching is 25%.
3. If your probability of catching is 25%, then your probability of not catching is $100\% - 25\%$ or 75%.
4. How much is in the pot? $2,000.
5. Determine your Expected Value.

Expected Value = (Probability of winning)(Pot size)
$$- \text{(Probability of losing)(Amount you must call)}$$

$$EV = (25\%)(\$2,000) - (75\%)(\$200)$$
$$= \$500 - \$150$$
$$= \$350.$$

You have a clear positive Expected Value of $350. You would at least call, probably raise. It is seldom as easy as this example. You are not always last to act and we haven't even talked about what happens when you are on the flop.

Special note: Some math experts will disagree with the Expected Value formula used. For example, the amount you can win, that is how much is in the pot, is not adjusted by the size of your bet. I recommend a basic method as there is not enough time at the table for too many mental mathematical gymnastics. Admittedly, this simplified formula is not the precise equivalent of pot odds, but is sufficient to give you a consistent edge.

The amount you can win is not only the amount in the pot when you bet, but includes any additional estimated, that is implied, amounts you think will be in the pot after all the betting is complete.

This is where both position and knowing your opponents comes into play. The less you know your opponents and the earlier you are to act, the more difficult it is to imply how much will be in the pot and how much more you must invest. Conversely, the more you know your opponents and the later your position, the easier it is to imply how much will be in the pot and what your investment will probably be.

Example 2

You have the same cards as the previous example, except now you are in early position. The pot is $800. You check. A player bets $400. Another player raises another $400. Everyone else folds and it comes to you. It will cost you $800 to call. The pot is now $2,000. Would you call to see the river?

1. How many outs do you have? 9 flush cards plus 3 cards to pair the overcard gives you 12 outs.
2. What is your probability of catching? From 11.12.a your probability of catching is 25%.
3. If your probability of catching is 25%, then your probability of not catching is 100% − 25% or 75%.

4. How much is in the pot? $2,000.
5. Determine your Expected Value.

Expected Value = (Probability of winning)(Pot size)
                 − (Probability of losing)(Amount you must call)

$$EV = (25\%)(\$2,000) − (75\%)(\$800)$$
$$= \$500 − \$600$$
$$= -\$100.$$

In this example you not only have a negative Expected Value, you still have another player to act behind you. And he could raise. Using only Expected Value you would fold. Many experts would not fold this hand even with a negative Expected Value, as they would factor in the implied size of the pot and call.

Example 3

Same cards and same draw but this time you have not yet seen the turn. You are in early position. The pot is $400. You check. One player bets $800. Another player calls the $800. Everyone else folds. The pot is now $2,000. It comes to you. It will cost you $800 to call. You know your opponents and believe, if you don't catch on the turn, someone will bet enough to make you fold. In other words, you know you will not be able to see two more cards cheaply.

1. How many outs do you have? 9 flush cards plus 3 cards to pair the overcard gives you 12 outs.
2. What is your probability of catching? From 11.12.a your probability of catching is 25%.
3. If your probability of catching is 25%, then your probability of not catching is 100% − 25% or 75%.
4. How much is in the pot? $2,000.
5. Determine your Expected Value.

Expected Value = (Probability of winning)(Pot size)
                 − (Probability of losing)(Amount you must call)

$$EV = (25\%)(\$2,000) − (75\%)(\$800)$$
$$= \$500 − \$600$$
$$= -\$100.$$

If you used Expected Value alone, you would fold. This is where estimating, or educated guessing, is used. You will estimate how much will be in the pot if you catch and what your Expected Value will be if you do hit on the turn. As stated at the start of this example, you know that if you do not catch on the turn at least one of your opponents will bet enough to force you to fold.

Mentally assume you hit on the turn, then imply how much will be in the pot whether you decide to bet out or check-raise. For this example assume the opponent to your left always uses a continuation bet, even if he misses, and the other opponent calls more than he should. You decide, if you hit, to check and let the others build the pot for you.

The pot currently stands at $2,000. Using the implied size of the pot, you make a decision whether or not to make the $800 call. For example, you imply that if you do catch and check, the person to your left will bet $1,000 and the next player will call the $1,000. We figure out the pot size from the bets of our opponents and ignore our possible $800 call for now. In other words, the size of the pot will then be the $2,000 that's in now, plus the $1,000 you guess the aggressive bettor will bet, and the $1,000 the calling station will put in, bringing the total in the pot on the turn to $4,000. Now using the implied bets of our opponents we go through the same procedure to see if you should stay in.

1. How many outs do you have? 9 flush cards plus 3 cards to pair the overcard gives you 12 outs.
2. What is your probability of catching? From 11.12.a your probability of catching is 25%.
3. If your probability of catching is 25%, then your probability of not catching is 100% − 25% or 75%.
4. How much do you imply in the pot from the opponents for the next round of betting? $4,000.
5. Determine your Expected Value.

Expected Value = (Probability of winning)(Pot size)
$$- \text{(Probability of losing)(Amount you must call)}$$

$$EV = (25\%)(\$4{,}000) - (75\%)(\$800)$$
$$= \$1{,}000 - \$600$$
$$= \$400.$$

Implying a bigger pot gives you a positive Expected Value. And with our oversimplified example, there is no one behind you left to raise so you would call.

Using Expected Value when your opponent is on a draw to see one more card

So far we have discussed using Expected Value when you are on a draw. But can we use Expected Value when we think an opponent is on a draw? You bet we can. If you believe you are ahead in the hand and you smell a draw, you can use Expected Value to get opponents to fold. Good players on a draw know Expected Value and will not call if your bet is sufficiently high.

Not losing money is the same as winning it. You want to make your bet high enough to put your opponent into negative Expected Value territory and discourage him from staying in the hand. If he does call a big bet, he'll be taking the worst of it. You also want to avoid a bet too big for the times when you are wrong and misread your opponent. For example, if you thought he was on a straight draw, but he had a set and your top pair was second place. Using Expected Value will help you accomplish this.

For the rest of this discussion we will assume you have one opponent; however, if you have more than one opponent, in order to take a conservative approach, outs will mean the sum of the outs for all of your remaining opponents. Using this conservative approach will require a heavier bet to get multiple drawers to fold.

You will use a similar procedure when you are on a draw:
1. Estimate how many outs you think your opponent has.
2. From 11.12.a, find out his probability of catching based on your estimate of how many outs you think he has.
3. Calculate his probability of not catching.
4. See how much is in the pot.
5. Mentally bet an amount you think would give him a negative Expected Value. This will take some practice but after you do it often enough, it will become easier. Then calculate his Expected Value.
6. If necessary, keep increasing your mental bet until you are sure he has a negative Expected Value.
7. Then add a sufficient amount to make sure he will fold. A 25% increase should theoretically get him to fold.

Warning 1. The reason we say theoretically is because many players claim they understand pot odds, but some will call a heads up bet of 100% of the pot with only a few outs. If they truly understood pot odds, they would fold. You must know your opponents; who understands and uses pot odds and who doesn't.

Warning 2. So far the discussion has just focused on seeing the next card. If you are on the flop and might see two more cards, this presents an entirely different situation, one we will cover in the next section.

Warning 3. If there is more than one opponent still in the hand, at least one of them will be thinking in terms of implied odds. They are implying, just as you would do if you had the cards they had, a much greater pot than what exists at the current moment. This opponent is using that implied amount to help make his decision. Even if you are heads up, he may imply a much bigger pot and continue in the hand. This is where knowing your opponent helps. As stated before, you want to bet enough to get your opponent far enough into negative Expected Value territory to get him to fold or have very negative Expected Value if he calls, but not so much that you lose too much if you misread his hand and you are second best.

Example

On the turn you have pocket QQ in late position, heads up. The board is a two flush with no overcard or straight possibility. You smell a flush draw. You know your opponent well enough to realize that unless he had suited connectors, he would only play suited cards if one was an A or K. You assume he has an overcard. There is $600 in the pot. He checked to you.

1. Estimate how many outs you think your opponent has. 9 flush cards and 3 overcards means there are 12 outs.

2. From 11.12.a find out his probability of catching, based on your estimate of how many outs you think he has. If he has 12 outs his probability of catching is 25%.
3. Calculate his probability of not catching. $100\% - 25\% = 75\%$.
4. See how much is in the pot. $600.
5. Mentally bet an amount you think would give him a negative Expected Value. Let's try $200, which would bring the pot to $800. We will now calculate his Expected Value.

$$EV = (25\%)\ (\$800) - (75\%)\ (\$200)$$
$$= \$200 - \$150$$
$$= \$50.$$

Your opponent has a positive Expected Value of $50 if you bet $200. Not good for you.

6. Keep increasing your mental bet until you are sure he is in negative Expected Value territory.

Let's try a bet of $400, which now brings the theoretical pot to $1,000.

$$EV = (25\%)\ (\$1,000) - (75\%)\ (\$400)$$
$$= \$250 - \$300$$
$$= -\$50.$$

We know a bet of $400 will give him a slightly negative Expected Value.

7. We then add a sufficient amount to try to get him to fold. A 25% increase will theoretically get him to fold. 25% of $400 is $100. Add that $100 to our mental bet of $400 and we get $500. A bet of $500 should get him to fold if our out guess is right and our evaluation of him knowing pot odds is correct. Even if he calls we make a profit, because he has negative Expected Value.

Using Expected Value on the flop when you are drawing

A special situation arises on the flop when you can see two more cards. The probabilities and Expected Values change dramatically. Figure 11.12.b shows how the probability of catching changes significantly if you are going to see two more cards.

% probability if you see both the turn and river	Outs on the flop
65.0	19
62.4	18
59.8	17
57.0	16
54.1	15
51.2	14
48.1	13
45.0	12
41.7	11
38.4	10
35.0	9
31.5	8
27.8	7
24.1	6
20.4	5
16.5	4
12.5	3
8.4	2
4.3	1

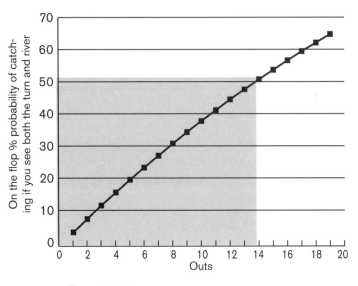

Figure 11.12.b

When you are drawing after you have seen the flop with two more cards to come, you are going to use the same procedure as before:

1. Determine how many outs you have.
2. Use 11.12.b to find out your probability of catching.
3. Calculate your probability of not catching.
4. See how much is in the pot.
5. Determine your Expected Value. If positive, stay in with either a call or a raise; if negative, fold.

Example

On the flop you have a four flush with no overcards and no straight possibility. You are in late position. The pot is $300. An opponent bets $100 and brings the pot to $400.

1. You have 9 outs.
2. From 11.12.b find out your probability of catching. With two cards to come you have a 35% chance.
3. Calculate your probability of not catching. If you have a 35% chance of catching, you have a 65% of not catching.
4. See how much is in the pot. $400.
5. Determine your Expected Value. If positive stay in with either a call or a raise; if negative fold.

$$EV = (35\%) (\$400) - (65\%) (\$100)$$
$$= \$140 - \$65$$
$$= \$75.$$

You have a positive Expected Value and should call or raise.

Extremely important point. Notice from 11.12.b that if you have 14 or more outs, you have a better than 50-50 chance of winning. You are favored to win. Although rare, **if you have 14 or more outs on the flop, you should not be afraid of a Big Foot bet or all in**.

Using Expected Value on the flop when your opponent is drawing

If it works to your advantage to see two more cards on a draw, it works to your opponent's advantage in exactly the same manner.

To get an opponent who is on a draw on the flop to fold, get ready to bet big. As before, you want to bet enough to get him to fold immediately, but not so much that you lose everything if he is not on a draw, but has a better hand than you right now.

We will use the same general procedure used when we want our opponent to fold with only one card to come:

1. Estimate how many outs you think your opponent has.
2. From 11.12.b find out his probability of catching, based on your estimate of how many outs he has.

3. Calculate his probability of not catching.
4. See how much is in the pot.
5. Mentally bet an amount you think would give him a negative Expected Value.
6. Keep increasing your mental bet until you are sure he is in negative Expected Value territory.
7. Then add a sufficient amount to try to make him fold.

Example

1. You estimate your opponent has 9 outs on the flop.
2. With two cards to go, using 11.12.b his probability of catching is 35%.
3. If his probability of catching is 35%, his probability of not catching is 65%.
4. The pot is $300.
5. You consider betting $200. If you did, the pot would then be $500.

   His Expected Value would be

   $$EV = (35\%)\ (\$500) - (65\%)\ (\$200)$$
   $$= \$175 - \$130$$
   $$= \$45.$$

   Not enough to put him into negative Expected Value territory.

6. You consider betting $400. The pot would be $700. His Expected Value would then be

   $$EV = (35\%)\ (\$700) - (65\%)\ (\$400)$$
   $$= \$245 - \$260$$
   $$= -\$15.$$

   A bet of $400 would give your opponent a negative Expected Value.

7. How much to increase your bet to get your drawing opponent to fold is more difficult on the flop.

Smart opponents will think in terms of the implied money in the pot, as opposed to the amount you might bet right now. This is especially true if there are several opponents in the hand. Some opponents will call almost any bet with AK because they believe in the hand. As always, our objective is to try to bet enough to get the drawer to fold, but not so much we lose too much when we are wrong. At a minimum, you should increase your bet by 50% and possibly more depending on your opponent. In step 6 above, we mentally bet $400 and that put him into a slight negative Expected Value territory. 50% of $400 is $200. So you would bet at least $600.

Some shortcuts

By now you are wondering if you will need a calculator or charts and graphs when you play. No reason not to if you are online, but hardly acceptable at a live table.

For one card to come

The graph in 11.12.a for seeing one card is a straight line. Anytime a graph is a straight line, an easy to use factor can be derived to help you calculate your probability of hitting.

The 2.1% One Card Rule. For one card to come, take the number of outs and multiply it by 2.1%. As figure 11.12.a is a straight line, this 2.1% will give you the probability of hitting.

Examples

$$8 \text{ outs} \times 2.1\% = 17\%$$
$$10 \text{ outs} \times 2.1\% = 21\%$$
$$12 \text{ outs} \times 2.1\% = 25\%$$
$$14 \text{ outs} \times 2.1\% = 29\%$$
$$16 \text{ outs} \times 2.1\% = 34\%$$

On the flop with two cards to come

Figure 11.12.b, showing the chance of hitting on the flop with two cards to come is not a straight line. This means the factor you will use will not be nearly as exact as with one card to come, but it will still allow you to approximate the break even percentage. As always, you are better off knowing the exact numbers, but below you will see some rules that will give you a reasonably close approximation to the actual probability.

The 4% Flop Rule. For two cards to come on the flop, take the number of outs and multiply that by 4%. Here, since the 4%

factor assumes a straight line in figure 11.12.b, which there isn't, the probability you get is just reasonably close to the actual one, not exact.

Examples 4% Flop Rule

	Actual
8 outs X 4% = 32%	31%
10 outs X 4% = 40%	38%
12 outs X 4% = 48%	45%
14 outs X 4% = 56%	51%
16 outs X 4% = 64%	57%

Using math shortcuts

For some, especially those who have used a calculator all their life, it is not easy to do mental multiplication with exact numbers. If that's your situation, getting close is as good as you will be able to do at a table. But close will be close enough.

Here's what we mean by close:

Instead of the 2.1% One Card Rule multiply the number of outs by 2%. 9 outs X 2 would be an 18% probability.

The 4% Flop Rule is already a shortcut. Multiply the number of outs by 4%. 9 outs X 4% would be a 36% probability.

A probability of 18% is close enough to 20% or $\frac{1}{5}$.

A probability of 24% is close enough to 25% or $\frac{1}{4}$.

A probability of 36% is close enough to 33% or $\frac{1}{3}$.

A probability of 48% is close enough to 50% or $\frac{1}{2}$.

A bet of $110 is close enough to $100.

A pot of $530 is close enough to $500.

The examples we have used so far are close to exact. Let's go through two of the examples and use numbers easier to mentally manipulate than the exact numbers.

Example 1

On the turn you have pocket QQ in late position, heads up. The board is a two flush with no obvious straight possibility. You smell a flush draw. You think your opponent has the 9 flush cards as outs, but you know your opponent well enough to realize unless he had suited connectors, he would only play suited cards if one was an A or K. The high card on the board is a Jack. You assume he has an overcard.

1. Your best guess is that he has 12 outs.
2. Shortcut. 12 outs X 2% = 24% probability of him catching. 24% is close enough to 25% or ¼.
3. There is $520 in the pot. $500 is close enough.
4. What happens if you bet $200? First, using our close enough, there would then be $700 in the pot.
5. His Expected Value would then be

   $$EV = (25\%)(\$500 + \$200) - (75\%)(\$200)$$
   $$= \$175 - \$150$$
   $$= \$25$$

   That's no good. He has a $25 positive Expected Value.
6. Let's increase the bet to $400 and see what happens.

   $$EV = (25\%)(\$500 + \$400) - (75\%)(\$400)$$
   $$= \$225 - \$300$$
   $$= -\$75$$
7. OK, he's in negative Expected Value territory, but only by $75. Increase our supposed bet by 25%, to $500.

   $$EV = (25\%)(\$500 + \$500) - (75\%)(\$500)$$
   $$= \$250 - \$375$$
   $$= -\$125$$

   If our read is right, and he is on a draw, a $500 bet should get him to fold.

Example 2

1. On the flop you think you have the better hand. You believe your heads up opponent is on a draw and has 9 outs.
2. Using the shortcut his probability of winning is 9 X 4% = 36%. Being no math wiz you say 33% or ⅓ is close enough.
3. The pot is $500.

4. You consider betting $100.
5. That would take the pot to $600.
6. His Expected Value is $600 X ⅓ = $200. It would cost him $100 to call. He would have a positive Expected Value. That tells you your bet of $100 is not nearly high enough.
7. Let's increase your bet to $400.
8. The pot would then be $900.
9. His Expected Value is $900 X ⅓ or $300. It would cost him $400 to call. He has a negative Expected Value.

Obviously you do not get the same numbers as you would if you could do the exact math in your head. But, you will almost always come to the correct conclusion using the shortcuts.

A formula to get your opponent's Expected Value to 0

By now you have figured out it takes a few seconds to do the mental math to put your opponent into negative Expected Value, especially if you try one amount and that doesn't work, then another, and then perhaps still another. That's the way we've presented it so far, because that's the method many players use.

We're now going to give you another way to figure out the same thing. But instead of gradually increasing bets to make sure your opponent has a negative Expected Value, we will find out where the break even Expected Value is; that is where your bet would leave your opponent with a 0 Expected Value. Once we do that we can then increase our bet beyond that to try to get him to fold.

First we start off with the definition of Expected Value.

$$\text{Expected Value} = (\text{Probability of winning})(\text{Pot} + \text{Your bet}) - (\text{Probability of losing})(\text{Your bet})$$

You may have noticed that we multiply the probability of winning by not just the pot before you bet, but by the sum of the existing pot and your bet. The reason we do this is because we have to look at it from your opponent's view. And he would view what he could win as the sum of the existing pot plus your bet.

Just as we turned hands into Win Factors and then back into

hands, to do some calculations we're going to change these terms into symbols. When we get an answer we'll turn it back into a formula you can use:

Pw means the probability of winning

Pl means the probability of losing

P means the size of the pot before you make your bet

B means your bet

Now if we want to find the break even Expected Value, that is when the Expected Value is 0.

$$0 = (Pw)(P + B) - (Pl)(B)$$

We want to find out how much your bet, that's B, must be for a 0 Expected Value. No need to bore you with the math, but here's the answer.

$$B = \frac{(Pw)(P)}{1 - 2Pw}$$

$$\text{Your bet} = \frac{(\text{Probability of winning})(\text{Pot})}{1 - 2(\text{Probability of winning})}$$

Example 1

Suppose your opponent has a 25% chance of winning a $1,000 pot. What is the amount you must bet to give your opponent a 0 Expected Value?

$$\text{Your bet} = \frac{(\frac{1}{4})(\$1,000)}{1 - 2(\frac{1}{4})}$$

$$= \frac{(\$250)}{1 - \frac{1}{2}}$$

$$= \frac{(\$250)}{\frac{1}{2}}$$

$$= \$500$$

So you must bet in excess of $500 to put your opponent in negative Expected Value territory.

Example 2

Your opponent has a 33% chance of winning a $900 pot. How much must you bet so your opponent has a 0 Expected Value?

$$\text{Your bet} = \frac{(\frac{1}{3})(\$900)}{1 - 2(\frac{1}{3})}$$

$$= \frac{(\$300)}{1 - \frac{2}{3}}$$

$$= \$900$$

Example 3

You have JJ. The flop comes. There are no overcards but three in sequence. The pot is $650.

Your opponent bets $200. You decide to stay in and believe he has an open-ended straight draw.

How much do you have to bet to get him to fold?

We will use close enough math shortcuts and then our 0 Expected Value formula.

You think he has 8 outs. Applying the 4% Flop Rule his probability of winning is 32%. 33% or $\frac{1}{3}$ is close enough.

The pot is $850 but $900 is close enough.

$$\text{Your bet} = \frac{(\frac{1}{3})(\$900)}{1 - 2(\frac{1}{3})}$$

$$= \$900$$

If you bet $900 he would have a 0 Expected Value. If you increased that $900 bet by 50% your bet would be another $450, let's say $500, for a total of $1,400. If our read is right, a $1,400 bet might get him to fold.

Example 4

The turn card has arrived. You have top pair with a King kicker. You believe your opponent has a flush draw with an Ace overcard for a total of 12 outs. The pot currently stands at $1,100.

You are first to act. How much should you bet to get him to fold?

If he has 12 outs with one card to come we can use the 2% rule and say he has a 24% probability of winning. 24% is close to 25%, so he has a ¼ chance of winning.

$1,100 is not easy to divide by 4 so we will say $1,200 is close enough.

$$\text{Your bet} = \frac{(¼)(\$1,200)}{1 - 2\,(¼)}$$

$$= \$600$$

If you bet $600 he would have a 0 Expected Value. With one card to come we should be able to increase the break-even bet by 25% to get him to fold. 25% of $600 is $150. If our read is correct, a bet of $750 should get him to fold.

Break even Expected Value graphs

These next two graphs in figure 11.13 are important, not just for the numbers, but for the understanding. Both graphs use the same scale, so you can compare one to another. The top graph shows what multiple of the pot you must bet if your opponent has one card to come so that your opponent will have a 0 Expected Value, depending on how many outs you think he has. The bottom graph shows the same thing, but for the flop, with two cards to come.

Study the bottom graph carefully. Notice how the flop multiples explode with the number of outs, just to get your opponent to a break even Expected Value. We have only shown the results for the first 13 outs, as the flop graph starts to run off the page. If he has 14 or more outs on the flop there is no amount you can bet to put him into a negative Expected Value. Careful of the high card sequenced suited flop and beware of that QJT suited flop.

Pot Multiple	Outs
0.62	13
0.52	12
0.44	11
0.37	10
0.31	9
0.26	8
0.21	7
0.17	6
0.13	5
0.10	4
0.07	3
0.05	2
0.02	1

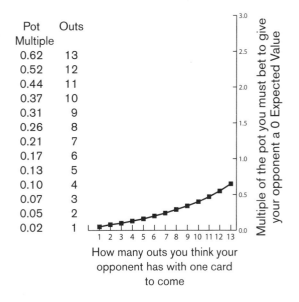

How many outs you think your opponent has with one card to come

Pot Multiple	Outs
12.66	13
4.50	12
2.34	11
1.66	10
1.17	9
0.85	8
0.63	7
0.47	6
0.34	5
0.25	4
0.17	3
0.10	2
0.05	1

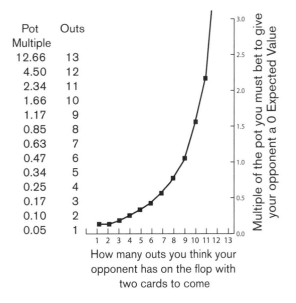

How many outs you think your opponent has on the flop with two cards to come

Figure 11.13

You now have an easy, but perhaps not too simple, method to use to find out the threshold amount you must bet. Yes, it does take practice, but to become world class you must learn how to do this.

A strong draw

You will recall that when we discussed betting in the previous chapter, we introduced the concept of building the pot with a draw preflop or on the flop. We can follow the same principle in cash no limit and in tournaments where the blinds go up fast when we are on the flop. You know anytime you have 14 or more outs on the flop, get your money all in. With two other callers, you can go all in on the flop, or at least make a huge bet, with 10 to 13 outs.

Implying the size of the pot

This is much more difficult in no limit than limit. In limit the size of bets is fixed, and on the flop you can usually imply, depending on the style of play of the remaining opponents, somewhere between 1 and 6 more big bets going into the pot. Implying no limit pots is not something that lends itself to exact mathematical calculations, as you don't know what your remaining opponent or opponents will do. If you are in the rare situation where you feel you know your opponents well enough to imply the future size of the pot, use the same procedures shown above to determine your play. Otherwise your decision will be based primarily on your psych skills.

Conclusion to Expected Value

To use Expected Value to your advantage when you are on a draw, you must be convinced that any of your outs will win the hand. As always, care must be taken to deduct bad outs and avoid double counting outs. When you are on a draw you should only continue in the hand with a positive Expected Value or when you can imply a positive Expected Value.

When your opponent is on a draw you need to make your bet big enough to get him to fold, but not so big that you lose too much when you misread his hand. Understanding and using Expected Value allows you to calculate correct betting decisions. On the flop, since there are two cards to come, the probabilities of catching almost double. Getting a drawing opponent to fold on the flop requires heavy betting. Anyone, you or your opponent, who has 14 or more outs on the flop has a better than 50-50 chance of winning the hand. Anytime a player has a better than 1 in 2 chance of winning, he should bet heavy or go all in.

Also, it is more difficult to determine how much to bet to get a drawing opponent to fold on the flop.

You can use the 2.1% One Card Rule to determine probabilities of catching for one card to come. Until you have memorized the numbers in 11.12.b, the 4% Flop Rule will give you an approximation of the flop probabilities with two cards to come. Implying the size of a no limit pot does not lend itself to easy math.

Another word to the math experts

If you use Expected Value in your everyday work, you may have noticed that we have not used the traditional definition for Expected Value, or always used the precise expected gain. At times when we needed to choose between being exactly correct or what is sufficient to be successful, we chose the sufficient.

Tournament table size

From the WFs as well as the Relative Strength Chapter, you have been exposed to the concept of fewer opponents requiring different play. In a tournament situation, if you are fortunate enough to get to the final table, your play must shift to the right in the PATL. Figure 11.14 shows the shifts required as the table becomes smaller.

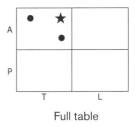

Full table

4-6 players

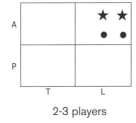

2-3 players

Table size
Figure 11.14

Short handed

You must play many more hands and make extremely aggressive moves on the pot preflop or on the flop. This is where understanding the relative strength graphs in Chapter 8 pays off. The fewer opponents, the more questionable hands you must play, even if the WFs are not correct.

Heads up

You must play almost every hand, approximately 80%; if you don't the blinds will eat you alive. Again, use the relative strength graphs to recognize how valuable high cards are. Although this will not be the determining factor heads up, look ahead in the next chapter to figure 12.4.a and you will see which hands have a positive or negative Expected Value heads up. This figure shows how powerful Ax, Kx, and most Qx hands are heads up.

Although we have mentioned it several times, if you and your opponent both have unpaired cards heads up, both of you have a ⅓ chance of catching a pair on the flop, or said another way, there is only a ½ chance of either of you catching a pair. Even if the flop missed you, it probably missed him too. Your Ace high is likely still good.

Heads up hands

Often you will be up against only one opponent. Figure 11.15 shows you heads up percentage wins.

Slightly different win/loss percentages are possible. For example, JT has a slightly higher chance to make a straight than 98 because, as you know, a straight must contain a T or 5 and with JT one of the T cards is used.

Some hands are repeated for easier comparison. If the win/loss percentages do not add up to 100%, the balance are ties.

Some heads up comparisons might surprise you. For example, notice how much stronger suited cards are against the same hand unsuited, with the AKs versus AK. Also, even with a trash hand such as 83 against AA, the 83 will still win 13% of the time.

Pair versus two lower

JJ	67	JJ	67s
82%	18%	78%	22%

JJ	68	JJ	68s
83%	17%	79%	21%

JJ	69	JJ	69s
84%	16%	80%	20%

JJ	49	JJ	49s
87%	13%	83%	17%

Dominated

AK	AQ	AKs	AQ
72%	24%	73%	22%

AKs	AQs	AK	AQs
69%	29%	68%	28%

Higher pair versus lower pair

JJ	99	AA	22
81%	19%	81%	18%

Two higher versus two lower

A9	83	A9	83s
67%	33%	63%	37%

A9s	83s	A9s	83
65%	35%	69%	31%

JT	83	JT	83s
69%	31%	65%	35%

JTs	83s	JTs	83
67%	32%	71%	28%

One higher, one lower

A9	K8	A9s	K8
64%	36%	66%	34%

A9s	K8s	A9	K8s
62%	38%	60%	40%

Suited versus unsuited

AKs	AK	Q6s	Q6
7%	2%	7%	2%

Pair versus one higher and one lower

JJ	QT	JJ	QTs
71%	29%	67%	33%

JJ	Q6	JJ	Q6s
72%	28%	68%	32%

Pair versus AK

22	AK	22	AKs
52.7%	46.7%	49.6%	49.8%
33	AK	**33**	AKs
53.5%	46.0%	50.3%	49.1%
44	AK	**44**	AKs
54.2%	45.4%	51.0%	48.5%
55	AK	**55**	AKs
54.8%	44.8%	51.6%	48.0%
66	AK	**66**	AKs
55.2%	44.5%	51.9%	47.7%
77	AK	**77**	AKs
55.2%	44.5%	52.0%	47.7%
88	AK	**88**	AKs
55.4%	44.3%	52.1%	47.5%
99	AK	**99**	AKs
55.5%	44.2%	52.2%	47.4%
TT	AK	**TT**	AKs
57.1%	42.6%	53.7%	45.9%
JJ	AK	**JJ**	AKs
57.1%	42.6%	53.7%	45.9%
QQ	AK	**QQ**	AKs
57.0%	42.7%	53.6%	46.0%
KK	AK	**KK**	AKs
69.6%	29.6%	65.5%	33.7%
AA	AK	**AA**	AKs
91.9%	6.8%	87.2%	11.5%

Pair versus inside connectors

22	98	22	98s
48.2%	49.7%	45.4%	52.6%
33	98	**33**	98s
48.9%	49.4%	46.0%	52.3%
44	98	**44**	98s
49.5%	49.2%	46.6%	52.1%
55	98	**55**	98s
51.2%	47.7%	48.3%	50.7%
66	98	**66**	98s
52.6%	46.7%	49.5%	49.7%
77	98	**77**	98s
53.7%	45.7%	50.6%	48.8%
88	98	**88**	98s
63.7%	34.2%	59.9%	38.0%
99	98	**99**	98s
85.0%	12.0%	80.7%	16.3%
TT	98	**TT**	98s
84.9%	14.0%	80.9%	18.6%
JJ	98	**JJ**	98s
83.4%	16.3%	79.6%	20.1%
QQ	98	**QQ**	98s
82.1%	17.7%	78.3%	21.4%
KK	98	**KK**	98s
81.3%	18.5%	77.5%	22.1%
AA	98	**AA**	98s
81.0%	18.8%	77.2%	22.5%

Heads up % win/loss

Figure 11.15

Here are general rules for you to use for heads up hands:

1. A higher pair will win 4 times more often than the lower pair.
2. A higher pair will win 4 times more often than two lower cards.
3. A pair will win 2½ times more often than one higher and one lower.
4. A pair has a slight advantage over most two higher cards.
5. Suited cards gain a few percentage points in strength against a pair.
6. Connected cards gain a few percentage points in strength against a pair.
7. Suited connectors gain percentage points in strength against a pair. Unless they are at or close to the top end, such as AKs, suited connectors are slightly favored against pairs 66 or lower.
8. With the exception of 22, pairs have a slight advantage over AKs.
9. If both players have the same cards, but one has suiteds, they will probably end up in a tie. If not, the suited cards have a tremendous advantage.
10. Two higher cards will win 2 times as often as two lower cards.
11. Just having one higher card will win 1½ times as often as lower cards.

Bluffing

We said a little bit about bluffing in the previous chapter, but now we will expand our discussion to include no limit bluffing as well as some principles that may be applied in limit.

Bluffing is used a lot less than most observers think. What is shown on television would indicate that the top players are bluffing all the time. Not so. Yes, good players do bluff, but seldom will you ever see a good player in no limit bluff all in. When the pot is big, and you have a good player against an average player, you will see the good player who goes all in or calls an all in has the hand. Good players do not bluff often postflop, but they will when it appears obvious to their opponents that the bluffer has the hand.

General times to bluff

As stated earlier, and repeated now because it is so important, you can't bluff loose players, only tight ones. This overrides everything else. Do not waste your chips trying to bluff bad, loose players.

You are actually more concerned about what they have or don't have than what you have. It is best if it is heads up. You can play the opponent, not your cards. It is profitable to pick on passive/tight opponents.

If your table image is passive/tight and you are the first to act or have position, a bluff can be pulled off against tight opponents.

If you find yourself at the worst of all tables, a Mega-Tight table, you must bluff to stay ahead of the rake.

As the number of players dealt cards goes down, bluffing is used more liberally. Bluffing should not be part of your game when several players are dealt cards except when you have position, the remaining opponents are tight, and there are only the blinds and perhaps one other limper.

If you attempt to bluff on the turn or river, it will only be effective when you have been setting it up throughout the entire hand or when a scare card hits.

Small pots are always easier to win with a bluff than big ones. Therefore, a bluff preflop or on the flop has a better chance of succeeding before the pot expands.

Specific bluffing opportunities

- The button raised and you are the only other player. Unless the raiser is a passive, you will find the raiser usually does not have good cards, rather, he is playing position. Even though you are out of position, either re-raise or fold.
- The call bluff. Here you will call a preflop raise with nothing except position against one tight opponent. If the tight opponent checks, he is giving you the pot when you bet.
- You were the preflop aggressor, have position, missed, or only caught a piece, such as a bottom pair. Bluff if you are the first to act, there are only one or two tight opponents left on the flop, and your table image is not aggressive/loose.

- You were the big blind, got to see the flop for free, and all rags or a low pair flops. Especially effective against a few remaining tights.
- If you were one of the blinds, there has been a lot of checking, and a scare card hits. You will be surprised how often this works, especially when a low card pairs on the board.
- When no one seems interested in the pot and you are first to act.
- On the turn or river, if you have been the aggressor during all previous betting rounds, but even then if, and only if, you are up against a lone opponent. A dangerous play unless you know who will fold with a marginal hand.
- A river bluff has a better chance of working if you are in late position or, to a lesser extent, are first to act. If you are both first to enter the pot and in late position, the chances of success are increased.
- On the river, if you have been checking and calling all the way, indicating you were on a draw, and a scare card hits which fills an obvious draw. Works best when you are the first to act with only one remaining opponent.
- Similar to the above bluff, the thin value river bluff is an inexpensive play. It should be attempted only against a tight opponent. A scare card hits on the river and instead of you betting your usual percentage of the pot, you bet a smaller amount, inviting the opponent to call. If you are down to one opponent, he will think you are value betting, and may fold.
- When you have the nuts you obviously are not bluffing. But one play you can use effectively against a lone aggressive opponent, if you have the image of one who normally value bets when he has a monster, is the nut bluff. Go all in as opposed to smooth calling or betting for value. If you make it appear you don't want any callers, you might be fortunate to get one.
- The blocker bluff. A blocker is a card you hold which prevents your opponent from having a monster, generally the nuts. The most common example is if you hold an A of the same suit as a three flushed board, you know no one has the nut flush. Usually having a blocker lets you know when someone is

bluffing in no limit when an opponent represents the nuts by going all in. But you can use a blocker to bluff. If you have the A of the same suit of a three flushed board, you can represent the nut flush with a bluff. This works best if the third flushed card hits on the river.

No limit cash

You should often use the semi-bluff, a bet or raise with a good draw, with position.

Representing AA or KK preflop is a dangerous and expensive play, but has a good chance as long as you have position. You have AK or AQ or any other strong draw, including a medium to low pair, in late position. You raise, everyone folds, other than another player in front of you who re-raises. As long as this player is not a passive/tight, you should re-raise, attempting to take the pot down immediately. This is a play that should not be attempted in no limit tournaments using the tortoise strategy, as you would be risking too many of your chips.

No limit tournaments

In no limit tournaments, other than to steal small pots, you will not find much bluffing going on in the early stages by good players; however, when one of the following occurs, bluffing increases. If several are in play at the same time, bluffing becomes a big part of the game.

The time between rounds is short, 30 minutes or less.
The blinds and antes go up.
The table size becomes smaller.
A player's stack size goes down.

The semi-bluff should be used anytime the conditions mentioned above make tortoise play incorrect. It should not be used in small ball or tortoise tournament play as generally you want to see the next card cheaply, even though you may be giving a free card. The exception is if you believe you can win the pot immediately.

A bluffing opportunity opens up at bubble time as all but the best opponents tend to tighten up when they are close to the money. Bluff if you are the first to enter a pot and have late position.

Bluff outs

Since you will be playing such a wide range of hands, you are going to find opponents fear you if you are still in the hand postflop. With such a loose table image, Daniel Negreanu is always looking postflop, and particularly on the turn, to see what bluff outs may be available. Now you will too. Daniel not only counts the outs he really has, but additional cards which would make it appear he has made his hand. Once bluff outs are added to real outs, often you will stay in when the pure Expected Value would indicate you should fold.

Amount to bluff

Bet the same amount you would if you had the hand. Other than with the thin value bluff, an aggressive/tight will notice when you deviate from your usual bet, which will probably result in a call.

How often to bluff?

If you bluff too much, aggressive/tights will not let you get away with it. If you never bluff, the tight will know when to fold and the aggressive/tight will bluff you. So how often should you bluff? The 12%-13% level is recommended against a lone tight opponent. In order not to fall into any pattern, let your cards tell you what to do.

Examples

	river bluff %
The color of the river card	
Red	50%
The suit of the river card	
A heart	25%
The suit of the river card and the color of the turn	
The river is a heart and the turn is black	13%
Same color, i.e. river a heart and turn is red	12%
The suit of the river card and the suit of the turn	
The river card is a heart and turn is a diamond	6%

A few final words

As mentioned in a previous chapter, if you intend to bluff now and then at a tight table, show your strong cards whether or not there is a showdown, and muck your bluffs.

If you don't have much, a bluff has a higher Expected Value than a call. Either bluff or fold, don't call.

Heads up tournaments and cash games

Heads up is not a game of card strength. **It is a game of aggression. Constantly apply pressure.**

You must know your opponent's range of hands.

You must find out how little or how much it takes to get your opponent to fold preflop.

Postflop, find out how much of a raise it takes to get your opponent to fold. When re-raising, start off with twice the raise. If that doesn't work, keep increasing your re-raises until you find where he will fold.

When in position, raise every time.

No matter what the flop, if first to act, continuation bet.

Do not defend your blind with any hand that has less than a Win Factor of 1.2. Many good players will have a minimum Win Factor of 1.3 or 1.4.

Steal the blinds.

Bankroll swings are extremely high playing heads up. Buckle up.

Go all in with any hand when your chip stack reaches five times your cost per orbit. If your opponent's chip stack is five times his cost per orbit, call with almost anything.

No limit betting summary

You have read a complete chapter on betting and you have found some more betting recommendations throughout this chapter. This section summarizes specific amounts to bet or raise depending on the blinds, stack size, type of opponent, or pot size. A few new amounts are introduced.

Preflop

If a beginner raises 5 times the big blind, he is trying to win the pot immediately.

If a beginner raises a caller by 7 times the big blind, he is trying to win the pot immediately.

In a deep stack no limit tournament, the standard raise is 3 to 4 times the big blind. Some players consistently raise 5 times the big blind.

A raise of 2.5 times the big blind will force the poor hands to fold and ask mediocre hands to call.

In a deep stack no limit tournament, a small ball tortoise player will raise 2.5 to 3 times the big blinds. The 2.5 amount is used when blinds go up slowly or in the early stages of a tournament where the blinds go up fast. The 3 times amount is used in the middle and late stages of a tournament where the blinds go up fast.

If you have a tight lone opponent to your left you want to fold, increase your raise to 4 to 5 times the big blind.

With low suited connectors or low one gap suiteds, the most you should risk is 10% of your chip stack.

If you are short stacked and decide to play a hand, go all in if your chip stack is 4 times or less your cost per orbit.

Postflop

In the absence of the special situations presented below, bet sizes or re-raises should be ⅔ of the pot.

If a beginner bets the pot size, he is probably just using good beginner raise or fold strategy.

Flop

You raised preflop. If you decide to steal against a lone opponent, bet 33% to 50% of the pot against an average opponent. Against a tight opponent, bet 50% to 80% of the pot.

Turn

Against a tight opponent who checks to you, bet 100% of the pot for a steal.

If you are out of position but plan to call if a lone opponent bets, a bet of 50% to 75% of what you think your opponent would bet will often result in your opponent just calling.

A dangerous and expensive play: To get a lone loose opponent to fold, check-raise 2 times of his turn bet.

River

You have a strong hand and believe you have the winner. Bet 75% of the pot for value.

You have a strong hand and are against a math player. You want to give him good pot odds to call. In this case a thin value bet of 25% to 50% of the pot is in order.

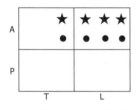

Distribution of no limit
hare winners
Figure 11.16

The "it" factor

Some great traditional no limit players will pooh pooh a lot of the mathematics. Other than pot odds, they think probability and statistical approaches are for the academic, not for them. They go by feel and instinct. That instinct is predominately a heightened psych skill, honed by decades of experience. Several of the younger internet players likewise go by feel and instinct, but their instinct is driven mostly by betting patterns. One thing all great no limit players have is **fearless targeted aggression**.

Targeted aggression

The targeted portion is knowing who you can run over, beat up, and pound into submission. This superior psych skill is the result of playing thousands and thousands of hands against different opponents. It is there whether intuitive or learned, from internet or casino, or from reading and understanding betting patterns or body language. This part of the equation can only be learned by experience.

Aggression

Take a look at figure 11.16. for an important lesson. This is where all good and great no limit hare players fall. Unlike limit where aggressive/tight is by far the most profitable, many of the best tournament no limit players are loose. **Hare winners seldom adjust their aggression, but do adjust their tightness and looseness depending on the type of no limit played.** Even the tortoise will, as he makes his way to the end of the tournament or as the size of the table decreases, shift to aggressive. Very Aggressive play is difficult, but possible, to learn.

Fearlessness

There is a big difference between landing a jet on a simulator compared to a carrier. One is fake; one is your life. In no limit it is easier when you are just betting with fake tournament chips, but if the prizes are big, many can't handle it. As you get closer to the real money, that's when you find out who is fearless. Being fearless cannot be taught. It is either part of one's personality or it isn't.

Summary

- Becoming great at limit is a step towards becoming good at no limit.
- No limit is a different game than limit.
- A lot of what you learn in limit is transferable to no limit.
- A winning strategy is to pick up several small pots with aggressive play and win a few big ones.
- Always build the pot when you have a good hand.
- The first to enter the pot with a raise puts great pressure on the rest of the table.
- When shorthanded, especially heads up, the first aggressor wins more than his fair share of the pots.
- The continuation bet is used often by aggressive players.
- Many hands are over on the flop.
- New dimensions are the type of no limit game, stack size, and unlimited betting.
- Betting deception is a powerful tactic.
- Traditional aggressive/tight play works best in cash no limit.
- You will need to shift gears from aggressive/tight to aggressive/loose when playing tournaments.
- Luck plays a big part in tournaments when the blinds increase quickly.
- No limit requires educated guessing and gambling.
- **The best players in the world constantly use pot odds or Expected Value in no limit.**
- You must use Expected Value when you are drawing.
- When you think opponents are on a draw, you want to bet enough to get them to fold, but you want to avoid betting too much for the times you misread their hand.
- You must use Expected Value to get drawing opponents to fold.
- **The best players show fearless targeted aggression.**

Homework

- If you skipped or just skimmed the first ten chapters, become an expert in limit before you attempt no limit.
- Create 100 situations where you are on a draw against an opponent or more than one opponent, and mathematically determine if you should stay in the hand or fold.
- Create 100 situations where you think you have the best hand against an opponent or more than one opponent who you believe to be on a draw, and mathematically determine how much you should bet to get others to fold.

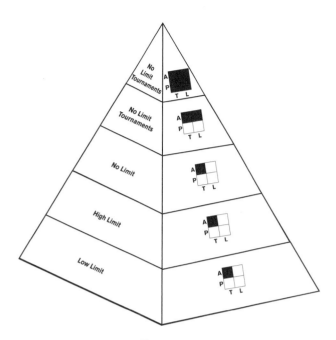

Figure 11.17

Now you are almost ready

You will have worked your way from low limit to high limit to no limit cash. During that time you found you must be aggressive/tight. As you progressed to no limit tournaments where the blinds go up fast, you saw you had to adjust your style of play to include aggressive/loose. Finally, as you were exposed to how to play professional deep stack tournaments where the blinds go up slowly, you were shown the tortoise or small ball strategy used by the top professionals. Here you learned you must vary your play all over the PATL depending on several different variables.

The right hand side of figure 11.17 summarizes the different styles you will employ depending on the game you are playing. Remember it.

I may not know all the answers, but I do know the questions

Most of this book has been focused on what to do when in specific situations. But before you start to play professional tournaments, you must develop your own series of questions to answer. You can use all of the previous chapters as a checklist for your questions, but with time you will come up with many of your own. Depending on the situation, and not in any specific order, these are the ones I use:

- Did I watch at least four orbits of play before I sat down at the table?
- How important is math in this game?
- How important are my psych skills in this game?
- How important is math during this round of betting?
- How important are my psych skills during this round of betting?
- Which players do I know? Which do I know well? Who are the strangers?
- How experienced is my opponent?
- Does my opponent like to gamble?
- Is my opponent a good or poor player?
- Does my opponent make few or lots of mistakes?
- Is my opponent a rock, calling station, maniac or professional?
- Am I one of the better players at this table?
- Where am I seated relative to the most aggressive/tight player?
- Where am I seated relative to the most aggressive/loose player?
- Am I seated between two aggressive players?
- Where am I seated relative to the loosest players?
- Where am I seated relative to the passive/tights?
- Will it cost me a lot or not much to stay in a hand at this table?
- What is the average pot size?
- Will this table have large or small pot size variations?
- Will I have large or small bankroll swings at this table?
- Will I be playing a lot of or only a few hands at this table?
- Is this the type of table I should play a lot of or only a few draws?
- Will I have lots of bad beats or only a few at this table?
- Which opponents value and use position?
- Which opponents take control of a hand?
- Which opponents are raisers? Which are callers?
- Which opponents bluff and how often?
- Is his range of hands easy or hard to discern?
- Does he use deception?
- Will deception work against him?

- What are his tells for a good hand?
- What are his tells for a marginal hand?
- What are his tells for a bluff?
- Should I use advanced or straightforward play against him?
- Does he usually fold, raise, or call preflop?
- How many opponents usually see the flop at this table?
- Does he usually fold, raise, or call postflop?
- Will he fold if I bet a draw?
- Will the free card play work?
- Will there be few or a lot of showdowns at this table?
- Do I need to worry about a scare card on the river against this opponent?
- Would he play runner runner?
- Is there anyone at the table who would check-raise with only a medium or low pair?
- Is there anyone at the table who would check-raise with anything less than a set?
- Does he fold when he knows he is beat?
- Does he let me know if he is going to fold before it is his turn to act?
- Does he tilt?
- Is he on tilt?
- Did he fast check?
- Did he fast call?
- Do I know exactly what cards he has shown on previous showdowns?
- Does he forget to read the board?
- Does he look at his hole cards when the flop is two or three suited?
- Does he look at his hole cards when there is a straight draw on the board?
- Does he play beyond what cards he has?
- How far beyond his cards does he play?
- How likely is it that my hand will improve?
- How often does he look at his hole cards?
- Does he have a betting pattern?
- Does he always raise when he catches?

- If he raised preflop, does he continuation bet or check on the flop if he missed?
- If he raised preflop, does he continuation bet or check on the flop if he catches?
- Does he vary his hands played depending on position?
- Does he vary his betting depending on position?
- Do I have a profile from previous experience with this opponent?
- Can I put him on a hand?
- Will the table react if I play poor cards to the river?
- Will the table react if I show good cards when I steal the blinds?
- Does this opponent only see the board card that helped him?
- What straight draws are on the board?
- How likely is it my opponent would play cards which fit a straight draw?
- What flush draw is on the board?
- How likely is it my opponent would play a flush draw with anything other than A, K or Q?
- If online, how many other tables is he playing?
- What is the nuts?
- What is the 2nd nuts?
- What is the 3rd nuts?
- What is the 4th nuts?
- What is the 5th nuts?
- Does he defend his blind?
- If he does defend his blind, does he call or re-raise?
- Does he control the size of the pot?
- Does he try to steal blinds?
- How does he react if reraised when he tries to steal the blind?
- Does he play a rush?
- Does he understand odds?
- Does he understand probability?
- Does he understand and use pot odds?
- Does he understand and use Expected Value?
- Does he play trash with lots of opponents in a hand?
- Does he bet hard with a flush when he has less than Q high?
- Does he understand the probability of what others will hold preflop?

- What is the lowest kicker he plays with his A?
- Does he play A-9?
- Does he play A-rag?
- If I have A-rag, what is the probability an opponent also has an A?
- If I have a pocket pair, what is the probability an opponent has a higher pair?
- Does he understand flop overcard probabilities?
- Does he understand overcard probabilities if played to the river?
- Does he continue to bet hard on the river with nothing but high pair?
- Is he a math player?
- Does he adjust his play depending on how tight or loose the table is?
- Does he adjust his play depending on how passive or aggressive the table is?
- Does he adjust his play depending on his card strength?
- Does he adjust his play depending on the number of opponents dealt cards?
- Does he adjust his play depending on his position?
- Does he adjust his play depending on the horse?
- Does he adjust his play depending on pot size?
- Exactly where is this table in the Advanced PATL?
- Exactly where is each opponent in the Advanced PATL?
- Where in the Advanced PATL is he most comfortable playing?
- What is in my player profile of this opponent?
- How much time does he take before he acts?
- Based on the count of how many hands he plays, what range of hands will he play?
- Based on information from a showdown, what adjustments should be made to the range of hands he will play?
- Have I made the proper horse adjustments?
- Have I made the proper adjustments for the pot size?
- Will he chase even when the pot size is too small?
- What are my implied odds?
- Does he use implied odds?
- Do I always know the pot size?
- Does he know or use the pot size?

- If he is a beginner, does he understand raise or fold poker?
- Does he understand how important aggression is?
- Can I run over him?
- Does he use bets to find out information?
- Does he fold to aggressive play?
- Does he build the limit pot preflop and on the flop with a draw?
- Does he continue to bet heavy with a draw on the turn?
- Does he try to buy the button?
- How often does he raise?
- When he raises, what does it mean?
- How often have I raised at this table?
- What does he think when I raise?
- How often does he check-raise?
- When he check-raises, what does it mean?
- How often have I check-raised at this table?
- When I check-raise, what does he think it means?
- If I am in this hand, will I be pot committed?
- What percentage of my chip stack am I risking if I stay in?
- Would he bluff in this situation?
- How often has he seen me bluff?
- Would he put me on a bluff in this situation?
- Does he make a continuation bet when he catches?
- Does he continuation bet when he misses?
- Does he think I have it when I make a continuation bet?
- Does he understand pot equity?
- Does he have a betting pattern with a draw?
- Does he stay in when the pot is big?
- Does he raise to get rid of the blinds?
- Does he try to isolate?
- Does he continue to bet strong when he has an opponent isolated?
- How does he react when he is isolated?
- How often does he raise from the blind?
- What hands will he raise with from the blind?
- Does he raise or call when defending his blind?
- Does he try to steal the blinds?
- Does he bet with nothing when no one seems interested in the pot?

- Does he try to steal posts?
- Does he check to the preflop raiser?
- How does he play a monster?
- How does he play top pair or a pocket overpair on the flop?
- How does he play second pair?
- Does he call with overcards?
- How does he play two pair or better on the flop?
- How does he play two pair or better on the turn and river?
- How does he play his overpair when a scare flop hits?
- Does he have the ability to smell weakness?
- Does he take advantage of weakness?
- Does he call on the river if he has any chance of winning?
- Why did he raise that amount?
- What does he think I have?
- What did he have when he check-raised?
- Who check-raises with a draw?
- Is he aggressive or tight close to the bubble?
- Does his range of hands change depending on table size?
- How often does the small blind defend?
- When defending his small blind, does he call or re-raise?
- How often does the big blind defend?
- When defending the big blind, does he call or re-raise?
- How much of a raise do I need to make to get the information I want?
- What is the stack size for each of my opponents?
- What range of hands do my opponents think I play?
- Does my hand play best in a multi-way pot or against few opponents?
- How many outs do I have?
- How many outs do I think he has?
- How much must I bet to isolate him?
- If I raise and a short stack goes all in, am I pot committed?
- If I raise and then get re-raised, can I fold?
- Who are the players who might call my raise?
- Is my opponent predictable?
- Does my opponent think I am loose?
- Does my opponent think I am tight?
- What cards have I shown?
- What hands have I been forced to show on the river?

- What hands has he been forced to show on the river?
- How does he play when he flops the nuts?
- How often does he slowplay?
- How likely is he to bet if I check?
- Will he be pot committed?
- Should I give a free card?
- How often does he give a free card?
- If I raise, can I win the pot now?
- What are the scare cards that will make my opponent think I made my hand?
- What are my bluff outs?
- Does he put me on what I have?
- If I call, will he know I'm on a draw?
- Does he play the same hands the same way all the time?
- How does he play second pair?
- What backdoor outs do I have?
- How often does he limp?
- Does he limp with a monster?
- How often does he play runner runner?
- Does he bet or check on the turn with a draw?
- Does he bet or check on the flop with a draw?
- Does he understand and use thin value betting?
- Does he understand how the rules of the game change how he can play?
- Does he use a consistent strategy?
- How often is he the first aggressor?
- Does he try to get the hand over fast?
- Does he understand how to play stack size compared to his cost per orbit?
- How does he play with a big stack?
- How does he play with a middle stack?
- How does he play with a short stack?
- Does he vary his bet sizes?
- Does he adjust his style of play during each phase of the tournament?
- Does he play differently when blinds go up slowly or fast?
- Does he understand small ball?
- Does he use small ball?
- When does he abandon small ball?

- How much does he bet when he wants a lone opponent to fold?
- Does he vary his style depending on the betting round?
- How much does he vary his style depending on position?
- Does he vary his bet sizes depending on an opponent's style?
- Does he vary his style between cash games and tournaments?
- Does he use a check-raise to neutralize poor position?
- Does he use a defensive bet to neutralize poor position?
- Does he use Expected Value when he is drawing?
- Does he understand Expected Value on the flop?
- Does he use Expected Value to get an opponent to fold?
- Does he vary his style depending on how many opponents are at the table?
- Does he use bluff outs?
- Does he vary his bet size when he bluffs?
- When did I last bluff?
- Should I vary my bet size against this opponent when I bluff?
- What will I do if he checks?
- What will I do if he bets?
- What will I do if he raises?
- What will I do if I am re-raised?
- Does he watch the board or other players as cards come out?
- Is he fearless?
- Does he know which opponents to target?
- Is he naturally aggressive?
- Does he ask himself questions before he acts?

Homework

Come up with a minimum of 100 questions you will use. Add to the list the more you play.

You now have an advanced degree, and are ready to make a living playing hold'em.

Final Exam

1. Hold'em is made for:
   - ❏ A. Playing as many hands as possible
   - ❏ B. Calling when you are in a hand
   - ❏ C. Being aggressive when you are in a hand
   - ❏ D. Checking and calling

2. Preflop, the best hold'em players do what most often, next most often, least often:
   - ❏ A. Bet, Call, Fold
   - ❏ B. Call, Fold, Bet
   - ❏ C. Fold, Bet, Call
   - ❏ D. Bet, Fold, Call

3. In limit, preflop or on the flop, if you are unsure if you have the best hand, what should you do?
   - ❏ A. Check and call
   - ❏ B. Bet or raise
   - ❏ C. Wait to see the turn
   - ❏ D. Call to the river

4. This opponent folds the most to aggressive play on the river:
   - ❏ A. passive/tight
   - ❏ B. aggressive/loose
   - ❏ C. passive/loose
   - ❏ D. aggressive/tight

5. This opponent folds the most to aggressive play preflop:
   - ❏ A. passive/tight
   - ❏ B. aggressive/loose
   - ❏ C. passive/loose
   - ❏ D. aggressive/tight

6. Most opponents will fold to aggressive betting:
   - ❏ A. Preflop
   - ❏ B. On the flop
   - ❏ C. On the turn
   - ❏ D. On the river

7. The best way to build a limit pot against aggressive/loose players is to:
   - ❏ A. Play straightforward
   - ❏ B. Check-raise on the flop
   - ❏ C. Slowplay on the flop and then raise if in position or check-raise on the turn
   - ❏ D. Slowplay to the river and then raise if in position or check-raise on the river

8. The best way to build a limit pot against aggressive players is to:
   - ❏ A. Play straightforward
   - ❏ B. Check-raise on the flop
   - ❏ C. Slowplay on the flop and then raise if in position or check-raise on the turn
   - ❏ D. Slowplay to the river and then raise or check-raise on the river

9. What is the advantage of check-raising?
   - ❏ A. Trap the aggressives
   - ❏ B. Neutralize poor position
   - ❏ C. Get checkers and drawers to fold
   - ❏ D. Build the pot
   - ❏ E. All of the above

10. When you are check-raised, your best play is usually to:
    - ❏ A. Re-raise
    - ❏ B. Call
    - ❏ C. Fold

11. The continuation bet works best:
    - ❏ A. Against many callers
    - ❏ B. Against many callers in no limit
    - ❏ C. Against few callers in no limit
    - ❏ D. Against few callers in limit

12. In limit, you are up against one opponent who bets on the flop and you have an open-ended straight. Using the concept of pot equity, you would:
    - ❏ A. Raise
    - ❏ B. Call
    - ❏ C. Check-call
    - ❏ D. Fold

13. Which is better to use, pot equity or Expected Value?
    - ❏ A. Pot equity
    - ❏ B. Expected Value
    - ❏ C. Both are the same

14. In limit, what is the best strategy preflop and on the flop when you are on a draw with position in a multi-way pot?
    - ❏ A. Check and call
    - ❏ B. Fold
    - ❏ C. Bet and raise
    - ❏ D. Raise and fold

15. Against this type of player, you could actually bet yourself out of the pot.
    - ❏ A. passive/tight
    - ❏ B. aggressive/loose
    - ❏ C. passive/loose
    - ❏ D. aggressive/tight
    - ❏ E. Two of the above

16. The lower your WF:
    - ❏ A. The more chances you can take
    - ❏ B. The more callers you want
    - ❏ C. The less important position is
    - ❏ D. The smaller the pot you want

17. This hand is ranked higher at a Tight table than any other type of table.
    - ❏ A. AKs
    - ❏ B. 99
    - ❏ C. A4s
    - ❏ D. 87s

18. This hand is ranked higher at a Mega-Loose table than any other type of table.
    - ❏ A. QJs
    - ❏ B. JJ
    - ❏ C. AK
    - ❏ D. Two of the above
    - ❏ E. None of the above

19. Which of the following hands is not among the top 40 hands regardless of the type of table?
    ❏ A. A5s
    ❏ B. A6s
    ❏ C. AK
    ❏ D. AQ
    ❏ E. None of the above

20. Top pair with an Ace kicker:
    ❏ A. Is favored in big pots
    ❏ B. Is favored in small pots
    ❏ C. Will win more pots than it will lose
    ❏ D. Will lose more pots than it will win
    ❏ E. Two of the above

21. If you let both blinds in the hand and they both have unpaired cards, what is the probability at least one of them will have a pair or better on the flop?
    ❏ A. 25%
    ❏ B. 33%
    ❏ C. 54%
    ❏ D. 64%
    ❏ E. 75%

22. In limit, if there are 8 big bets in the pot on the river and you have a marginal hand, how many times do you have to be right to call?
    ❏ A. 1 out of 5
    ❏ B. 1 out of 7
    ❏ C. 1 out of 9
    ❏ D. 1 out of 12
    ❏ E. None of the above

23. In limit, if you are the first to act on the river and you plan to call, what should you do?
    ❏ A. Bet out
    ❏ B. Check and call
    ❏ C. Check and raise
    ❏ D. Raise and re-raise

24. You usually don't have to worry about this opponent check-raising you.
    ❏ A. passive/tight
    ❏ B. aggressive/loose
    ❏ C. passive/loose
    ❏ D. aggressive/tight

25. With a no limit value bet, you should vary your bet size based on:
    ❏ A. The deception method using the suit of your cards
    ❏ B. Whether you think your opponent has a strong hand or a weak hand
    ❏ C. Whether your opponent is tight or loose
    ❏ D. Whether your opponent is passive or aggressive

26. How many big bets per hour should you be consistently winning when playing high limit hold'em before moving on to no limit?
    ❏ A. 0.5 big bets
    ❏ B. 1 big bet
    ❏ C. 1.5 big bets
    ❏ D. None of the above

27. The tortoise strategy is most effective in a no limit tournament when:
   - ❏ A. The blinds go up at a fast rate and everyone starts off with a deep stack
   - ❏ B. The blinds go up slowly and everyone starts off with a short stack
   - ❏ C. The blinds increase at a fast rate and everyone starts off with a short stack
   - ❏ D. The blinds go up slowly and everyone starts off with a deep stack

28. Which of the following is NOT true when comparing limit hold'em to no limit hold'em?
   - ❏ A. The pot size has a greater fluctuation in no limit
   - ❏ B. The cost to stay in a no limit hand is higher than limit
   - ❏ C. There are fewer showdowns in limit than no limit
   - ❏ D. Deception is much more important in no limit

29. Which of the following is true when comparing limit hold'em to no limit hold'em?
   - ❏ A. Stealing preflop with position is much more prevalent in no limit
   - ❏ B. Utilizing a "no tell routine" is less important in no limit
   - ❏ C. The number of hands you play will generally be more in no limit compared to the number of hands played in limit
   - ❏ D. All of the above

30. Which of the following is the least important when playing no limit?
   - ❏ A. Win Factors
   - ❏ B. Truth Drawing Numbers
   - ❏ C. Position
   - ❏ D. Pot size

31. True or False: In no limit, high pairs or overpairs tend to lose more big pots than they win.
   - ❏ A. True
   - ❏ B. False

32. In a no limit tournament, as your chip stack diminishes and the number of orbits you can afford decreases, your style of play must become:
   - ❏ A. More passive and more loose
   - ❏ B. More passive and more tight
   - ❏ C. More aggressive and more loose
   - ❏ D. More aggressive and more tight

33. Unless you are very confident your hand is the winner, you should not risk more than what percentage of your chip stack when utilizing the no limit tortoise strategy?
   - ❏ A. 5%
   - ❏ B. 10%
   - ❏ C. 15%
   - ❏ D. 20%

34. Typically, how big should your preflop raise size be when first to act in a deep stack no limit tournament with the tortoise strategy?
    ❏ A. 2 ½ times the big blind
    ❏ B. 3 ½ times the big blind
    ❏ C. 4 times the big blind
    ❏ D. 5 times the big blind

35. During flop play and using the no limit tortoise strategy, how should you normally play when the board is sequenced or flushed?
    ❏ A. aggressive/loose
    ❏ B. aggressive/tight
    ❏ C. passive/tight
    ❏ D. passive/loose

36. When using the tortoise strategy, about what percentage of the pot should you raise postflop if you want a tight player out of the hand?
    ❏ A. 25%-35%
    ❏ B. 33%-50%
    ❏ C. 50%-80%
    ❏ D. 100%-125%

37. When using the tortoise strategy, how much should you normally raise preflop when you want an experienced player to fold?
    ❏ A. 2 ½ times the big blind
    ❏ B. 3-3 ½ times the big blind
    ❏ C. 4-5 times the big blind
    ❏ D. 6-7 times the big blind

38. You have AKs and you flop a four flush and an inside straight draw. You believe that if you hit a straight or a flush you will be the winner. Your passive opponent bets $300. You believe if you call he will not bet on the turn and you will get a free card if you need one. Which of the following is closest to your Expected Value if you see both the turn and the river. The pot, before you call, is $1,500.
    ❏ A. $380
    ❏ B. $580
    ❏ C. $680
    ❏ D. $780
    ❏ E. None of the above is close

39. If you have to call $500 to stay in and you have a 15% chance of winning the hand, which of the following pot sizes, including your opponent's bet, is closest to a zero Expected Value?
    ❏ A. $1,833
    ❏ B. $2,633
    ❏ C. $2,833
    ❏ D. $3,233
    ❏ E. None of the Above

40. To find out your break even probability of catching one of your outs on the next card, you should multiple the number of outs you have by:
    ❏ A. 1.1%
    ❏ B. 2.1%
    ❏ C. 3.1%
    ❏ D. 4%

41. In heads up play, which hand is the statistical favorite?

    ❏ A. 44
    ❏ B. AKs
    ❏ C. Each hand has a 50% chance of winning the hand

42. In heads up play, which hand is the statistical favorite?

    ❏ A. 22
    ❏ B. 89s
    ❏ C. Each hand has a 50% chance of winning the hand

43. On average, a pair will win _____ times more often than one higher and one lower when heads up.

    ❏ A. 1 ½
    ❏ B. 2 ½
    ❏ C. 3 ½
    ❏ D. 4 ½
    ❏ E. None of the above

44. True or False: It is often considered a profitable bluffing opportunity when you are in the big blind, got to see the flop for free, and the flop is ragged or a low pair flops.

    ❏ A. True
    ❏ B. False

45. Approximately what percentage of the time should you be bluffing against tight opponents?

    ❏ A. 4-5%
    ❏ B. 7-8%
    ❏ C. 12-13%
    ❏ D. 22-23%
    ❏ E. 28-29%

46. If a beginner raises a caller by 7 times the call, what is he trying to accomplish?

    ❏ A. Build the pot
    ❏ B. Isolation
    ❏ C. Win the pot immediately
    ❏ D. All of the above
    ❏ E. None of the above

47. On the river you have a strong hand and believe you are the winner. Without taking into account how strong you think your opponent's hand is, and whether your opponent is a math player or not, what percentage of the pot should you bet for value?

    ❏ A. 25%
    ❏ B. 33%
    ❏ C. 50%
    ❏ D. 75%
    ❏ E. 100%

48. On the turn against a tight opponent, what percentage of the pot should you bet if you are trying for a steal?

    ❏ A. 25%
    ❏ B. 33%
    ❏ C. 50%
    ❏ D. 75%
    ❏ E. 100%

49. On the river you have a strong hand and believe you are the winner. Your lone opponent is a math player. What percentage of the pot should you bet for value?

    ❏ A. 12.5% to 25%
    ❏ B. 25% to 50%
    ❏ C. 50% to 75%
    ❏ D. 75% to 100%
    ❏ E. None of the above

50. In a no limit hand, you have AK of hearts and the flop comes 8h 5s 2h. You believe that your hand will be the winner if you either hit your flush or make a pair. The size of the preflop pot is $400 and you decide to bet $200 on the flop from early position against two loose opponents who call your bet. The turn misses you and you check. One of your opponents bets $300 and the other opponent folds. With just the river to come, ignoring implied odds, which of the following is closest to your Expected Value?

❏ A. $74
❏ B. $114
❏ C. $222
❏ D. $310
❏ E. $500

51. You are in the small blind in no limit. The blinds are $50 and $100. Everyone folded and you tried to steal the big blind with a raise of $225. The big blind calls. On the flop you have an open-ended straight draw with one overcard. You are confident that if you hit your straight or overcard on the turn you will win the hand. If you check on the flop and your opponent bets $600, ignoring implied odds, which of the following is closest to your Expected Value?

❏ A. $208
❏ B. $125
❏ C. -$21
❏ D. -$179
❏ E. -$210

See Appendix E for answers

CHAPTER 12

Ultimate Texas Hold'em

Casino game. Ultimate Texas Hold'em. As with every casino game, the odds favor the house. But there is an element to this game which allows you to be the equivalent of a blackjack card counter. One area where, at times, you have a mathematical edge.

The game

The game is played with a single deck. You play heads up against the dealer. You can't bluff the dealer out and likewise the dealer can't bluff you out. You both play to the river and unless you fold after all the cards are out, there is a showdown. If there are other players at the table they are also heads up against the dealer. Your cards play only against the dealer's, not against any other players.

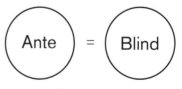

Figure 12.1.a

To play, you first put down two bets. One bet goes in the "ante" circle and one goes in the "blind" circle. These bets must be equal to each other. See figure 12.1.a.

Before play starts you also have the option to place a bet in the "trips" square. Most casinos allow you to place a bet in the trips square greater than the one you placed in the ante and blind. Some casinos even allow you to play only the trips square without having to play the ante/blind. They should. The trips bet has a negative Expected Value and over the long run you will lose a lot with this bet. Figure 12.1.b.

Figure 12.1.b

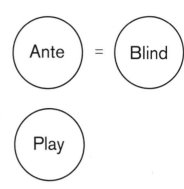

Figure 12.1.c

You then receive two cards and the dealer gets two cards, both face down. The dealer does not look at his cards.

After you receive your cards you have the option of checking or betting. The rules of this game are set up in such a way that the earlier you bet, the more you may bet. If you decide to bet at this point you must bet either three times or four times the amount of your ante. It is your choice whether you bet three or four bets or check. If you bet you are finished until all the board cards are out. You can't bet any more and you can't take back your bet. Bets are placed in the "play" circle shown in Figure 12.1.c.

Then the flop is dealt. If you bet preflop you may not do anything. If you checked preflop, you may now either check or bet. If you bet now you must bet exactly two times your ante. You cannot bet more or less. This bet goes in the play circle. If you bet now you are finished until all the community cards are out.

Then both the turn and river are dealt at once. If you have checked up to this point you now may either place a bet equal to your ante or fold. If you fold you lose both your ante and blind. You also lose any trips bet you may have made.

The dealer then flips over his two hole cards and it is you against the dealer.

You have four ways to win. The first three, you must beat the dealer to be paid.

1. You win even money for the amount of your ante if you beat the dealer and the dealer has "qualified." Some casinos say a dealer has qualified with at least a pair. Others classify qualification as an A high; your odds are better with casinos who go with the A high. If the dealer doesn't qualify your ante is returned to you. Your blind bet is still in play. If the dealer qualifies and you push, you keep your ante and blind.

2. If you beat the dealer you win even money for the amount you bet in the play circle. In this area you have an advantage. More on this in a minute. If you push you do not lose or win.

3. You also win if you have beaten the dealer and have certain hands such as a straight or above. Figure 12.1.d shows these payouts for your blind bet.

Royal Flush	500 to 1
Straight Flush	50 to 1
Quads	10 to 1
Full House	3 to 1
Flush	3 to 2
Straight	1 to 1

Figure 12.1.d

4. This last way for you to be paid off does not require you to beat the dealer. If you placed a bet in the trips square — that was the optional bet you can make before play begins — you will be paid if you hit three of a kind or better, even if all the cards are on the board. Figure 12.1.e.

Trips	
Royal Flush	50 to 1
Straight Flush	40 to 1
Quads	30 to 1
Full House	8 to 1
Flush	7 to 1
Straight	4 to 1
Trips	3 to 1

Figure 12.1.e

Where does the house have the advantage?

1. The optional trips bet. It can be maddening to see someone cash in big, but you must resist the temptation to make this bet. For every $10 you bet, you will win $8.16 or, said another way, lose $1.84. Figure 12.2 shows the calculations.

2. The ante and blind bets are also in the house's favor. They are your entry fee to play the hand. The blind bet heavily favors the house; if you lose the house takes the bet; if you win you don't get paid anything unless you have a straight or better. But, if you play this game you must make the blind bet. The blind bet is designed to eat the elephant, that's you, one bite at a time. It is not as bad on the ante, these are nibbles at the elephant, but the house wins here too.

Expected Value when betting trips

	Occurs once every so many	Probability of occurring %	Payoff from trips bet	Expected Value % (Payoff X Probability of hands occurring)
Royal flush	33,333	0.003	50 to 1	0.15
Straight flush	3,226	0.031	40 to 1	1.24
Quads	595	0.168	30 to 1	5.04
Full house	41	2.460	8 to 1	19.68
Flush	28	3.057	7 to 1	21.40
Straight	21	4.824	4 to 1	19.30
Trips	20	4.925	3 to 1	14.77
				81.59 %

Figure 12.2

Where do you have an advantage?

1. Choosing to bet or check preflop.
2. Choosing to bet or check on the flop.
3. Choosing to bet or fold when all community cards are out.

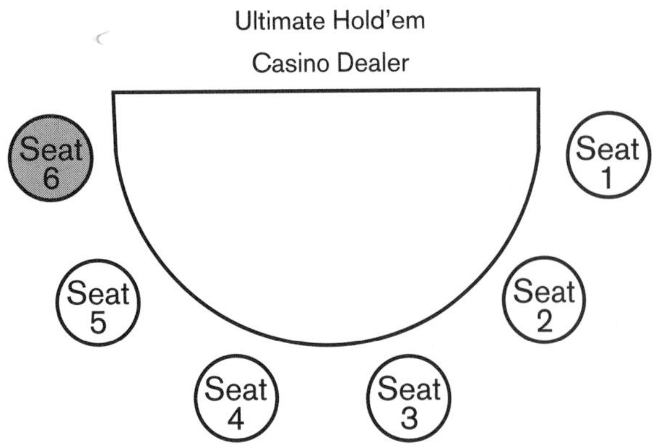

Ultimate Hold'em Casino Dealer

Figure 12.3

Choosing your seat

As with blackjack, third base is the place to be. Few players understand this. If you can't get to seat 6 when you sit down, find the furthest left position available. Immediately ask the dealer to allow you to move to the left, until you get to seat 6, if any seats become available.

Valuable future information

You will be able to gain an extraordinary amount of information from all of the other players. Info which would take several hours to obtain at a regular hold'em game, you can glean in 15 minutes. Why? Unless a player folds, you get to see his cards. If you pay attention to when he bets, you will quickly learn how aggressively or passively each player acts when they hold certain cards.

Preflop information is the most valuable. Your primary objective is to learn when your fellow players bet or check with each of the following:

1. A high card, Ax, Kx, Qx.
2. Two high cards not paired.
3. High pairs.
4. Middle pairs.
5. Low pairs.

On the flop you must learn whether your opponents check or bet if they hit a pair or are still on a draw, especially a four flush or open-ended straight.

Last, when the turn/river cards come out, what do they stay with? You can also find out what they folded with after the hand just by asking them.

Once you have this information, you can apply it with hand specific info.

Valuable hand specific information

Preflop all the players will be focusing on their cards and bets. Not you. As with regular hold'em you must focus on the players as they get their first two cards. You should wait before you bet until you have seen all of the checks or bets from earlier seats.

Preflop almost everyone will indicate how they will bet as they will be focused on their cards alone, no matter what their position. You should not. Wait to bet until after you have determined if others are going to bet or check.

Using the information

Preflop, your information should give you a good idea of how many high cards are already in play by others at the table.

If you read there are few high cards out, you bet as you normally would.

If several players bet preflop it is logical to assume they hold high cards. Three things come into play.

1. There are fewer high cards for the dealer to have.
2. If you have a hand you would normally check with, say J7, this now becomes a betting hand preflop. Why? Precisely because there are fewer high cards available for the dealer.
3. Most important, if you have high unpaired cards and it is apparent there are several high cards out, you should check even if you have normally extremely strong cards such as AKs. With more high cards out it is less likely for you to hit your high cards.

For the first few minutes at the table, until you know how others bet, a preflop hesitation before checking tells you they probably have a high card. A preflop bet means they probably have at least one high card or a pair.

Flop information will let you know who probably hit a pair. It is good for you when another player hits a pair. It means there is at least one less card the dealer might have to pair one of the board cards.

Turn/river information is only marginally valuable, but still can help. If a player folds, you should conclude he had low cards, and certainly did not hit a pair. If several fold, they probably all had low cards, which means there are higher cards available to be in the dealer's hand.

Preflop hands to bet

What strategy should you employ preflop? You have a mathematical edge for every probability 50.1% or higher.

Three strategies are presented. Under all three you will never play the trips bet.

Very aggressive. Using this approach you will win or lose the most. Bankroll needs to adjust for chance variations: 100 bets; if the bets are $5 for the ante and small blind, you need $500 to have a chance to win at this game.

You will bet the maximum, 4 bets, every time you have cards with a 50.1%+ probability of winning. When you have the odds in your favor, even slim odds, you will play your advantage. Bet the max.

Aggressive. Medium wins; medium losses. Bankroll: 60 bets. An aggressive approach says you will bet as follows:

> 4 bets when you have a 60% or greater probability of winning.
>
> 3 bets when you have a 55%-59% chance of winning.
>
> Waiting to see the flop before deciding to bet with a probability of anything less than 55%.

Passive. Bankroll: 40 bets. Minimal wins; minimal losses.

> 4 bets when you have a 66% or better chance of winning.
>
> 3 bets when you have a 61-65% probability.
>
> Waiting to see the flop with less than a 60% chance of winning.

Another way to look at the same hands is to put the probabilities in the form of a distribution. See figure 12.4.a. The shaded hands are all 50% or less. Those hands in the 51-55% column are marginally above 50%, while the remaining hands in the left columns are strong preflop betting hands.

It is important for you to understand these numbers are for a particular hand against a random hand which is what the dealer has. Some results are counter intuitive when compared to the strength of a specific hand against another specific hand that you reviewed in figure 11.15 in Chapter 11. For example, the figure below says AK will win 61-65% against a random hand. It also says 22 will win between 46-50% against a random hand. But you know from the previous chapter if you have 22 against AK the 22 has a 53% chance of winning as opposed to the AK which only has a 47% chance of winning. So, AK is better than 22 against a random hand, but is a statistical loser if heads up against 22.

% win distribution of heads up play against a random hand played 100% to the river

81 +	80-76	75-71	70-66	65-61	60-56	55-51	50-46	45-41	40-36	35-31
							J7			
					A5s	K7	22			
					A6s	A2	Q2s			
					A8	K4s	J5s	85s		
					55	J8s	T8	T2s		
					KT	K6	Q5	J3		
					QTs	T9s	97s	96	73s	
					A4s	Q7s	T6s	J2	82s	
					A7	K3s	J4s	75s	65	
					QJ	Q6s	Q4	94s	93	
					A3s	33	87s	T5	43s	
					K8s	Q8	Q3	T4	84	
				AK	A6	K5	98	65s	92	
				77	JTs	J9	J3s	93s	74	
				ATs	Q9s	K2s	T7	86	52s	
				AQ	A2s	Q5s	J6	84s	62s	
				AJ	K7s	T8s	96s	95	72s	
				KQs	K9	J7s	J2s	T3	54	
				KJs	A5	T9	T5s	74s	64	
				A9s	QT	Q4s	T4s	92s	42s	
				AT	44	K4	J5	76	83	
				66	K6s	Q7	Q2	T2	73	
				KTs	A4	J8	86s	54s	82	
				A8s	A3	K3	95s	64s	32s	
				KQ	J9s	98s	T3s	75	53	
				A7s	Q8s	T7s	97	94	63	
			88	A9	K5s	J6s	T6	83s	43	
	KK		AKs	KJ	K8	Q3s	J4	85	72	
	QQ	TT	AQs	QJs	JT	Q6	76s	53s	52	42
AA	JJ	99	AJs	K9s	Q9	K2	87	63s	62	32
% win 81 +	80-76	75-71	70-66	65-61	60-56	55-51	50-46	45-41	40-36	35-31

Figure 12.4.a

Betting preflop

Figures 12.4.b.a-c show all of the hands you should bet preflop depending on whether you choose to play very aggressively, aggressively, or passively. Copy and laminate the card of your choice. Most casinos will allow you to refer to this helper before

```
                    AA
                AKs KK  AK
            KQs AQs QQ  AQ  KQ
        QJs KJs AJs JJ  AJ  KJ  QJ
    JTs QTs KTs ATs TT  AT  KT  QT  JT
T9s J9s Q9s K9s A9s 99  A9  K9  Q9  J9  T9
98s T8s J8s Q8s K8s A8s 88  A8  K8  Q8  J8
T7s J7s Q7s K7s A7s 77  A7  K7  Q7
    J6s Q6s K6s A6s 66  A6  K6  Q6
        Q5s K5s A5s 55  A5  K5
        Q4s K4s A4s 44  A4  K4
        Q3s K3s A3s 33  A3  K3
            K2s A2s     A2  K2
```

VERY AGGRESSIVE PLAY-SWAYNE'S ULTIMATE HOLD'EM HANDS
BOLD 50.1%+
Figure 12.4.b.a

```
                AA
            AKs KK  AK
        KQs AQs QQ  AQ  KQ
    QJs KJs AJs JJ  AJ  KJ | QJ
JTs QTs KTs ATs TT  AT  KT | QT  JT
J9s Q9s K9s A9s 99  A9    K9  Q9
    Q8s K8s A8s 88  A8    K8
        K7s A7s 77  A7
        K6s A6s 66  A6
        K5s A5s 55  A5
            A4s 44  A4
            A3s     A3
            A2s
```

AGGRESSIVE PLAY-SWAYNE'S ULTIMATE HOLD'EM HANDS
BOLD 60%+; NOT BOLD 55.1-59.9%
Figure 12.4.b.b

```
            AA
        AKs KK  AK
    KQs AQs QQ  AQ  KQ
QJs KJs AJs JJ  AJ  KJ
    KTs ATs TT  AT
    K9s A9s 99  A9
        A8s 88
        A7s 77
            66
```

PASSIVE PLAY-SWAYNE'S ULTIMATE HOLD'EM HANDS
BOLD 66%+; NOT BOLD 61.1-65.9%
Figure 12.4.b.c

you bet. The hands in italics in figure 12.4.b.a, the Very Aggressive Play, are only slightly above 50% and some players may wish to check with these hands.

Reading hands on flop bets

Again, late position allows you to watch who bets on the flop. Unless you have developed a different profile for a particular player, if a player bets with a rainbow board you should assume they paired one of the top two board cards. With a two flush or two in sequence you need to learn who bets with those draws and who checks.

Your flop action

Let's suppose you checked your 50% or less hand preflop. You may either make two bets or check. It gets a little more complicated to decide what to do. As opposed to overwhelming you with tons of numbers, we have developed the following rules for you to follow. A key to remember is this is a game of high cards and pairs. It is not a game of draws.

1. On the flop bet if you make a pair of 66 or better. Otherwise check.
2. Do not bet if you have a four flush or an open-ended straight. Your probability of making the flush is 35% and the straight is 31%. Wait for the turn/river.

Reading hands on the turn/river

If another player has checked to the end and then bets on the turn/river cards you can assume they just made a pair or possibly have an A or face in their hand. This information helps you because if others have just paired their cards that means there are fewer cards for the dealer to pair. If several players fold, or several players are crabbing because they bet earlier and didn't hit, that tells you the dealer has more cards with which to make a pair.

In regular hold'em you are probably watching your opponents when the cards are dealt. In this game, when the turn/river cards come out, you must watch the cards. Unlike regular hold'em, dealers in many casinos immediately start to rearrange the cards in sequential order, and if you are watching the others at the table as opposed to the cards as they are dealt, you will probably forget what those last two cards were.

Your play at the end

What should you do if you have checked to the turn/river? You must find the number of net countable outs the dealer has. Figure 12.5 shows what is meant by countable outs. Three unusual twists for countable outs.

1. If there is a straight draw, other than an open-ended straight which you would count as 8 outs, this will count as 1 countable out.

2. If there is a three flush on the board, not a four flush, which would count as 9 countable outs, this also will count as 1 countable out.

3. If you have a low kicker — 7 or lower — you have to take into account the possibility the dealer has the same card as you with a higher kicker. The way this is done is to add 3 countable outs.

Dealer countable outs

A four flush on the board	9
A four card open-ended straight	8
A double inside straight draw	8
Each overcard not shown	4
An inside straight draw	4
Each unpaired card on the board	3 per card
You have a 7 or lower kicker with your high card	3
Both a three flush and a straight possible	3
Each paired card	2
Each tripped card	1
A three flush on the board	1
Any other possible straight	1

Figure 12.5

If the board has paired or better and the dealer has 22 or more net countable outs, fold. Otherwise bet.

If the board has not paired and the dealer has 18 or more net countable outs, fold. Otherwise, bet. Using the net countable outs will allow you to stay at least some of the time.

When the rules of 22/18 outs were derived, you should know the following factors were taken into account:

1. The Expected Value of your bet. This is the reason the number of countable outs depends on whether the board is paired or not. If the board is paired, and you win, you will win even money on your ante bet. If the board is not paired, and the dealer doesn't qualify — which is the only way you can win — the dealer pushes back your ante bet and you do not receive even money if you win.
2. The chance the dealer has a pocket pair, which occurs 1 out of every 17 hands.
3. Over 150,000,000 calculations.

Make sure you read and understand 12.6.a-b.

Playing the board
You might have nothing but the board is strong, i.e. all high cards. Use the rule of 18 outs as discussed above, and hope for a push.

Catching up
When you're down there is a tendency to start to increase your ante and blind bets to try to catch up. Don't do it.

A word of caution
Although this game is available at the time of writing, the publication and use of these findings might cause the house to change the rules, and thus the odds, or even eliminate the game. The house doesn't like it when a player has an advantage and loses its sense of humor when lots of players have an advantage.

Similar games
There are similar games at different casinos; usually the difference is the game has a variation of the trips bet. If so, avoid this house bet.

Ultimate Texas Hold'em Dealer Countable Outs
Examples

You have Q ♦ 8♣
    The board shows:

        J♦   T♣   7♠   3♦   2♥

    Dealer outs

Any one of four Aces	4
Any one of four Kings	4
Possible straight	1
Each unpaired card on the board	<u>15</u>
Total dealer countable outs	24

You have Q♦ 2♣
    The board shows

        A♥   J♠   8♥   7♥   3♥

    Dealer outs

Any Queen with a higher kicker	3
Any one of 4 Kings	4
Any heart	9
Possible straight	1
Each unpaired card on the board	<u>15</u>
Total dealer countable outs	32

You have T♣ 9♦
    The board shows

        A♠   7♦   Q♣   Q♠   Q♥

    Dealer outs

The remaining Queen	1
Any one of 3 Aces	3
Any one of 4 Kings	4
Any one of 3 Sevens	3
Any one of 4 Jacks	<u>4</u>
Total dealer countable outs	15

You have K♦ 4♣
    The board shows

        9♠   8♠   7♠   6♥   2♠

    Dealer outs

Any one of 4 Aces	4
Any one of 9 spades	9
Open-ended straight	8
Each unpaired card	15
A King with a higher kicker	<u>3</u>
Total dealer countable outs	39

Figure 12.6.a

Ultimate Texas Hold'em Dealer Net Countable Outs
Examples

You have Q♦ 8♣

    The board shows:

        J♦   T♣   7♠   3♦   2♥

    You are sure two other Aces are out with other players

Dealer outs

Any one of four Aces	4
Deduct 2 Aces	-2
Any one of four Kings	4
Possible straight	1
Each unpaired card on the board	15
Total dealer net countable outs	22

You have Q♦ 2♣

    The board shows

        A♥   J♠   8♥   7♥   3♥

    Three other players have paired

Dealer outs

Any one of 3 Aces	3
Any Queen with a higher kicker	3
Any one of 4 Kings	4
Possible straight	1
Any heart	9
Each unpaired card on the board	15
Deduct three paired	-3
Total dealer net countable outs	32

You have T♣ 9♦

    The board shows

        A♠   7♦   Q♣   Q♠   Q♥

    Another player has an Ace

Dealer outs

The remaining Queen	1
Any one of 3 Aces	3
Deduct 1 Ace	-1
Any one of 4 Kings	4
Any one of 3 Sevens	3
Any one of 4 Jacks	4
Total dealer net countable outs	14

You have K♦ 4♣

    The board shows

        9♠   8♠   7♠   6♥   2♠

    Two players hit a straight

Dealer outs

Any one of 4 Aces	4
Any one of 9 spades	9
Open-ended straight	8
Deduct straight cards	-2
Any one of 3 fours	3
Any one of 3 twos	3
A King with a higher kicker	3
Total dealer net countable outs	28

Figure 12.6.b

Summary

- Ultimate Hold'em is a casino game with the odds in favor of the house; not a big surprise.
- Seat 6 is your best spot.
- The trips bet is a sucker bet; don't make it.
- The ante and blind bets are the house's edge.
- Your edge is how much you bet and when you bet.
- Knowing other cards which are out and how other players bet helps you decide what to do.
- The probabilities of each of the 169 hands played 100% to the river heads up have been calculated.
- You may choose to be very aggressive, aggressive, or passive when you play.
- Don't try to catch up.
- At the end, if the board has paired or better and the dealer has 22 or more net countable outs, fold. Otherwise bet.
- At the end, if the board has not paired and the dealer has 18 or more net countable outs, fold. Otherwise bet.

CHAPTER 13

Preface/Postface/Conclusion

This chapter contains many of the things that would normally go in the front of a book, but I didn't think they were important enough to put there.

Language

Although my English teacher of a ½ century ago would go nuts (Sister Catherine is probably dead by now), here are some examples of the shorthand language and grammar I use:

- He and him are generic for he/she and him/her. In this politically correct world no offense is meant and I hope none is taken.
- I write as I talk. I've written college texts. Formal. Boring.
- Some important things are repeated. If you think you read it earlier, you probably did.
- Often you will be told a topic will be covered or repeated later.
- Sentence fragments are used.
- New words and terms are coined such as "unsuiteds" and "boardology."
- Some sentences end with a preposition or a verb.
- AA means two Aces.
- AK means Ace King unsuited.
- A♥ means the Ace of hearts.

- A-face means an A with a K or Q or J.
- When writing a one digit number sometimes it is shown as "7" and other times "seven."
- T means the card Ten, but it is not written as Ten or 10.
- WF stands for Win Factor. WFs means the plural of a WF.
- As means Ace suited. It does not mean 2 Aces.
- "Re-raise" is written as opposed to "reraise."
- To indicate an open-ended straight sometimes the phrase "open-ended" is used.
- A table in this book could refer to two different things. It could mean the poker table. It could mean a data display. To avoid confusion, when the word "table" is used, it means the poker table.
- If we are somewhere in a quadrant of the PATL matrix I will use "passive/loose," with a small "p" for passive and a small "l" for loose. When referring to a specific plot point within the Advanced PATL matrix I will use capital letters such as "Passive/Very Loose." Oftentimes, when talking about a specific plot point within an Advanced PATL quadrant, a chart will also be shown. An example is figure 13.1.
- When describing either a general quadrant or a specific plot point in the PATL matrix, I use the words in the order of the letters P, A, T, L. For example, I will say "passive/tight" since the p comes before the t, as opposed to "tight/passive." Or "Very Aggressive/Mega-Loose" because the A comes before the L, as opposed to "Mega-Loose/Very Aggressive."
- An inside straight is called an "inside straight," not a "gutshot" nor a "belly buster." A double inside straight is called a "double inside straight."
- Early position in a 10-handed game means the blinds and seats 3 and 4.

    Middle position means seats 5, 6 and 7.

    Late position means seats 8, 9 and the button.

    This is not the same as some other authors use.

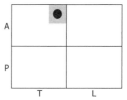

Figure 13.1
PATL Matrix –
Mini PATL plot points

Button	Seat 9	Seat 8	Seat 7	Seat 6	Seat 5	Seat 4	Seat 3	Big Blind	Small Blind
Late position			Middle position			Early position			

Figure 13.2.a

- Early position in a 6-handed game means the blinds.
  Middle means seats 3 and 4.
  Late position means seat 5 and the button.
  Again, this is not the same as some other authors use.

Button	Seat 5	Seat 4	Seat 3	Big Blind	Small Blind
Late position		Middle position		Early position	

Figure 13.2.b

Presentation of hands

Hands are presented in an order easiest to remember as opposed to the traditional lumping of hands by strength or type. Often the same hand is repeated because it will fall into several categories. The general pattern of presentation is:

- Axs, Kxs, Qxs.
- Ax, Kx.
- Suited connectors, One gap suiteds, Two gap suiteds, Three gap suiteds.
- Unsuited connectors, One gap unsuiteds, Two gap unsuiteds.
- Pairs.

Research

Many hours went into the research. Some of the research team have favorite hands they like to play. But, in many cases those hands didn't pass the rigorous research WFs. Facts are stubborn things. We presented what we found, not what we would have liked to find.

Simulation aberrations

What did I do when the simulation numbers weren't smooth? Sometimes sophisticated mathematical techniques such as correlation or regression were used. If that didn't work we would do several do overs. Other times I just used common sense.

How about if the results didn't seem right? Lots of do overs. Lots of scratching my head. Lots of individual calculations. Usually I found the answer and you see the result. A few times I couldn't. What to do? Publish results I think might be wrong? If the results seemed incorrect, and I couldn't find any mathematical reason to correct them, I gave you a more conservative answer than I actually found. For example, for a few simulations the results indicated some hands with a playable WF that I, nor few of the experts I consulted, would play. I didn't want you to play a hand that might not have a positive Expected Value, so I changed the results to indicate a non-playable WF. As I do further research, if I find these simulations were accurate, I will make the revisions in future editions.

Too many charts and graphs

Perhaps. Some graphs appear simple, but many times the simple needs a picture to be understood. We retain images better than numbers. Whenever possible, an attempt has been made to turn numbers or concepts into a graph or chart, even though some are obvious.

Numbers different than those in other books

There are some differences between our numbers and those in other books. Most of the time the difference is insignificant. When one of our numbers differed from another author, unless I was sure their number was incorrect, I chose to publish the more conservative one. We have checked our numbers over and over, but we may have some errors. If you arrive at a different number, or several different numbers than we have, please write me.

When numbers were consciously used from other books, with or without our independent calculations, they are given credit in Appendix A, the endnotes section.

Winning all the time in limit

Forget it. You will not win all the time. It's always the dealer's fault. You may have several bad days and lose a lot. That's all part of chance and probability. And you may have several extremely profitable days in a row and think you are the greatest poker player in the world. Garbage. Both losing and winning are part of probability. This is not a zero sum game unless all your opponents are aggressive/tights; if they are it is less than a zero sum game as the rake will be against you. If you are playing against opponents who are anything other than aggressive/tights you will know more than they do. You should be winning more than you are losing. How much? As mentioned in the introduction, an average of 1.5 big bets per hour at a casino and slightly more per table on the net. As you exceed 2 big bets per hour you are becoming an expert. If you aren't up to the 1.5 big bets per hour, focus on these areas:

1. Your opponents are better than you. Way back in Chapter 2 we told you the most important strategic decision you could make is whether to get in a game or get out of it. Until you are an expert, avoid aggressive/tight tables.

2. Chasing.

    a. You chase your money when you are losing by playing low WF hands.

    b. You chase a draw when you should have folded on the flop or turn.

3. Ensure you are not playing too many hands for the table.

4. Do not play a low WF hand out of position. Too many of my students tend to play plot points looser and more passive than their position indicates.

5. You try to steal the blind with nothing, one of the blinds re-raises, and you won't give up. In limit you'll almost always call one more bet, but that's definitely not the case in no limit. If you have nothing, fold.

6. Analyze whether you are staying in too many hands too long. In other words, you chase when you should have folded on the flop or turn.

7. Last, ask yourself if you are a betting wuss. Perhaps you don't isolate with high cards and high pairs. You are not getting enough money with a good draw in the first two betting rounds with position. You call when you should be raising, which is what too many rocks do.

Remember Miller, Sklansky, and Malmuth when they say, "Raising when you should call can cost you a bet, calling when you should have raised can cost you a pot."

Hand rankings

One question I often get is what hand ranking system I use. By now you know there is no one set of rankings as the strength of the hands depends on several factors. But, to satisfy those who want an overall ranking system, figure 13.3 is a good one. These rankings come primarily from the Pro Academy Pro 2.5 computer software; however, I have made some inconsequential adjustments.

Hand Rankings using primarily the computer program Poker Academy Pro 2.5

1	AA	41	A2s	81	54s	121	92s	161	93
2	KK	42	Q8s	82	J5s	122	42s	162	73
3	QQ	43	T8s	83	A6	123	76	163	42
4	JJ	44	K7s	84	K8	124	K3	164	92
5	AKs	45	J8s	85	33	125	Q6	165	83
6	AQs	46	98s	86	T8	126	83s	166	62
7	TT	47	K6s	87	85s	127	62s	167	32
8	KQs	48	66	88	J4s	128	86	168	82
9	AJs	49	K5s	89	A3	129	32s	169	72
10	AK	50	A9	90	98	130	82s		
11	KJs	51	87s	91	22	131	K2		
12	ATs	52	K4s	92	Q8	132	65		
13	QJs	53	Q7s	93	J8	133	Q5		
14	KTs	54	T7s	94	64s	134	96		
15	AQ	55	97s	95	J3s	135	72s		
16	99	56	K9	96	K7	136	T6		
17	QTs	57	J7s	97	95s	137	Q4		
18	JTs	58	K3s	98	T5s	138	54		
19	KQ	59	T9	99	J2s	139	75		
20	A9s	60	Q6s	100	53s	140	J6		
21	AJ	61	A8	101	A2	141	Q3		
22	K9s	62	55	102	T4s	142	J5		
23	KJ	63	Q9	103	74s	143	85		
24	88	64	J9	104	T3s	144	64		
25	A8s	65	K2s	105	43s	145	Q2		
26	QJ	66	76s	106	K6	146	J4		
27	Q9s	67	Q5s	107	84s	147	95		
28	T9s	68	86s	108	87	148	53		
29	J9s	69	A7	109	T2s	149	J3		
30	AT	70	Q4s	110	63s	150	T5		
31	A7s	71	44	111	K5	151	74		
32	A5s	72	A5	112	97	152	T4		
33	KT	73	96s	113	94s	153	J2		
34	A4s	74	65s	114	T7	154	43		
35	A6s	75	T6s	115	52s	155	T3		
36	QT	76	J6s	116	Q7	156	84		
37	A3s	77	Q3s	117	J7	157	63		
38	K8s	78	Q2s	118	93s	158	T2		
39	JT	79	75s	119	K4	159	94		
40	77	80	A4	120	73s	160	52		

Figure 13.3

Complaining not allowed

Let's take a look at the raw data for AA before I turned that data into a WF. This raw data indicates the chances of you winning the hand. You see against 9 opponents your highest probability of winning is at a Mega-Loose table and your chance of winning is 30%. 30% of the time you will win. 70% of the time you will lose. When your AA is cracked on the river that's part of the 70%. You can't sweat it. It happens. It is worth repeating. No whining. Move on to the next hand.

When an opponent wins a hand with a 43 unsuited, either compliment him or say nothing. Let it go. He won but will lose in the long run. When a hotshot complains to you about you winning with a Q5s, feel free to say, "You shouldn't criticize my play when I'm stacking your chips. It makes one of us look stupid."

Number of opponents	Mega-Tight Opponents play 20% of their hands	Tight Opponents play 35% of their hands	Loose Opponents play 50% of their hands	Very Loose Opponents play 65% of their hands	Mega-Loose Opponents play 80% of their hands
	% wins	% wins	% wins	% wins	% wins
1	84	84	85	85	85
2	72	73	73	73	73
3	62	63	63	63	63
4	54	54	54	55	55
5	47	47	47	48	48
6	40	42	42	42	43
7	35	37	37	37	38
8	31	32	32	33	33
9	28	28	28	29	30

Raw % win data for AA before conversion to Win Factor
Figure 13.4

A home field advantage

Why do most teams play better at home? Is it the crowd? Familiar surroundings? It doesn't matter. What matters is they do. You can create your own home field advantage. You will need to keep track of your performance, and all of the variables you think influence your performance, every day you play. You are going to create your poker diary or journal or log. **The most important part of your journal is your win rate per hour** as all other factors will be measured against this number. It will be expressed as the number of big bets to two decimal places. For example +1.86 would mean you won 1.86 big bets per hour of play. Variables to document are:

How much money you made or lost per session
The table PATL, including how often the table PATL changed and how it changed

Betting amounts such as $5/$10

Location played

Time started

Time ended

Breaks taken

Day of the week

Month of the year

What you had to eat before and during play

Hours of sleep night before play

Type of exercise before play

Number of opponents; if it's changed, by how many and when

Mistakes you know you made

A profile of every opponent including where they fall in the Advanced PATL

Any other variable you believe affects your win rate.

You will then correlate your results with variables that seem to occur when you have your best sessions as well as those which correlate with your worst sessions. You then attempt to play with the same variables that appear to help you play better and avoid those that seem to hinder your play.

There is a big difference between correlation and causation. Correlation just says when certain things occur, you play better. That doesn't mean they actually cause you to play better, but as with the home field advantage, it doesn't matter. They could influence how you play, but they might not. What matters is you will come to believe certain factors help you play better. Your mind reacts positively and, in fact, you will play better.

Tilt

You see it all the time. Someone loses their focus and self-control. Why? It could be he loses a hand on the river and can't control himself. It doesn't matter why, but it is unmistakable when he does. Immediately he becomes the aggressor, straddling, playing poor cards, raising and re-raising. There is a natural psychological reaction to an unexpected loss. Many equity traders on Wall Street have the same reaction when they have a big loss. For many, the brain thinks aggressive action will result in making up for a previous loss, or a series of losses. Sometimes it does. Most of the time, since he is playing poor cards, the result is more losses. The more experienced you become, the less you will tilt. After 250,000 hands you know there are players who will play anything, call a re-raise with A6, stay all the way to the river, and win some big pots you thought should have been yours. Over the long run those players will lose, but they can and do win in the short run. It is just part of the game.

To be a great player you must control your mind. You need focus to win. You need focus to play your best game all the time. Leave your personal problems in the parking lot. If you are the kind of person who goes on tilt, even a little bit, here's what you must do after a bad beat, something you perceive to be a bad beat, or anything which pulls you away from playing your top game. Tell the dealer you are going to sit out a few hands. Take a few laps around the casino. Several deep breaths. And return to play. Your head will be clearer, and you will have a better chance of playing your best game.

Fatigue

The only thing you can do well when you are tired is sleep. Play hold'em when you are tired and you are guaranteed to lose concentration, play poorly, make mistakes, and lose money. Keep your body in shape. Work out at least an hour a day.

The internet

Playing on the net, especially if you are playing several speed tables at once, gives you the advantage of being able to wait for the right hands. Sitting in a casino you can go well more than an hour and not play one hand. You won't have to wait long for a playable hand when you are on multiple internet speed tables simultaneously. By now you should have concluded that your winning in limit, especially low limit, is a function of the quantity of hands you play. With the net you can play many, many, many more hands than you could in a casino during the same period of time.

There are some disadvantages. Physical tells, other than the speed of an opponent's bet, are gone. Collusion, as discussed in the next section, is possible. When you find the same opponent on many tables he too is waiting for good hands. Reading the board can be difficult with several warnings going off at the same time telling you have a few seconds to act or your hand will be folded. Becoming one with your computer screen can lead to no real life. But, on balance, the advantages of the net outweigh the disadvantages.

Problems

A problem with publishing this data is that someone could easily write a computer program to win on the internet. With a clever programmer, the chances of winning would be remarkable. Within the foreseeable future, a computer in your pocket, a wireless heads up display on your glasses, optical recognition software, and you may be able to use the exact numbers at a casino.

Knowing some cards in players' hands gives players a great advantage. I know students who collude on the internet. Instant messaging, telephone, several players playing in the same room. Even if an online site can track Internet Service Providers, or players who play the same tables as others, this is a game of spy versus spy. Students are remarkable at keeping one step ahead of being honest (these students will probably turn out to be lawyers).

Swayne this, Swayne that

I have put my name with some of the things I believe are original, not just to feed my ego, but also so you can identify new ideas. If it turns out you have seen any of the following before, let me know and I will not only apologize to the originator but make corrections in future editions (anything in parentheses indicates a figure number):

Ch 1   Relative importance of math and psych skills depending on type of hold'em played (1.1)

Importance of math and psych skills during each round of betting (1.2)

Degree of difficulty during each round of betting (1.3)

Experience numbers

Ch 2   The concept of the basic PATL matrix

Tables and players (2.3.a)

Target size (2.4.b)

Chance to recoup losses (2.5.e)

Deception (2.8.b)

Preflop raising and calling (2.9.a)

Flop folding (2.10.b)

Ch 3   Combination of play difficulty and skills needed during each round of betting (3.1)

The inexperienced bettor (3.2)

Ch 4   The concept of how to use cards for random deception

Ch 5   The concept of focusing on possible straight draws first

Ch 6   Risk during rounds of betting (6.1)

Ch 7   The hand pyramid (7.1). I used a figure created by Burton, extrapolated it into a pyramid

Breaking various types of hands apart using the hand pyramid (7.2.d)

Preflop straight and flush draws (7.4.c)

What players will have at a 10-handed table (7.4.e)

Overcard probabilities with all five cards (7.5.b.d)

Outs converted into minimum bets needed in pot (7.6.3)

How does this chart help me?

Ch 8   The entire chapter

Ch 9   All figures. Almost the entire chapter. I used Sam Bradis' book (see Appendix A) as the basis for most of the seven critical factors.

Ch 10   Relative importance when betting (10.1)

Frequency of folding when faced with aggressive play (10.2)

Betting yourself out of a pot (10.7.b)

Betting yourself into a pot

The betting figures (10.8)

Postflop betting (10.12)

If you are ahead on the flop (10.13)

When to go for a free card with a strong draw (10.14.a)

When to go for a free card with a weak draw (10.14.b)

Big pot on the river (10.15)

Ch 11   Explanation of style of play depending on type of limit game (11.1.a)

Explanation of style of play depending on type of tournament (11.1.b)

Use of the PATL to explain style of play depending on stack size compared to the cost per orbit (11.3)

Use of the PATL to explain style of play depending on stack size compared to other players (11.4)

Swayne deceptive betting (11.11)

Using Expected Value (11.12)

Use of the PATL to explain style of play depending on tournament table size (11.14)

The "it" factor.

Ch 12   The entire chapter

Conclusion

At the beginning I said the concepts in this book would be simple to understand but not easy to implement. I hope I have made some very complex concepts appear simple. Easy to implement? No. If you want to be a better than average to good limit player you may use a cafeteria approach. Pick those concepts which you are good at or like to do.

If you intend to become a great limit player you must not only build on your strengths, but compensate for weaknesses. The great player goes way beyond the good player. The great player understands it will take thousands of hours of study and play, play and study. Below is a summary of the details the great player needs to know. Before you will be able to see everything at a glance, it is like climbing a ladder. Learn and do. Do and learn. The only thing stopping you is you.

Here are the things you must reinforce, understand, or learn as you play:

- The importance of math and psych skills during each round of betting.
- The flop and turn are the most challenging rounds to play.
- Do not play for real money until you are experienced.
- Use the basic PATL matrix to identify players and tables.
- Always try to play at passive/loose tables.
- Sit to the left of the most aggressive players.
- Against loose opponents, straightforward play is best.
- Some loose players draw to the river and that will cause bad beats to happen.

- There are folding patterns on the flop, depending on a player's PATL.
- You can only bluff good players; on the turn or heads up on the river is the best time.
- Beware of a scare card on the river or runner runner against loose opponents.
- An opponent's PATL indicates the types of hands he will play.
- There are physical tells certain players may give you.
- Specific betting patterns are associated with a player's PATL.
- Position affects players' betting.
- As the hand develops put each opponent on a hand or a small range of hands.
- Develop a no tell routine.
- Create your own method of deception when playing at a tight table.
- Become an expert boardologist.
- Blinds are risky.
- Never play as though you are on a rush.
- Certain hands come up more or less frequently than others.
- Odds and probability are the same thing said in a different way.
- Suited connectors and gapped suiteds are a better draw than connectors.
- An Ace in the hole without a good kicker is not very powerful against more than a couple opponents.
- An average 10-handed table distribution will have a draw for almost every player.
- Overcard probabilities on the board are extremely high for medium pairs.
- The outs chart in the Numbers Chapter is extremely important.
- An overpair or top pair with a good kicker will win most of the pots.
- The relative strength of hands changes with the number of opponents.
- Some hands increase in strength with the number of opponents and some decrease.
- There are seven critical factors which determine hands you will play.

- There are mathematical definitions for how tight or loose a player or table is.
- There are mathematical definitions for how aggressive or passive a player or table is.
- Calculating where a table falls on the Advanced PATL is the basis for playable hands.
- Calculating where a table falls on the Advanced PATL takes time to learn.
- A Win Factor shows you the relative Expected Value of starting hands.
- A Win Factor accounts for the number of opponents and how tight or loose the table is.
- The minimum acceptable WF is 1.1.
- Hold'em is position. The WFs for starting hands are adjusted for position.
- Few hands are played in early position; more hands are played in later position.
- Few hands are played at an aggressive table; more hands are played at a passive one.
- WFs are converted into potential playable hands.
- There is a basic adjustment for the horse and there are advanced adjustments.
- Postflop pot size will form the basis of whether to stay in or fold with a drawing hand.
- The Truth Drawing Numbers must be memorized for limit.
- Betting is where the money is made.
- Implying how many bets will be in the future pot helps you win big pots.
- Hold'em rewards aggression.
- Preflop the PATL of the table has more importance than an individual's PATL.
- Postflop where each opponent falls in the PATL is extremely important.
- Recommendations are given for your limit betting depending on the PATL of opponents.
- Fold as soon as you know you are beat.
- Stealing blinds and/or posts is worthwhile.
- If you are ahead on the flop, bet like the pot is yours.
- The more turn cards that can harm you, the more aggressive you must be on the flop.

- No limit is a different game than limit, although you must know limit before you should play no limit.
- In no limit pick up several small pots with aggressive play and go for a few big ones.
- The first to act in no limit can put great pressure on the rest of the table.
- Stack size adds a completely new dimension in no limit.
- Luck and gambling are part of no limit.
- No limit deep stack tournaments where blinds go up slowly require tortoise play.
- Understanding how to use Expected Value will help you win more and lose less.
- The best no limit players have fearless targeted aggression.
- Everything in this book is simple, but not easy.
- Learn and do; do and learn.
- Poker is sand, not pebbles, never golf balls. Please read Appendix D now.

I hope this has been worth your while to read. There is much more to discover. You should read every poker book and article you can. You should keep track of plays or concepts you learn as you play. My address is in the first section of Chapter 1 and the last part of Appendix A. I ask you to let me know the things you have discovered, or things you feel need to be discovered. Also, if you do not agree with anything presented, or have found mistakes, please let me know.

Bibliography

Read everything you can. When ordering books I recommend Mr. Howard Schwartz, Schwartz's Gambler's Book Shop, 630 S. 11th Street, Las Vegas, Nevada, 89101. To see what is contained in each book he has personally read everything and summarized his thoughts on his web site www.gamblersbook.com. Mr. Schwartz has everything you need. This is a list of material I either used for this book or have used in the past. To the left is a number and letter to identify each, as later there will be an endnote section, and the letters and numbers are used to identify the source.

Books

A1 Chen, B., Ankenman, J., 2006, *The Mathematics of Poker*, ConJelCo, Pittsburgh, Pennsylvania.

B1 Barboianu, C., 2005, *Texas Hold'em Odds*, Infarom.

B2 Badizadegan, M., 1999, *Texas Hold'em Flop Types*, Goldstar Books, Los Angeles, California.

B3 Braids, S., 2003, *The Intelligent Guide to Texas Hold'em Poker*, Intelligent Games Publishing, Towson, Maryland.

B4 Brunson, D., 2002, *Super System*, 3rd edition, Cardoza Publishing, New York.

B5 Brunson, D., 2005, *Super System 2*, Cardoza Publishing, New York.

B6 Burton, B., 2005, *Get the Edge at Low-Limit Texas Hold'em*, Bonus Books, Los Angeles, California.

C1 Caro, M., 2003, *Caro's Book of Poker Tells*, Cardoza Publishing, New York.

G1 Gordon, P., November 2008, World Series of Poker Camp, Las Vegas.

H1 Hellmuth, P., 2005, *Phil Hellmuth's Texas Hold'em*, Harper Collins, New York.

H2 Hilger, M, 2003, *Internet Texas Hold'em*, Dimat Enterprises, Inc.

H3 Hilger, M., 2006, *Texas Hold'em Odds and Probabilities*, Dimat Enterprises, Inc.

H4 Harrington, D., Robertie, B., 2006, *Harrington on Hold'em Volume I Strategic Play*, Two Plus Two Publishing, Nevada.

H5 Harrington, D., Robertie, B., 2005, *Harrington on Hold'em Volume II The Endgame*, Two Plus Two Publishing, Nevada.

J1 Jones, L., 2005, *Winning Low Limit Hold'em*, ConJelCo, Pittsburgh, Pennsylvania.

K1 Krieger, L., 1999, *Hold'Em Excellence*, ConJelCo, Pittsburgh, Pennsylvania.

L1 Largay, A., 2006, *No-Limit Texas Hold'em*, ECW Press, Toronto, Ontario, Canada.

M1 Maroon, M., 2005, *Winning Texas Hold'em*, Sterling Publishing, Toronto, Ontario, Canada.

M2 McKenna, J., 2005, *Beyond Tells*, Kensington Publishing, New York.

M3 McEvoy, T., Cloutier, T., 2005, *Championship Hold'em Tournament Hands*, Cardoza Publishing, New York.

M4 Miller, E., Sklansky, D., Malmuth, M., 2005, *Small Stakes Hold'em*, Two Plus Two Publishing, Henderson, Nevada.

M5 Miller, E., 2005, *Getting Started in Hold'Em*, Two Plus Two Publishing, Henderson, Nevada.

N1 Nelson, A., 1993, *Poker – Hold'em: Intermediate*, Pokerbook Press, Lafayette, Colorado.

N2 Negreanu, D., 2007, *Hold'Em Wisdom for all players*, Cardoza Publishing, New York.

N3 Negreanu, D., 2008, *PokerVT.com*.

N4 Negreanu, D., 2005, *Learning to Win*, MTV Networks.

P1 Petriv, M., 1996, *Hold'em's Odds Book*, The Objective Observer, Ontario, Canada.

S1 Sklansky, D., 2000, *Hold'em Poker*, 5th edition, Two Plus Two Publishing, Henderson, Nevada.

S2 Sklansky, D., Malmuth, M., 2004, *Hold'em Poker for Advanced Players*, 3rd edition, Two Plus Two Publishing, Henderson, Nevada.

W1 Warren, K., 2004, *Ken Warren Teaches Texas Hold'Em*, Cardoza Publishing, New York.

W2 Wenzel, J., 2006, *The Everything Texas Hold'em Book*, Adams Media, Avon, Massachusetts.

Computer programs
C-P1 Poker Academy Pro 2.5 at *www.poker-academy.com*
C-W1 Wilson Turbo Texas Hold'em software

Video
V1 Texas Hold'em Poker Fundamentals for Winning, 1989, Fifth Street Video, Los Angeles, California.

Acknowledgments

The final product could not have been completed without all of the following. My sincere thanks go to:

Luke Bakemeier

Andy Blum

Jordan Fischer

Andrew Gleason

Cody Goble

Phil Gordon

Florence Heintz-Aliesch

Cody Jones

Charlie Kline

Stewart Klugman

Jerry Krause

Warren Luckner

Rich Maresh

Bob Masternak

James Murray

Lisa Nason

John Nebeck

Daniel Negreanu

Dave Nelson

Robert Newberry

Scott Paetzold

Greg Polt

Zach Raff

Andy Readleaf

Jim Scherrer

Mark Seif

Kevin Selberg

Brian Swayne

Chuck Swayne

Joe Swayne

Sherwin Toribio

Sasha Tregebov

Jordan Williams

The Author

Charley Swayne considers himself to be a lifelong learner. One of his passions is teaching. At the university level he has taught mathematics, statistics, economics, industrial engineering, operations research, total quality management, strategic thinking, ethics, marketing and finance. He has presented seminars on business policy and strategy, organizational behavior, business communication, entrepreneurship, cost control, investments, money and banking, real estate, compensation, choosing a career, building on strengths, and yes, poker. His teaching and seminar presentations have been at the University of Michigan, Virginia Tech, Radford University, Upper Iowa University, University of Wisconsin-La Crosse, Winona State, Viterbo University, Michigan State, Babson College, Lake Forest College and the University of Toronto. He has appeared on over 100 media shows, authored many magazine articles and several books. He has received emeritus status from the University of Wisconsin-La Crosse and the "Excellence in Teaching" award from Upper Iowa. He is a frequent speaker at the World Series of Poker camps. You may contact him at Advanced Degree Poker, LLC, N. 1964 Crestview Place, La Crosse, WI, 54601, USA.

Seminars

If you wish to book Charley for a seminar or private coaching contact either James Sullivan, President of Poker Royalty, 8691 W. Sahara Avenue, Suite 200, Las Vegas NV 89117, *pokerroyalty.com*; or Brian Lammi, president of Lammi Sports, 161 S. 1st Street, Milwaukee, WI 53204, *lammisports.com*.

Endnotes

I don't use footnotes because I personally find they break my concentration when I'm trying to learn something. But I did use the ideas, concepts, or exact quotes from others. This endnote section is my equivalent of traditional footnotes.

Here's a list of those whose ideas I have quoted or used. If you are an author and I failed to give you credit, it was not intentional. Please write me and I'll make the corrections in future editions. I have read and benefited from many authors, including those listed in the bibliography. However, I don't always remember where I got a general understanding of a concept or who gave me certain ideas first. I may have included passages from others that I couldn't improve, but I have used my best efforts to give each author appropriate acknowledgement. When there is a number under the source column that means the source is the book or other material listed in the bibliography.

Chapter	Section	Figure	Concept, phase, or quote	Source
1	Introduction to the introduction		whole section inspired by Braids	B3 p4, p26
	How important is poker?		story adapted from term paper	Kellie Kramer, Upper Iowa U, Oct 06
	Knowledge and skill		wheel	W2 p69
			psych skills	C1 p11
			two skills: math and psych	M1 p99
			need to have both skills	M2 p102
	Experience		experience	S2 p3
			patience and discipline	H1 pxii
	Good or World Class		discipline	S2 p108
	Gambling		catch and release	P1 p113
			following the numbers	M2 p21
2	Passive vs Aggressive		passive player doesn't raise much	B6 p198
			aggressive raises a lot	B6 p198
	Tight versus loose		tight play few hands	B6 p198
	Creating the Matrix	2.1.c	entire figure	B3 p53-54
		2.1.d	passive/tight table means few in hand, little raising	W2 p154
	Mistakes		profit comes from mistakes	M2 p21, W1 p124, M5 p184
			against loose players	L1 p35
	Their names		names	L1 p71
		2.2.c	Professional	B3 p75, W2 p149-150
			Maniac	W2 p147-149
			Rock	W1 p407, W2 p146-147
			Calling station	B6 p198, W2 p144-145
	The chip clue		messy chips equals loose player	C1 p49
			neat chips equals passive/tight	C1 p47
			tall precise stacks	Andy Blum
	Cost to benefit	2.4.a	passive/loose game equals low cost and high benefit	S2 p152
	Get in or get out		avoid aggressive/tight games	W2 p155
			want loose players	Charlie Kline
			adapt to changing table	B3 p113-115
	Reduce your risk		sit to the left of most aggressive	J1 p25
	Make more money		have loosest players on your right	W1 p125, B6 p199
			money flows to the left	W2 p76, Mike Caro
			loose/aggressive players to their left	S2 p131
	Best of both worlds	2.4f	passive/tights on left	N2 p102, H4 p21, L1 p35 and p73
			aggressive/loose on right	M5 p189
	Cost to stay in the hand	2.5a	aggressive/tight equals high cost	B3 p85
			aassive/loose equals low cost	B3 p76
	Pot size fluctuation	2.5b	smallest pots are at passive/tight tables	B6 p202
	Bankroll swing	2.5c	extreme bankroll swings at aggressive/loose	B3 p78, W2 p153-154

Chapter	Section	Figure	Concept, phase, or quote	Source
	Wins		accumulating small wins	W2 p154
	Bad Beats		bad beats happen	B3 p64
	General comment		cut losses with good position	W1 p95
		2.6.b	position importance at both loose tables	B3 p76
	Opponents	2.7.a	aggressive/tights take control	S1 p39
	When players raise or call	2.7.b	passive/loose calls	B3 p76
	Bluff		passive loose calls bluff; "wants to see it"	B6 p199, W2 p150
		2.7.c	A/T sometimes bluff, A/L often bluff	W2 p150
	Type of play		straightforward play	S2 p237
		2.8.c	straightforward play works best at loose tables	B5 p 378
	Preflop	2.9.a	folding preflop at passive/tight	B3 p82
	Preflop pot size	2.9.b	very small preflop pot size at passive/tight	B3 p82
	Preflop raising and calling		caw, caw, caw	Andy Blum
	Winning hands	2.9.e	P/L pairs and draws	W2 p153
	Flop folding		P/L flop folding	W1 p179
	Bet draws to get these to fold	2.10.c	A/L will not fold to draw betting	B3 p78
	Showdowns	2.11.a	many showdowns at loose tables	B3 p76-78
	What to do if heads up on the river and you missed		good players can be bluffed, poor players can't	M2 p17
	The player you will become		an aggressive/tight	S2 p205
3	Entire chapter		Andy Blum helped me write much of the chapter	
	Taking good to great – knowing when to hold them;	3.4	math allows you to maximize expected value	W2 p61
			when to fold to physical tells	Mike Caro
	Ease of reading summary	3.8	parts of figure	S2 p237
	Tell trends		great players pay attention to tells	C1 p41
			observing others when they get cards	B6 p203, L1 p101
	Stops conversation		stops conversing with another	C1 p107
	Bad hand – Chip action		bad hand – throws chips in	W1 p197
	Tilt		players foolish	N2 p17-21
			tilt provides profit	M2 p51 and 69, B6 p176
	Good hand – Chips come in slowly		player's hands	H4 p85-86
	Two or three suited on flop		look at cards when flush card hits river	W1 p22
	Unusual tells from loose players		acts strong when weak, weak when strong	C1 p12, B6 p205
			disappointment	C1 p12
			calls immediately on flop with 2 flush on board	S1 p84
			shaky hand is a good hand	C1 p73, B6 p206
			looks at card then looks at chips – going to bet	C1 p99
			looks away he has a better hand	C1 p147, B6 p205
	Position betting gives more clues		continuation bet	M1 p168
		3.27	turn/river position betting clues	S2 p228-229

Chapter	Section	Figure	Concept, phase, or quote	Source
	Showdown information		pay attention	H4 p89-90
	Put each opponent on a hand		use logic to reduce and eliminate possibilities	H4 p171
			betting pattern/position clues	S2 p225, N2 p26
	No Tell Routine		no tell routine concept	W1 p201, H4 p87
			follow exact routine every time	M2 p59
			only look at hand preflop when it is your turn	W1 p22
4	Introduction		same hands every time, players will know	W2 p6, M2 p45-46 and p72, p133
		4.1	deception importance	S2 p149
	Playing bad cards		appear loose by playing bad cards	H3 p12, H4 p142
			bad play within first few minutes	H1 p142
			keep opponents off balance	S2 p12
	Summary		playing bad cards helps win bigger pots	W2 p48
5	The Expensive Mistake		many good books have reading the board	S1 p28-29, B6 p145-154
			losing the pot	L1 p21
	How to clearly see the board		making reading the board part of your game	W1 p35-45
	Practice on every hand		you get practice on every hand	B6 p145
	The flop		easiest to miss	L1 p22
			flop questions	S1 p28
			if play stopped now, nuts? 2nd nuts?....	W1 p34-45
	The answer is yes		straight draw on flop	W2 p118
	Straight possibilities on the flop		different types	B4 p514-7
	Straight flop conclusions		look out for 3 high card flop, closer sequence	K1 p33, M3 p26
6	Blinds are risky		inexperienced players perceive blinds as cheap	W1 p163
		6.1.a-d	risk during rounds	S1, B6 p61
			least amount of info for turn/river	S2 p18
	The Swayne risk/position graph	6.2	highest risk in small blind	W1 p168
			early position poses most risk	S1 p112
7	Probability and a rush		you should never experience a rush	K1 p26
			never play on a rush	M2 p158
	Each betting round		preflop 1,326 possible starting hands	K1 p63, P1 p37 and p113
			19,600 flops	W1 p74, W2 p119, P1 p37 and p43
	50-50		169 hands	M3 p46, W1 p73
	The Swayne hand pyramid	7.1	I took the chart which looked like an arrow in Burton's book, B6 inside cover, extrapolated and flipped it up to create the hand pyramid.	

Chapter	Section	Figure	Concept, phase, or quote	Source
	Hand frequency		AK suited can happen 4 ways	W1 p72
			pocket pairs can happen 6 ways	W1 p72
			AA once in every 221 hands	W1 p73, H3 p20, P1 p86, B3 p43
			AK frequency slightly different	P1 p86
			AKs frequency slightly different	P1 p86
	Hand frequency first look		unpaired/unsuited hole cards 70% of time	M5 p67, B6 p75
			suited hole cards 24% of time	W1 p72
	Presentation of probabilities	7.3.a	32%	H3 p23
	Odds and probability		odds definition	J1 p32
			probability definition	H3 p20, 33
		7.3.b	entire figure	H3 p21
	Pot odds		pot odds concept	M1 p38, W1 p319, B6 p72, B3 p46, L1 p42, H4 p123
			comparing pot odds to probability of winning	W2 p64, M2 p20, B3 p46
	The Swayne preflop straight and flush draws		suited hole cards hit flush 6.5% of time	S1 p20
			includes runner runner, which you should never play	S1 p20
	Preflop	7.4.d.a	any specific pair = .45%	H3 p175
			AKs = .3%	H3 p175, B1 p124
			any pocket pair = 6%	H3 p175, B1 p124
			connectors = 16%	H3 p175
			suited connectors = 4%	H3 p175, B1 p126
		7.4.d.b	connectors in the middle = 8%	P1 p150
	Ace in the hole		75% someone else has an Ace	W1 p206, W2 p65
		7.4.f	shared Ace chart	B6 p40
	Significance of preflop numbers		loose players play A-anything and K-anything	K1 p37
	Flop folding	7.4.g	exactly a pair 17%	P1 p90
			exactly three of a kind .24%	P1 p90
			you will flop at least a set 12%	P1 p119, H3 p24 and p186, B3 p48
			flop two pair with two unpaired hole cards 2%	P1 p74
			at least a pair with two unpaired hole cards 32%	B6 p107
			flushes, the flop will contain…	P1 p91
			you hold two of a suit, flop shows two of your suit 11%	H3 p186, W1 p76, B6 p43, P1 p 46-47
			you hold two of a suit, flop shows three of your suit 1%	B6 p43, C1 p18, B3 p47

Chapter	Section	Figure	Concept, phase, or quote	Source
			you will flop a straight with middle connectors 1%	B3 p47
	Overcard Probabilities	7.5.b.a	overcard probabilities on the flop	W1 p76, H3 p196, B3 p49
		7.5.b-d	overcard probabilities on the turn/river	W1 p83
			70% chance of overcard when holding TT	B3 p49
			probability of overcard increases fast once below JJ	P1 p99
	The Gordon Rule	7.6.a-b	chance of holding the best hand	Toribio, Klugman, Luckner, and Nebeck
	Postflop draws	7.7.a	a set improving to boat or better 33%	P1 p119, B6 p117, B3 p 50
			a set improving to exactly a boat on turn 13%	P1 p119
			a set improving to exactly a boat on river 20%	P1 p119
		7.7.c	entire figure	W1 p82
	Other numbers	7.7.d	entire figure	W1 p69
			5 cards similar to but not exactly the same as	W2 p20
	Five card hand frequency		2,598,960 five card hands	W1 p69, B6 p103
		7.7.e	entire figure	P1 p187
			frequency	B4, p568
	How does this chart help me?		be aggressive with overpair/top pair	J1 p69
8			suited connectors gain in strength	L1 p136
9	Introducing the seven critical factors		factors	B3 p70, L1 p123
			passive/aggressive – amount of calling/raising	B3 p38
			card strength factor	W2 p95
9 Part III	Hold'em is position		hold'em is a game of position	B6 p17, K1 p62, W1 p95, H4 p87
			does the work of betting	H4 p25
			importance of position	H1 p27 and 87, N1 p5
			good position gives you most info and control	K1 p23, B3 p44
			early position equals less hands you can play; late position equals more	W1 p95, B3 p45, W2 p73-76
9 Part VII	Introduction		take into account pot size before staying in a hand	B3 p61
	Postflop pot size		bet if you have positive Expected Value	H4 p120
	Deducting bad outs		deducting bad outs concept	H3 p65, L1 p25
	What about implied odds?		implied odds concept	B3 p62, S1 p80-83, B5 p254, M5 p80, J1 p34, B6 p72

Chapter	Section	Figure	Concept, phase, or quote	Source
	The beginner player in no limit			N4
			pot odds concept	B5 p266
10	Aggression is rewarded		hold'em made for aggression	W2 p177, K1 pvii
			"raising/calling" quote	N2 p47
			"save pots, not bets" quote	M5 p104
			aggression is selective and targeted	K1 p19 and 39
			requires more skill	H5 p 1
			any hand that is worth a call is worth a raise	S1 p42, N1 p45, W2 p170
			best hand equals be aggressive	K1 p21
			be aggressive against drawing hands	B5 p244
	Calling is punished		calling indicates weakness	W2 p170
			callers lose	L1 p55 and p152
			aggressives punish callers by raising	S1 p39
	Checking and calling is punished more		checking and calling is punished	S1 p50, S2 p63
	Taking the lead is rewarding		controlling the hand is rewarding	B5 p268-269
	What happens if your personality isn't aggressive		winnings not at full potential while not playing aggressive	M2 p49
	Asking what he has		find out what he has when bets are small	H1 p47, M2 p124
	Opponents who fold to aggressive play		players fold to aggressive betting mostly on the turn	S2 p170
	Building the pot		play straightforward with the best hand	N1 p29
	Buying the button		heavy betting with late position	M1 p151, W2 p76
			best position is on the button; most info and most control	S1 p42
	When you check-raise		possibility of giving away a free card	J1 p83
	You are check-raised		when check-raised, fold unless you have a great hand	J1 p88
	Overcall		overcall concept	W1 p249
	Beware boards with high cards		beware boards	M3 p26
	Bluffing		only bluff against good players	W2 p175
			bluff when it was set up throughout the entire hand or scare card	M2 p17, W1 p352, B5 p273
	The continuation bet		continuation bet concept	M1 p168, H1 p90, p98, H4 p22, H5 p9
			bets out against three or more	H5 p14
	Your betting pattern with a draw		miss on the turn, free card or just call	W1 p333
	Pot equity			M4 p52; L1 p67
	Steals		small pots are easier to steal	W1 p353
	Betting yourself out of a pot		stay in a hand	Charlie Kline
	Fold when beat		if you know you are beat, fold as early as possible	W1 p148

Chapter	Section	Figure	Concept, phase, or quote	Source
	Attack loose players, or fold		aggressive play wins the most money	B3 p56
			loose players will call one more bet when already in the hand	B6 p45
	Get rid of the blinds		raise to get rid of the blinds' trash hands	W1 p179
	Specific preflop hand recommendations		raise or re-raise to find out who has the better hand when bets are small	W1 p144-5
			raise with high pairs	B5 p232
	Isolation		isolation strategy	S1 p42, H2 p73, H1 p95, B5 p221
			one player raised, a re-raise will result in isolation	M1 p117
	Raising from the blinds or early position		raising from early position represents strong cards	W1 p300
	Stealing the blinds		stealing the blinds concept	W1 p136, W2 p77, S2 p32-33
			stealing the blinds is worthwhile	W1 p190
			further away from the big blind, better chance of deception	H1 p88
			a re-raise from blinds means experienced player	H1 p148
			initial caller won't fold to another raise	W1 p301
	Flop	10.12	bet and raise with high board pair	B4 p388
	Whether you hit or miss on the flop		fold when you miss	M1 p140
			"ragged" board doesn't help you	W2 p119-124
	If you are ahead on the flop		71% of hand has been played on the flop	K1 p28
			whoever is ahead on the flop is the clear favorite to win hand	B2 p9, B3 p46 and 58
			build pot when you are ahead on the flop	W1 p150, W2 p124
	Flop a monster		bet, raise, and re-raise when you flop a monster	B3 p62
	You have top pair or pocket overpair on the flop		top pair with good kicker wins more than it loses	B3 p56
			more opponents you have, more likely to be outdrawn	M3 p25, S1 p42
	Bet aggressive to thin herd with top pair			B5 p233, W2 p124-125
	You have 2nd high pair on the flop with no other draw		first to act bet	M3 p58 and p82
	You flop trips; straight or flush draw on the board		bet/raise, make it expensive	S2 p121
	You flop a set (bottom board card)		go aggressive	W1 p139
	You flop a set; straight or flush draw on the board		bet, make it expensive for drawers	S1 p79
	You flop a flush but your pocket high card isn't very good		go aggressive	W1 p139-140

Chapter	Section	Figure	Concept, phase, or quote	Source
	Going for a free card		free card concept	W1 p140, S1 p55, B5 p223, B3 p76, W2 p77
	When high cards flop		not good unless the flop hits you	M3 p26, B3 p60
	When the board pairs		a paired board is dangerous	B6 p147, B3 p59
	When a three flush appears on the flop		24% of all hands are suited	B6 p43
			if passive/loose leads betting, assume a flush was made	B3 p60, B6 p148
	Anytime there is heavy betting and you have less than a top dog hand			B5 p270
	Anytime you smell weakness and you have nothing		bet out against loose players on the turn	W2 p175
	Anytime you smell weakness and you have second or third high pair		bet out, raise against tights	W2 p130-131
	The river		either in or out on river	W2 p134-140
	Big pot on the river		call if you have any chance of winning when pot is big	W1 p152, J1 p86, K1 p10, H1 p32, M5 p95, H4 p32
			win 1 out of 9 hands to be profitable	B6 p167, S1 p69
	The final bet heads up		check and call if opponent called all the way to river with straight/flush card	L1 p146
	The no limit value bet		25% and 75%	N3
	Summary		turn is where players face most aggressive play	B5 p268-269
			bet like the pot is yours when you are ahead	B3 p63
11	The first ten chapters – Chapter 9		implied dominate role	L1 p130
	A word on the extremely important		avoid all ins unless you have isolation	W2 p204
	What's different?		rules dictate type of play	H4 p54
			see flops cheaply then outplay	N2 p32
			heavy betting	N2 p32
			control Expected Value	H5 p12 and p346-347 L1 p45 and p148
			first bettor usually wins	W2 p194
			flop is where bets are made	H4 p27
			educated guess	H4 p27
			stack size compared...short stack preflop moves...first to act...all in	H1 p231
	Swayne deceptive betting		impossible to read	H5 p52
	Philosophy of tortoise		increase your stack	N3
			winning blinds and antes	N3
			10% of chip stack	N3
			avoid coin flops	N3
			straights and flushes	N3
			small pots aggressively	N3
			what your opponent has	N3
			worm at the end of a pole	N3
			control the pot size	N3
			more callers	N3

Chapter	Section	Figure	Concept, phase, or quote	Source
	General preflop tortoise tactics		re-raised a lot and forced to fold	N3
			outplay opponents after the flop	N3
			cheap with your raises	N3
			2½ times the big blind	N3
			bet 1.5-2 times the pot	N3
			bet the same	N3
	General postflop tortoise tactics		calls on the turn	N3
	Specific flop tortoise tactics		get to the turn cheap	N3
			control the size of the pot...½ the pot	N3
			50%-80% of the pot	N3
			all right to give a free card	N3
	Specific turn tortoise tactics		60% of the pot	N3
	Tortoise raises		4 or 5 times	N3
			50% to 80% of the pot	N3
			33% to 50%	N3
	Using Expected Value		get drawing player to fold	H5 p14 and p22
	Bluffing		less than most people think	N3
	General times to bluff		concerned what they have or don't have	N3
			setting it up	N3
	Specific bluffing opportunities		thin value river	N3
			blocker	N3
	Bluff outs		additional cards	N3
	Amount to bluff		same amount	N3
	No limit betting summary preflop		5 times	N3
			7 times	N3
			3 to 4 times	N3
			2.5 times	N3
			4 to 5 times	N3
			10% of chip stack	N3
	No limit betting summary postflop		⅔ of the pot	N3
	No limit betting summary flop		50% to 80%	N3
	No limit betting summary turn		100% of the pot	N3
			50% to 75%	N3
			check-raise 200%	N3
	No limit betting summary river		75% of the pot	N3
			thin value bet	N3
12	4-5 times the initial raise			N3
	Preflop hands to bet	12.4.a	We compared our calculations to those found in Hilger's Odds and Probabilities	H3 p226
			While all were the same or close, where there was a conflict, the more conservative number was used.	
13	Language		early, middle, and late position	B4 p362, B5 p213
	Research		"Facts are stubborn things."	John Adams
	Winning all the time		you will not win all the time	M2 p37

Chapter	Section	Figure	Concept, phase, or quote	Source
	Hand rankings	13.3	most derived from Poker Academy 2.5 computer program	
	Complaining not allowed		"You shouldn't criticize..."	Verlyn Schmitt
	A home field advantage		keep track of performance with a poker diary/journal	B6 p217, B3 p104, BW1 p50
	Tilt		a player on tilt happens frequently	N2 p17-21
			many think aggressive action will make up for losses	M2 p51 and 69
			being on tilt usually results in more losses	B6 p176
	Fatigue		being fatigued will negatively affect your game	M2 p59, N2 p17
	The internet		quantity of hands	A1 p73
Appendix D			difference between world class player and compulsive gambler	M2 p23
Glossary			Backraise	W1 p401
			Calling station	J1 p25
			Caught speeding	M2 p55
			Collecting bullets	N2 p105
			Cold call	S1 p79
			Drawing dead	B6 p155
			Freerolling	W1 p157
			Limp raise	J1 p67
			Paint	B6 p278
			Rainbow	B6 p278
			Snowmen	C1 p55
			Soft playing	N1 p40
			Straightforward play	W1 p339
			Straddle	W1 p407

Appendix B

Boardology You have permission to copy this page.

Flop	Turn	River
☐ ☐ ☐	☐	☐

FLOP

Straights

Is there a straight possible?   Y N

Highest   ____ ____ ____ ____ ____

2nd highest____ ____ ____ ____ ____

3rd highest____ ____ ____ ____ ____

Is there a straight draw on the board? Y N

Highest draw____ ____ ____ ____ ____

2nd highest ____ ____ ____ ____ ____

3rd highest ____ ____ ____ ____ ____

4th highest ____ ____ ____ ____ ____

Flushes

Could someone have made a flush? Y N

Could someone have a flush draw? Y N

Pairs, sets, trips or better

What is the top ranked card on the board?_____

Are two pairs possible?   Y N

Are trips possible?   Y N

Is a set possible?   Y N

Is a boat or better possible?   Y N

If play stopped now

Best hand?____ ____ ____ ____ ____

The 2nd nuts?____ ____ ____ ____ ____

The 3rd nuts?____ ____ ____ ____ ____

The 4th nuts?____ ____ ____ ____ ____

The 5th nuts?____ ____ ____ ____ ____

From what has happened so far

Which player appears to have the best hand?

What do you think he has?

TURN

Straights

Is there a straight possible?   Y N

Highest   ____ ____ ____ ____ ____

2nd highest____ ____ ____ ____ ____

3rd highest____ ____ ____ ____ ____

Is there a straight draw on the board? Y N

Highest draw____ ____ ____ ____ ____

2nd highest ____ ____ ____ ____ ____

3rd highest ____ ____ ____ ____ ____

4th highest ____ ____ ____ ____ ____

Flushes

Could someone have made a flush? Y N

Could someone have a flush draw? Y N

Pairs, sets, trips or better

What is the top ranked card on the board?_____

Are two pairs possible?   Y N

Are trips possible?   Y N

Is a set possible?   Y N

Is a boat or better possible?   Y N

If play stopped now

Best hand?____ ____ ____ ____ ____

The 2nd nuts?____ ____ ____ ____ ____

The 3rd nuts?____ ____ ____ ____ ____

The 4th nuts?____ ____ ____ ____ ____

The 5th nuts?____ ____ ____ ____ ____

From what has happened so far

Which player appears to have the best hand?

What do you think he has?

RIVER

Straights

Could someone have a straight? Y N

Highest   ____ ____ ____ ____ ____

2nd highest____ ____ ____ ____ ____

3rd highest____ ____ ____ ____ ____

4th Highest ____ ____ ____ ____ ____

Runner runner required?   Y N

Which?

Flushes

Is the board 3 or more flushed?   Y N

Runner runner required?   Y N

Pairs, sets, trips or better

What is the top ranked card on the board?_____

Are two pairs possible?   Y N

Are trips possible?   Y N

Is a set possible?   Y N

Is a boat or better possible?   Y N

Hand ranking

Best hand?____ ____ ____ ____ ____

The 2nd nuts?____ ____ ____ ____ ____

The 3rd nuts?____ ____ ____ ____ ____

The 4th nuts?____ ____ ____ ____ ____

The 5th nuts?____ ____ ____ ____ ____

Before the cards are turned over

Which player appears to have the best hand?

What do you think he has?

Which player do you think is in 2nd place?

What do you think he has?

Winning Probabilities for Specific Hands and Flops

Further research needed

In Chapter 9 we took the raw data of not just making a preflop hand, but winning with the hand, and converted those probabilities into WFs.

Wouldn't it be great if we could give you the probability of winning a hand once the flop is shown? All you would have to do is multiply the probability of winning by the amount in the pot, or the implied amount to be in the pot, and use Expected Value to determine if you should bet. That would be so much better than using the Truth Drawing Numbers because those numbers only tell the minimum number of bets that must be in the pot if you think your draw will win the hand. OK, I've started to do just that.

The reason I say started is this is not something which can be done overnight. Naturally, the probability of winning changes with the cards; that's 169 possible hands, the number of opponents who see the flop, anywhere between 1 and 9 at a 10-handed table, and the flop itself, a mere 19,600 different flops. To be a complete study that translates into almost 30,000,000 probabilities, although some short cuts could be taken. You can imagine this might take some time. I can't guarantee when all of the calculations will be complete. It may take years. If you are the head of a math department at a university with a very high speed computer and need a project for some students, or someone who needs a research publication, I know what to do and it is not nearly as complex as you might expect; I just have a hard time finding the time to do it.

Another problem. Once all the results are complete, for every flop, every hand, and each opponent who might see the flop, I'm not sure if they can be presented as anything more than a bunch of numbers. The results could certainly be used for a clever internet program, but I don't know if they can be converted into easy to understand formulas or rules for a casino player to use.

On the next few pages you will find the probabilities of you winning with some sample hands, not just making your hand, for two points on a loose table; one point will be when 5 opponents see the flop; the other point will be when all 9 opponents see the flop. The right hand columns next to the flop show you the probability of winning the hand for those two points. The sample hands are AK, TT, and 76s. To keep this appendix under a few thousand pages, only selected flops are shown, not all 19,600.

Perhaps I should have included a magnifying glass with each copy of the book. The font is small.

AK
Selected flops

Flop Type: Suit Type	Flop			6 see flop	10 see flop
Rainbow	Q	Q	3	13%	5%
2 suited not yours	Q	Q	3	11%	4%
2 suited yours	Q	Q	3	15%	7%
Rainbow	9	9	3	14%	5%
2 suited not yours	9	9	3	12%	4%
2 suited yours	9	9	3	16%	7%
Rainbow	6	6	3	15%	6%
2 suited not yours	6	6	3	13%	5%
2 suited yours	6	6	3	17%	8%
Rainbow	A	Q	3	50%	29%
2 suited not yours	A	Q	3	43%	23%
3 suited not yours	A	Q	3	25%	11%
2 suited yours	A	Q	3	49%	29%
3 suited yours	A	Q	3	61%	46%
Rainbow	A	9	3	53%	31%
2 suited not yours	A	9	3	46%	25%
3 suited not yours	A	9	3	26%	11%
2 suited yours	A	9	3	52%	31%
3suited yours	A	9	3	63%	48%
Rainbow	A	6	3	53%	31%
2 suited not yours	A	6	3	46%	25%
3 suited not yours	A	6	3	26%	11%
2 suited yours	A	6	3	53%	31%
3 suited yours	A	6	3	63%	47%
Rainbow	A	Q	T	41%	23%
2 suited not yours	A	Q	T	36%	18%
3 suited not yours	A	Q	T	22%	8%
2 suited yours	A	Q	T	41%	23%
3 suited yours	A	Q	T	56%	44%
Rainbow	A	9	7	46%	26%
2 suited not yours	A	9	7	40%	21%
3 suited not yours	A	9	7	23%	9%
2 suited yours	A	9	7	46%	27%
3 suited yours	A	9	7	59%	45%
Rainbow	A	6	4	51%	29%
2 suited not yours	A	6	4	44%	23%
3 suited not yours	A	6	4	25%	10%
2 suited yours	A	6	4	50%	29%
3 suited yours	A	6	4	61%	46%
Rainbow	K	Q	3	49%	28%
2 suited not yours	K	Q	4	42%	23%
3 suited not yours	K	Q	5	24%	11%
2 suited yours	K	Q	6	49%	29%
3 suited yours	K	Q	7	60%	46%
Rainbow	K	9	3	51%	31%
2 suited not yours	K	9	3	45%	25%
3 suited not yours	K	9	3	26%	12%
2 suited yours	K	9	3	51%	31%
3 suited yours	K	9	3	62%	47%
Rainbow	K	6	3	53%	31%
2 suited not yours	K	6	3	46%	25%
3 suited not yours	K	6	3	26%	11%
2 suited yours	K	6	3	52%	31%
3 suited yours	K	6	3	63%	47%
Rainbow	K	Q	T	36%	18%
2 suited not yours	K	Q	T	31%	15%
3 suited not yours	K	Q	T	18%	7%
2 suited yours	K	Q	T	36%	20%
3 suited yours	K	Q	T	52%	40%
Rainbow	K	9	7	43%	24%
2 suited not yours	K	9	7	37%	19%
3 suited not yours	K	9	7	22%	9%
2 suited yours	K	9	7	44%	26%
3 suited yours	K	9	7	57%	45%

Flop Type: Suit Type	Flop			6 see flop	10 see flop
Rainbow	K	6	4	50%	28%
2 suited not yours	K	6	4	43%	23%
3 suited not yours	K	6	4	25%	10%
2 suited yours	K	6	4	49%	29%
3 suited yours	K	6	4	61%	46%
Rainbow	J	T	7	19%	13%
2 suited not yours	J	T	7	16%	10%
3 suited not yours	J	T	7	9%	4%
2 suited yours	J	T	7	21%	15%
3 suited yours	J	T	7	41%	35%
Rainbow	Q	9	8	9%	4%
2 suited not yours	Q	9	8	8%	3%
3 suited not yours	Q	9	8	4%	1%
2 suited yours	Q	9	8	12%	8%
3 suited yours	Q	9	8	36%	31%
Rainbow	Q	6	5	12%	6%
2 suited not yours	Q	6	5	10%	4%
3 suited not yours	Q	6	5	5%	2%
2 suited yours	Q	6	5	14%	8%
3 suited yours	Q	6	5	40%	34%
Rainbow	Q	J	5	21%	15%
2 suited not yours	Q	J	5	18%	11%
3 suited not yours	Q	J	5	10%	5%
2 suited yours	Q	J	5	23%	16%
3 suited yours	Q	J	5	44%	39%
Rainbow	9	8	7	7%	2%
2 suited not yours	9	8	7	6%	2%
3 suited not yours	9	8	7	3%	1%
2 suited yours	9	8	7	10%	6%
3 suited yours	9	8	7	32%	25%
Rainbow	6	5	4	9%	3%
2 suited not yours	6	5	4	7%	2%
3 suited not yours	6	5	4	4%	1%
2 suited yours	6	5	4	12%	6%
3 suited yours	6	5	4	34%	25%
Rainbow	Q	J	T	75%	66%
2 suited not yours	Q	J	T	66%	52%
3 suited not yours	Q	J	T	37%	22%
2 suited yours	Q	J	T	72%	59%
3 suited yours	Q	J	T	69%	55%
Rainbow	2	3	4	13%	4%
2 suited not yours	2	3	4	10%	3%
3 suited not yours	2	3	4	6%	1%
2 suited yours	2	3	4	15%	7%
3 suited yours	2	3	4	38%	30%
Rainbow	Q	T	5	21%	14%
2 suited not yours	Q	T	6	18%	11%
3 suited not yours	Q	T	7	10%	5%
2 suited yours	Q	T	8	23%	16%
3 suited yours	Q	T	9	44%	38%
Rainbow	2	4	8	14%	6%
2 suited not yours	2	4	8	11%	5%
3 suited not yours	2	4	8	6%	2%
2 suited yours	2	4	8	16%	9%
3 suited yours	2	4	8	41%	34%
Rainbow	9	2	7	12%	6%
2 suited not yours	9	2	7	10%	5%
3 suited not yours	9	2	7	5%	2%
2 suited yours	9	2	7	15%	9%
3 suited yours	9	2	7	40%	34%
Rainbow	6	T	4	13%	6%
2 suited not yours	6	T	4	11%	5%
3 suited not yours	6	T	4	5%	2%
2 suited yours	6	T	4	15%	10%

AK
Selected flops

Flop Type: Suit Type	Flop			6 see flop	10 see flop
3 suited yours	6	T	4	40%	34%
Rainbow	A	A	5	78%	65%
2 suited not yours	A	A	5	71%	57%
2 suited yours	A	A	5	76%	61%
Rainbow	K	K	5	81%	68%
2 suited not yours	K	K	5	73%	60%
2 suited yours	K	K	5	78%	64%
Rainbow	Q	Q	Q	18%	8%
Rainbow	9	9	9	20%	8%
Rainbow	6	6	6	20%	9%
Rainbow	A	K	Q	58%	44%
2 suited not yours	A	K	Q	52%	37%
3 suited not yours	A	K	Q	35%	23%
2 suited yours	A	K	Q	57%	42%
Rainbow	A	K	9	58%	44%
2 suited not yours	A	K	9	52%	37%
3 suited not yours	A	K	9	43%	28%
2 suited yours	A	K	9	70%	55%
Rainbow	A	K	6	73%	58%
2 suited not yours	A	K	6	65%	49%
3 suited not yours	A	K	6	42%	28%
2 suited yours	A	K	6	70%	55%

Selected flops ranked for 6-handed

Flop Type: Suit Type	Flop			6 see flop	10 see flop
Rainbow	K	K	5	81%	68%
Rainbow	A	A	5	78%	65%
2 suited yours	K	K	5	78%	64%
2 suited yours	A	A	5	76%	61%
Rainbow	Q	J	T	75%	66%
2 suited not yours	K	K	5	73%	60%
Rainbow	A	K	6	73%	58%
2 suited yours	Q	J	T	72%	59%
2 suited not yours	A	A	5	71%	57%
2 suited yours	A	K	9	70%	55%
2 suited yours	A	K	6	70%	55%
3 suited yours	Q	J	T	69%	55%
2 suited not yours	Q	J	T	66%	52%
2 suited not yours	A	K	6	65%	49%
3 suited yours	A	9	3	63%	48%
3 suited yours	A	6	3	63%	47%
3 suited yours	K	6	3	63%	47%
3 suited yours	K	9	3	62%	47%
3 suited yours	A	Q	3	61%	46%
3 suited yours	A	6	4	61%	46%
3 suited yours	K	6	4	61%	46%
3 suited yours	K	Q	7	60%	46%
3 suited yours	A	9	7	59%	45%
Rainbow	A	K	Q	58%	44%
Rainbow	A	K	9	58%	44%
3 suited yours	K	9	7	57%	45%
2 suited yours	A	K	Q	57%	42%
3 suited yours	A	Q	T	56%	44%
Rainbow	A	9	3	53%	31%
Rainbow	A	6	3	53%	31%
2 suited yours	A	6	3	53%	31%
Rainbow	K	6	3	53%	31%
2 suited yours	A	9	3	52%	31%
2 suited yours	K	6	3	52%	31%
3 suited yours	K	Q	T	52%	40%
2 suited not yours	A	K	Q	52%	37%
2 suited not yours	A	K	9	52%	37%
Rainbow	A	6	4	51%	29%
Rainbow	K	9	3	51%	31%

Flop Type: Suit Type	Flop			6 see flop	10 see flop
2 suited yours	K	9	3	51%	31%
Rainbow	A	Q	3	50%	29%
2 suited yours	A	6	4	50%	29%
Rainbow	K	6	4	50%	28%
2 suited yours	A	Q	3	49%	29%
Rainbow	K	Q	3	49%	28%
2 suited yours	K	Q	6	49%	29%
2 suited yours	K	6	4	49%	29%
2 suited not yours	A	9	3	46%	25%
2 suited not yours	A	6	3	46%	25%
Rainbow	A	9	7	46%	26%
2 suited yours	A	9	7	46%	27%
2 suited not yours	K	6	3	46%	25%
2 suited not yours	K	9	3	45%	25%
2 suited not yours	A	6	4	44%	23%
2 suited yours	K	9	7	44%	26%
3 suited yours	Q	J	5	44%	39%
3 suited yours	Q	T	9	44%	38%
2 suited not yours	A	Q	3	43%	23%
Rainbow	K	9	7	43%	24%
2 suited not yours	K	6	4	43%	23%
3 suited not yours	A	K	9	43%	28%
2 suited not yours	K	Q	4	42%	23%
3 suited not yours	A	K	6	42%	28%
Rainbow	A	Q	T	41%	23%
2 suited yours	A	Q	T	41%	23%
3 suited yours	J	T	7	41%	35%
3 suited yours	2	4	8	41%	34%
2 suited not yours	A	9	7	40%	21%
3 suited yours	Q	6	5	40%	34%
3 suited yours	9	2	7	40%	34%
3 suited yours	6	T	4	40%	34%
3 suited yours	2	3	4	38%	30%
2 suited not yours	K	9	7	37%	19%
3 suited not yours	Q	J	T	37%	22%
2 suited not yours	A	Q	T	36%	18%
Rainbow	K	Q	T	36%	18%
2 suited yours	K	Q	T	36%	20%
3 suited yours	Q	9	8	36%	31%
3 suited not yours	A	K	Q	35%	23%
3 suited yours	6	5	4	34%	25%
3 suited yours	9	8	7	32%	25%
2 suited not yours	K	Q	T	31%	15%
3 suited not yours	A	9	3	26%	11%
3 suited not yours	A	6	3	26%	11%
3 suited not yours	K	9	3	26%	12%
3 suited not yours	K	6	3	26%	11%
3 suited not yours	A	Q	3	25%	11%
3 suited not yours	A	6	4	25%	10%
3 suited not yours	K	6	4	25%	10%
3 suited not yours	K	Q	5	24%	11%
3 suited not yours	A	9	7	23%	9%
2 suited yours	Q	J	5	23%	16%
2 suited yours	Q	T	8	23%	16%
3 suited not yours	A	Q	T	22%	8%
3 suited not yours	K	9	7	22%	9%
2 suited yours	J	T	7	21%	15%
Rainbow	Q	J	5	21%	15%
Rainbow	Q	T	5	21%	14%
Rainbow	9	9	9	20%	8%
Rainbow	6	6	6	20%	9%
Rainbow	J	T	7	19%	13%
3 suited not yours	K	Q	T	18%	7%

AK
Selected flops

Flop Type: Suit Type	Flop			6 see flop	10 see flop
2 suited not yours	Q	J	5	18%	11%
2 suited not yours	Q	T	6	18%	11%
Rainbow	Q	Q	Q	18%	8%
2 suited yours	6	6	3	17%	8%
2 suited yours	9	9	3	16%	7%
2 suited not yours	J	T	7	16%	10%
2 suited yours	2	4	8	16%	9%
2 suited yours	Q	Q	3	15%	7%
Rainbow	6	6	3	15%	6%
2 suited yours	2	3	4	15%	7%
2 suited yours	9	2	7	15%	9%
2 suited yours	6	T	4	15%	10%
Rainbow	9	9	3	14%	5%
2 suited yours	Q	6	5	14%	8%
Rainbow	2	4	8	14%	6%
Rainbow	Q	Q	3	13%	5%
2 suited not yours	6	6	3	13%	5%
Rainbow	2	3	4	13%	4%
Rainbow	6	T	4	13%	6%
2 suited not yours	9	9	3	12%	4%
2 suited yours	Q	9	8	12%	8%
Rainbow	Q	6	5	12%	6%
2 suited yours	6	5	4	12%	6%
Rainbow	9	2	7	12%	6%
2 suited not yours	Q	Q	3	11%	4%
2 suited not yours	2	4	8	11%	5%
2 suited not yours	6	T	4	11%	5%
2 suited not yours	Q	6	5	10%	4%
3 suited not yours	Q	J	5	10%	5%
2 suited yours	9	8	7	10%	6%
2 suited not yours	2	3	4	10%	3%
3 suited not yours	Q	T	7	10%	5%
2 suited not yours	9	2	7	10%	5%
3 suited not yours	J	T	7	9%	4%
Rainbow	Q	9	8	9%	4%
Rainbow	6	5	4	9%	3%
2 suited not yours	Q	9	8	8%	3%
Rainbow	9	8	7	7%	2%
2 suited not yours	6	5	4	7%	2%
2 suited not yours	9	8	7	6%	2%
3 suited not yours	2	3	4	6%	1%
3 suited not yours	2	4	8	6%	2%
3 suited not yours	9	2	7	5%	2%
3 suited not yours	Q	6	5	5%	2%
3 suited not yours	6	T	4	5%	2%
3 suited not yours	Q	9	8	4%	1%
3 suited not yours	6	5	4	4%	1%
3 suited not yours	9	8	7	3%	1%

Selected flops ranked for 10-handed

Flop Type: Suit Type	Flop			6 see flop	10 see flop
Rainbow	K	K	5	81%	68%
Rainbow	Q	J	T	75%	66%
Rainbow	A	A	5	78%	65%
2 suited yours	K	K	5	78%	64%
2 suited yours	A	A	5	76%	61%
2 suited not yours	K	K	5	73%	60%
2 suited yours	Q	J	T	72%	59%
Rainbow	A	K	6	73%	58%
2 suited not yours	A	A	5	71%	57%
2 suited yours	A	K	9	70%	55%
2 suited yours	A	K	6	70%	55%
3 suited yours	Q	J	T	69%	55%
2 suited not yours	Q	J	T	66%	52%

Flop Type: Suit Type	Flop			6 see flop	10 see flop
2 suited not yours	A	K	6	65%	49%
3 suited yours	A	9	3	63%	48%
3 suited yours	A	6	3	63%	47%
3 suited yours	K	6	3	63%	47%
3 suited yours	K	9	3	62%	47%
3 suited yours	A	Q	3	61%	46%
3 suited yours	A	6	4	61%	46%
3 suited yours	K	6	4	61%	46%
3 suited yours	K	Q	7	60%	46%
3 suited yours	A	9	7	59%	45%
3 suited yours	K	9	7	57%	45%
Rainbow	A	K	Q	58%	44%
Rainbow	A	K	9	58%	44%
3 suited yours	A	Q	T	56%	44%
2 suited yours	A	K	Q	57%	42%
3 suited yours	K	Q	T	52%	40%
3 suited yours	Q	J	5	44%	39%
3 suited yours	Q	T	9	44%	38%
2 suited not yours	A	K	Q	52%	37%
2 suited not yours	A	K	9	52%	37%
3 suited yours	J	T	7	41%	35%
3 suited yours	2	4	8	41%	34%
3 suited yours	Q	6	5	40%	34%
3 suited yours	9	2	7	40%	34%
3 suited yours	6	T	4	40%	34%
Rainbow	A	9	3	53%	31%
Rainbow	A	6	3	53%	31%
2 suited yours	A	6	3	53%	31%
Rainbow	K	6	3	53%	31%
2 suited yours	A	9	3	52%	31%
2 suited yours	K	6	3	52%	31%
Rainbow	K	9	3	51%	31%
2 suited yours	K	9	3	51%	31%
3 suited yours	Q	9	8	36%	31%
3 suited yours	2	3	4	38%	30%
Rainbow	A	6	4	51%	29%
Rainbow	A	Q	3	50%	29%
2 suited yours	A	6	4	50%	29%
2 suited yours	A	Q	3	49%	29%
2 suited yours	K	Q	6	49%	29%
2 suited yours	K	6	4	49%	29%
Rainbow	K	6	4	50%	28%
Rainbow	K	Q	3	49%	28%
3 suited not yours	A	K	9	43%	28%
3 suited not yours	A	K	6	42%	28%
2 suited yours	A	9	7	46%	27%
Rainbow	A	9	7	46%	26%
2 suited yours	K	9	7	44%	26%
2 suited not yours	A	9	3	46%	25%
2 suited not yours	A	6	3	46%	25%
2 suited not yours	K	6	3	46%	25%
2 suited not yours	K	9	3	45%	25%
3 suited yours	6	5	4	34%	25%
3 suited yours	9	8	7	32%	25%
Rainbow	K	9	7	43%	24%
2 suited not yours	A	6	4	44%	23%
2 suited not yours	A	Q	3	43%	23%
2 suited not yours	K	6	4	43%	23%
2 suited not yours	K	Q	4	42%	23%
Rainbow	A	Q	T	41%	23%
2 suited yours	A	Q	T	41%	23%
3 suited not yours	A	K	Q	35%	23%
3 suited not yours	Q	J	T	37%	22%
2 suited not yours	A	9	7	40%	21%

AK
Selected flops

Flop Type: Suit Type	Flop			6 see flop	10 see flop
2 suited yours	K	Q	T	36%	20%
2 suited not yours	K	9	7	37%	19%
2 suited not yours	A	Q	T	36%	18%
Rainbow	K	Q	T	36%	18%
2 suited yours	Q	J	5	23%	16%
2 suited yours	Q	T	8	23%	16%
2 suited not yours	K	Q	T	31%	15%
2 suited yours	J	T	7	21%	15%
Rainbow	Q	J	5	21%	15%
Rainbow	Q	T	5	21%	14%
Rainbow	J	T	7	19%	13%
3 suited not yours	K	9	3	26%	12%
3 suited not yours	A	9	3	26%	11%
3 suited not yours	A	6	3	26%	11%
3 suited not yours	K	6	3	26%	11%
3 suited not yours	A	Q	3	25%	11%
3 suited not yours	K	Q	5	24%	11%
2 suited not yours	Q	J	5	18%	11%
2 suited not yours	Q	T	6	18%	11%
3 suited not yours	A	6	4	25%	10%
3 suited not yours	K	6	4	25%	10%
2 suited not yours	J	T	7	16%	10%
2 suited yours	6	T	4	15%	10%
3 suited not yours	A	9	7	23%	9%
3 suited not yours	K	9	7	22%	9%
Rainbow	6	6	6	20%	9%
2 suited yours	2	4	8	16%	9%
2 suited yours	9	2	7	15%	9%
3 suited not yours	A	Q	T	22%	8%
Rainbow	9	9	9	20%	8%
Rainbow	Q	Q	Q	18%	8%
2 suited yours	6	6	3	17%	8%
2 suited yours	Q	6	5	14%	8%
2 suited yours	Q	9	8	12%	8%
3 suited not yours	K	Q	T	18%	7%
2 suited yours	9	9	3	16%	7%
2 suited yours	Q	Q	3	15%	7%
2 suited yours	2	3	4	15%	7%
Rainbow	6	6	3	15%	6%
Rainbow	2	4	8	14%	6%
Rainbow	6	T	4	13%	6%
Rainbow	Q	6	5	12%	6%
2 suited yours	6	5	4	12%	6%
Rainbow	9	2	7	12%	6%
2 suited yours	9	8	7	10%	6%
Rainbow	9	9	3	14%	5%
Rainbow	Q	Q	3	13%	5%
2 suited not yours	6	6	3	13%	5%
2 suited not yours	2	4	8	11%	5%
2 suited not yours	6	T	4	11%	5%
3suited not yours	Q	J	5	10%	5%
3suited not yours	Q	T	7	10%	5%
2 suited not yours	9	2	7	10%	5%
Rainbow	2	3	4	13%	4%
2 suited not yours	9	9	3	12%	4%
2 suited not yours	Q	Q	3	11%	4%
2 suited not yours	Q	6	5	10%	4%
3suited not yours	J	T	7	9%	4%
Rainbow	Q	9	8	9%	4%
2 suited not yours	2	3	4	10%	3%
Rainbow	6	5	4	9%	3%
2 suited not yours	Q	9	8	8%	3%
Rainbow	9	8	7	7%	2%

Flop Type: Suit Type	Flop			6 see flop	10 see flop
2 suited not yours	6	5	4	7%	2%
2 suited not yours	9	8	7	6%	2%
3 suited not yours	2	4	8	6%	2%
3 suited not yours	Q	6	5	5%	2%
3 suited not yours	6	T	4	5%	2%
3 suited not yours	9	2	7	5%	2%
3 suited not yours	2	3	4	6%	1%
3 suited not yours	Q	9	8	4%	1%
3 suited not yours	6	5	4	4%	1%
3 suited not yours	9	8	7	3%	1%

Selected flops with 50% or higher probability of winning ranked for 6-handed

Suit Type	Flop			6 see flop	10 see flop
Rainbow	K	K	5	81%	68%
Rainbow	A	A	5	78%	65%
2 suited yours	K	K	5	78%	64%
2 suited yours	A	A	5	76%	61%
Rainbow	Q	J	T	75%	66%
2 suited not yours	K	K	5	73%	60%
Rainbow	A	K	6	73%	58%
2 suited yours	Q	J	T	72%	59%
2 suited not yours	A	A	5	71%	57%
2 suited yours	A	K	9	70%	55%
2 suited yours	A	K	6	70%	55%
3 suited yours	Q	J	T	69%	55%
2 suited not yours	Q	J	T	66%	52%
2 suited not yours	A	K	6	65%	49%
3 suited yours	A	9	3	63%	48%
3 suited yours	A	6	3	63%	47%
3 suited yours	K	6	3	63%	47%
3 suited yours	K	9	3	62%	47%
3 suited yours	A	Q	3	61%	46%
3 suited yours	A	6	4	61%	46%
3 suited yours	K	6	4	61%	46%
3 suited yours	K	Q	7	60%	46%
3 suited yours	A	9	7	59%	45%
Rainbow	A	K	Q	58%	44%
Rainbow	A	K	9	58%	44%
3 suited yours	K	9	7	57%	45%
2 suited yours	A	K	Q	57%	42%
3 suited yours	A	Q	T	56%	44%
Rainbow	A	9	3	53%	31%
Rainbow	A	6	3	53%	31%
2 suited yours	A	6	3	53%	31%
Rainbow	K	6	3	53%	31%
2 suited yours	A	9	3	52%	31%
2 suited yours	K	6	3	52%	31%
3 suited yours	K	Q	T	52%	40%
2 suited not yours	A	K	Q	52%	37%
2 suited not yours	A	K	9	52%	37%
Rainbow	A	6	4	51%	29%
Rainbow	K	9	3	51%	31%
2 suited yours	K	9	3	51%	31%
Rainbow	A	Q	3	50%	29%
2 suited yours	A	6	4	50%	29%
Rainbow	K	6	4	50%	28%

Selected flops with 50% or higher probability of winning ranked for 10-handed

Suit Type	Flop			6 see flop	10 see flop
Rainbow	K	K	5	81%	68%
Rainbow	Q	J	T	75%	66%
Rainbow	A	A	5	78%	65%
2 suited yours	K	K	5	78%	64%

AK
Selected flops

Flop Type: Suit Type	Flop			6 see flop	10 see flop
2 suited yours	A	A	5	76%	61%
2 suited not yours	K	K	5	73%	60%
2 suited yours	Q	J	T	72%	59%
Rainbow	A	K	6	73%	58%
2 suited not yours	A	A	5	71%	57%
2 suited yours	A	K	9	70%	55%
2 suited yours	A	K	6	70%	55%
3 suited yours	Q	J	T	69%	55%
2 suited not yours	Q	J	T	66%	52%

Top ten flops for 6-handed					
Rainbow	K	K	5	81%	68%
Rainbow	A	A	5	78%	65%
2 suited yours	K	K	5	78%	64%
2 suited yours	A	A	5	76%	61%
Rainbow	Q	J	T	75%	66%
2 suited not yours	K	K	5	73%	60%
Rainbow	A	K	6	73%	58%
2 suited yours	Q	J	T	72%	59%
2 suited not yours	A	A	5	71%	57%
2 suited yours	A	K	9	70%	55%

Top ten flops for 10-handed					
Rainbow	K	K	5	81%	68%
Rainbow	Q	J	T	75%	66%
Rainbow	A	A	5	78%	65%
2 suited yours	K	K	5	78%	64%
2 suited yours	A	A	5	76%	61%
2 suited not yours	K	K	5	73%	60%
2 suited yours	Q	J	T	72%	59%
Rainbow	A	K	6	73%	58%
2 suited not yours	A	A	5	71%	57%
2 suited yours	A	K	9	70%	55%

TT
Selected flops

Flop Type: Suit Type	Flop			6 see flop	10 see flop
Rainbow	A	7	4	15%	7%
2 suited not yours	A	7	4	13%	5%
3 suited not yours	A	7	4	8%	3%
2 suited yours	A	7	4	16%	7%
3 suited yours	A	7	4	23%	10%
Rainbow	Q	7	4	18%	8%
2 suited not yours	Q	7	4	16%	6%
3 suited not yours	Q	7	4	9%	3%
2 suited yours	Q	7	4	18%	8%
3 suited yours	Q	7	4	24%	10%
Rainbow	Q	Q	4	30%	15%
2 suited not yours	Q	Q	4	27%	13%
2 suited yours	Q	Q	4	29%	14%
Rainbow	9	9	4	30%	16%
2 suited not yours	9	9	4	27%	14%
2 suited yours	9	9	4	29%	14%
Rainbow	6	6	4	29%	15%
2 suited not yours	6	6	4	26%	14%
2 suited yours	6	6	4	28%	14%
Rainbow	T	A	2	80%	69%
2 suited not yours	T	A	2	72%	61%
3 suited not yours	T	A	2	53%	42%
2 suited yours	T	A	2	72%	61%
Rainbow	T	Q	2	76%	66%
2 suited not yours	T	Q	2	69%	58%
3 suited not yours	T	Q	2	51%	41%
2 suited yours	T	Q	2	72%	60%
Rainbow	T	9	3	75%	66%
2 suited not yours	T	9	3	70%	59%
3 suited not yours	T	9	3	53%	44%
2 suited yours	T	9	3	72%	61%
Rainbow	T	6	2	83%	73%
2 suited not yours	T	6	2	83%	73%
3 suited not yours	T	6	2	56%	47%
2 suited yours	T	6	2	78%	67%
Rainbow	T	A	K	66%	53%
2 suited not yours	T	A	K	60%	48%
3 suited not yours	T	A	K	45%	33%
2 suited yours	T	A	K	64%	50%
Rainbow	T	Q	J	48%	37%
2 suited not yours	T	Q	J	45%	34%
3suited not yours	T	Q	J	36%	27%
2 suited yours	T	Q	J	48%	36%
Rainbow	T	7	8	62%	51%
2 suited not yours	T	7	8	58%	47%
3 suited not yours	T	7	8	45%	36%
2 suited yours	T	7	8	59%	48%
Rainbow	T	6	5	78%	67%
2 suited not yours	T	6	5	72%	60%
3 suited not yours	T	6	5	54%	44%
2 suited yours	T	6	5	74%	61%
Rainbow	A	K	3	11%	5%
2 suited not yours	A	K	3	9%	4%
3 suited not yours	A	K	3	5%	2%
2 suited yours	A	K	3	12%	6%
3 suited yours	A	K	3	26%	15%
Rainbow	7	8	3	29%	13%
2 suited not yours	7	8	3	26%	11%
3 suited not yours	7	8	3	15%	6%
2 suited yours	7	8	3	28%	13%
3suited yours	7	8	3	27%	10%
Rainbow	6	5	2	24%	10%
2 suited not yours	6	5	2	21%	8%

Flop Type: Suit Type	Flop			6 see flop	10 see flop
3 suited not yours	6	5	2	12%	4%
2 suited yours	6	5	2	24%	10%
3suited yours	6	5	2	24%	8%
Rainbow	Q	J	2	14%	6%
2 suited not yours	Q	J	2	12%	5%
3 suited not yours	Q	J	2	7%	2%
2 suited yours	Q	J	2	14%	6%
3 suited yours	Q	J	2	25%	13%
Rainbow	9	8	2	31%	15%
2 suited not yours	9	8	2	27%	12%
3 suited not yours	9	8	2	16%	6%
yours	9	8	2	29%	14%
3 suited yours	9	8	2	27%	10%
Rainbow	A	K	Q	11%	7%
2 suited not yours	A	K	Q	13%	8%
3 suited not yours	A	K	Q	8%	4%
2 suited yours	A	K	Q	16%	9%
3 suited yours	A	K	Q	34%	25%
Rainbow	6	5	4	16%	7%
2 suited not yours	6	5	4	15%	5%
3 suited not yours	6	5	4	9%	3%
2 suited yours	6	5	4	16%	6%
3suited yours	6	5	4	19%	6%
Rainbow	9	8	7	35%	20%
2 suited not yours	9	8	7	30%	17%
3 suited not yours	9	8	7	18%	8%
2 suited yours	9	8	7	32%	18%
3 suited yours	9	8	7	33%	19%
Rainbow	9	7	2	31%	15%
2 suited not yours	9	7	2	27%	12%
3 suited not yours	9	7	2	16%	6%
2 suited yours	9	7	2	30%	14%
3 suited yours	9	7	2	27%	11%
Rainbow	6	4	2	26%	11%
2 suited not yours	6	4	2	22%	9%
3 suited not yours	6	4	2	13%	5%
2 suited yours	6	4	2	25%	10%
3 suited yours	6	4	2	25%	9%
Rainbow	K	K	K	39%	23%
Rainbow	Q	Q	Q	41%	24%
Rainbow	7	7	7	40%	24%
Rainbow	6	6	6	40%	25%

Selected flops ranked for 6-handed

	Flop				
Rainbow	T	6	2	83%	73%
2 suited not yours	T	6	2	83%	73%
Rainbow	T	A	2	80%	69%
2 suited yours	T	6	2	78%	67%
Rainbow	T	6	5	78%	67%
Rainbow	T	Q	2	76%	66%
Rainbow	T	9	3	75%	66%
2 suited yours	T	6	5	74%	61%
2 suited not yours	T	A	2	72%	61%
2 suited yours	T	A	2	72%	61%
2 suited yours	T	Q	2	72%	60%
2 suited yours	T	9	3	72%	61%
2 suited not yours	T	6	5	72%	60%
2 suited not yours	T	9	3	70%	59%
2 suited not yours	T	Q	2	69%	58%
Rainbow	T	A	K	66%	53%
2 suited yours	T	A	K	64%	50%
Rainbow	T	7	8	62%	51%
2 suited not yours	T	A	K	60%	48%

TT
Selected flops

Flop Type: Suit Type	Flop	6 see flop	10 see flop
2 suited yours	T 7 8	59%	48%
2 suited not yours	T 7 8	58%	47%
3 suited not yours	T 6 2	56%	47%
3 suited not yours	T 6 5	54%	44%
3 suited not yours	T A 2	53%	42%
3 suited not yours	T 9 3	53%	44%
3 suited not yours	T Q 2	51%	41%
Rainbow	T Q J	48%	37%
2 suited yours	T Q J	48%	36%
3 suited not yours	T A K	45%	33%
2 suited not yours	T Q J	45%	34%
3 suited not yours	T 7 8	45%	36%
Rainbow	Q Q Q	41%	24%
Rainbow	7 7 7	40%	24%
Rainbow	6 6 6	40%	25%
Rainbow	K K K	39%	23%
3 suited not yours	T Q J	36%	27%
Rainbow	9 8 7	35%	20%
3 suited yours	A K Q	34%	25%
3 suited yours	9 8 7	33%	19%
2 suited yours	9 8 7	32%	18%
Rainbow	9 8 2	31%	15%
Rainbow	9 7 2	31%	15%
Rainbow	Q Q 4	30%	15%
Rainbow	9 9 4	30%	16%
2 suited not yours	9 8 7	30%	17%
2 suited yours	9 7 2	30%	14%
2 suited yours	Q Q 4	29%	14%
2 suited yours	9 9 4	29%	14%
Rainbow	6 6 4	29%	15%
Rainbow	7 8 3	29%	13%
2 suited yours	9 8 2	29%	14%
2 suited yours	6 6 4	28%	14%
2 suited yours	7 8 3	28%	13%
2 suited not yours	Q Q 4	27%	13%
2 suited not yours	9 9 4	27%	14%
3 suited yours	7 8 3	27%	10%
2 suited not yours	9 8 2	27%	12%
3 suited yours	9 8 2	27%	10%
2 suited not yours	9 7 2	27%	12%
3 suited yours	9 7 2	27%	11%
2 suited not yours	6 6 4	26%	14%
3 suited yours	A K 3	26%	15%
2 suited not yours	7 8 3	26%	11%
Rainbow	6 4 2	26%	11%
3 suited yours	Q J 2	25%	13%
2 suited yours	6 4 2	25%	10%
3 suited yours	6 4 2	25%	9%
3 suited yours	Q 7 4	24%	10%
Rainbow	6 5 2	24%	10%
2 suited yours	6 5 2	24%	10%
3 suited yours	6 5 2	24%	8%
3suited yours	A 7 4	23%	10%
2 suited not yours	6 4 2	22%	9%
2 suited not yours	6 5 2	21%	8%
3 suited yours	6 5 4	19%	6%
Rainbow	Q 7 4	18%	8%
2 suited yours	Q 7 4	18%	8%
3 suited not yours	9 8 7	18%	8%
2 suited yours	A 7 4	16%	7%
2 suited not yours	Q 7 4	16%	6%
3 suited not yours	9 8 2	16%	6%
2 suited yours	A K Q	16%	9%

Flop Type: Suit Type	Flop	6 see flop	10 see flop
Rainbow	6 5 4	16%	7%
2 suited yours	6 5 4	16%	6%
3 suited not yours	9 7 2	16%	6%
Rainbow	A 7 4	15%	7%
3 suited not yours	7 8 3	15%	6%
2 suited not yours	6 5 4	15%	5%
Rainbow	Q J 2	14%	6%
2 suited yours	Q J 2	14%	6%
2 suited not yours	A 7 4	13%	5%
2 suited not yours	A K Q	13%	8%
3 suited not yours	6 4 2	13%	5%
2 suited yours	A K 3	12%	6%
3 suited not yours	6 5 2	12%	4%
2 suited not yours	Q J 2	12%	5%
Rainbow	A K 3	11%	5%
Rainbow	A K Q	11%	7%
3 suited not yours	Q 7 4	9%	3%
2 suited not yours	A K 3	9%	4%
3 suited not yours	6 5 4	9%	3%
3 suited not yours	A 7 4	8%	3%
3 suited not yours	A K Q	8%	4%
3 suited not yours	Q J 2	7%	2%
3 suited not yours	A K 3	5%	2%

Selected flops for 10-handed

Flop Type: Suit Type	Flop	6 see flop	10 see flop
Rainbow	T 6 2	83%	73%
2 suited not yours	T 6 2	83%	73%
Rainbow	T A 2	80%	69%
2 suited yours	T 6 2	78%	67%
Rainbow	T 6 5	78%	67%
Rainbow	T Q 2	76%	66%
Rainbow	T 9 3	75%	66%
2 suited yours	T 6 5	74%	61%
2 suited not yours	T A 2	72%	61%
2 suited yours	T A 2	72%	61%
2 suited yours	T 9 3	72%	61%
2 suited yours	T Q 2	72%	60%
2 suited not yours	T 6 5	72%	60%
2 suited not yours	T 9 3	70%	59%
2 suited not yours	T Q 2	69%	58%
Rainbow	T A K	66%	53%
Rainbow	T 7 8	62%	51%
2 suited yours	T A K	64%	50%
2 suited not yours	T A K	60%	48%
2 suited yours	T 7 8	59%	48%
2 suited not yours	T 7 8	58%	47%
3 suited not yours	T 6 2	56%	47%
3 suited not yours	T 6 5	54%	44%
3 suited not yours	T 9 3	53%	44%
3 suited not yours	T A 2	53%	42%
3 suited not yours	T Q 2	51%	41%
Rainbow	T Q J	48%	37%
2 suited yours	T Q J	48%	36%
3 suited not yours	T 7 8	45%	36%
2 suited not yours	T Q J	45%	34%
3 suited not yours	T A K	45%	33%
3 suited not yours	T Q J	36%	27%
Rainbow	6 6 6	40%	25%
3 suited yours	A K Q	34%	25%
Rainbow	Q Q Q	41%	24%
Rainbow	7 7 7	40%	24%
Rainbow	K K K	39%	23%
Rainbow	9 8 7	35%	20%

TT
Selected flops

Flop Type: Suit Type	Flop	6 see flop	10 see flop
3 suited yours	9 8 7	33%	19%
2 suited yours	9 8 7	32%	18%
2 suited not yours	9 8 7	30%	17%
Rainbow	9 9 4	30%	16%
Rainbow	9 8 2	31%	15%
Rainbow	9 7 2	31%	15%
Rainbow	Q Q 4	30%	15%
Rainbow	6 6 4	29%	15%
3 suited yours	A K 3	26%	15%
2 suited yours	9 7 2	30%	14%
2 suited yours	Q Q 4	29%	14%
2 suited yours	9 9 4	29%	14%
2 suited yours	9 8 2	29%	14%
2 suited yours	6 6 4	28%	14%
2 suited not yours	9 9 4	27%	14%
2 suited not yours	6 6 4	26%	14%
Rainbow	7 8 3	29%	13%
2 suited yours	7 8 3	28%	13%
2 suited not yours	Q Q 4	27%	13%
3 suited yours	Q J 2	25%	13%
2 suited not yours	9 8 2	27%	12%
2 suited not yours	9 7 2	27%	12%
3 suited yours	9 7 2	27%	11%
2 suited not yours	7 8 3	26%	11%
Rainbow	6 4 2	26%	11%
3 suited yours	7 8 3	27%	10%
3 suited yours	9 8 2	27%	10%
2 suited yours	6 4 2	25%	10%
3 suited yours	Q 7 4	24%	10%
Rainbow	6 5 2	24%	10%
2 suited yours	6 5 2	24%	10%
3 suited yours	A 7 4	23%	10%
3 suited yours	6 4 2	25%	9%
2 suited not yours	6 4 2	22%	9%
2 suited yours	A K Q	16%	9%
3 suited yours	6 5 2	24%	8%
2 suited not yours	6 5 2	21%	8%
Rainbow	Q 7 4	18%	8%
2 suited yours	Q 7 4	18%	8%
3 suited not yours	9 8 7	18%	8%
2 suited not yours	A K Q	13%	8%
2 suited yours	A 7 4	16%	7%
Rainbow	6 5 4	16%	7%
Rainbow	A 7 4	15%	7%
Rainbow	A K Q	11%	7%
3 suited yours	6 5 4	19%	6%
2 suited not yours	Q 7 4	16%	6%
3 suited not yours	9 8 2	16%	6%
2 suited yours	6 5 4	16%	6%
3 suited not yours	9 7 2	16%	6%
3 suited not yours	7 8 3	15%	6%
Rainbow	Q J 2	14%	6%
2 suited yours	Q J 2	14%	6%
2 suited yours	A K 3	12%	6%
2 suited not yours	6 5 4	15%	5%
2 suited not yours	A 7 4	13%	5%
3 suited not yours	6 4 2	13%	5%
2 suited not yours	Q J 2	12%	5%
Rainbow	A K 3	11%	5%
3 suited yours	6 5 2	12%	4%
2 suited not yours	A K 3	9%	4%
3 suited not yours	A K Q	8%	4%
3 suited not yours	Q 7 4	9%	3%

Flop Type: Suit Type	Flop	6 see flop	10 see flop
3 suited not yours	6 5 4	9%	3%
3 suited not yours	A 7 4	8%	3%
3 suited not yours	Q J 2	7%	2%
3 suited not yours	A K 3	5%	2%

Selected flops for 10-handed

Flop Type: Suit Type	Flop	6 see flop	10 see flop
Rainbow	T 6 2	83%	73%
2 suited not yours	T 6 2	83%	73%
Rainbow	T A 2	80%	69%
2 suited yours	T 6 2	78%	67%
Rainbow	T 6 5	78%	67%
Rainbow	T Q 2	76%	66%
Rainbow	T 9 3	75%	66%
2 suited yours	T 6 5	74%	61%
2 suited not yours	T A 2	72%	61%
2 suited yours	T A 2	72%	61%
2 suited yours	T 9 3	72%	61%
2 suited yours	T Q 2	72%	60%
2 suited not yours	T 6 5	72%	60%
2 suited not yours	T 9 3	70%	59%
2 suited not yours	T Q 2	69%	58%
Rainbow	T A K	66%	53%
Rainbow	T 7 8	62%	51%
2 suited yours	T A K	64%	50%
2 suited not yours	T A K	60%	48%
2 suited yours	T 7 8	59%	48%
2 suited not yours	T 7 8	58%	47%
3 suited not yours	T 6 2	56%	47%
3 suited not yours	T 6 5	54%	44%
3 suited not yours	T 9 3	53%	44%
3 suited not yours	T A 2	53%	42%
3 suited not yours	T Q 2	51%	41%
Rainbow	T Q J	48%	37%
2 suited yours	T Q J	48%	36%
3 suited not yours	T 7 8	45%	36%
2 suited not yours	T Q J	45%	34%
3 suited not yours	T A K	45%	33%
3 suited not yours	T Q J	36%	27%
Rainbow	6 6 6	40%	25%
3 suited yours	A K Q	34%	25%
Rainbow	Q Q Q	41%	24%
Rainbow	7 7 7	40%	24%
Rainbow	K K K	39%	23%
Rainbow	9 8 7	35%	20%
3 suited yours	9 8 7	33%	19%
2 suited yours	9 8 7	32%	18%
2 suited not yours	9 8 7	30%	17%
Rainbow	9 9 4	30%	16%
Rainbow	9 8 2	31%	15%
Rainbow	9 7 2	31%	15%
Rainbow	Q Q 4	30%	15%
Rainbow	6 6 4	29%	15%
3 suited yours	A K 3	26%	15%
2 suited yours	9 7 2	30%	14%
2 suited yours	Q Q 4	29%	14%
2 suited yours	9 9 4	29%	14%
2 suited yours	9 8 2	29%	14%
2 suited yours	6 6 4	28%	14%
2 suited not yours	9 9 4	27%	14%
2 suited not yours	6 6 4	26%	14%
Rainbow	7 8 3	29%	13%
2 suited yours	7 8 3	28%	13%
2 suited not yours	Q Q 4	27%	13%

TT
Selected flops

Flop Type: Suit Type	Flop			6 see flop	10 see flop
3 suited yours	Q	J	2	25%	13%
2 suited not yours	9	8	2	27%	12%
2 suited not yours	9	7	2	27%	12%
3 suited yours	9	7	2	27%	11%
2 suited not yours	7	8	3	26%	11%
Rainbow	6	4	2	26%	11%
3 suited yours	7	8	3	27%	10%
3 suited yours	9	8	2	27%	10%
2 suited yours	6	4	2	25%	10%
3 suited yours	Q	7	4	24%	10%
Rainbow	6	5	2	24%	10%
2 suited yours	6	5	2	24%	10%
3 suited yours	A	7	4	23%	10%
3 suited yours	6	4	2	25%	9%
2 suited not yours	6	4	2	22%	9%
2 suited yours	A	K	Q	16%	9%
3 suited yours	6	5	2	24%	8%
2 suited not yours	6	5	2	21%	8%
Rainbow	Q	7	4	18%	8%
2 suited yours	Q	7	4	18%	8%
3 suited not yours	9	8	7	18%	8%
2 suited not yours	A	K	Q	13%	8%
2 suited yours	A	7	4	16%	7%
Rainbow	6	5	4	16%	7%
Rainbow	A	7	4	15%	7%
Rainbow	A	K	Q	11%	7%
3 suited yours	6	5	4	19%	6%
2 suited not yours	Q	7	4	16%	6%
3 suited not yours	9	8	2	16%	6%
2 suited yours	6	5	4	16%	6%
3 suited not yours	9	7	2	16%	6%
3 suited not yours	7	8	3	15%	6%
Rainbow	Q	J	2	14%	6%
2 suited yours	Q	J	2	14%	6%
2 suited yours	A	K	3	12%	6%
2 suited not yours	6	5	4	15%	5%
2 suited not yours	A	7	4	13%	5%
3 suited not yours	6	4	2	13%	5%
2 suited not yours	Q	J	2	12%	5%
Rainbow	A	K	3	11%	5%
3 suited not yours	6	5	2	12%	4%
2 suited not yours	A	K	3	9%	4%
3 suited not yours	A	K	Q	8%	4%
3 suited not yours	Q	7	4	9%	3%
3 suited not yours	6	5	4	9%	3%
3 suited not yours	A	7	4	8%	3%
3 suited not yours	Q	J	2	7%	2%
3 suited not yours	A	K	3	5%	2%

Flop Type: Suit Type	Flop			6 see flop	10 see flop
Selected flops with a 50% or higher probability of winning ranked for 10-handed					
Rainbow	T	6	2	83%	73%
2 suited not yours	T	6	2	83%	73%
Rainbow	T	A	2	80%	69%
2 suited yours	T	6	2	78%	67%
Rainbow	T	6	5	78%	67%
Rainbow	T	Q	2	76%	66%
Rainbow	T	9	3	75%	66%
2 suited yours	T	6	5	74%	61%
2 suited not yours	T	A	2	72%	61%
2 suited yours	T	A	2	72%	61%
2 suited yours	T	9	3	72%	61%
2 suited yours	T	Q	2	72%	60%
2 suited not yours	T	6	5	72%	60%
2 suited not yours	T	9	3	70%	59%
2 suited not yours	T	Q	2	69%	58%
Rainbow	T	A	K	66%	53%
Rainbow	T	7	8	62%	51%
2 suited yours	T	A	K	64%	50%
Top ten flops for 6-handed					
Rainbow	T	6	2	83%	73%
2 suited not yours	T	6	2	83%	73%
Rainbow	T	A	2	80%	69%
2 suited yours	T	6	2	78%	67%
Rainbow	T	6	5	78%	67%
Rainbow	T	Q	2	76%	66%
Rainbow	T	9	3	75%	66%
2 suited yours	T	6	5	74%	61%
2 suited not yours	T	A	2	72%	61%
2 suited yours	T	A	2	72%	61%
Top ten flops for 10-handed					
Rainbow	T	6	2	83%	73%
2 suited not yours	T	6	2	83%	73%
Rainbow	T	A	2	80%	69%
2 suited yours	T	6	2	78%	67%
Rainbow	T	6	5	78%	67%
Rainbow	T	Q	2	76%	66%
Rainbow	T	9	3	75%	66%
2 suited yours	T	6	5	74%	61%
2 suited not yours	T	A	2	72%	61%
2 suited yours	T	A	2	72%	61%

76s
Selected flops

Flop Type: Suit Type	Flop	6 see flop	10 see flop
Rainbow	K 5 3	18%	16%
2 suited not yours	K 5 3	16%	13%
3 suited not yours	K 5 3	9%	5%
2 suited yours	K 5 3	38%	30%
3 suited yours	K 5 3	60%	45%
Rainbow	Q 5 3	19%	16%
2 suited not yours	Q 5 3	16%	12%
3 suited not yours	Q 5 3	9%	5%
2 suited yours	Q 5 3	37%	30%
3 suited yours	Q 5 3	61%	45%
Rainbow	9 5 2	17%	14%
2 suited not yours	9 5 2	15%	11%
3 suited not yours	9 5 2	8%	5%
2 suited yours	9 5 2	38%	31%
3 suited yours	9 5 2	60%	45%
Rainbow	A A T	2%	1%
2 suited not yours	A A T	2%	1%
2 suited yours	A A T	20%	13%
Rainbow	Q Q T	2%	0%
2 suited not yours	Q Q T	1%	0%
2 suited yours	Q Q T	21%	13%
Rainbow	9 9 Q	3%	1%
2 suited not yours	9 9 Q	3%	1%
2 suited yours	9 9 Q	22%	14%
Rainbow	4 4 Q	5%	3%
2 suited not yours	4 4 Q	4%	2%
2 suited yours	4 4 Q	24%	16%
Rainbow	7 K 2	18%	10%
2 suited not yours	7 K 2	15%	8%
3 suited not yours	7 K 2	10%	5%
2 suited yours	7 K 2	40%	29%
Rainbow	7 Q 2	18%	10%
2 suited not yours	7 Q 2	20%	12%
3 suited not yours	7 Q 2	10%	5%
2 suited yours	7 Q 2	40%	28%
Rainbow	7 9 2	18%	9%
2 suited not yours	7 9 2	19%	11%
3 suited not yours	7 9 2	10%	4%
2 suited yours	7 9 2	40%	28%
Rainbow	7 5 2	23%	12%
2 suited not yours	7 5 2	20%	10%
3 suited not yours	7 5 2	12%	5%
2 suited yours	7 5 2	42%	29%
Rainbow	7 A K	13%	8%
2 suited not yours	7 A K	11%	7%
3 suited not yours	7 A K	7%	4%
2 suited yours	7 A K	38%	29%
Rainbow	7 Q J	13%	7%
2 suited not yours	7 Q J	11%	6%
3 suited not yours	7 Q J	7%	4%
2 suited yours	7 Q J	37%	28%
Rainbow	7 9 8	17%	8%
2 suited not yours	7 9 8	15%	7%
3 suited not yours	7 9 8	9%	4%
2 suited yours	7 9 8	40%	31%
Rainbow	6 A 3	16%	9%
2 suited not yours	6 A 3	15%	7%
3 suited not yours	6 A 3	9%	5%
2 suited yours	6 A 3	39%	29%
Rainbow	6 Q 3	18%	10%
2 suited not yours	6 Q 3	15%	8%
3 suited not yours	6 Q 3	10%	5%
2 suited yours	6 Q 3	39%	29%
Rainbow	6 9 3	19%	10%
2 suited not yours	6 9 3	16%	8%
3 suited not yours	6 9 3	10%	5%
2 suited yours	6 9 3	39%	29%
Rainbow	6 5 2	20%	11%
2 suited not yours	6 5 2	18%	9%
3 suited not yours	6 5 2	11%	5%
2 suited yours	6 5 2	40%	28%
Rainbow	6 A K	13%	8%
2 suited not yours	6 A K	11%	6%
3 suited not yours	6 A K	11%	6%
2 suited yours	6 A K	37%	30%
Rainbow	6 Q J	11%	8%
2 suited not yours	6 Q J	11%	6%
3 suited not yours	6 Q J	7%	3%
2 suited yours	6 Q J	37%	29%
Rainbow	6 9 8	24%	14%
2 suited not yours	6 9 8	21%	12%
3 suited not yours	6 9 8	13%	6%
2 suited yours	6 9 8	45%	35%
Rainbow	A K 3	3%	2%
2 suited not yours	A K 3	3%	2%
3 suited not yours	A K 3	1%	1%
2 suited yours	A K 3	27%	21%
3 suited yours	A K 3	60%	43%
Rainbow	Q J 3	3%	2%
2 suited not yours	Q J 3	3%	2%
3 suited not yours	Q J 3	2%	1%
2 suited yours	Q J 3	27%	21%
3 suited yours	Q J 3	59%	43%
Rainbow	9 3 2	7%	5%
2 suited not yours	9 3 2	6%	4%
3 suited not yours	9 3 2	3%	1%
2 suited yours	9 3 2	29%	22%
3 suited yours	9 3 2	56%	41%
Rainbow	9 8 Q	15%	9%
2 suited not yours	9 8 Q	13%	7%
3 suited not yours	9 8 Q	7%	3%
2 suited yours	9 8 Q	35%	26%
3 suited yours	9 8 Q	65%	50%
Rainbow	5 4 Q	29%	26%
2 suited not yours	5 4 Q	26%	21%
3 suited not yours	5 4 Q	14%	8%
2 suited yours	5 4 Q	44%	35%
3 suited yours	5 4 Q	63%	50%
Rainbow	A K Q	1%	1%
2 suited not yours	A K Q	1%	0%
3 suited not yours	A K Q	1%	0%
2 suited yours	A K Q	27%	21%
3 suited yours	A K Q	63%	47%
Rainbow	Q J T	1%	0%
2 suited not yours	Q J T	1%	0%
3 suited not yours	Q J T	1%	0%
2 suited yours	Q J T	27%	20%
3 suited yours	Q J T	62%	45%
Rainbow	A 2 3	4%	2%
2 suited not yours	A 2 3	3%	2%
3 suited not yours	A 2 3	2%	1%
2 suited yours	A 2 3	28%	22%
3 suited yours	A 2 3	56%	39%
Rainbow	5 4 3	80%	65%
2 suited not yours	5 4 3	70%	54%
3 suited not yours	5 4 3	38%	23%

76s
Selected flops

Flop Type: Suit Type		Flop		6 see flop	10 see flop
2 suited yours	5	4	3	79%	65%
3 suited yours	5	4	3	100%	100%
Rainbow	5	Q	3	18%	16%
2 suited not yours	5	Q	3	16%	12%
3 suited not yours	5	Q	3	9%	5%
2 suited yours	5	Q	3	37%	29%
3 suited yours	5	Q	3	60%	45%
Rainbow	Q	T	3	4%	2%
2 suited not yours	Q	T	3	3%	2%
3 suited not yours	Q	T	3	2%	1%
2 suited yours	Q	T	3	28%	21%
3 suited yours	Q	T	3	59%	42%
Rainbow	7	7	A	71%	56%
2 suited not yours	7	7	A	65%	48%
Rainbow	7	7	Q	71%	55%
2 suited not yours	7	7	Q	65%	48%
Rainbow	7	7	9	67%	49%
2 suited not yours	7	7	9	61%	43%
Rainbow	7	7	5	75%	59%
2 suited not yours	7	7	5	69%	53%
Rainbow	6	6	A	72%	57%
2 suited not yours	6	6	A	66%	49%
Rainbow	6	6	Q	72%	55%
2 suited not yours	6	6	Q	65%	48%
Rainbow	6	6	9	71%	53%
2 suited not yours	6	6	9	64%	46%
Rainbow	6	6	5	75%	59%
2 suited not yours	6	6	5	68%	52%
Rainbow	A	A	A	6%	2%
Rainbow	Q	Q	Q	7%	3%
Rainbow	9	9	9	6%	3%
Rainbow	5	5	5	8%	3%

Selected flops ranked for 6-handed

3 suited yours	5	4	3	100%	100%
Rainbow	5	4	3	80%	65%
2 suited yours	5	4	3	79%	65%
Rainbow	7	7	5	75%	59%
Rainbow	6	6	5	75%	59%
Rainbow	6	6	A	72%	57%
Rainbow	6	6	Q	72%	55%
Rainbow	7	7	A	71%	56%
Rainbow	7	7	Q	71%	55%
Rainbow	6	6	9	71%	53%
2 suited not yours	5	4	3	70%	54%
2 suited not yours	7	7	5	69%	53%
2 suited not yours	6	6	5	68%	52%
Rainbow	7	7	9	67%	49%
2 suited not yours	6	6	A	66%	49%
3 suited yours	9	8	Q	65%	50%
2 suited not yours	7	7	A	65%	48%
2 suited not yours	7	7	Q	65%	48%
2 suited not yours	6	6	Q	65%	48%
2 suited not yours	6	6	9	64%	46%
3 suited yours	5	4	Q	63%	50%
3 suited yours	A	K	Q	63%	47%
3 suited yours	Q	J	T	62%	45%
3 suited yours	Q	5	3	61%	45%
2 suited not yours	7	7	9	61%	43%
3 suited yours	K	5	3	60%	45%
3 suited yours	9	5	2	60%	45%
3 suited yours	A	K	3	60%	43%
3 suited yours	5	Q	3	60%	45%

Flop Type: Suit Type		Flop		6 see flop	10 see flop
3 suited yours	Q	J	3	59%	43%
3 suited yours	Q	T	3	59%	42%
3 suited yours	9	3	2	56%	41%
3 suited yours	A	2	3	56%	39%
2 suited yours	6	9	8	45%	35%
2 suited yours	5	4	Q	44%	35%
2 suited yours	7	5	2	42%	29%
2 suited yours	7	K	2	40%	29%
2 suited yours	7	Q	2	40%	28%
2 suited yours	7	9	2	40%	28%
2 suited yours	7	9	8	40%	31%
2 suited yours	6	5	2	40%	28%
2 suited yours	6	A	3	39%	29%
2 suited yours	6	Q	3	39%	29%
2 suited yours	6	9	3	39%	29%
2 suited yours	K	5	3	38%	30%
2 suited yours	9	5	2	38%	31%
2 suited yours	7	A	K	38%	29%
3 suited not yours	5	4	3	38%	23%
2 suited yours	Q	5	3	37%	30%
2 suited yours	7	Q	J	37%	28%
2 suited yours	6	A	K	37%	30%
2 suited yours	6	Q	J	37%	29%
2 suited yours	5	Q	3	37%	29%
2 suited yours	9	8	Q	35%	26%
2 suited yours	9	3	2	29%	22%
Rainbow	5	4	Q	29%	26%
2 suited yours	A	2	3	28%	22%
2 suited yours	Q	T	3	28%	21%
2 suited yours	A	K	3	27%	21%
2 suited yours	Q	J	3	27%	21%
2 suited yours	A	K	Q	27%	21%
2 suited yours	Q	J	T	27%	20%
2 suited not yours	5	4	Q	26%	21%
2 suited yours	4	4	Q	24%	16%
Rainbow	6	9	8	24%	14%
Rainbow	7	5	2	23%	12%
2 suited yours	9	9	Q	22%	14%
2 suited yours	Q	Q	T	21%	13%
2 suited not yours	6	9	8	21%	12%
2 suited yours	A	A	T	20%	13%
2 suited not yours	7	Q	2	20%	12%
2 suited not yours	7	5	2	20%	10%
Rainbow	6	5	2	20%	11%
Rainbow	Q	5	3	19%	16%
2 suited not yours	7	9	2	19%	11%
Rainbow	6	9	3	19%	10%
Rainbow	K	5	3	18%	16%
Rainbow	7	K	2	18%	10%
Rainbow	7	Q	2	18%	10%
Rainbow	7	9	2	18%	9%
Rainbow	6	Q	3	18%	10%
2 suited not yours	6	5	2	18%	9%
Rainbow	5	Q	3	18%	16%
Rainbow	9	5	2	17%	14%
Rainbow	7	9	8	17%	8%
2 suited not yours	K	5	3	16%	13%
2 suited not yours	Q	5	3	16%	12%
Rainbow	6	A	3	16%	9%
2 suited not yours	6	9	3	16%	8%
2 suited not yours	5	Q	3	16%	12%
2 suited not yours	9	5	2	15%	11%
2 suited not yours	7	K	2	15%	8%

76s
Selected flops

Flop Type: Suit Type	Flop			6 see flop	10 see flop
2 suited not yours	7	9	8	15%	7%
2 suited not yours	6	A	3	15%	7%
2 suited not yours	6	Q	3	15%	8%
Rainbow	9	8	Q	15%	9%
3 suited not yours	5	4	Q	14%	8%
Rainbow	7	A	K	13%	8%
Rainbow	7	Q	J	13%	7%
Rainbow	6	A	K	13%	8%
3 suited not yours	6	9	8	13%	6%
2 suited not yours	9	8	Q	13%	7%
3 suited not yours	7	5	2	12%	5%
2 suited not yours	7	A	K	11%	7%
2 suited not yours	7	Q	J	11%	6%
3 suited not yours	6	5	2	11%	5%
2 suited not yours	6	A	K	11%	6%
3 suited not yours	6	A	K	11%	6%
Rainbow	6	Q	J	11%	8%
2 suited not yours	6	Q	J	11%	6%
3 suited not yours	7	K	2	10%	5%
3 suited not yours	7	Q	2	10%	5%
3 suited not yours	7	9	2	10%	4%
3 suited not yours	6	Q	3	10%	5%
3 suited not yours	6	9	3	10%	5%
3 suited not yours	K	5	3	9%	5%
3 suited not yours	Q	5	3	9%	5%
3 suited not yours	7	9	8	9%	4%
3 suited not yours	6	A	3	9%	5%
3 suited not yours	5	Q	3	9%	5%
3 suited not yours	9	5	2	8%	5%
Rainbow	5	5	5	8%	3%
3 suited not yours	7	A	K	7%	4%
3 suited not yours	7	Q	J	7%	4%
3 suited not yours	6	Q	J	7%	3%
Rainbow	9	3	2	7%	5%
3 suited not yours	9	8	Q	7%	3%
Rainbow	Q	Q	Q	7%	3%
2 suited not yours	9	3	2	6%	4%
Rainbow	A	A	A	6%	2%
Rainbow	9	9	9	6%	3%
Rainbow	4	4	Q	5%	3%
2 suited not yours	4	4	Q	4%	2%
Rainbow	A	2	3	4%	2%
Rainbow	Q	T	3	4%	2%
Rainbow	9	9	Q	3%	1%
2 suited not yours	9	9	Q	3%	1%
Rainbow	A	K	3	3%	2%
2 suited not yours	A	K	3	3%	2%
Rainbow	Q	J	3	3%	2%
2 suited not yours	Q	J	3	3%	2%
3 suited not yours	9	3	2	3%	1%
2 suited not yours	A	2	3	3%	2%
2 suited not yours	Q	T	3	3%	2%
Rainbow	A	A	T	2%	1%
2 suited not yours	A	A	T	2%	1%
Rainbow	Q	Q	T	2%	0%
3 suited not yours	Q	J	3	2%	1%
3 suited not yours	A	2	3	2%	1%
3 suited not yours	Q	T	3	2%	1%
2 suited not yours	Q	Q	T	1%	0%
3 suited not yours	A	K	3	1%	1%
Rainbow	A	K	Q	1%	1%
2 suited not yours	A	K	Q	1%	0%
3 suited not yours	A	K	Q	1%	0%

Flop Type: Suit Type	Flop			6 see flop	10 see flop
Rainbow	Q	J	T	1%	0%
2 suited not yours	Q	J	T	1%	0%
3 suited not yours	Q	J	T	1%	0%

Selected flops ranked for 10-handed

Flop Type: Suit Type	Flop			6 see flop	10 see flop
3 suited yours	5	4	3	100%	100%
Rainbow	5	4	3	80%	65%
2 suited yours	5	4	3	79%	65%
Rainbow	7	7	5	75%	59%
Rainbow	6	6	5	75%	59%
Rainbow	6	6	A	72%	57%
Rainbow	7	7	A	71%	56%
Rainbow	6	6	Q	72%	55%
Rainbow	7	7	Q	71%	55%
2 suited not yours	5	4	3	70%	54%
Rainbow	6	6	9	71%	53%
2 suited not yours	7	7	5	69%	53%
2 suited not yours	6	6	5	68%	52%
3 suited yours	9	8	Q	65%	50%
3 suited yours	5	4	Q	63%	50%
Rainbow	7	7	9	67%	49%
2 suited not yours	6	6	A	66%	49%
2 suited not yours	7	7	A	65%	48%
2 suited not yours	7	7	Q	65%	48%
2 suited not yours	6	6	Q	65%	48%
3 suited yours	A	K	Q	63%	47%
2 suited not yours	6	6	9	64%	46%
3 suited yours	Q	J	T	62%	45%
3 suited yours	Q	5	3	61%	45%
3 suited yours	K	5	3	60%	45%
3 suited yours	9	5	2	60%	45%
3 suited yours	5	Q	3	60%	45%
2 suited not yours	7	7	9	61%	43%
3 suited yours	A	K	3	60%	43%
3 suited yours	Q	J	3	59%	43%
3 suited yours	Q	T	3	59%	42%
3 suited yours	9	3	2	56%	41%
3 suited yours	A	2	3	56%	39%
2 suited yours	6	9	8	45%	35%
2 suited yours	5	4	Q	44%	35%
2 suited yours	7	9	8	40%	31%
2 suited yours	9	5	2	38%	31%
2 suited yours	K	5	3	38%	30%
2 suited yours	Q	5	3	37%	30%
2 suited yours	6	A	K	37%	30%
2 suited yours	7	5	2	42%	29%
2 suited yours	7	K	2	40%	29%
2 suited yours	6	A	3	39%	29%
2 suited yours	6	Q	3	39%	29%
2 suited yours	6	9	3	39%	29%
2 suited yours	7	A	K	38%	29%
2 suited yours	6	Q	J	37%	29%
2 suited yours	5	Q	3	37%	29%
2 suited yours	7	Q	2	40%	28%
2 suited yours	7	9	2	40%	28%
2 suited yours	6	5	2	40%	28%
2 suited yours	7	Q	J	37%	28%
2 suited yours	9	8	Q	35%	26%
Rainbow	5	4	Q	29%	26%
3 suited not yours	5	4	3	38%	23%
2 suited yours	9	3	2	29%	22%
2 suited yours	A	2	3	28%	22%
2 suited yours	Q	T	3	28%	21%

76s
Selected flops

Flop Type: Suit Type	Flop			6 see flop	10 see flop
2 suited yours	A	K	3	27%	21%
2 suited yours	Q	J	3	27%	21%
2 suited yours	A	K	Q	27%	21%
2 suited not yours	5	4	Q	26%	21%
2 suited yours	Q	J	T	27%	20%
2 suited yours	4	4	Q	24%	16%
Rainbow	Q	5	3	19%	16%
Rainbow	K	5	3	18%	16%
Rainbow	5	Q	3	18%	16%
Rainbow	6	9	8	24%	14%
2 suited yours	9	9	Q	22%	14%
Rainbow	9	5	2	17%	14%
2 suited yours	Q	Q	T	21%	13%
2 suited yours	A	A	T	20%	13%
2 suited not yours	K	5	3	16%	13%
Rainbow	7	5	2	23%	12%
2 suited not yours	6	9	8	21%	12%
2 suited not yours	7	Q	2	20%	12%
2 suited not yours	Q	5	3	16%	12%
2 suited not yours	5	Q	3	16%	12%
Rainbow	6	5	2	20%	11%
2 suited not yours	7	9	2	19%	11%
2 suited not yours	9	5	2	15%	11%
2 suited not yours	7	5	2	20%	10%
Rainbow	6	9	3	19%	10%
Rainbow	7	K	2	18%	10%
Rainbow	7	Q	2	18%	10%
Rainbow	6	Q	3	18%	10%
Rainbow	7	9	2	18%	9%
2 suited not yours	6	5	2	18%	9%
Rainbow	6	A	3	16%	9%
Rainbow	9	8	Q	15%	9%
Rainbow	7	9	8	17%	8%
2 suited not yours	6	9	3	16%	8%
2 suited not yours	7	K	2	15%	8%
2 suited not yours	6	Q	3	15%	8%
3 suited not yours	5	4	Q	14%	8%
Rainbow	7	A	K	13%	8%
Rainbow	6	A	K	13%	8%
Rainbow	6	Q	J	11%	8%
2 suited not yours	7	9	8	15%	7%
2 suited not yours	6	A	3	15%	7%
Rainbow	7	Q	J	13%	7%
2 suited not yours	9	8	Q	13%	7%
2 suited not yours	7	A	K	11%	7%
3 suited not yours	6	9	8	13%	6%
2 suited not yours	7	Q	J	11%	6%
2 suited not yours	6	A	K	11%	6%
3 suited not yours	6	A	K	11%	6%
2 suited not yours	6	Q	J	11%	6%
3 suited not yours	7	5	2	12%	5%
3 suited not yours	6	5	2	11%	5%
3 suited not yours	7	K	2	10%	5%
3 suited not yours	7	Q	2	10%	5%
3 suited not yours	6	Q	3	10%	5%
3 suited not yours	6	9	3	10%	5%
3 suited not yours	K	5	3	9%	5%
3 suited not yours	Q	5	3	9%	5%
3 suited not yours	6	A	3	9%	5%
3 suited not yours	5	Q	3	9%	5%
3 suited not yours	9	5	2	8%	5%
Rainbow	9	3	2	7%	5%
3 suited not yours	7	9	2	10%	4%

Flop Type: Suit Type	Flop			6 see flop	10 see flop
3 suited not yours	7	9	8	9%	4%
3 suited not yours	7	A	K	7%	4%
3 suited not yours	7	Q	J	7%	4%
2 suited not yours	9	3	2	6%	4%
Rainbow	5	5	5	8%	3%
3 suited not yours	6	Q	J	7%	3%
3 suited not yours	9	8	Q	7%	3%
Rainbow	Q	Q	Q	7%	3%
Rainbow	9	9	9	6%	3%
Rainbow	4	4	Q	5%	3%
Rainbow	A	A	A	6%	2%
2 suited not yours	4	4	Q	4%	2%
Rainbow	A	2	3	4%	2%
Rainbow	Q	T	3	4%	2%
Rainbow	A	K	3	3%	2%
2 suited not yours	A	K	3	3%	2%
Rainbow	Q	J	3	3%	2%
2 suited not yours	Q	J	3	3%	2%
2 suited not yours	A	2	3	3%	2%
2 suited yours	Q	T	3	3%	2%
Rainbow	9	9	Q	3%	1%
2 suited not yours	9	9	Q	3%	1%
3 suited not yours	9	3	2	3%	1%
Rainbow	A	A	T	2%	1%
2 suited not yours	A	A	T	2%	1%
3 suited not yours	Q	J	3	2%	1%
3 suited not yours	A	2	3	2%	1%
3 suited not yours	Q	T	3	2%	1%
3 suited not yours	A	K	3	1%	1%
Rainbow	A	K	Q	1%	1%
Rainbow	Q	Q	T	2%	0%
2 suited not yours	Q	Q	T	1%	0%
2 suited not yours	A	K	Q	1%	0%
3 suited not yours	A	K	Q	1%	0%
Rainbow	Q	J	T	1%	0%
2 suited yours	Q	J	T	1%	0%
3 suited not yours	Q	J	T	1%	0%

Selected flops with 50% or higher probability of winning ranked for 6-handed

Flop Type: Suit Type	Flop			6 see flop	10 see flop
3 suited yours	5	4	3	100%	100%
Rainbow	5	4	3	80%	65%
2 suited yours	5	4	3	79%	65%
Rainbow	7	7	5	75%	59%
Rainbow	6	6	5	75%	59%
Rainbow	6	6	A	72%	57%
Rainbow	6	6	Q	72%	55%
Rainbow	7	7	A	71%	56%
Rainbow	7	7	Q	71%	55%
Rainbow	6	6	9	71%	53%
2 suited not yours	5	4	3	70%	54%
2 suited not yours	7	7	5	69%	53%
2 suited not yours	6	6	5	68%	52%
Rainbow	7	7	9	67%	49%
2 suited not yours	6	6	A	66%	49%
3 suited yours	9	8	Q	65%	50%
2 suited not yours	7	7	A	65%	48%
2 suited not yours	7	7	Q	65%	48%
2 suited not yours	6	6	Q	65%	48%
2 suited not yours	6	6	9	64%	46%
3 suited yours	5	4	Q	63%	50%
3 suited yours	A	K	Q	63%	47%

76s
Selected flops

Flop Type: Suit Type	Flop			6 see flop	10 see flop
3 suited yours	Q	J	T	62%	45%
3 suited yours	Q	5	3	61%	45%
2 suited not yours	7	7	9	61%	43%
3 suited yours	K	5	3	60%	45%
3 suited yours	9	5	2	60%	45%
3 suited yours	A	K	3	60%	43%
3 suited yours	5	Q	3	60%	45%
3 suited yours	Q	J	3	59%	43%
3 suited yours	Q	T	3	59%	42%
3 suited yours	9	3	2	56%	41%
3 suited yours	A	2	3	56%	39%

Selected flops with 50% or higher probability of winning for 10-handed

Flop Type: Suit Type	Flop			6 see flop	10 see flop
3 suited yours	5	4	3	100%	100%
Rainbow	5	4	3	80%	65%
2 suited yours	5	4	3	79%	65%
Rainbow	7	7	5	75%	59%
Rainbow	6	6	5	75%	59%
Rainbow	6	6	A	72%	57%
Rainbow	7	7	A	71%	56%
Rainbow	6	6	Q	72%	55%
Rainbow	7	7	Q	71%	55%
2 suited not yours	5	4	3	70%	54%
Rainbow	6	6	9	71%	53%
2 suited not yours	7	7	5	69%	53%
2 suited not yours	6	6	5	68%	52%
3 suited yours	9	8	Q	65%	50%

Flop Type: Suit Type	Flop			6 see flop	10 see flop
Top ten flops for 6-handed					
3 suited yours	5	4	3	100%	100%
Rainbow	5	4	3	80%	65%
2 suited yours	5	4	3	79%	65%
Rainbow	7	7	5	75%	59%
Rainbow	6	6	5	75%	59%
Rainbow	6	6	A	72%	57%
Rainbow	6	6	Q	72%	55%
Rainbow	7	7	A	71%	56%
Rainbow	7	7	Q	71%	55%
Rainbow	6	6	9	71%	53%

Top ten flops for 10-handed

Flop Type: Suit Type	Flop			6 see flop	10 see flop
3 suited yours	5	4	3	100%	100%
Rainbow	5	4	3	80%	65%
2 suited yours	5	4	3	79%	65%
Rainbow	7	7	5	75%	59%
Rainbow	6	6	5	75%	59%
Rainbow	6	6	A	72%	57%
Rainbow	7	7	A	71%	56%
Rainbow	6	6	Q	72%	55%
Rainbow	7	7	Q	71%	55%
2 suited not yours	5	4	3	70%	54%

Hobby, Profession or More!

I ask you take a minute to read this, even though you may not want to. There is a chance someone you know, and maybe even you, could be or become one of the 2,000,000 Americans addicted to gambling.

Check off any that apply:

- ❏ Have you ever put off having a meal because you were playing?
- ❏ Has it ever been difficult for you to leave the casino or internet site?
- ❏ Do you continue to play when you are tired?
- ❏ Has life at home ever been negatively affected because of your playing?
- ❏ Do you continue to play when you are down trying to recoup losses?
- ❏ Do you play trying to pay your bills?
- ❏ Have you ever borrowed so you could play?
- ❏ Have you ever stolen so you could play?
- ❏ Have you ever sold something so you could afford to play?
- ❏ Have you ever hidden how much you play from others?

There is a difference between being driven to become a world class player and being a compulsive gambler. If you have three checks you need to know there is a chance you are compulsive. Four, you are borderline.

Five or more checks and poker has become golf balls. What to do?

1. The first step is to realize you are addicted. You can't change what you don't acknowledge. You are addicted.
2. Accept you have a problem. You do, but you are not alone.
3. Once you accept you have a problem, realize you need help, now.
4. Then get help, now. It is available and for free. What a deal.

If you did check off more than three above, I ask you to contact Gamblers Anonymous **today**. It doesn't help to wait. Addiction doesn't go away by itself or with time. It gets worse.

Gamblers Anonymous provides — and yes, you can remain anonymous — substantial help to gamblers all over the world. They are experts at helping you, with numerous self-help group meetings as well as helpful online resources.

www.gamblersanonymous.org

or

Gamblers Anonymous International Service Office
P.O. Box 17173
Los Angeles, CA 90017
213.386.8789

Appendix E

Test and Final Exam Answers

Test 1
1. C
2. A
3. D
4. B
5. A
6. C
7. D
8. C
9. D
10. D
11. A
12. C
13. B
14. C
15. B
16. A
17. D
18. B
19. C
20. A
21. B
22. C
23. D
24. D
25. B
26. C
27. D
28. A
29. B
30. A
31. B
32. B
33. B
34. C
35. A
36. C
37. B
38. A
39. D
40. B
41. C
42. A
43. B
44. A
45. D
46. A
47. D
48. B
49. A
50. A
51. B
52. C
53. C
54. B
55. D
56. A
57. D
58. B

Test 2
1. A
2. B
3. B
4. A
5. B
6. D
7. D
8. B
9. A
10. B
11. C
12. A
13. C
14. A
15. B
16. C
17. D
18. C
19. D
20. C
21. A
22. A
23. B
24. D
25. B
26. B
27. A
28. A
29. B
30. D
31. A
32. C
33. D
34. E
35. D
36. A
37. A
38. D
39. E
40. C
41. E
42. C
43. B
44. A
45. D
46. C
47. B
48. C
49. B
50. A
51. E
52. B
53. B
54. A
55. D
56. C
57. E
58. A
59. B
60. D
61. A
62. B
63. E
64. A
65. E
66. B
67. A
68. C
69. B
70. D
71. C
72. C
73. D
74. C
75. D
76. D
77. A
78. D
79. D
80. D
81. D
82. E
83. A
84. A
85. E
86. E
87. E
88. C
89. A
90. B
91. E
92. A
93. D
94. C
95. B
96. B
97. C

Test 3
1. D
2. E
3. D
4. D
5. D
6. D
7. E
8. E
9. E
10. C

11. D	50. C	13. B	
12. E	51. D	14. C	
13. E	52. E	15. E	
14. E	53. D	16. B	
15. E	54. D	17. B	
16. C	55. E	18. D	
17. C	56. A	19. E	
18. E	57. D	20. E	
19. B	58. E	21. C	
20. E	59. C	22. C	
21. E	60. D	23. A	
22. E	61. D	24. C	
23. E	62. A	25. B	
24. E	63. E	26. C	
25. E	64. D	27. D	
26. D	65. E	28. C	
27. B	66. A	29. A	
28. B	67. C	30. B	
29. B	68. A	31. A	
30. D	69. C	32. C	
31. A	70. A	33. D	
32. A	71. B	34. A	
33. D	72. B	35. C	
34. C	73. E	36. C	
35. C	74. C	37. C	
36. E		38. B	
37. E	**Final Exam**	39. C	
38. E	1. C	40. B	
39. D	2. C	41. A	
40. D	3. B	42. B	
41. D	4. C	43. B	
42. E	5. A	44. A	
43. E	6. C	45. C	
44. D	7. A	46. C	
45. D	8. C	47. D	
46. E	9. E	48. E	
47. D	10. C	49. C	
48. A	11. D		
49. C	12. D		

50. C

15 total outs (3 Aces, 3 Kings, and 9 hearts) gives you a 32.6% chance of making your hand with one card to come. The pot size is $1,300 and you have to invest $300 to see the next card. (32.6)($1,300) − (.674)($300) = $221.60.

51. D

11 total outs (8 cards for the open-ended straight draw and 3 cards for the overcard pair) gives you 23.4% chance of making your hand on the turn. The pot size is $1,200 ($150 in blinds + $450 in pre-flop raises + $600 from your opponent's bet on the flop) and you have to invest $600. (.234)($1,200) − (.766)($600) = -$178.80

2nd pair	A pair of whatever is the 2nd highest card on the board.
Aces full of tens	Three of a kind Aces with two tens.
Aces up	A pair of aces with another pair. Tens up would mean a pair of tens with another pair lower than tens.
Act	To make a play; fold, bet, or raise.
Advertise	To represent a certain hand, usually by the way a person is betting.
Aggressive	A player who raises more than most others.
All in	When a player puts all of his remaining chips in the pot.
American Airlines	Aces, usually meant as pocket Aces.
Ammo	Chips.
Ante	Money, not the blinds, put into the pot before play begins.
Back door	Making a hand on the turn or river secondary to your primary draw.
Backraise	A player calls. Another raises. Then the player who originally called re-raises.
Bad beat	A loss to a player who received a miracle river card.
Bankroll	How much money you have available to play.
Behind	A player is behind if another player has a better hand.
Belly buster	An inside straight. Also known as a gutshot.
Bicycle	The straight A 2 3 4 5, also known as a wheel.
Big bet	A bet in the second two rounds of betting, which are twice as much as the first two rounds in limit.
Big blind	The position two to the left of the dealer. Also, the amount which must be put in the pot from the Big Blind.
Big Foot bet	A very large, but less than all in, bet.
Big slick	An Ace and a King as hole cards.
Big stack	A player who has more chips than anyone else at the table.
Blank	A card, usually on the turn or river, which probably doesn't affect the hand; also known as a brick or rag.
Blind	A forced bet before play; made by the two players to the left of the dealer.
Blocker	A card in your hand which prevents an opponent from having the nuts.
Bluff	Betting to pretend you have a good hand when you don't.
Board	The community cards on the table.
Boardologist	A person who studies the board.

Boardology	The study of the board.
Boat	A full house. Three cards of one rank and two of another.
Brick	A turn or river card which probably doesn't affect the hand; also known as a blank or rag.
Broadway	An Ace high straight.
Brunson	A 2 and a T.
Bullet	An Ace.
Bullets	Hole card Aces.
Bully	An aggressive player, usually the player with a large stack of chips.
Burn or burn card	A card the dealer puts in the muck after dealing all players their cards but before dealing the flop. A card put in the muck before exposing the turn or river card.
Burton arrow	A method of showing suggested preflop hands to play depending on position; the result resembles an arrow.
Button	The white puck placed in front of the player who assumes the position of the dealer.
Call	Betting the same amount as the previous bettor.
Calling station	A loose player who stays with many hands by calling, not raising. A passive/loose.
Calling two bets	One player raises and then another player re-raises. The next player who has not yet bet calls two bets. Also termed cold calling.
Cap	The maximum number of raises allowed during a round of betting.
Capped	You are no longer allowed to raise once the dealer announces capped.
Cards speak	Whatever you have is what counts, not what you say you have.
Case card	The fourth card of a specific rank. If you have pocket Aces, with one on the board, if another comes that is the case Ace.
Catching air	Missing completely, usually on the flop.
Caught speeding	A bluffer gets caught.
Chase	To stay in a hand with only a draw.
Check	A player does not bet when it is his turn to do so.
Check-raise	Checking, allowing another to bet, and then raising.
Chopping	With regard to a dealer tip, it means ½ of the chip goes to the dealer; preflop, with only the blinds remaining, it means both the blind players take back their bets and no hand is played.
Clock	A request for the dealer to tell a slow player to speed up his play on a hand.
Cold call	One player raises and then another player re-raises. A cold call is when the next player calls both raises. Also termed calling 2 bets.
Collecting bullets	Trapping an aggressive player by slowplaying.
Collusion	Players working together to cheat others.
Come over the top	To raise or re-raise.

Community cards	Cards placed in the middle of the card table for all players to use as part of their hands, the board.
Completed hand	A hand that has already been made.
Connectors	Hole cards in sequence: AK, KQ, QJ, JT, T9, 98, 87, 76, 65, 54, 43, 32, A2
Counterfeit	Your lower pair, of the two pair, is no longer playable as there are two higher pair on the board.
Covered	An all in bet is "covered" by an opponent who has more chips than the bet.
Cowboy	A King.
Crabs	Hole cards are a pair of threes.
Cracked	You have a big hand at the start, but someone outdraws you.
Customer	An opponent who calls, usually against a better hand.
Dead man's hand	Aces and eights.
Dead money	Money left in the pot by the players who have folded.
Dead money grab	An attempt to win the pot with an aggressive bet, usually by a player in late position without a made hand.
Deep stack poker	When each player starts off with a stack of chips which is a large multiple of the initial big blind. If each player started off with a stack of chips equal to 250 times the big blind, this would be an example of deep stack poker.
Defending the blind	Calling or raising when you are seated at either blind.
Dog	A player with a low chance of winning the hand.
Dominated hand	A player who has a lower pair or kicker than another player. His hand is dominated.
Donkey	A poor player.
Double belly buster	A draw to a double inside straight, that is, there are two possible straights which can be made.
Dout	An out which may give another player a better hand. A discounted out.
Drawing dead	No matter what card you get, you can't possibly win.
Drawing hands	A hand which needs another card or cards to be a possible winner.
Duck	A 2.
Early position	Players immediately to the left of the button. I refer to the small blind, big blind, and seat 3 in a 10-handed game as early position.
End connectors	Hole cards in sequence at the end: AK, A2.
Face	K, Q, or J.
Family pot	A pot where all the players are in.
Fast playing	Aggressive play.
Fifth street	The last betting round; the river.
Fish	A poor player. Usually inexperienced.
Floating	Calling with nothing with the intention of stealing the pot on the turn or river. Used primarily in no limit.
Floor	The casino pit boss.

Flop	The first community cards dealt. Three in number.
Flopping a set	You have a pair in your hand, and one of those cards is dealt on the flop.
Flush	Five of the same suit.
Flush card	A card of a suit needed to make a flush.
Flush draw	You have four suited cards and need the fifth on the turn or river to make a flush.
Fold	Get out of the hand.
Four flush	You have four cards suited cards.
Four of a kind	Four cards all of the same rank. Quads.
Fourth street	The turn card.
Free card	It doesn't cost you anything to see the next card, as everyone checked.
Freerolling	Preriver, having the nuts with a draw to an even better hand.
Full house	A hand with three of a kind and another pair.
Good drawing	In this book ATs, A9s, KJ, KTs, QJs, QTs, AQ, AJ, KQ, QTs and 99.
Gutshot	An inside straight; also known as a belly buster.
Hand pyramid	A modification and extrapolation of the Burton arrow, showing all possible 169 hands.
Hare	A term used to describe fast or aggressive play.
Heads up	Only two players left in the hand.
Heater	Winning several hands in a row. A rush.
High pair	A pair matching the highest card on the board.
Hole cards	The two cards you are dealt face down.
Hook	A Jack.
Horse	The last one who bets or raises.
Implied odds	Estimating the future pot size and using that estimate to determine if you will stay in a hand.
In the dark	Checking or betting without seeing your cards; also betting or checking before you see the next card or cards dealt.
Inducing a bet	Checking a strong hand trying to get an opponent to bet.
Inside straight draw	A drawing hand where only one card of a specific rank can compete the straight.
Isolate	Using aggressive betting to attempt to get heads up.
Jam	Aggressive play; raising or re-raising.
Kicker	A card used to decide ties. The higher kicker wins.
Kicker trouble	Two players have paired a card on the board, but one does not have a high kicker.
King crab	Hole cards are a King and a 3.
Lady	A Queen.
Late position	The button or close to the right of the button. Seats 8, 9 and the button in a 10-handed game.
Lay down	To get out of a pot, usually on the turn or river. Folding your cards.

Lead	To be the first to bet.
Limit	The maximum bet or raise. Limit hold'em means you must bet or raise a specified amount.
Limp	To call.
Limp in	Calling, not raising preflop.
Limp-raise	During the same round of betting calling and then re-raising after a raise.
Loose	A player who plays more hands than most others.
Made hand	A hand which is not on a draw, which can stand alone.
Middle connectors	Hole cards in sequence more than three from the end: JT, T9, 98, 87, 76, 65, 54.
Middle position	The seats in the middle of the table relative to the dealer. I refer to seats 4, 5, 6 and 7 in a 10-handed game as middle position.
Middle stack	A player's chips are about the average of those at the table.
Miss	A player was drawing and did not receive the card he wanted.
Monster	The best hands. In this book AA or KK. After the flop, an extremely good hand.
Muck	To fold your hand. Also the pile of discarded cards in front of the dealer.
Multiway	A pot with more than two players in.
Multi-table	Playing several tables at the same time.
Newbie	A beginner.
No cap	In limit, when it is you and just another player, allowing each of you to keep raising as long as both wish to do so.
No limit	A player may bet any amount.
Nut bluff	A player going all in or making a big bet when he has the nuts, hoping to get a call.
Nuts	A hand that cannot be beaten.
Off suit	Hole cards not suited.
On the button	The last person to act in the last three rounds of betting.
One from end connectors	Hole cards in sequence one away from the end: KQ, 32.
One gap connectors	Hole cards separated in sequence by one rank: AQ, KJ, QT, J9, T8, 97, 86, 75, 64, 53, 42, A3.
One gap suiteds	Hole cards suited separated in rank by one, such as AQs.
One gap unsuited	Hole cards separated in rank by one, such as AQ.
Open-ended straight	You have four cards in sequence and you could make a straight with a card above or below your cards.
Outs	Cards which will allow a player to improve his hand.
Overcall	You call a bet that has already been called.
Overcard	A hole card higher than any on the board.
Overpair	A pocket pair higher than any card on the board.
Overlay	When the pot odds are in your favor; when the Truth Drawing Numbers are in your favor.

Overs	Two hole cards higher than any on the board.
Paint	A face card.
Passive	A player who raises less than most others.
PATL	Pronounced "paddle." A box-like representation showing passive, aggressive, tight, and loose.
Pocket	The cards in your hand; does not include any of the community cards.
Pocket rockets	Hole card Aces.
Position bet	A player either bets or raises because he has good position.
Post	To put a required bet in the pot. Blinds are posts. If a player enters the game out of turn he may choose to post and play the next hand.
Pot equity	Ratio of your share of the betting in a round to how often you expect to win if you play to the river.
Pot odds	The ratio of how much a player must bet to the size of the pot.
Premium hand	A top hand. In this book AKs, AQs, QQ. In other books the top 10 hands.
Put	Inferring a player has a good or bad hand or on a specific hand; also known as a read.
Quack	A 2.
Quads	Four cards all the same rank.
Rabbit card	After all the players have folded preriver, the next card that would have been dealt.
Rabbit hunting	After all players have folded preriver a request to the dealer to show the next card.
Rag	A turn or river card which probably doesn't affect the hand; also known as a blank or brick.
Ragged flop	A flop without an A or face card, not suited, with no straight draw possible.
Rainbow	A flop without any two cards suited.
Rake	The house take on each hand.
Read	Inferring a player has a good or bad hand or is on a specific hand; also known as putting a player on a hand.
Represent	To make it appear you have a hand. Similar to advertise.
Re-raise	To raise after another player has raised. Spelled in other books as reraise.
Ring game	A game with all or almost all of the seats filled.
River	The fifth and last community card dealt.
Rock	A passive/tight player.
Rounder	A professional poker player.
Royal or royal flush	An Ace high straight flush.
Royal straight flush	Same as a royal flush. An Ace high straight which is also suited.
Runner runner	The turn and river cards. Usually indicates you made your hand because of the turn and river cards.
Rush	Several good hands in a short period of time.

Scare card	A card on the turn or river which could give anyone a good hand.
Semi-bluff	Betting on a drawing hand which has a good chance of becoming the best hand.
Set	Your pocket pair turns into three of a kind with one of the community cards.
Shorthanded	Fewer players than allowed at the table.
Short stack	A player who has less chips than anyone at the table.
Show one, show all	In a live game, at the end of a hand, if you show your cards to one player, you must show them to every player.
Showdown	After the river when all remaining players show their cards.
Side pot	A player has run out of chips, but is still in the pot. A side pot is the pool of money the remaining players bet.
Slowplay	To play a strong hand as though it were a weak hand.
Small ball	A style of play in certain no limit tournaments focused on low risk.
Small bet	The first two rounds of betting have a limit for a bet. These are called small bets.
Small bet poker	The same thing as small ball. A style of play in certain no limit tournaments focused on low risk.
Small blind	The player to the left of the dealer button. An amount smaller than the big blind to be put in before betting starts.
Smooth call	To call without raising; the term is usually used when slowplaying.
Snowing	A stone cold bluff from preflop all the way to the river.
Snowmen	Hole cards are a pair of eights.
Soft playing	Failure to get the most money from your opponents. Normally done when an opponent is a friend.
Splash the pot	Throwing chips in so that some go into the pot.
Split pot	The pot won by two or more players which must be split between all winners.
Split two pair	Your hole cards are two different ranks and the board pairs both.
Squeezer	A very tight player.
Stack	The number of chips a player has.
Staying ahead of the rake	Trouble making a profit because of the house take.
Steal	To get opponents to fold with aggressive betting, not good cards.
Steal the blinds	To win the blinds with a bluff, usually done in late position.
Steel wheel	Straight flush 5 high.
Straddle	The player to the left of the big blind doubles the big blind bet before any cards are dealt.
Straight	Five cards in sequence which do not also form a flush.
Straightforward play	Betting when strong; checking when weak.
Straight draw	Drawing on the turn or river to make a straight.

Straight flush	Five cards in sequence which also form a flush.
Street	One of the last two betting rounds. The turn is 4th street. The river is 5th street.
String bet	Putting an amount of chips in equal to a call, then putting more chips in to raise. Usually not allowed.
Strong hand	Not a premium or monster hand; but next in line. In this book AJs, KQs, AK, JJ, TT.
Structured	A player may only bet or raise a fixed amount during a betting round.
Suited connectors	Two suited cards also in sequence.
Swayne hand pyramid	A method, in the shape of a pyramid, showing all 169 possible hands.
Swayne PATL matrix	A box-like representation showing Passive or Aggressive and Tight or Loose.
Swayne Win Factor	A number for preflop hole cards indicating the chances of winning or losing with the hand.
Table personality	The style of play at the table, directly related to one of the PATL's quadrants.
Table texture	Same as table personality but may also refer to the cards shown on the board.
Tell	An action or mannerism which lets an opponent know something about the person's hand.
Ten year old boy hand	Jacks and fives.
Texture	Usually refers to the cards shown on the board. Sometimes means the style of play at the table.
Thin bet	A low bet in no limit on the river.
Third base	In the casino game Ultimate Hold'em, this position bets or checks after all others at the table have checked or bet.
Three gap suiteds	Hole cards suited separated in rank by three, such as ATs.
Three gaps	Cards separated by three in sequence, such as T6.
Three of a kind	Three cards of the same rank.
Tight	A player who plays less hands than most others.
Tilt	Playing poor cards or too aggressively when upset.
Toke	A tip to the dealer.
Tortoise	A style of play in certain no limit tournaments which is slow and steady and focuses on low risk.
Treetop	An Ace high straight.
Trips	A card in your hand with a pair on the board which makes three of a kind.
Truth drawing numbers	The minimum number of bets in the pot for you to consider betting on the turn or river.
Turn	The card turned up by the dealer after the flop.
Two gap suiteds	Suited hole cards separated in rank by two, such as AJs.

Two gap unsuited	Hole cards separated in rank by two, such as AJ.
Two gaps	Cards separated by two in sequence, such as T7.
Two pair	Two cards of the same rank and another two cards which have the same rank but one different than the first.
Under the gun	The first player to act.
Underpair	One of your hole cards pairs on the board, but there is a higher card on the board.
Value bet	Betting or raising with a strong hand in order to build the pot.
Weak	Same as passive.
Weak tight	A tight player who folds quickly if he doesn't hit. Same as passive/tight.
Wheel	The straight A 2 3 4 5.
Win Factor	Used to determine whether or not to play a preflop hand.
Wired pair	A pair in your hand.
Woolworth	Hole cards are a 5 and a T.
Zero board	The board is not paired and shows no possible straight or flush draws.